foreign policy, trade, and defence, 1968-84

Trudeau's World

Robert Bothwell and J.L. Granatstein

Trudeau's World
Insiders Reflect on Foreign Policy,
Trade, and Defence, 1968-84

UBCPress · Vancouver · Toronto

© UBC Press 2017

All rights reserved. No part of this publication may be reproduced, stored in a retrieval system, or transmitted, in any form or by any means, without prior written permission of the publisher, or, in Canada, in the case of photocopying or other reprographic copying, a licence from Access Copyright, www.accesscopyright.ca.

26 25 24 23 22 21 20 19 18 17   5 4 3 2 1

Printed in Canada on FSC-certified ancient-forest-free paper (100% post-consumer recycled) that is processed chlorine- and acid-free.

Library and Archives Canada Cataloguing in Publication

Bothwell, Robert, author
    Trudeau's world insiders reflect on foreign policy, trade, and defence, 1968-84 / Robert Bothwell and J.L. Granatstein.

Includes bibliographical references and index.
Issued in print and electronic formats.
ISBN 978-0-7748-3637-1 (hardcover). – ISBN 978-0-7748-3639-5 (PDF)

    1. Trudeau, Pierre Elliott, 1919-2000. 2. Canada – Foreign relations – 1945-.
3. Canada – Economic policy. 4. Canada – Military policy. 5. Canada – Politics and government – 1963-1984. I. Granatstein, J.L., author II. Title.

FC625.B68 2017   971.064'4   C2017-904615-2
                                                           C2017-904616-0

Canadä

UBC Press gratefully acknowledges the financial support for our publishing program of the Government of Canada (through the Canada Book Fund), the Canada Council for the Arts, and the British Columbia Arts Council.

Printed and bound in Canada by Friesens
Set in Helvetica Condensed, Minion, and Baskerville 10
by Artegraphica Design Co. Ltd.
Copy editor: Deborah Kerr
Proofreader: Carmen Tiampo
Indexer: Jennifer Levin Bonder

UBC Press
The University of British Columbia
2029 West Mall
Vancouver, BC V6T 1Z2
www.ubcpress.ca

Contents

Acknowledgments | ix

Abbreviations | xi

Introduction | 3

I   Advisers and Ministers | 13
   Hon. Marc Lalonde | 16
   Hon. R. Gordon Robertson | 21
   Hon. Michael Pitfield | 28
   Marshall Crowe | 42
   Hon. Gérard Pelletier | 46
   Ivan Head | 49
   Rt. Hon. Paul Martin | 63
   Hon. Mitchell Sharp | 70
   Reeves Haggan | 73
   Hon. Mark MacGuigan | 75

II   Deputy Ministers and Senior Diplomats | 85
   A. Edgar Ritchie | 87
   Allan Gotlieb | 91
   William Barton | 100
   Alan Beesley | 103
   John Halstead | 107
   Gordon Smith | 110
   Hon. Gordon Osbaldeston | 113
   de Montigny Marchand | 116
   Thomas Delworth | 121

III The Defence and Foreign Policy Reviews and After | 126

Hon. Mitchell Sharp | 129
Hon. Léo Cadieux | 132
Hon. Paul Hellyer | 134
Hon. Donald Macdonald | 136
Hon. Otto Lang | 137
Ross Campbell | 139
John F. Anderson | 142
H. Basil Robinson | 146
John Halstead | 152
Michael Shenstone | 154
Rear Admiral Robert Murdoch | 157
Gordon Smith | 159
Hon. Donald Macdonald | 163
Sylvain Cloutier | 166
General Jacques Dextraze | 171

IV Canada and the United States | 175

Ivan Head | 180
Rufus Smith | 186
A. Edgar Ritchie | 189
Emerson Brown | 191
Marshall Crowe | 196
Peter Towe | 197
Hon. Mitchell Sharp | 200
Russell McKinney | 201
Richard Post | 206
Thomas Enders | 207
Robert Duemling | 211
Hon. Donald Macdonald | 215
Allan Gotlieb | 216
Edward Nef | 224
Robert Hunter | 225

Hon. Mark MacGuigan | 226
Paul H. Robinson, Jr. | 227
Richard Smith | 230

V Canada and Europe | 232
Hon. Gérard Pelletier | 234
François Leduc | 237
Max Yalden | 238
Pierre-Marc Siraud | 241
Hon. Léo Cadieux | 243
John Halstead | 245
Jacques Viot | 247
Michel Dupuy | 249
de Montigny Marchand | 254
Jean Béliard | 258
Drs. Heinz Schneppen and Rüdiger von Lukowitz | 259

VI Canada and the Soviet Union | 262
Rt. Hon. Paul Martin | 265
Robert Ford | 267
John Halstead | 279
Peter Roberts | 280
William Hooper | 282
Peter Hancock | 289
Vernon Turner | 290
James (Si) Taylor | 291
Geoffrey Pearson | 294

VII Canada and the Far East | 297
Rt. Hon. Paul Martin | 299
Yao Guang | 301
John Fraser | 304
Maurice Copithorne | 307
Yu Zhan | 309

Yasuhiko Nara | 312
Thomas Delworth | 314
Richard Gorham | 316
Michel Gauvin | 317

VIII Canada, the United Kingdom, and Patriation | 321
Rt. Hon. Paul Martin | 323
Hon. Mark MacGuigan | 328
Sir John Ford | 331
Reeves Haggan | 334
Peter Meekison | 338
Daniel Gagnier | 340
Thomas Wells | 345
Rt. Hon. Lord Pym | 347
Eddie Goldenberg | 348

IX The Peace Initiative | 351
Louis Delvoie | 355
Peter Hancock | 359
Thomas Delworth | 367
de Montigny Marchand | 368
Allan Gotlieb | 369
Geoffrey Pearson | 372

X The Trudeau Conversation | 374
Rt. Hon. Pierre Trudeau | 375

Conclusion | 383

Index | 391

Acknowledgments

THE INTERVIEWS FOUND IN this volume – and the many others for which we regrettably had no space – were facilitated by numerous people. We are grateful to all those officials and politicians who talked to us and answered our queries and who permitted us to make use of their thoughts and recollections. A full list of the interviews we conducted at the end of the 1980s is printed in the bibliography of *Pirouette*. The complete texts of the interviews can be found in Robert Bothwell's papers at the University of Toronto archives and in the archives of the Canadian War Museum in Ottawa. Only a very few of the interviews remain closed to researchers.

We have also made use here of an interview that was done for us by Paul Litt. In addition, Bothwell did some interviews with John Kirton in Washington, and Granatstein did interviews in Beijing with Bernie Frolic.

The authors cheerfully admit that they are of a certain generation, the generation that seeks the assistance of the young to find its way through the electronic marvels invented in the 1990s and after – that is, after the interviews were done. At the time, they were typewritten on paper, by the authors directly, and eventually placed in files and deposited in archives. When we decided to create this volume, we resorted to the knowledge and artistry of Katie Davis, a graduate student in history at the University of Toronto, who transferred often barely legible typescript into a shining digital product. We are most grateful for her time, trouble, and skill. In many respects she made this volume possible. Jennifer Levin Bonder, also a graduate student in history at the University of Toronto, did the painstaking job of proofreading and on the way rescued the authors from more technical glitches they did not understand. She also tackled the intensive and thankless job of indexing. We owe them both heartfelt thanks.

Alison Smith of the University of Toronto History Department did interpretation of another kind, helping us with a semantic quibble raised by one of our interviewees, about a treaty text. Jeremy Kinsman, Allan Gotlieb, and

Peter Hancock came to the rescue by giving identities to some of the names herein.

Linda McKnight of Westwood Creative Associates acted for us with UBC Press, and we enjoyed working out the details of this volume with Emily Andrew and her successor, Randy Schmidt, at the press. We are grateful to Holly Keller and Deborah Kerr for their fine work on the manuscript.

Abbreviations

ADM	Assistant deputy minister
ACCT	Agence de coopération culturelle et technique
CDS	Chief of the defence staff
CF	Canadian Forces
CSCE	Conference on Security and Cooperation in Europe
DEA	Department of External Affairs
DND	Department of National Defence
EC	European Community
EEC	European Economic Community
FCO	Foreign and Commonwealth Office, United Kingdom
FIRA	Foreign Investment Review Agency
FLQ	Front de libération du Québec
FPC	*Foreign Policy for Canadians*
FPRO	Federal-Provincial Relations Office
FSO	Foreign service officer
GATT	General Agreement on Tariffs and Trade
ICER	Interdepartmental Committee on External Relations
ITC	Department of Industry, Trade and Commerce
LOS	Law of the Sea
MBFR	Mutual and Balanced Force Reductions
NATO	North Atlantic Treaty Organization
NDHQ	National Defence Headquarters, Ottawa
NEP	National Energy Programme
NORAD	North American Air Defence Command
P&P	Cabinet Committee on Priorities and Planning
PC	Progressive Conservative Party

PCO	Privy Council Office
PMO	Prime Minister's Office
PQ	Parti Québécois
PRC	People's Republic of China
SACEUR	Supreme Allied commander in Europe
SALT	Strategic Arms Limitation Talks/Treaty
SSEA	Secretary of state for external affairs
STAFEUR	Special Task Force on Europe
TCS	Trade Commissioner Service
USSEA	Under secretary of state for external affairs
VCDS	Vice chief of the defence staff

Trudeau's World

Introduction

THIS BOOK IS A COLLECTION of interviews done between 1986 and 1988 with individuals who were connected with, or informed about, Canadian foreign relations under Prime Minister Pierre Elliott Trudeau. Subsequently, the information in the interviews formed the basis, along with other research, for a book, *Pirouette: Pierre Trudeau and Canadian Foreign Policy,* that we published with the University of Toronto Press in 1990. Thirty years have now passed since the interviews and twenty-five and more since the book, the span of a generation. "The Trudeau government" now means something quite different to Canadians – no longer Pierre, but Prime Minister Justin Trudeau, his son, who was born in the period covered by this book. The Trudeau past is even more distant, and different, than we imagined when we published our history.

As any scholar who has done interviews knows, memory is fallible. Some of our interviewees wanted to protect themselves or settle old scores with their long-dead enemies, some quite sincerely misremembered events, and others simply could not recall them with any clarity. Unless they had memoranda close at hand (and some happily did), what most could best recall was their reaction to the personalities of those with whom they had worked or served under. Our task was to be well prepared but also resilient, in case we encountered the unexpected, able to help with chronology and names but not to lead our interlocutors where they did not want to go or into expressing views that they genuinely did not hold. We did many interviews together but often singly as circumstances dictated. Whether we worked alone or together, we did not use a tape recorder, believing that it inhibited conversation. Instead, we jotted notes and, as soon as the interview ended, wrote up a memorandum with key comments in quotes. The collected interviews are edited here for coherence and an attempted minimization of irrelevant subjects, diplomatic and military jargon, and the governmental alphabet soup of abbreviations.

The interviews ranged widely over issues and personalities, as well as the battles around the cabinet table, in international meetings, and within departments and the bureaucracy in Ottawa. Some interviews that covered several subjects and spanned many years have been divided with parts in various chapters. Those who were interviewed are indicated in **boldface** when they are mentioned in others' interviews. For *Pirouette*, we did some 180 interviews, as listed in that volume's bibliography. We have had to be very selective in this volume, reducing the quarter-million words in our original interview memoranda by some 60 percent. Copies of the original memoranda, almost all now available for research, can be found in Robert Bothwell's papers in the University of Toronto archives and in the archives of the Canadian War Museum in Ottawa.

The interviews presented here vary in length and quality, as might be expected, but many are superb in content and revealingly frank. There is repetition in the interviewees' opinions of some politicians and senior officials in Canada and elsewhere, of course, not least in the views expressed on Trudeau, Presidents Richard Nixon, Gerald Ford, Jimmy Carter, and Ronald Reagan, Prime Minister Margaret Thatcher, President Charles de Gaulle, and others. There are also some startlingly blunt assessments of the key figures. There is much on the enormous difficulties that Canada faced in dealing with the United States, the European Union, NATO, the Soviet Union, and China. There is substantial material on defence policy and, not least, on the efforts to patriate the Constitution, which involved the Thatcher government in London and the Provinces here. We have interviews that go into detail on Trudeau's Peace Initiative, his last hurrah. Unfortunately, we did not hear very much on foreign aid or the Third World problems that sometimes greatly interested Trudeau. In all, nonetheless, these interviews tell us much about Canada and the world from 1968 to 1984 and about the key departments and officials who made foreign and defence policy.

Our interviews took us where the veterans of the Trudeau era had settled. The largest number were in and around Ottawa, and after that Montreal, Vancouver, Victoria, and Calgary within Canada, and the United States, Britain, France, China, Japan, and what was then the Soviet Union outside. Interviewees who were still serving as diplomats, other public servants, or politicians who did not wish to make attributable comments were listed in *Pirouette*'s bibliography by date but not name.

During the Trudeau period, virtually all the senior officials and ministers in the Privy Council Office, the Prime Minister's Office, National Defence, and External Affairs were men, and this explains the absence of interviews with women. However, Margaret Meagher (1911-99), then residing in Nova Scotia, had been a senior diplomat for many years and was ambassador to Sweden when negotiations with the People's Republic of China on recognition occurred. Jean Wadds (1920-2011) was high commissioner in London during the patriation controversy. We erred in not interviewing these able women.

Our interviews and our book touched on Trade, with a capital T, because Trade was a very lively and obvious issue in Canadian external affairs, as it always had been and still is. We did not, however, venture into larger questions of financial policy, and we did not interview any officials from the Bank of Canada or the Finance Department.

If there was and is repetition, there are major differences in attitudes and reactions too, and these differences, though they certainly complicate the historians' task of attempting to make sense of past events, add much interest to the story. We were also very conscious of the fact that old men do forget and that there are factual mistakes in some of the interviews. We have corrected in footnotes the most egregious errors.

The interviews were conducted while Pierre Trudeau was very much alive, and his unseen presence is discernible in many of the comments from his colleagues. When we began, the Trudeau government was only three years in the past, and Trudeau himself was still a lively contemporary presence. He was not content to stay retired. Between 1987 and 1990, just as we were researching and writing, he inspired a successful campaign to derail the Mulroney government's constitutional amendments – the so-called Meech Lake affair. The Meech Lake Accord was very much on the mind of every Canadian who was interested in public affairs and, it must be admitted, on our minds as well. We tried as best we could to keep contemporary politics out of our work, but it may have affected attitudes and recollections among our subjects, depending on their contemporary view of Trudeau's constitutional activity.

The world from the perspective of the twenty-first century looks rather different from the world that Canadians knew in 1986-89. In the first place, they saw the Cold War. The historians of that day quibbled among themselves about *when* the Cold War began and *who* began it, but they did not dispute that it remained the dominant fact in international relations. Virtually nobody, including ourselves and our interviewees, realized that it was on the verge of ending. None of us had a clear memory of the world before the Cold

War, and it seemed at the time that it would go on forever. This fact places our interviews squarely in Cold War Canada, and careful readers should remember the adage, "The past is a foreign country; they do things differently there."

Trudeau's World

Pierre Elliott Trudeau came to power in April 1968, determined to make a break with the past – or what he saw as the past. "No more helpful fixers," he quipped, a jibe at Canada's busy role in patching, repairing, connecting, and enabling out-of-kilter parts of the international system. The fixer-in-chief was Trudeau's predecessor, Prime Minister Lester B. Pearson, who understandably took Trudeau's remark as a slur on his forty years of patching, repairing, and enduring the idiocies of international relations.

It was not the first time that Trudeau and Pearson had differed. In 1963, private citizen Trudeau, infuriated when Pearson committed his Liberal Party to accepting American nuclear warheads for Canada's armed forces, described him as "the defrocked pope of peace." Pearson swallowed hard and accepted the same Trudeau as a Liberal candidate in the federal election of 1965. The issue then was not foreign policy but national unity, and Trudeau was a fierce defender of Canadian unity inside Quebec. The crisis of Quebec – the rapid rise of separatism as a political force inside that province – catapulted Trudeau into the cabinet as minister of justice, made him a contender for the Liberal leadership to succeed Pearson, and then won him that leadership. On 21 April 1968, Trudeau became prime minister and promptly called a general election for 25 June, which he won, with a parliamentary majority. The Liberals had not won a majority since 1953, and thereafter they gazed at Trudeau respectfully.

"We looked down the cabinet table," commented Mitchell Sharp, the minister of external affairs, "and said to ourselves, 'We're here because he's here.'"[1] From 1968 until he retired in 1984, Trudeau was the dominant power

---

[1] The full quote compared the Liberal cabinets under Lester (Mike) Pearson and Pierre Trudeau: "We [the ministers] looked down the table at Mike and we said, 'He's here because we're here.' We looked down the table at Trudeau, and said, 'We're here because he's here.'" Sharp made the comment to Bothwell in 1993 or 1994, when the latter was editing Sharp's autobiography, *Which Reminds Me ... A Memoir* (Toronto: University of Toronto Press, 1994). It was a memorable comment.

in his party. His leadership was essentially uncontested, a fact that was reflected in our interviews. There is little or nothing here of intra-party scandals or struggles: differences of opinion abound, as do disagreements over policy, but there was no question then, and no expression in the interviews, of plots and coups. Such matters were left to a later generation.

The Shape of Events

Trudeau's views and actions on foreign policy changed considerably over time. Trudeau never believed that he could shape the world as he desired, though his view of what Canada could and should do in the world changed greatly with experience. As leader of the Canadian government, he had to construct his country's reactions to events over which it had little or no control, and sometimes not even advance notice. Once he was done reacting, there might be some time and space left over to put a Canadian spin on proceedings.

Trudeau became prime minister at a time of political upheaval in the United States and Western Europe – not to mention separatism in Quebec. Latin America seemed poised on the brink of revolutionary change inspired by Fidel Castro's Cuba. In France, riots and strikes almost overthrew the government of President Charles de Gaulle. The Israeli victory in the Six-Day War of 1967 weakened the Arabs and discredited their leadership, but what would follow was most unclear. The United States had not achieved its objectives in the Vietnam War, and the Soviet Union was driving for parity in strategic arms – nuclear weapons stockpiles and the means to deliver them. At the end of the year, the Republican Richard Nixon was elected the American president, bringing with him as national security adviser a Harvard political scientist, Henry Kissinger.

Over the next five years – Trudeau's first and second terms in office – the political horizon darkened. The United States was compelled to make peace in Vietnam, leaving its anti-communist ally, South Vietnam, at the far end of an uncertain flow of aid from an unwilling Congress in Washington. Another Arab-Israeli war in October 1973 did not reproduce the clear-cut Israeli victory of 1967. The United States backed Israel in this new war, crucially replacing depleted Israeli stocks of weapons, whereas the Soviet Union supplied and advised Arab governments and threatened direct intervention to forestall the collapse of Egypt. As significant, Arab oil producers wielded the weapon of an oil boycott against the West and against the United States in particular. This was the signal, though not the cause, of an economic earthquake that fundamentally altered relations between oil-producing and oil-consuming states.

The 1970s saw a spectacular increase in petroleum prices. Not coincidentally, the early 1970s marked the end of the decades-long rise in the American standard of living; that this would be a permanent condition would take years if not decades to be understood. Despite this setback, the American economy remained the world's largest and the United States the world's most prosperous nation. At the same time, most Western European economies were growing too, along with Japan's, meaning that Canada's gross domestic product, relative to those of France, West Germany, and Japan, was less important than it had been during the twenty years after the Second World War.

The United States abandoned the effort to regulate the international economic system at the beginning of the 1970s and instead used a series of blunt unilateral moves to shore up its own economic position, floating the US dollar and placing a series of emergency tariffs on imports. (The world adopted the term *Nikuson shokku,* or Nixon shock, from the Japanese.) The shokku did not, however, signal a fundamental change in US economic policy. The Americans had abandoned responsibility for maintaining the world economy, but they did not relinquish their leading role in shaping it. Instead, nudged by Kissinger, the United States stressed *interdependence* and, later, *globalization,* vague but positive words that defined American policy as anything but unilateral.

The economic troubles of the mid-1970s gave birth to the G7 – the Group of Seven – the United States, Japan, West Germany, France, Great Britain, and Italy, plus, at American insistence, Canada, which was the world's sixth- or seventh-largest economy at the time and, as important, the close neighbour and ally of the United States. These events, as we shall see in Chapter IV, had a major impact on Canada, and they influenced the Trudeau government's policies, both domestic and foreign.

Western Europe, North America, Australasia, and Japan formed what was called the First World – fully developed capitalist economies that as a partial consequence were also politically stable and generally liberal in character, using the term in both its economic and political senses, as they were understood at the time. Trudeau's Canada had no problem with a First World identity (or a liberal-capitalist identity). Despite occasional twitches, Canadians, and Trudeau, did not consider their country to be part of the Third (or economically undeveloped) World, especially because it was usually politically illiberal as well. The poverty and aspirations of the Third World engaged Trudeau's sympathies, and those of many Canadians, but not enough to budge Canada from its primary role as part of the First World.

The Second World, the Communist bloc, had fallen into incoherence. The two great Communist countries, the Soviet Union and China, had divorced politically at the end of the 1950s. The Chinese Communist government spent the 1960s in political isolation, free to indulge in the economically self-defeating and politically catastrophic Cultural Revolution (1966-76). Meanwhile, most Western countries ignored or avoided China as much as they could, following a fearful United States, which treated Beijing throughout the 1950s and 1960s as the ultimate communist menace. Fortunately for the West, though not for China, the lunatic policies of Mao Zedong ensured that China remained economically chaotic and politically retarded. But it still had the world's biggest population and a large and strategically significant geography. Though economically weak, China was too large to be ignored. Pierre Trudeau and Henry Kissinger, in their different ways, were determined to modify its isolation. Canada accordingly recognized the Beijing government in 1970, and the two countries exchanged embassies. Kissinger, strongly supported by Nixon, soon arrived in Beijing and established a form of diplomatic contact that resulted in Communist China joining the United Nations. Having ended its fruitless confrontation with China, the United States could deal more confidently with the Soviet Union, which it did through the policy of détente.

The position of the Soviet Union differed to some extent from that of China. An oil and gas producer, it benefitted hugely from the rise in petroleum prices during the 1970s. Western Europeans welcomed new Russian supplies of oil and natural gas, despite American misgivings that dependence on Soviet supply could undermine Western solidarity. Much of the income from oil and gas sales went to feed the Soviet military-industrial complex, another negative. Yet it was not as negative as observers in the 1970s and 1980s believed. Some Canadian commentators noticed that the civilian side of the economy was obviously contracting as the Soviets strove desperately to modernize their military to cope with rapidly advancing Western technology. (They were unsuccessful, though that was not entirely clear by 1984.) At the same time, the Soviets were having increasing trouble keeping their European satellites quiescent. Ironically, their economic situation was still superior to that of the Soviet Union itself. Since they were unable to squeeze more subsidies out of their hegemonic power, the satellite governments turned to the West for loans; by 1984, they were substantially indebted, with no obvious means of ever paying off their Western creditors. As long as oil prices remained high, the whole creaking structure could be held together, but when prices started to decline in 1981, the Soviet Union and its satellites were more and more dangerously exposed.

From the outside, the Soviet Union looked fierce and seemed dangerous. During Kissinger's détente, the peril receded, but relations cooled when the Soviets invaded Afghanistan in 1979, becoming glacial when Ronald Reagan was elected to the American presidency in 1980. The Trudeau Peace Initiative (Chapter IX) in 1983-84 reflected the temper of the times, which was even more hazardous than Trudeau knew or imagined.

What Trudeau did know was that Canada was on the Western side in the Cold War. At first, he underestimated what that meant. What's in it for Canada? Trudeau and his entourage asked about NATO in 1968-99. Could Canada not be more effective out of NATO or with a significantly reduced defence burden? At the time, some answered yes, whereas Trudeau himself balanced between yes and no, reluctantly convinced that Canada would be worse off if it were out – of NATO, of Europe, of the arms race, of the Cold War – than it would be as a participant in all of those things.

Key to Trudeau's change of heart and choice of political options was his attempt to reconfigure Canada's external economic connections – to move away from a dangerous dependence on the United States for trade and investment by invoking Europe and Japan, and by increasing Canada's trans-Atlantic and trans-Pacific trade – what was called the Third Option (Chapter V). As Trudeau discovered, the Europeans would play ball only if Canada gave them something in return by maintaining and modernizing its defence linkage to NATO, and in particular Germany. And so the unmilitarist Trudeau found himself purchasing German tanks to keep alive a Canadian tank regiment confronting the Soviets across a line in Germany.

Seen in this perspective, Pierre Trudeau's time in office was an interval in the continuing Cold War, and not surprisingly that is what our interviews show. There were, however, other themes in Canadian foreign relations. American investment, the development of natural resources, the Autopact that established a version of free trade in automotive products across the 49th parallel – all proceeded largely independent of Cold War considerations. Relations with the Third World did have a Cold War backdrop, given a desire either to counteract Soviet influence or to shore up underdeveloped economies in order to remove the temptation of too close a relationship with the Soviet Union on the part of Third World governments.

The change that Trudeau hoped for when he became prime minister in 1968 did not occur. What changed, instead, was his conception of the world. Canada was and remained a First World country and a firm member of the Western alliance. As Trudeau came to see, however, Canada's participation in the Commonwealth and activities at and through the United Nations mitigated that fact, providing both himself and Canada with a bridge to the world outside the West.

What's in the Interviews?

Readers will expect that the interviews deal with foreign and defence policy, and up to a point that is true. Interviewees give their views on the Cold War, Ronald Reagan, and such questions as French interference in Quebec with an eye to breaking up Canada, trade, exchange rates, and so forth. However, much of the material deals not so much with policy as a finished product, as with the making of foreign and defence policy.

That reflects what actually consumed time and effort under the Trudeau governments. Trudeau and his close associates, particularly Michael Pitfield, were convinced that getting process right would, eventually, produce the right policy or, at worst, a better policy. Pitfield, and behind him Trudeau, moved the civil service, including the diplomats, around like pieces on a chessboard. The pieces, however, were intelligent and often eloquent human beings, and they did not appreciate being fed into organizational streams or becoming way stations on a policy conveyor belt. Their irritation (and it was mostly irritation) is very evident.[2] We think their sentiments are worth preserving as a piece of human documentation. For contemporary diplomats and general officers, some of what their predecessors experienced in the 1970s and 1980s may ring true – the shock of recognition.

As historians judging from the evidence, we sometimes felt it a miracle that any rational policy at all emerged from Trudeau's rationalistic slicing

---

2 In 1984, the UK high commissioner to Ottawa, Lord Moran, put his own particular spin on Canada's Department of External Affairs (DEA) bureaucracy, which was, he said, once "widely respected in the world." Unfortunately, it had "undergone changes which are converting it all too rapidly into a huge, sluggish bureaucratic conglomerate dominated by a French-Canadian mafia, ignorant of diplomacy, who have pushed aside the leading English-speaking professionals." Paul Waldie, "Files Show What British Diplomats Really Thought of Canada in the 1980s," *Toronto Globe and Mail*, 24 August 2016, A8.

and dicing. His motives were high – unexceptionable, really. But the result may have been disproportionate – disproportionately small – compared to the effort expended.

This book, therefore, aims to explain not just the *what* of Canadian foreign and defence policy, but the *how* as well. Survivors may find that we have resurrected gruesome memories of organizational issues expressed as personal conflicts. But that in our opinion is the reality of life in a world of large organizations. Although, after reading this book, one may conclude that we cannot do much with the functions and politics of bureaucracy, what is even clearer is that we cannot do without them.

I
Advisers and Ministers

PIERRE TRUDEAU SERVED FIFTEEN years and five months as Canada's prime minister, from April 1968 to June 1979, and from March 1980 to June 1984. He won three elections with a parliamentary majority and one with a minority. He was voted out of office in June 1979, resulting in a minority Progressive Conservative government. That government, led by Joe Clark, was soon defeated, first in Parliament and then in a general election.

In his fifteen years, Trudeau had four secretaries of state for external affairs (abbreviated here as SSEA): Mitchell Sharp (1968-74), Allan MacEachen (1974-76 and 1982-84), Don Jamieson (1976-79), and Mark MacGuigan (1980-82). Two, MacEachen and Jamieson, were powerful regional politicians, MacEachen for Nova Scotia and Jamieson for Newfoundland. Mitchell Sharp was a significant politician, though in a region (Greater Toronto) that was heavy with significant politicians. But Sharp's background – twenty years as a senior Ottawa bureaucrat – and reputation as a senior businessman after he left the civil service had helped clinch the Liberal leadership for Trudeau in 1968. Mark MacGuigan, considered one of the most talented Liberal backbenchers, was astounded to be appointed minister of external affairs. Others were astounded too, and though MacGuigan was by no means insignificant or unsuccessful as a minister, he was not politically powerful. Two of the four ministers are interviewed here.

By the time we conducted our interviews, Jamieson was dead. We did have two good and productive interviews with Allan MacEachen, which will eventually be available in our papers. We regret that we could not include them here.

Trudeau had come to Ottawa in 1965 with two friends, Gérard Pelletier and Jean Marchand, both of whom entered his cabinet in 1968. Pelletier, interviewed here, was arguably more influential than Marchand, both before 1965 and after. His relationship with Trudeau was always close.

To manage his government, Trudeau relied on two organizations. One, the Privy Council Office, or PCO, was a regular government department that dated back to Confederation in 1867. In the 1940s, it was significantly expanded so as to organize and regularize cabinet business. (Trudeau himself was employed in it, in 1949-50.) Its permanent head, the clerk of the privy council and secretary to the cabinet, became Canada's senior civil servant. Gordon Robertson, Trudeau's first clerk, is interviewed below.

The prime minister's personal staff was organized into the Prime Minister's Office, or PMO, whose functions were explicitly political and whose employees were not part of the civil service. The post of principal secretary was of long standing, but until the 1940s it would have seemed strange that the principal secretary also had secretaries, who would multiply and change into specialists, advisers, and, of course, more secretaries. The principal secretary eventually morphed into the chief of staff and became under Trudeau an important personage in political and official Ottawa. Because of his proximity to the prime minister, even ministers could not safely ignore him. Trudeau's first principal secretary was Marc Lalonde, who became a senior minister in Trudeau's later cabinets. Also in the PMO was Ivan Head, a former officer in External Affairs and law professor who quickly became Trudeau's main foreign policy adviser. Interviews with both Lalonde and Head follow.

The various ministers had their own offices and staffs. We include in this section part of an interview with Reeves Haggan, Sharp's departmental assistant in External Affairs, which sheds light on how Sharp (and by extension other ministers) carried out his duties and on his relations with his under secretaries, or deputy ministers, especially the formidable Marcel Cadieux. (On Cadieux, who had died by the time *Pirouette* was composed, see especially Chapters 1 and 2 of this volume.)

The confrontation between old and new, orthodox and unorthodox, played out on the struggle over NATO and defence policy that consumed the spring of 1969, and which is embodied in interviews with Ivan Head and his senior opponents. It was a battle that Trudeau won and Cadieux lost – inevitably, considering their respective positions in the governmental hierarchy. The bureaucracy was reoriented as Pitfield, supported by Trudeau, desired. Cadieux's version of professionalism gave way to a personnel policy that was directed from the centre and aimed at the general good of the civil service and more broadly, the country.

It should not be assumed that because Cadieux lost he was wrong. The conclusion is rather mixed. The foreign service endured years of tinkering, followed by a major convulsion in the early 1980s, when various foreign affairs agencies were shoehorned into a single department, headquartered in External Affairs in the Pearson Building. Doing it required a heavy commitment of time and talent, represented by two deputy ministers, Gordon Osbaldeston and Marcel Massé. The Osbaldeston interview in this chapter is very revealing; the Massé interview will eventually be opened in our papers. Pitfield's system is essentially still in force, and after forty years some of its effects are apparent. Senior civil servants move about from department to department. Peripatetic deputy ministers often arrive with no knowledge of the institutional culture of the organization they have come to head or the specific precedents and history that govern its behaviour. Not surprisingly, decisions are often taken in ignorance. Talent without knowledge is not indefinitely transferable.

As our interviews show here and in Chapter III, Canada reduced its NATO commitment and did so with scant consideration for its allies. This asserted Canada's self-interest, as defined by Canadians, a major point with Trudeau in 1968-72. But sovereignty is not purely a domestic plant. Canadian sovereignty existed – exists – in a larger world, and as Trudeau learned, there were consequences to Canada's exercise of its sovereign power. As a consequence, Trudeau ended up re-equipping the Canadian Forces, keeping some troops in Europe while demonstrating, in a variety of spheres, that Canada could indeed be useful – a helpful fixer, as it were.

Before we turn to Trudeau's policy making, we should explain what the policy was about. In 1951 and later, Canadian governments placed and sustained a reinforced army brigade and (initially) an air division in Europe. The air component had gradually dwindled, but it was still there in 1968. The army dwelt in northern Germany and operated with British forces to block (it was hoped) any Soviet offensive across the north German plain. When we say "dwelt," we mean to convey that Canada's overseas garrison included not just soldiers and air personnel, but also their wives and children – the equivalent of two small, prosperous Canadian towns. And, we should add, expensive Canadian towns. The presence of family members no doubt boosted morale, though one of the brigade commanders, Major General James Tedlie, was not sure what his troops would do if they thought their families were in danger, as they must be if war broke out. As to their military function, in terms of an attack by a much larger Soviet army, Tedlie hoped that his troops could manage to hold out for a couple of days, using conventional weapons.[1]

During the winter of 1968-69, it was this force that was the centre of a debate in Ottawa about Canada's commitment to NATO and its European allies.

HON. MARC LALONDE (1929-)
INTERVIEW | MONTREAL, 30 NOVEMBER 1987

Like Trudeau a lawyer, a Montrealer, and a fierce federalist, Lalonde worked as an adviser to Progressive Conservative justice minister Davie Fulton and in Lester Pearson's PMO. In 1968, he became Trudeau's principal secretary, a position he held until election to Parliament in 1972. He then served in a variety of key ministerial posts, most notably Justice, Energy, and Finance.

Lalonde began with his time in Trudeau's PMO
In 1968, **Trudeau** and company were "a whole bunch of amateurs who were given the Liberal Party by its members." Trudeau had very definite ideas about the way that affairs should be run. Lalonde himself had had experience in Pearson's office, which he characterized as being like a train station, where anybody could walk in but only one man knew where the trains were going. The office was perpetually in a "nice state of disorganization."

Trudeau did not want an office like that, the more so because, unlike Pearson, he was not an expert in government; he wanted an office that was more structured, more organized ...

External Affairs as a reservoir of talent
Lalonde believed that there was a great reservoir of talent in the Department of External Affairs (DEA). It had not changed in that respect with the generations; rather, circumstances had changed. The proof lay in the attraction of employment in the department. Every year, many of the most talented people

---

1 Bothwell-Granatstein interview with Major General James Tedlie, 5 March 1988, Victoria, British Columbia (not published).

in the country struggled to get in. The department was not like its earlier manifestation: in 1940-60, it was small. By the late 1960s, it was very much bigger. But there were too few challenging jobs, so first-class minds ended up as third secretaries, stamping passports. Why not move these people elsewhere to employ them in more challenging work? Lalonde expected that this opportunity would be welcomed, as it was by some, at least the people affected. But the establishment in the department saw it as an offence to the proper conduct of life. When **Allan Gotlieb** and **Max Yalden** told Marcel Cadieux that they were leaving DEA,[2] Cadieux told them they need not expect ever to return ...

Trudeau was determined not to be constrained by established customs or (in a non-pejorative sense) prejudices. As mentioned earlier, he wanted his office to be better organized than Pearson's, and "I was put in charge of the office to do that." As for foreign policy, "I obviously had more experience in domestic policy."

Ivan Head

Ivan Head was brought in to write speeches and to be an in-house legal expert. Lalonde then got him to take a larger and larger role, handing over more and more responsibility. True, he did not hand over the Quebec-France file. That would have been unfair to Head, who was unilingual and fresh from Alberta, and who, moreover, did not know the personalities and the context. (Lalonde said he had already handled the matter under Pearson.)

New policies for DEA

In 1968, a number of issues cried out for a fresh approach. One was the imbalance between Canada's treatment of English-speaking Commonwealth states and its virtual non-relations with the new French-speaking nations. More generally, there was the sense that Canadian foreign policy as it was

---

2   Marcel Cadieux (1915-82) trained as a lawyer and joined the Department of External Affairs during the Second World War. He became USSEA in 1964 and remained in that position until 1970, when he became ambassador to the United States. The major part of Cadieux's career is ably covered by Brendan Kelly, "Marcel Cadieux, the Department of External Affairs, and Canadian International Relations: 1941-1970" (PhD thesis, University of Toronto, 2016). Cadieux's relations with Trudeau himself are examined in Brendan Kelly, "The Politician and the Civil Servant: Pierre Trudeau, Marcel Cadieux, and the Department of External Affairs (1968-1970)," *International Journal* 72, 1 (March 2017): 5-27.

expounded under Pearson did not properly represent the particular Canadian national interest or, better, the national policies we wished to pursue. We also felt that English Canadians had always taken a rather snobbish attitude toward Latin America; Latin countries were banana republics ruled by dictators, and close contact with them would pervert Canada's moral standing. This attitude entirely ignored French Canada's historic ties to Latin America through missionaries and through education. Even if those things were irrelevant, how could one ignore a whole continent?

Additionally, we were coming out of the Cold War. On that score, Lalonde made no claim to have invented the wheel: productive relations with Cuba dated back to Diefenbaker. We thought we could pursue a policy that did not need to copy the Americans. In short, we should pursue our own national interest. It was this attitude that underlay the Foreign Policy Review – the complete re-evaluation of Canada's foreign policy.

Marcel Cadieux and Trudeau saw eye to eye on separatism, nationalism, Quebec-France, and similar issues. There was considerable intellectual respect between them, as well as similarity of views. Where they differed was over organization and the role of DEA in government.

But there was increased respect for DEA, and it grew out of the Quebec nationalist question in the late 1960s. In 1969-70, PMO and DEA officials met very, very regularly, with **Gordon Robertson** and **Michael Pitfield** in attendance. During the FLQ kidnapping crisis of October 1970, they found themselves meeting twelve hours a day for weeks or months on end. The experience showed how closely linked domestic politics and international relations were.

The episode "confirmed our view" that foreign policy in Canada had been developed in a vacuum without due regard for our own national interests. While pursuing world peace, we should take Canada's own interests more into account. Lalonde had developed this view in a speech he gave much later to the Ottawa branch of the Canadian Institute of International Affairs. In effect, by 1968 "we had become the boy scouts of the world." All this made DEA pretty nervous in those years.

Quite clearly, DEA was not sure where it stood. The foreign service officers (FSOs) were demoralized by seeing Yalden and Gotlieb quitting and going to domestic departments. (From the PMO's point of view, Lalonde said, this was really an improvement in DEA's prospects.) It was interpreted as a dark plot to downgrade the department.

The Foreign Policy Review

Trudeau's early relations with DEA were not helped by the Foreign Policy Review. It became obvious that the department did not question itself enough. It wrote draft after draft of the review report, which were sent back as inadequate; they were obviously the lowest common denominator of committee work. The review became a large structural operation, with each division doing its own thing and contributing the result to the common draft. Letting just one person write the review report would have been better, Lalonde stated, Yalden or Gotlieb, for example.

Mitchell Sharp was not the man to impose novelty on DEA; he was very much a product of its environment, a junior member of the old establishment. He was not one to challenge the system. He found it extremely difficult to stand back and view his department from a distance. Lalonde, however, would not agree that Sharp did not contend for his department's interests. He argued strongly and persistently in the cabinet. On the other hand, he was a very, very loyal team player and would accept the common decision.

Department of National Defence problems

As for the Department of National Defence (DND), Lalonde shook his head. As with DEA, the PMO was trying to get DND to re-examine its policies. In 1968, defence policy was simply a series of increments: you just kept on adding new things every year without examining why. DND was very much isolated in the government, which put it at a comparative disadvantage.

The department was not always represented by strong ministers, and it was seriously handicapped by a dim-witted chief of defence staff, General Jean V. Allard. As for Deputy Minister Elgin Armstrong, Lalonde said, "I don't even remember him." There were no first-class policy people at DND. **Donald Macdonald** was a strong minister, but his successor, Jim Richardson, was out of his depth in terms of questioning the existing policy. Gilles Lamontagne was a nice, decent fellow, but as a minister he was extremely weak. Barney Danson was alright, but he was very much part of the gang: "He was not the kind of guy keen to develop a new policy."

Lalonde's only comment on **Sylvain Cloutier,** the new deputy minister in DND, was that it was "interesting that we had to create a civilian position on top of the chief of defence staff" (CDS). Fortunately, General **Jacques Dextraze** was first class as CDS, a born leader of men. Generals Gerry Thériault and Ramsey Withers were both good CDSs. No, he had not heard that Withers had been fired, and Gilles Lamontagne would not have had the authority to do it. Perhaps Withers asked for a transfer.

With DND, it was the same process as with DEA, he said. We had to get DND out of the frame of mind that Canada had to be in everything. Trudeau developed a lot of respect for DND Minister **Léo Cadieux**, but Cadieux was stuck with Allard, a bull in a china shop: "I remember Allard coming to make presentations to cabinet committees, and it was pathetic." His style of presentation was well (though unconsciously) calculated to stimulate Trudeau's faculty for asking rational questions, not to mention his intellectual arrogance. The Cabinet Committee on Priorities and Planning (P&P) meetings on defence were "long and numerous."

France and Canada

As for France, any claim that the French embassy did not interfere in Canada's internal affairs was "bullshit." Anybody who read the story of Charles de Gaulle's 1967 visit to Canada could not believe they were not interfering.[3] "We're not naive and they're not naive," Lalonde said. At the same time, it was true that not every single French bureaucrat was devoted to the cause of Quebec independence. (In July 1967, Lalonde said, most of de Gaulle's cabinet did not support his initiative.) There was a "coterie d'agitateurs au Quai d'Orsay," true believers in a separate Quebec, and the others stood around and acted noncommittal and confused. Bernard Dorin, the head of the American section at the Quai, was one of the true believers. Dorin was crazy, weird, obsessed with ideas of an Anglo-Saxon conspiracy. He would do anything to annoy, and so would his coterie ... Couve de Murville, de Gaulle's factotum, was used quite cleverly by these zealots ...

There were far-right Gaullist politicians too, such as Xavier Deniau. And Philippe Rossillon was involved through the Elysée. (Georges Pompidou as prime minister was not involved.) It was the radical Gaullists who gave the rapprochement with Quebec its impulse, and true enough, it was a costless affair for the French. It had the advantage for the French government that it kept the loonies busy. The Délégation Général du Québec in Paris also played a role.

French ambassador **Pierre-Marc Siraud** in Ottawa did not control all French activities in Canada. The consul-general in Quebec City reported

---

3 During his calamitous official visit to Canada in 1967, French president de Gaulle encouraged Quebec separatism.

directly to the Quai. The same situation obtained under Ambassador **Jacques Viot,** who was a decent fellow; he wanted things to work and did his best to make it so. But it was his successor, **Jean Béliard,** who made the real difference.

The French government was not supported by anybody. The British and the Americans thought the whole thing was tasteless and outrageous. But was Canada supported by anyone? We did not ask, Lalonde said; it was a purely Canadian affair. Was it not true that the Americans had lent us their communications from the 1970 conference of La Francophonie in Niamey? Perhaps, because we did not want the French to know our every move.

Was Quebec premier J.J. Bertrand an improvement on Daniel Johnson? Yes, because one knew that he and Julien Chouinard, the secretary-general of the Executive Council and his right-hand man, were strong and open federalists. With Claude Morin and Jacques Parizeau around, it was like the Quai d'Orsay all over again; and there was Jean-Guy Cardinal, Johnson's education minister, who collected medals from all over Africa and thought it was all for real.

HON. R. GORDON ROBERTSON (1917-2013)
INTERVIEW | OTTAWA, 19 JANUARY 1988

Robertson joined DEA in 1941, worked in Mackenzie King's PMO and Louis St. Laurent's PCO, served as deputy minister of northern affairs, and became clerk of the privy council in 1963. He held that post to 1975, when he became secretary to the cabinet for federal-provincial relations. He retired in 1979.[4]

Trudeau wanted options
On defence and foreign policy issues, Robertson began, **Trudeau** was very irritated at his inability to get either DND or DEA to really put up options. Each department was operating on the basis of well-settled policy. They weren't deliberate obstructionists, but intellectually it was very, very difficult for them to admit that there were alternatives. Robertson had remonstrated

---

[4] Robertson's autobiography is *Memoirs of a Very Civil Servant: Mackenzie King to Pierre Trudeau* (Toronto: University of Toronto Press, 2000).

with DND types, at first mildly and then more forcefully, trying to get them to understand what Trudeau wanted. Trudeau went behind the backs of the departments and got **Ivan Head** to produce the real options only after experiencing disappointment with DND and DEA. He knew that ministers by themselves did not have the capacity to produce useful results, and that bothered him. And no, the reviews were not just an intellectual exercise.

Robertson was aware that Head was working on something for Trudeau, though he was not at all certain that he knew its full extent. Normally, he would have tried to ensure that a department did not get something sprung on it, but on the other hand, he could not be, and could not be seen to be, a leak to the departments from the PCO/PMO. There had to be "a nice, neat line" between disclosure and retaining the confidence of the PMO.

The PCO and the PMO

There was no revolutionary change between Pearson and Trudeau's cabinet committee system. The main thing Trudeau did was give power of decision to cabinet committees, subject to reconsideration before the full cabinet, the latter requiring notice. The second change was Trudeau's insistence on options being presented.

Robertson and **Marc Lalonde** tried to clarify the relationship between the PCO and the PMO in two papers presented to the P&P in 1970 or 1971. The basic purpose was to clarify the respective roles.

The days started with a meeting *à trois* – Trudeau, Marc Lalonde, and Robertson. One more person was added later, possibly someone handling the public relations function.

Now, this was not really different from the Pearson period. It remained "indefinable" where the politics stopped and the policy began.

Anyway, the meetings were the easiest way to have a complete exchange of information. Lalonde had the advantage, since he got the minutes of the cabinet and the agendas; only occasionally did Robertson hanker after more. Lalonde, Robertson said, had to be the judge of what was political and what was policy.

Trudeau's biases on foreign policy

When Trudeau came in as prime minister, he had a lot of prejudices on foreign policy issues and biases, "but damn little experience in the foreign field." He had not worked on foreign policy when he was at the PCO. He had worked with and for Robertson in preparation for the British North America Act Number 2 of 1949,[5] and in preparing the two dominion-provincial conferences of 1950. He was very good at that, but he had no foreign policy assignment.

One of Trudeau's early prejudices was his "scorn" for the Commonwealth, Robertson noted. He did not even want to go to the Commonwealth Conference in London in 1969, asking why **Mitchell Sharp** could not attend instead, and he was presumably expressing his scorn with his dating behaviour and his pirouettes while there. But then Trudeau showed his capacity for change and growth by changing his mind about the Commonwealth. It was, he realized, a major forum for a good part of the Third World, and the Third World was a good part of the world. He discovered that there was and could be a genuine exchange of views and information.

There was obviously real compatibility between Trudeau and Ivan Head. Trudeau looked to Head as a visible alternative to DEA and drew on him to pique and poke DEA (of course, he liked to poke in general and not just at DEA). Yes, Trudeau had a genuine resentment of DEA, which Robertson believed derived from his treatment by missions during his world voyaging. But there was no resentment of the PCO, no hard feelings dating back to the 1950s. The contrary was the case. Robertson and Trudeau had "an extremely happy relationship," meaning "I liked him, he liked me." (Yet they were not friends, the way **Michael Pitfield** and Trudeau later were: that close friendship led to trouble, as it did for Pitfield, and blame, whether justified or not.)

Trudeau greatly respected Norman Robertson;[6] he was genuinely diffident as to whether he should impose on Mrs. Robertson after her husband's death in 1968. Robertson eventually insisted that Trudeau must go, and at Trudeau's request, he accompanied him. While there, Robertson did most of the talking. Diffidence was a real part of Trudeau's character, as much as intellectual arrogance.

---

5 The BNA Act (No. 2) of 1949 dealt with procedures for amendment of the BNA Act.
6 A major figure in DEA history, Norman Robertson (1904-68) was twice under secretary of state for external affairs (USSEA). He held senior diplomatic posts in London and Washington. See J.L. Granatstein, *A Man of Influence: Norman A. Robertson and Canadian Statecraft, 1929-68* (Ottawa: Deneau, 1981).

Trudeau's circle

Trudeau's innermost circle was French speaking, people he had known since youth, who were part of his milieu ... The next circle out included such people as Robertson himself and Pitfield, in both of whom Trudeau reposed "complete confidence." Among the ministers, Bud Drury was the closest on the English side because of his intelligence and utter straightforwardness. He could analyze things so clearly and straightly, and doubtless Trudeau admired Bud intellectually. He never had to doubt his purposes. **Otto Lang** was another for whom Trudeau had regard and **Donald Macdonald** too.

Trudeau was never won to an idea or a decision just because he admired its author. Take Norman Robertson, for example, whom he would have seen as both an architect and a prisoner of the foreign policy system. That was why he would not have given much credence to Robertson's analysis of foreign policy.

Trudeau had two *idées fixes*: a prejudice against DEA and the view that its policy was unqualified dogma. He revolted against dogma.

Trudeau's work habits did not vary much. He was always a very hard worker and always did his homework; you could count on Trudeau being the best prepared at any cabinet. He read all his briefs and cogitated while tramping around the Gatineau. Even when apparently not working, he was.

In the late 1960s and early 1970s, P&P was clearly the top committee. It had more influence than any other, although a committee's influence did not depend on its control over spending. Such things as chairmanship by the prime minister counted, as in the case of the Cabinet Committee on Federal-Provincial Relations. Trudeau's decisions counted there. But it was also true that the Cabinet Committee on External Affairs and National Defence was not functioning as well as it might. It was known that the prime minister had his own strong views on these matters, and so the committee's efforts were to some degree undermined. Trudeau attended it at times, as did Robertson because of his view that if something – some issue, some item – greatly interested the prime minister, he himself should know of it.

There were many differences between Trudeau and Mitchell Sharp, who was in a very uncomfortable position, caught between his department, with whose views he was in basic sympathy, and the government. It could also be, Robertson thought, that Sharp saw the Foreign Policy Review as more of "a formalistic exercise" than a genuine re-examination of policy. Robertson had more liking for **Léo Cadieux**, perhaps because he thought that Sharp "should have known better and done better." Cadieux was a good man, who tried to do well by his department and the best he could for the government.

Intelligence about Quebec

Robertson turned next to intelligence. Trudeau chaired the Cabinet Committee on Security and Intelligence, and Robertson chaired the mirror committee of deputy ministers. The problem for him was knowing how much to bring to the prime minister's attention, since Trudeau largely relied on him to do that. There must have been small sessions of Marcel Cadieux, Marc Lalonde, and Robertson to consider this or that French transgression – the French were generally being "pretty damn pretentious and obnoxious" at this time. They knew of Philippe Rossillon's activities stirring up separatist sentiment in Quebec and among the Acadians;[7] they often had to consider whether it was best to conceal what they knew or whether they should intervene to stop it. How far should the RCMP go?

Unfortunately, the RCMP had no great expertise in or on Quebec during the late 1960s. They probably should have hired somebody good as assistant commissioner but had not. The RCMP were thin in Quebec because they were not the provincial police and therefore had no ears to the ground, and they had very few French Canadians. Those they did have were from the police side, not from intelligence.

Robertson said that intelligence at the top was not always structured formally; if you let things go to the cabinet committee, the decisions tended to take on some shape, some substance, requiring action, such as the expulsion of foreign diplomats. The government never actually had to expel a Frenchman during this time.

They did have sessions at the cabinet level on the question of dealing with members of the Parti Québécois (PQ). Should a Péquiste be treated the same as a member of the Communist Party of Canada (CPC)? The answer, to the dismay of the RCMP, was no: they should have access to the public service,

....

7 Philippe Rossillon (1931-), a French functionary, started his public career as a supporter of "French Algeria" before Algerian independence and moved on to promote the French language in Canada and elsewhere, a desperate quest because of his belief that French was losing ground everywhere and must be sustained against its main adversary, English. He was known to be a strong supporter of Quebec separatism.

even confidential jobs, but nevertheless the fact of their membership should be brought to the attention of the deputy minister of the relevant department. This was, in a phrase, "relevant information." The treatment of the PQ and the CPC was interesting: both were legal parties. The RCMP had to be strictly instructed to do as they were told over this.

Discussing the RCMP claim that Ottawa had been informed regarding the FLQ before the October Crisis of 1970 – "I've heard them say afterwards that they warned the government" – Robertson remarked that he'd "read their documents" at the time. All the RCMP did was list organizations, list groups, even those like the FLQ that we now know to have been very disorganized independent cells. He recalled a 1967 meeting in which the RCMP were sharply criticized for spending all their money on communists and nothing on the much greater threat posed by violent separatist groups. The RCMP concentration on communism was the equivalent of the unqualified dogma of DND and DEA. He was not sure that they would have known how to change. Putting in a Marcel Cadieux type would have helped, but they didn't.

Robertson didn't think that Trudeau had great confidence in the police on this issue or on the communist one either. The police were good at pursuing people, thorough and meticulous, but Trudeau had no respect for their judgment. They were not intellectually subtle at all. He relied instead on Robertson and Marcel Cadieux. And any idea that Trudeau had any leftist or communist tendencies is "rot." Nobody who believed in political freedom, in the individual, as Trudeau did could possibly be attracted to authoritarianism.

True, Trudeau was not a military sympathizer; his wartime activities, the German helmet story,[8] probably drove "great big wedges" between him and the military. He had formally correct relations with General Allard, but the two men were not intellectually close.

Remaking the public service
When DEA began to be used as a milch cow source for personnel, Cadieux and others did complain that they were being plundered. But Robertson had absolutely no sympathy for their point of view. He told them that DEA had a great resource of talented people, who could be replaced. The head hunting

---

[8] Trudeau apparently drove a motorcycle around Montreal while wearing a German helmet.

was not an attack on the department and was not related to policy. The fact was that a lot of departments did not have quality people. The Golden Age was limited to Finance, the Bank of Canada, and DEA – too "damn few." Other departments were pretty bleak ...

The Senior Appointments Secretariat originated with Bob Bryce keeping a file in his desk drawer.[9] As cabinet secretary, Robertson personally handled senior appointments: "I did most of it myself." There was no interdepartmental committee; that came later. The business of formal evaluation at the top also came later. He did have a bit of help, derived from informal discussions with other departments. He would then meet personally with the prime minister, with only the latter's principal secretary present. And, finally, perhaps appointments did become more formal, even before he ceased to be cabinet secretary ...

The separate mandates sent to deputy ministers from the PCO, Robertson admitted, made him uncomfortable. This practice ultimately derived from Mackenzie King's appropriation of the sole responsibility for nominating deputy ministers. After Robertson's time, it developed into Pitfield sending a mandate letter, a practice that is fraught with the possibility of difficulty. What then is the role of the minister? To whom is the deputy minister responsible? Fortunately, that practice seemed to have dribbled away, at least in part.

The concentration of power in the PCO, the formalizing and extension of its influence, did occur. Robertson had a close relationship with Trudeau, but not as close as Pitfield's. It meant that Pitfield took the blame for some things that were not his responsibility.

The Federal-Provincial Relations Office
As for the Federal-Provincial Relations Office (FPRO), he was secretary from January 1975 to December 1979. Quebec's foreign dimension was a major part of its concern, as it had been since at least 1967, with Premier Daniel Johnson. Claude Morin there was the evil genius. At first, Robertson and Morin were relatively close, through Jean Lesage, his minister back in the 1950s.[10] There is no doubt that Morin was one of the most astute schemers

---

9 R.B. Bryce (1910-97) was clerk of the privy council, 1954-63, and deputy minister of finance, 1963-70.
10 Liberal premier of Quebec, 1960-66, and a former federal minister.

he'd ever encountered. Morin used to phone Robertson frequently, and he was even helpful in setting up a Quebec version of the PCO, at Lesage's behest. Soon Robertson came to realize that Morin was the motive force, the catalyst for the expansion of the role of the Quebec government: "He was the one who wrote the ticket." He was a master of creating a situation where it was no-win for his opponent, either way or any way. Robertson gradually became distrustful of him and was not surprised when Morin officially declared himself a Péquiste. He was a very astute man.

After 1976 and the PQ election victory, the FPRO tried to develop plans to meet whatever strategy the PQ might develop abroad and domestically. The office consistently considered such matters, whether interior or exterior to the country. Robertson set up Paul Tellier's unit to do nothing but cope with the problems posed by the PQ government.[11] Inevitably, much if not most of the counter-effort was francophone, though "I was up to my neck in it." Robertson was the chairman throughout of a committee that had to vet federal strategy in the area. (There was one other senior anglophone, Frank Carter, Robertson's number two.) As to the ministers involved, not all were francophone, but his memory had lapsed as to exactly who they were. Because he had spent four months in Quebec City during 1967 (he had to return prematurely to Ottawa), he learned French and knew many people there; his French and his acquaintances were useful in the 1960s and 1970s.

During the Trudeau period, cabinet business was almost always in English. Cabinet documents could be in either language, and they were not translated. The fact is that the language of work was English.

HON. MICHAEL PITFIELD (1937-)

INTERVIEWS | OTTAWA, 20 JANUARY 1988, AND MONTREAL, 25 FEBRUARY 1988

Pitfield, a lawyer, worked for Progressive Conservative justice minister Davie Fulton, became assistant secretary in Pearson's PCO, and was then planification secretary under Trudeau. Clerk of the privy council from 1975 to 1979, he was fired by Joe Clark but returned after Trudeau won the 1980 election.

....

11 Tellier (1939-) occupied a series of increasingly senior posts in the civil service and eventually became clerk of the privy council, 1985-92.

INTERVIEW | OTTAWA, 20 JANUARY 1988

He began by speaking of DEA
Pitfield argued that the crisis in DEA reflected a larger crisis in Canadian central government that dated back to the end of the 1950s and had first been identified by the Glassco Royal Commission on Government Organization, which reported in 1962-63. If Glassco marked the end of an era, the era that began at that point had not yet ended.

One could look at Canada's status, a rich (relatively) powerful country at the end of the Second World War, sitting on all the important councils of the world. At that time, non-military government expenditure was less than 10 percent of the GNP. But with the recovery of Europe and the defeated powers, with the growth of non-military expenditures by a factor of three or four, the world had changed.

The old world was one in which government was small and the press was benign, where it was quite feasible to borrow a government plane every Friday, fly to Knowlton, Quebec, and get picked up on Monday – and no one would comment. The old world centred on Finance and on DEA, with Trade and Commerce halfway between them. In the new world, the old verities of macro-economics and commercial policy were no longer sufficient. Just taking a cadre or two from DEA or Finance to strengthen Trade and Commerce was not enough. We went from three economic departments to nine in Diefenbaker's time, to thirteen or fourteen under Pearson, and finally to seventeen under Trudeau. The personnel of these departments began to challenge Finance or DEA for expertise. Their problems were micro, not macro, but nobody in Finance did macro. Pitfield believed that in a fifteen-year period from the early 1960s, more change occurred than in any comparable span. The effort to accomplish it was highly rational, and a massive amount of paper was left behind to attest to it. Even bringing the Trade Commissioner Service over to DEA took up three full filing cabinets.

In 1968, the senior men in the civil service were the last to have known Clifford Clark and Norman Robertson.[12] They were trying to grapple with the new reality and with the view of systems that had imbued their predecessors.

---

12   Clifford Clark (1889-1952) was deputy minister of finance from 1932 to 1952. See Robert Wardhaugh, *Behind the Scenes: The Life and Work of Clifford Clark* (Toronto: University of Toronto Press, 2010).

The upcoming generation had no understanding of what had gone before, but (by implication) Pitfield did. He tried to direct policy toward consistency, toward preserving the (corporate) cultures of the experimentation on a Canadian foreign office. Yet unless there was change, he feared that DEA's very existence would be imperilled – at least as a significant department of government. Without access to the levers of foreign economic policy, it could not possibly flourish. Could one claim, he mused, that DEA had much influence on free trade or Meech Lake?

To what extent could you distinguish foreign policy from administration? Yet look at Marcel Cadieux's reaction to personnel competition and his attempt to erect a stone wall around his choice francophone personnel, who in DEA were supposed to carry out a policy that most of them were not in sympathy with. The level of attention that DEA got was pretty high throughout Pitfield's own tenure, and the consistency of the reform policies was also very high, with very little doubling back. He was trying to protect DEA as *the* expert adviser to the government on foreign policy.

He protected DEA against the development of counter-pressures, such as **Donald Macdonald** coming to the cabinet and demanding that DEA butt out of foreign energy policy and turn it all over to his department. Pitfield admitted that there had been a period when C.D. Howe had run his own foreign policy, but there was only one Howe;[13] in any case, his position was definitely ceded by 1958 and was gone altogether by 1961.

The force behind the pressures was the entry of the government into micro-economics. Since Finance had none at the outset, it could not prevent or control the establishment of competing departments of micro-economics. When you expand to welfare policy, you also expand to distribution and thus to regional policies.

Trade and Commerce personnel approached the problem in an old-fashioned way, and partly as a result the whole system was breaking down by the beginning of the 1980s. Pitfield had taken the position that he would do something only if the various deputies begged for a solution. **Gordon Osbaldeston**'s letters of the period testify to the near collapse of the system. Finally, the deputies did beg for mercy and got the amalgamated department as a result. If that had not been done, Pitfield or Osbaldeston could not have resolved the "irresolvable."

....

13   C.D. Howe was a senior Liberal cabinet minister, 1935-57.

So the 1980-82 reforms were not imposed from the centre, but the 1968-70 ones were, and by fiat and by stealth. Many costs were attached to these reforms in blighted careers. In fact, the later reforms were accomplished despite the objections of the centre. It will be interesting to see whether these reforms endure and whether the objectives remain valid. He reflected on the role of the Bank of Canada in international economic policy, given that (apparently) the Bank of International Settlements has more to do with actual economic trends and effects. But debate at the moment, pressure-centred, short-term, is not up to resolving these questions.

Trudeau on nationalism and foreign policy
Another way of looking at the era of change is to remember that Trudeau's hatred of nationalism was one basis for his distinctive foreign policy. His hatred of Quebec nationalism caused him to eschew demagogic excesses in the service of Canadian nationalism; yet his policies were designed to be protective of the Canadian nation and of Canadian nationalism. In this respect, he was in sync with Pearson.

Indeed, there were many continuities between Pearson's late views on foreign policy and those of Trudeau. As assistant secretary to the cabinet, Pitfield often heard Pearson exclaim on the arrogant Americans and sclerotic NATO policies. Pearson commonly remarked that our US policy was lily-livered and that it consisted of hand wringing. The similarities between Pearson and Trudeau were concealed by the hurt that Pearson's friends ascribed to him because of his treatment by Trudeau's entourage after 1968.

"When you get into Trudeau in terms of nuclear disarmament or the GATT Tokyo Round,[14] it seems to me you'll get into a discussion of the evolution of the intellectual content of Canadian policy that parallels the evolution of domestic decision making," Pitfield said. He again lamented that Canadians today were not up to that level of debate.

He sometimes thought that DEA was the frontline, the heart, of the defence of Canadian national interests because of Trudeau's reforms. Those who had known Norman Robertson carried the message of a certain view of Canada's place in the world, though it was increasingly difficult to do so, given the changes domestically and internationally.

....
14 The Tokyo Round (1973-79) was an international negotiation conducted under the auspices of the General Agreement on Tariffs and Trade (GATT). It reduced tariffs worldwide and tackled the problem of non-tariff barriers.

He wondered whether the late 1980s were a reaction against the Trudeau years. Now there was minimalism, paying the necessary dues to hide under the American umbrella. This was anathema to Robertson and to Klaus Goldschlag, his intellectual successor.[15] Why, he asked, had Canada discarded multilateralism as the best defence of its identity in favour of (today's) bilateralism?

Pitfield visualized an FSO image, "the **Ross Campbells**," people whose intransigence in debate helped make 1968-70 into a watershed. But was it a watershed? No, it carried on for fourteen years after that.

The problem was that DEA did not accept Trudeau's 1968 election as a mandate for change. In Pitfield's view, Pearson would have sympathized with the change more than the DEA old guard did. It was almost as if the "collectivity which was External failed to meet the challenge of 'reborning' itself." (He pondered the word and decided it was exactly what he meant.)

How did the old guard's 1968 performance compare with the way that DEA met the challenges of 1929 or 1931? In his view, not well at all. But in the previous generation, DEA had led the pack as Canada emerged as a middle power even though it had a population of only 12 million. Trudeau wanted Canada to have a foreign policy that would enable it to stand on its own two feet in an increasingly inclement world. And Pearson had wanted that too. Campbell and the others thought we could do it best by adhering to the same bias of policies that we had had in the 1940s. They said, we are the professionals, and foreign policy is different from domestic policy.

The Trudeau people's response was governed by their feeling that they were new; they didn't have any sense of the coming generation in DEA. Perhaps Trudeau and company would have handled the transition better if they'd been able to reach into the department and get the new leaders and use them constructively (in the best sense). But they didn't, and the result was at least partly botched.

It was just at this time [1968] that the connection between DEA and the PMO was weakened further by the exclusion of the departmental secondments that had been there since Mackenzie King's day. The idea that somebody from DEA had a relationship of some intimacy with the prime minister, as

---

15 Klaus Goldschlag (1922-2012) was a senior foreign service officer, ambassador to various countries including his native Germany, and deputy USSEA. His career ended prematurely when he was disabled as the result of a medical procedure while he was ambassador to Germany.

Basil Robinson had had with Diefenbaker, would have helped. [The relationship between the Trudeau government and DEA] was a long process, but 1968 was a key point in it ...

In summing up the Foreign and Defence Policy Reviews, Pitfield said, "I think the events of the late sixties were badly handled, were traumatic, were in a sense inevitable." Yet Pitfield felt they were mitigated to some extent over the next fourteen years. Still, a very important cadre in DEA never forgot and never forgave them. "What a tragedy," he said. You could write a play or a piece balancing the mishandling with the inevitability.

He wondered to what degree DEA's recruitment mechanisms in the 1960s helped create a department with an inherent sense of its priestly duties, the protector of NATO against the barbarians.

He warned that anyone who studied DEA and foreign policy should approach the cabinet documents with caution. If you look at the cabinet minutes, you'll see an extensive debate over the Third Option and whether its emphasis ought to be toward Europe or Japan. DEA, supported by francophone ministers, favoured Europe; ministers from Western Canada, conscious of their region and its myths, wanted Japan. That would be a bow to them. They wanted to be credible at home.

As to whether **Allan Gotlieb** could have been a link to DEA from Trudeau, that was impossible, because Gotlieb was very much an outsider. He was Cadieux's man, promoted fast and regarded with jealousy in his own department. His alliance with Trudeau was like Derek Burney's with Mulroney, the connection of talent to power.

Trudeau didn't buy DEA's assessment of its own self-worth. He may have tuned in to the experience of francophones in Ottawa, who were embittered at the way that DEA had treated people such as Jean Désy or Georges Vanier.[16] To those who believed that bilingualism was a remedy for Canada, this was a sin. As someone who'd been deeply involved in DEA appointments for twenty years, Pitfield could truthfully say that the treatment of francophones as second class was a great embarrassment. They were treated the same way the army treats its communications branch.

The overwhelming, overflowing cup of unhappiness was the way the "administrative officers" were treated by the mostly English-speaking political officers. Trudeau's own departure from Ottawa might have been looked on

....

16   Désy and Vanier were senior diplomats in the 1940s.

as desertion (presumably by the Anglo establishment). It might have been a disowning of what he left behind.

So Trudeau was arguing a certain view of the Canadian national interest, of national development, in the very important election of 1968.

The Foreign Policy Review
As for the Foreign Policy Review, Pitfield remarked that Trudeau was dedicated to the belief that high policy should emerge from rational discussion among men of goodwill. The early characteristic of his government was that it was in transition, and he didn't want to lose ministers in the process. It was the wearing down of one group by another. That was why the Foreign Policy Review was conducted by a committee, why it took so much time. Trudeau could have had it written by one man, but he might have lost six ministers in the process. He didn't.

Pitfield apologized for citing Ross Campbell as a type; he had a high regard for Campbell, and on NATO, Campbell's views were closer to the prime minister's than to many others.

INTERVIEW | MONTREAL, 25 FEBRUARY 1988

Trudeau's personality and work habits
Pitfield once again contended that the Pearson period was the one of radical change and that Trudeau inherited the mechanisms Pearson had left behind.

It was Pearson who assigned Pitfield to Trudeau over a ruckus between Quebec and France, on one side, and Canada on the other at a Francophonie conference on education in Gabon in early 1968. Pitfield thought that one should really study the Trudeau of the 1950s, and he recalled Norman Robertson's good opinion of Trudeau, which he had urged on Pearson – that though Trudeau was too eccentric to be a good foreign service officer, he had the capacity to be an exceptional something else.

Trudeau wasn't capricious or wilful. The Trudeau whom Pitfield knew had decided to put away childish things. For example, it was notorious before April 1968 that he was never on time for anything; afterward, he was never late for anything. Even his caprices were dictated by calculation. Take his famous 1977 pirouette in London: that was a protest against the protocol that was causing the British (with the Queen as their instrument) to make a distinction between the heads of state and the mere heads of government who were attending the Commonwealth summit.

Pearson, Pitfield said, had decided to reform the cabinet structure after reading Walter Goerlitz on the German general staff and Lord Hankey's diaries.[17] He took the assigned staff from DEA, etc., and made them non-partisan, whereas before they were expected to handle all kinds of political duties (except speech making). He created the distinction between the partisan PMO and the PCO. Trudeau benefitted from these changes and took to them like a duck to water.

In the cabinet, Trudeau was as well briefed as any other minister, but he had the great advantage of knowing every minister's brief, so he knew how they would react. He knew what Finance or DND were telling their ministers and could react. And his dialectical skill was greater than anybody's.

Trudeau has been criticized as "the imperial prime minister." Really, he was the least imperial. His ministers (especially John Roberts or Don Macdonald) would put him down, and he wouldn't mind; he liked a good fight. But on some issues, it was true that Trudeau knew more than any other member of the cabinet, and it showed. There were, as well, the subjects on which he was confident he was right. With them, he could be like "a bloody steamroller." And Trudeau "vacuumed up information and data from a machine set up by Pearson that could give it to him every night."

Pearson's changes
It was under Pearson that a distinction started to be made in cabinet business between policy and programs. Now, 70 percent of what interests the politicians are the programs, not the policies, even though the policy is a precondition to the program. But the cabinet was breaking down under the combined load, as witness Diefenbaker's endless cabinet meetings. You just cannot make decisions seriatim as Diefenbaker did. The cabinet was becoming a co-ordinating rather than a decision-making body, and so Pearson decided to create an executive committee, Priorities and Planning.

Pitfield knew what was in Pearson's mind during this period because Pearson came to the Vaniers' every Monday night for dinner, and the Vaniers had their official staff sit in. You might say that Pearson was a prime minister

---

17   Walter Goerlitz, *History of the German General Staff, 1657-1945* (New York: Praeger, 1953, and subsequent editions). Maurice (Lord) Hankey was the legendary British cabinet secretary of the 1910s and 1920s who practically invented the job. His diaries were published in 1961. See Stephen Roskill, *Hankey: Man of Secrets*, 3 vols. (London: Collins, 1970-74).

in rebellion against the very system he had benefitted from. He wanted to take the power he had had as USSEA with him; as prime minister, he was anxious to transfer it back from the civil servants to the ministers. In the cabinet committee system, he brought the civil servants to the table and made them speak up. But this was in aid of getting the ministers, not the civil servants, to make the decisions.

DEA is the department in which prime ministers naturally take the most interest, so **Paul Martin**, Pearson's SSEA, was at a disadvantage. Pearson had ended the seconding of FSOs to his personal office, people such as Jean Fournier, Jack Hodgson,[18] and Ross Martin. "By God, I tell you, what a difference of view" that was. But though making the distinction between the political and the administrative could be seen as an altruistic move, and Pitfield in his naïveté saw it as such at the time, he might now be tempted to say that it was also to have better control and better accountability. You could divide and rule so much better that way. Trudeau was the beneficiary of that too.

DND's bad situation

Pitfield traced the DND situation back to the 1950s. The cabinet office had everything in it, from the defence budget to ministerial decision making. In the event, everything disappeared down to National Defence Headquarters at Cartier Square. The deal in the 1960s was that DEA set the parameters of foreign policy, and Finance set the parameters of the budget; the PCO would monitor the co-ordination, and DND, within those limits, would run itself. The Cabinet Committee on External Affairs and National Defence hardly ever dealt with defence matters. It was not a significant part of any rethinking or of any speculation on the foreign policy side. It was just fed policy through DEA's Defence Liaison 1 or 2 divisions, and DEA liked it that way: "NATO set the policy and life went on."

"I thought this a tragedy," Pitfield said. It meant that a whole side of foreign policy was literally closed to the foreign policy people. It was terribly wasteful in terms of finance, for what it meant was the status quo plus annual increments. The money just escalated, and nobody worried.

The biggest tragedy was in Defence itself. The military felt isolated and insignificant. They felt rightly that their concerns were not ministers' concerns.

---

18 Misspelled as "Hodson" in the original transcript, Hodgson was Pearson's principal secretary. We are grateful to Jeremy Kinsman and Brendan Kelly for clarifying this.

The fact was that only three ministers were concerned: the prime minister, the minister of national defence, and the minister of external affairs. Their policy had "no roots, nobody who could stand up for you." Pitfield therefore sought to show DND that participating in the policy process would be in its own self-interest. One way was by establishing a posting at the PCO for a promising DND officer. It was the second such, the first having been for DEA. He went to the chief of the defence staff (CDS) and outlined the problem, as described above. He made it plain to the CDS that he wanted somebody in whom the CDS and the deputy minister had confidence, somebody to whom DND would listen, and someone destined for promotion.

He paused to reflect on the vicissitudes of fame: if you bring an arrangement out into the open, you are accused of overt power grabbing; if you do not, you are accused of being subtle. Really, a cabinet secretary has enough power without grabbing for more; he has enough demands on his time not to want more. And in this case, Pitfield strongly denied having any ulterior motive. You can't beat the rap; whatever you did, they thought you devious.

This time, he thought his ploy of seconding a prominent military officer to the PCO was successful. DND came, after ten years, to accept the arrangement in the terms he had used, and when he left Ottawa, Pitfield remembered, the DND people were the only ones who gave him a testimonial dinner.

The idea achieved many, though not all, of its objectives. On the financial side, DND's position improved. It got a 3 percent annual increase – an enormous achievement – "and we got it plus an escalation factor" of the rate of inflation. All this was because of greater ministerial involvement "and because of the confidence we pieced together."

His own view at this time was that life was not a zero-sum game. He was not then familiar (as he later became at Harvard) with Tom Schelling's game theories in which they teach that everything is confrontation and that nobody in a bureaucracy speaks for anything but his own department. That was not Pitfield's view, pre-1980, or the view of people such as Norman Robertson or Bob Bryce. "Now if I was to go back, I'd be somewhat more skeptical of departmental briefs than I was then," he stated.

DEA's problems
The problems of DEA existed because of history, because of events. There was the growth of the program side of DEA and the disappearance of its foreign policy thinkers. This was not the consequence of conscious decision making, however. By the late 1960s, early 1970s, some DEA people had come

to think that only by having big programs could you have big clout. Typical of game playing. But at the time, it seemed to Pitfield that men of goodwill could solve a problem by applying their minds to it. And, as he said in the last interview, when he did the reorganization of 1979-80, he got every single one of the deputies "on that committee" to request it in writing. Nevertheless, for about 20 percent, he had to use fiat to counter their turf defences.

Thinking in DEA
But to return to his defence arrangements, he thought they worked on the whole, and he was happier with them than he was on foreign policy.

To think out foreign and defence policy, all you needed was 30 or fewer people. Compare that to the 100,000-plus in DND or the 6,000 in DEA.

The idea was to use Klaus Goldschlag as associate USSEA and make him responsible for policy with a small staff. So Klaus was to come back and head the policy side. Allan Gotlieb was too program-oriented, not of the policy school, and though **Si Taylor** was bright and policy-capable, he was too much on the European side, or at least was so regarded. The **Tom Delworth**s and the **Geoffrey Pearson**s were too embittered to work.

Pitfield remembered meeting Klaus when he was on his way back from a meeting with younger FSOs in Cyprus, where officers from our Middle East posts had gathered. He and Klaus agreed on the need for a policy apparatus, and Klaus thought that at the outside, he needed fifteen officers. Pitfield added that none of our foreign policy thinkers, Pearson or Robertson, for example, had ever been good administrators.

What had sparked his interest in this kind of position? At summits, Pitfield had met "political directors" from other foreign offices, people who were number two or three in their departments, with great prestige and an accepted function. They were regarded as the "constructive mind" in their departments.

How could this be developed in Canada? He and Klaus knew that to pick fifteen first-class officers would be to make them loathed as privileged by their peers. And Klaus's group would have a call on funds that would be only 10-15 percent of what everybody else at Klaus's level would have. He added that this proposal was quite time-specific, 1975-81, and should not be confused with the larger or longer Policy Analysis Group problem.

The same problem occurred in DND. The question was, did you want them to have a capacity to think about defence policy? DEA was very much of two minds about that. The last thing some of them wanted was to allow

George Lindsay to exist.[19] This negative point was argued in DEA right up to the assistant USSEA and had to be resolved by Marcel Cadieux.

Cadieux's problem in dealing with any kind of reorganization, especially to create a thinking division, was that he had three-quarters of the department against him, including – especially – many of the francophones, who thought he was taking too hard a line on Quebec. The francophones were very split over de Gaulle, and they knifed Marcel. Plus, Marcel had to spend a lot of time defending Paul Martin from Mike Pearson, and he was being raided for good people. Remember, Pitfield said, that an FSO could hope to become an SX-2 in two years via the non-departmental route; inside the department, it could take twenty-five years. Marcel had his own large problems, therefore, and little time to spare for other things.

The whole problem of policy thinking related to the other question: Was DEA relevant? Would it continue to be a great department of state? Remember that Donald Macdonald demanded that DEA butt out of foreign energy policy. And it was true that the old instrument had failed to reorganize to service its market.

Allan Gotlieb's solution was to put DEA into programs and to enlarge its mandate. He did this against the background of those who felt slighted by the Defence and Foreign Policy Reviews. Allan's creation looked from the outside like a department that was all muscle and no brains. It couldn't even come up with new ideas for economic summitry or for Canadian-American relations; all we had was people who could run programs. But, Pitfield reminded, Klaus and Taylor in their own day were capable of thought.

Pitfield returned to the need for a political director. The word "political" triggered another thought. DEA was the most political of all departments in terms of individual politics. It was full of bright people bickering and quarrelling, like the Alpha colony in *Brave New World*.[20] The most devastating comment Trudeau made about the department came after his retirement.

....

19 Lindsay (1920-2011) was chief of operational research and analysis at DND from 1967 to 1987.
20 A novel by the British author Aldous Huxley, *Brave New World* depicts a future stratified according to intelligence. Chapter 16 mentions an experiment in which a colony of Alphas, members of the intelligentsia class, was founded on Cyprus. It failed because the colonists competed against each other and were unable to function as a team.

He and Pitfield had both read Strobe Talbott's *Deadly Gambits*.[21] What bothered Trudeau was that it was news to him, and it was news to Pitfield too. Trudeau's comment: "We're really not very good at what we think we're good at." If DEA wasn't about these things, who was? Now, it's a big order for a country like Canada to be innovative and fresh, but a lot of where we stood was not satisfactory.

Take the 1982 NATO summit meeting in Bonn, which was "an absolute and complete and total disaster," where everybody just gave set-pieces and walked out. Trudeau, the German chancellor Helmut Schmidt, and the Belgian prime minister remonstrated: was this what we came to NATO for? DEA should be the cutting edge. They knew what was going to happen at the meeting.

Foreign policy formulation is particularly a challenge for Canada, as the Canadian identity has become more assertive and must be imprinted on our policy.

It was a contradiction to have DEA tell you on the one hand that nobody listened, and on the other, that it didn't have anything to say. And by the way, there wasn't a problem of intermediaries or of transmission. People such as Klaus had immediate access to the prime minister.

Pitfield discussed time and schedules. He spent no more than 10 percent of his time on foreign affairs, and of that, half was devoted to problems of personnel and budget.

It wasn't that DEA was a constant disappointment to Trudeau from 1968 to 1984. He didn't mean that. One should guard against the tendency of the inner circle to denounce those in the outer darkness as anonymous bureaucratic bunglers. They would say this to the prime minister and give him possibly the wrong impression. But even now, DEA was not reconciled to what it is. There was also a danger in thinking that foreign policy can be summed up in neat formulas.

But if we are going to send the prime minister around the world on a Peace Initiative in hopes of diffusing Cold War tensions, thereby twisting the

---

21 Strobe Talbott, *Deadly Gambits* (New York: A.A. Knopf, 1984). Talbott recounted the arms control negotiations within the American government and with the Soviet Union. It was a story of frustration and intransigence, rich in detail. The gist of Trudeau's comment was that Talbott's history was better than anything his own diplomats had supplied him with.

American tail or plucking its feathers, we'd better have thought it through in terms of its impact on other aspects of Canadian-American relations. If we depart from the main thrust of our policy – multilateralism – we should think that through.

We tried even to get the department to think about free trade; but as recently as **Ed Ritchie**'s day, the reply was that there was no need because 80 percent of Canadian foreign policy dealt with the United States. "Unquote." Pitfield found this attitude astonishing.

Look at the Regan green paper on sectoral free trade.[22] It was a mish-mash. What happened was that the department produced a draft. Gotlieb came up from his kingdom in Washington and trashed it. Osbaldeston, who had no foreign policy experience, and whose appointment was therefore a mistake, couldn't put his foot down, and the result was a pastiche of compromises. The SSEA hadn't read it. It came up to the cabinet without any recommendations. The cabinet found that it didn't meet the political requirements of the situation and imposed its own conclusions, which are in the final chapter, but they are free floating with respect to the rest of the document. They are by themselves with respect to sectoral free trade. How could DEA send to the cabinet, nine months before the election of 1984, a paper without recommendations?

The National Energy Programme
It was not true that the National Energy Programme (NEP) was sprung on DEA without notice or warning. Quite untrue, Pitfield said. **Marc Lalonde** had a small backroom committee. It may not have been well known to DEA's directors general, but they had both the USSEA and an assistant USSEA on the committee – more than the PCO had: "Though they'd very much like [the fact] to be otherwise." But that's a book in itself, he said.

Sure, with the benefit of hindsight, people can denounce the NEP. But first, he considered that in 1980-84 Canada stood more effectively and forcefully for its own interests than ever before, and second, given the data as we had them in 1980, didn't the NEP make sense? Even on the Peace Initiative, wasn't Trudeau delivering a message that Canadians very much wanted to have delivered?

....
22   Gerald Regan was minister of state for international trade, 1983-84. A "green paper" is a public government discussion document.

The cabinet discussion of the NEP was contentious, and the minutes will be eloquent on the issue. Some people were nervous of twisting the tail of the American lion, but eventually the prime minister forced the issue.

It was within DEA's capacity to say whether the global oil or energy situation would last, and it said that it would. However, raiding had denuded the department of its first-rate economic capacity by then.

The lesson of the NEP was that it was the challenge you must expect and the situation you must avoid ...

MARSHALL CROWE (1921-2013)
INTERVIEW | OTTAWA, 14 MARCH 1988

Crowe served in the army during the Second World War, joined DEA, and had postings in New York, Moscow, and Washington. After working in banking, he became deputy cabinet secretary in 1967. Later, he was president of the Canada Development Corporation and the National Energy Board.

At the PCO
Crowe came back to Ottawa in 1967 to be assistant cabinet secretary on economic matters. Because **Gordon Robertson**, the secretary, was away, Gerry Stoner became acting secretary and Crowe, deputy secretary.[23]

The experience was "extraordinarily interesting," and he had no regrets for moving back. The cabinet committees were in place, as Pitfield claimed, but it was really **Trudeau** who made them work, an essential part of the process. Unfortunately, he also made all things go to committee, with the result that they took up too much time. Rooms were cluttered with officials, partly because some ministers did not dare show their faces without their official back-up team.

When the committees reached a conclusion, the cabinet agenda would list them. If a minister wanted to reopen something, he had to give the secretariat notice. Otherwise, at the end of the cabinet meeting, Trudeau would announce that they would be taken as read. That meant that they appeared

---

23 O. Gerald Stoner (1922-2008) worked in the public service from 1947 to 1987, most notably in the PCO and as deputy minister of transport.

as cabinet decisions in the records, even though they had not in fact been discussed at the cabinet.

Priorities and Planning

Michael Pitfield was the secretary of the P&P, and he tried to turn it into an inner cabinet. That meant evolving something like the British system, where there are all kinds of ministers who do not sit in the cabinet, though they can be fobbed off with the title of "Right Honourable." Oddly enough, Prime Ministers Joe Clark and Brian Mulroney bought it, despite their relations with Pitfield. But how, Crowe asked, can you in the Canadian system have an inner cabinet that doesn't include, for example, the minister of agriculture, or the minister of labour, or a minister representing the Prairies? It's just too difficult to fiddle. Crowe and Gordon Robertson fought the idea. There was another thing wrong with it: planning. Surely, the experience of the socialist countries shows us what to make of that idea. At any rate, some of Clark's and Mulroney's ministers thought they were not in the cabinet at all. We should have, instead, fewer ministers and a more efficient cabinet.

In the event, Gerry Stoner would have been a better choice for cabinet secretary than Pitfield; luckily, Crowe himself, by then deputy secretary, was out of the way. It was hard to know how they would have coped since he was, of course, senior to Pitfield.

Michael loved tinkering with machinery. Clever and articulate, he had too much influence on Trudeau. Because he liked to work in secret and because he had a horror of confrontation – he didn't like to argue with people or to have to defend a proposition – he shaped his appointments and appointment strategy accordingly. He simply wouldn't argue with Simon Reisman,[24] for example.

Pitfield would have P&P spend hours and hours on the most remote contingencies. He loved long woolly-minded memos, like those written by Buzz Nixon, the deputy secretary to cabinet for plans.[25] When somebody suggested that Nixon be sent for French-language training, Crowe objected that Nixon should learn English first. They all loved charts and would cover the walls with them. Most ministers were embarrassed by them, but Trudeau

---

24   Reisman (1919-2008) was successively deputy minister of industry and of finance in the 1960s and 1970s.
25   Nixon was later (1975) appointed deputy minister of national defence. He was renowned for his impenetrable prose.

seemed to take it seriously. Once, Simon Reisman entered the room when an economics chart was on the wall. He started asking questions – pointed, brutal questions – and showed that most of the chart's basic data were wrong. The upshot was that Reisman was never invited back. "One thing I know about plans," said Crowe, "is that they never work out ..."

In the early seventies, Crowe was deputy secretary, handling the economic and operational side of the PCO, which included social and commercial; Pitfield handled planning, legislative, and legal. Gordon Robertson kept charge of senior appointments, though Pitfield did his damnedest to take it over; like Stalin, he had the right instinct for where power lay ...

The Foreign Policy Review

The Foreign Policy Review was Geoff Murray's *Wheel of Fortune*. By the end, Murray, who was in charge of drafting, actually seemed to believe in it. A minister once asked Crowe why the United States was not included in the review. Oh, Crowe replied, that's a serious subject, so it can't be in there, but putting in Africa is okay. There was a Rasputin element to the whole P&P (Pitfield and Plans) business ...

The Non-Group

Crowe had been a member of the Non-Group committee examining defence policy in 1968; its mission was to develop an alternative to the orthodoxy produced by External Affairs and National Defence. The principal drafter of the Non-Group paper was Hume Wright, an ex-FSO.[26] Others involved were somebody who later became head of Export Development Canada, and Michael Shoemaker,[27] who became a deputy commissioner of the RCMP. "I don't remember **Ivan Head** being all that prominent," Crowe reflected. "He was just starting out then." He remembered the Non-Group paper was about cutbacks, but he couldn't recall which. Its argument was that the Europeans were big boys now and could defend themselves.

Their great cabinet ally was **Donald Macdonald**, who pushed for the paper very hard and took a strong stand against **Sharp**. But really procedurally, Sharp had the rights of it; he and **Léo Cadieux** had legitimate grounds for bitter complaint about the process. Cadieux was a very fine man and a very nice one.

....

26 Wright was assistant secretary to the cabinet for external affairs and defence.
27 Shoemaker was another ex-FSO who had joined the PCO.

The interesting thing about Donald Macdonald was how fast he switched position on defence when he became defence minister. He refused to take some of Crowe's proposals to cabinet committee and once even denounced Crowe in the cabinet for obstructing him; really, all Crowe wanted to do was put a paper on the cabinet agenda. In one portfolio, Macdonald worked for the Defence Review; as minister of national defence, he frustrated the same review.

Canada, France, and Quebec
Crowe spoke of France and security. That was handled separately in Trudeau's offices and belonged in **Marc Lalonde**'s bailiwick. Marcel Cadieux participated, as did **Gérard Pelletier** and Jean Marchand.[28]

"I have a feeling we threatened to break diplomatic relations once," Crowe recalled, "and Lalonde went over [to France] in secret to tell them to stop what Trudeau called 'bargain-basement Gaullism.'" This was under Pompidou rather than under de Gaulle himself.

The issues with Quebec and France all derived from Paul Gérin-Lajoie's 1965 dictum on the provinces' sovereign authority over the external aspects of their jurisdiction.[29] It led to very serious continuing rows, "but I only picked it up at the morning meetings," which consisted of Marc Lalonde and Roméo Leblanc on the PMO side, and Gordon Robertson and Crowe himself on the PCO delegation. The Quebec stuff was discussed in rapid French, which Crowe had some trouble following, and much slipped by; Lalonde confessed that he himself had some difficulty in following Leblanc's Acadian accent.

There was no question that under de Gaulle and Pompidou the French were playing a very tricky game. They would have recognized Quebec immediately if it declared independence, though probably the Americans would have beaten them to it.

Trudeau's Russian trip, 1971
Trudeau's 1971 visit to Russia was very good, very constructive in a lot of ways, except that he got out of control in a question-and-answer session when

....

28 A long-standing friend of Trudeau's, Jean Marchand was a labour leader in the 1950s and 1960s, and an MP and cabinet minister in the Pearson and Trudeau governments.
29 A constitutional lawyer, Gérin-Lajoie was minister of youth (1960-64) and of education (1964-66) in the Lesage Liberal government in Quebec. He was later appointed by Trudeau to head the Canadian International Development Agency.

asked a question by a Soviet journalist. He said the USSR was necessary to Canada to counter excessive American influence over the Canadian economy, culture, politics, and military life. And yes, he said it; it wasn't just something that was included in a draft speech. Journalist Charles Lynch was sitting beside Crowe and just about exploded, but he got it right, even if ever after Lynch kept returning to the topic.[30]

HON. GÉRARD PELLETIER (1919-97)
INTERVIEW | OTTAWA, 14 AUGUST 1987

A journalist and editor of La Presse, Pelletier was a close friend and political ally of Pierre Trudeau. He was elected to Parliament in 1965 and served in the Trudeau cabinet until 1975. He was then ambassador to France and permanent representative at the United Nations in New York.

Trudeau's knowledge and understanding of foreign policy
Pelletier criticized **Ivan Head** for telling George Radwanski, author of a biography of **Trudeau,** that the prime minister knew little of foreign policy; that was "totally stupid" of Head.[31] It was so untrue, so unfortunate. Trudeau, Pelletier well remembered, was assigned foreign policy duty when he worked at the PCO back in 1951-52. For eighteen months, it was one of his major duties, and Pelletier recalled finding him in the attic of the East Block, working on some paper on Korea for Prime Minister St. Laurent. Later, Trudeau wrote four major articles on foreign policy, and by the time he came to office in 1968, or even earlier by 1965, he had persuaded Pelletier that, for example, Canada had to be a member of an alliance and that it had to be in NATO, because unarmed neutrality would invite aggression or imposition by the Russians or the Americans, and armed neutrality with Canada's three coasts would be prohibitively expensive.

Trudeau had travelled, he had been to a great many Canadian missions. Pelletier felt that he had no particular prejudices against DEA. And he contrasted DEA's treatment of Trudeau when the latter was a parliamentary secretary, sending him to Latin America and to the United Nations, with its

---

30 Lynch was a prominent member of the Ottawa press corps.
31 George Radwanski, *Trudeau* (Toronto: Macmillan, 1978).

treatment of himself. After all, when Pelletier was **Paul Martin**'s parliamentary secretary, Marcel Cadieux had excluded him from any significant documents and had carefully kept him away from important meetings. After Martin had told Cadieux to behave better, he did send invitations; they always arrived after the meeting had been held, except for the unimportant ones ...

The Foreign Policy Review
The first summer of Trudeau's government was taken up with the Official Languages Act. Pelletier was busy, of course, working late at night, but he remembered dropping in on Trudeau just after the prime minister had received DEA's first reply to his demand for a re-examination of Canada's foreign policy. What had come in was a pure defence of the status quo. "My God," Trudeau said, "just look at this."[32] It took three drafts before DEA came up with an acceptable version.

Pelletier had no recollection of winter or spring cabinet meetings on the Defence Review. What he did remember were a whole series of meetings, probably without officials and running into the evening. This occurred, he thought, while he and his committee of lawyers were wrestling with the Official Languages Act. So he recollected a meeting at the end of the summer of 1968, which adjourned over the supper hour. He adjourned to the country club with his then ally Jim Richardson – the only time, he remarked, that he and Richardson ever agreed on something. The others who felt similarly about defence, NATO, and the possibility of neutrality were **Donald Macdonald** and Eric Kierans, who was very effective in the cabinet because he was systematic and well organized. **Sharp** he thought to be well disposed to change. Pelletier agreed that there was a range of options, but he said he did not think that neutrality was one; he did remember withdrawal from NATO being contemplated.

He knew that DEA officers were angry. When some ill-advised anonymous comments were repeated to Trudeau at a press conference, he said that he didn't presume to teach DEA officers how to eat olives out of their cocktails, and he intended them to learn that they must follow government policy. Pelletier also had an interview with **Ross Campbell**, sponsored by Jules Léger,[33] at which Campbell denounced Trudeau up and down. Pelletier replied

---

32   Pelletier's memoir is *L'aventure du pouvoir, 1968–1975* (Montreal: Stanké, 1992).
33   Jules Léger was USSEA, ambassador to France in the 1960s, and governor general.

that he assumed Campbell wanted him to repeat his comments verbatim to the prime minister; if this weren't the case, Campbell could ask him to refrain and then clear off. Campbell cleared off. Pelletier also remembered Léger saying that Campbell was actually a man of great talent with some peculiar characteristics.

On Trudeau
Pelletier talked about Trudeau and his cabinet. Trudeau hated long special meetings. He did hold meetings without officials (the summer 1968 meetings were an example), and on political matters the officials were not present. Trudeau hated special meetings. One was when Trudeau convened the cabinet for half an hour between phone calls to and from Pelletier in Niamey, to approve his tough line at the La Francophonie meeting.

Trudeau was punctual, though he was late for a 1969 cabinet meeting. Time passed and finally after twenty-five minutes, Sharp, as deputy prime minister, moved to the agenda. Five minutes later, Trudeau arrived and replaced Sharp, telling everyone that he wanted the advice of his elders on what he should do about **Paul Hellyer**'s resignation from the cabinet. George McIlraith spoke first, for twenty minutes of obscurity.[34] Then it was **Paul Martin**'s turn. For the first time, he showed a self-mockery that made him more attractive to Pelletier. He told Trudeau that he should table the resignation, table his reply if any, and then announce Hellyer's successor if any. So, Trudeau said in summary, "Mr. Martin would do thus and such if he were in my place." No, said Martin, "that's not what I meant. I would ... lose the letter in my suit at the cleaner's or drop it in the swimming pool. But you can't do that; it's not in your character."

In the cabinet or cabinet committee, Trudeau seldom argued. The position of prime minister is special, and he told Pelletier that he reserved his interventions for very special occasions. Pelletier remembered one incident when he was almost driven to resignation by a debate in P&P over the reception of Chilean refugees. Trudeau had said nothing. Afterward, he told Trudeau that he resented his silence. "Why?" Trudeau replied. "You won." Trudeau only came to the rescue of those who needed help – if they were on the right side, of course.

....

34 George McIlraith was a long-serving Liberal MP and a cabinet minister under Pearson and Trudeau.

IVAN HEAD (1930-2004)
INTERVIEWS | OTTAWA, 6 AUGUST 1987, AND TORONTO, 31 AUGUST 1987

A lawyer, academic, and briefly an FSO, Head became associate counsel to Justice Minister Trudeau, then his legal assistant, and, from 1970 to 1978, his special assistant for foreign policy. In 1978, he became head of the International Development Research Centre.

INTERVIEW | 6 AUGUST 1987

His acquaintance with Pierre Trudeau
Head's acquaintance with Trudeau went back to the days when they were both law professors and met at conventions. **Trudeau** knew that he was an international lawyer. In the mid-1960s, when Head got into the business of criticizing British Columbia's case on offshore rights, Trudeau responded by phoning him up and asking if he would come to work for him at the Department of Justice. Trudeau wanted him to come for two years, but Head had other commitments, first for the summer of 1967 and in the longer term to his existing career. So he finally agreed to come for one year, starting in the fall.

Trudeau had chosen him because he felt he could not rely entirely on the Department of Justice to prepare for a possible constitutional conference and review. So, although Head's entrée was through international law, he was swiftly co-opted to work on and about the Constitution ...

Head became associate counsel to the minister for the constitutional conference (Carl Goldenberg was counsel). **Allan Gotlieb** told him that in his view the Department of Justice was looking at the offshore issue in a purely constitutional way; he wanted somebody who could take it from an international law point of view.

Soon pressures began to mount for Trudeau to run for the leadership. Trudeau had established a good, informal atmosphere about him at Justice; it was bag lunches around the table, brainstorming, and first names. Head believed that Trudeau should run. One night, the two of them took a walk around Parliament Hill, and Head urged his case. There was a whole agenda of things to achieve: official recognition of China was one. Trudeau replied that Head's arguments were good; but, he wondered, if he took the plunge would Head do so as well and stay on? Cornered, Head said yes.

For Trudeau, the acquisition of the leadership was a turning point – the end of his naïveté and of informality. After the victory, **Marc Lalonde** asked

Head to take on the task of briefing Trudeau for question period under the title "legislative counsel to the prime minister." At first he covered the street, but gradually foreign policy came to predominate.

Commonwealth policy adviser

In 1968, Trudeau made some offhand remarks about Biafra, which were misinterpreted.[35] For example, when he asked "Where's Biafra?" he intended to convey that Biafra was an illegitimate separatist government that did not officially exist as far as Canada was concerned. In Trudeau's later speeches, Head inserted material to show that he did know where Biafra was, but it was too late. And also during that year, Trudeau got into trouble when he asked Saskatchewan farmers, "Why should I sell your wheat?" This was a rhetorical question, which he proceeded to answer, but all that people remembered was the question. Head found it necessary to call the publisher of the *Edmonton Journal* a liar on the matter, but explanations of any kind hardly helped. Trudeau's reaction to these contretemps was "why should I explain my references to people without any culture who can't understand my classical allusions?"

In the case of Biafra, DEA didn't know whether it was coming or going. But Head had met General Yakubo Gowon, the Nigerian leader, on his 1967 trip. He regarded him as sound, decent, impressive, and above all, trustworthy. So he started talking to Gowon. He added that people in the government had no impression of Biafran leader Odumegwo Ojukwu.

This coincided with the preparations for the January 1969 Commonwealth Heads of Government meeting in London. Nigeria was bound to be discussed, but the Nigerians would be reluctant to air their internal matters in an international forum. Canadian public opinion, however, expected something.

The trouble was that Trudeau was ill-prepared to cope with the session or the issues that were raised. Commonwealth conferences were the domain of the PCO, not External Affairs, and **Gordon Robertson** did not take any particular interest. By that point, Trudeau knew that Head could produce

....

35 A short-lived rebel state, Biafra seceded from Nigeria in 1967. During the ensuing conflict, the Nigerian government used starvation as a weapon of war. Biafra surrendered in 1970 and was reabsorbed into Nigeria. See generally, Ivan Head and Pierre Trudeau, *The Canadian Way: Shaping Canada's Foreign Policy, 1968-84* (Toronto: McClelland and Stewart, 1995).

material that sounded like him, and Head told Lalonde before the conference that if he could be useful, he would go.

At the conference, what struck both Trudeau and Head was that the British were still running the show. The government heads sat around a very big table, one place per country, but British prime minister Harold Wilson sat at the end, presiding, with his foreign secretary and his Commonwealth relations secretary on either side.

Nevertheless, the conference atmosphere made a good impression on Trudeau. He was struck by the quality of some of the leaders; in his mind, this came to justify the very large amount of time that had to be devoted to Commonwealth conferences. He believed that he got value from Julius Nyerere of Tanzania and Lee Kuan Yew of Singapore.[36] As the conference proceeded, things got a bit bogged down. Wilson insisted on discussing the Russian invasion of Czechoslovakia, even though that was far from the minds of most people at the table. And Trudeau had briefing problems.

Jimmy Walker, the MP for York Centre, was present as Trudeau's parliamentary secretary. He came to Head and said, "This is awful: nobody is doing the job of briefing the prime minister." So Head took on the task. He winged it, of course, without briefing materials. He remembered Trudeau's "soulful eyes" as he told Head that Canada must do better next time round.

But Trudeau was not without impact. When Nyerere went on and on about Rhodesia, Trudeau interrupted him and said, "But wait, why should we believe you? You haven't proved your case." And Kenneth Kaunda of Zambia was in the middle of his "crying days" – he had a handkerchief at the ready to begin his weeping and moaning over whatever perturbed him. Lee Kuan Yew had no patience with this behaviour or with the Africans in general. Lee had one of the toughest minds going; he used to say that if the Africans would stop whining and roll up their sleeves, they'd do better. Trudeau might not have agreed with everything Lee thought, but he admired his coherence and his discipline. The regard was reciprocated – when Trudeau barged in on Nyerere, Lee was plainly delighted ...

So that was the beginning. It led to Trudeau's resolve to get the conference moved but not to Canada the first time. It would be better if it went to another country farther down in the chronological hierarchy and then to Canada. So it went to Singapore first and then to Canada.

---

36   Julius Nyerere was the president of Tanzania.

Just to continue with the Commonwealth theme: Trudeau was determined to break up the prepared, stale nature of the conference. He could not prevent the heads of government from reading their prepared statements when the conference came to Canada, but he could and did control their staffs. Nobody but a head could read from notes, and he spirited away the heads with one staffer only (this could be a briefer, staffer, mistress, or bodyguard but just one). The result was splendid, and it helped lead to a Trudeau approach to foreign policy style ...

Trudeau's interests in foreign policy
Aspects of international affairs were attractive to Trudeau, but he wanted a rationale. The old one would not do. Trudeau wanted Canada to increase its place in the world, but in relation to its own interests, not those of the United States. The value of the old internationalist currency was steadily depreciating, and people were becoming cynical about it. It was time for something new, something fresh. Head never had any doubt as to Trudeau's internationalism, he just wanted it differently expressed.

Some things about foreign policy attracted Trudeau more than others. China was a prime example: official recognition made sense to him. Developing countries were of great interest as well. Head had Trudeau speak on this topic at the University of Alberta in May 1968. Head wrote the speech himself; it dealt with relations between the global North and the global South, and it said that the days of giveaways were over, that the products of less developed countries would compete in the Canadian market, and that Canadians must accept the fact. Trudeau had the crowd roaring with approval for developing countries.[37]

The Defence Review
And, after North-South, there was one other priority back in 1968 – defence policy. "I've always been an iconoclast with reference to NATO," Head stated. This feeling dated back to his own DEA service, the idea being that NATO didn't represent an exchange of real ideas and feelings. "It's got so turgid," Head said. He was not, however, a hawk on NATO: that was **Donald Macdonald,** and even somebody like Joe Greene could come up with offensive

---

37 Readers may detect in this comment an early expression of "globalization" of the kind that would cause so much controversy in the 2010s.

and silly anti-American speeches (or at any rate, very deprecatory ones) like the one he made in Denver in 1970.[38]

Withdrawal from NATO was genuinely considered. There were tensions with DEA anyway. Marcel Cadieux, "an anachronism," could not face up to what was asked of him in the way of budget cuts. It was true that DEA did not have the same leeway as other departments when cuts were made. Others can reduce their capital budgets, but DEA must cut personnel, having almost no capital expenditure. Cadieux used to say, "They don't understand us." And he would put on his best suit and march up to confront Marc Lalonde about the cuts. He would say, "I won't do it," but Lalonde would reply, "You will." So Cadieux made up a list of cuts, presented them to Lalonde, and said, "There, you see it's impossible, you can't cut this." But Lalonde simply answered, "It's just been done ..."

The DEA documents on NATO and Europe were a full-scale justification for the status quo. There were no variations, and they enraged the cabinet. DEA was asked to re-do its report, so after a suitable interval, it came back and said it had been right the first time. **Basil Robinson** was in charge of reviewing policy, and though Basil was a wonderful man, what he produced was not appropriate to the desires of the cabinet.

So the prime minister asked, "What to do?" The Defence Policy Review was proceeding, and there were two or three weeks left before it had to be considered. Trudeau asked Head to put together the Non-Group in secret to prepare a report that provided alternatives. He did so. He had somebody from the Treasury Board, somebody from DEA seconded to the PCO (this was **Marshall Crowe**), and a general whose name he refused to divulge. The general was willing to be more open-minded than most of his colleagues, evidently.

They prepared a range of options but argued in the end that Canada should stay in NATO and use its influence from inside to change the alliance. Head was especially keen on getting out of the nuclear strike role, for that made sense only as a first-strike capability. He could just imagine a drunken Russian artillery lieutenant seeing two CF-104s on his screen and wondering if this was it. The important thing was to raise the threshold of nuclear accidents ...

....

38 Joe Greene was minister of agriculture under Pearson and minister of energy under Trudeau.

The Non-Group paper went to the cabinet and raised shockwaves, but it was adopted, he claimed. **Léo Cadieux** and **Mitchell Sharp** had a tough row to hoe, but the pro-NATO group, Cadieux, Sharp, Drury, and **Hellyer,** were simply not running things as they once had done.

Head's role here was justified, he claimed, because he was separate from DEA. He worked for the prime minister. If the prime minister asked him to do something, he did it. The NATO issue might have come close to splitting the cabinet, though he denied knowledge of any resignation threats. "We were all new," he said. His actions did come close to ruining his relations with Basil Robinson, whom after all he liked. He said to Robinson, "It's a new government with new personalities, and when they say they want freshness, they mean it."

As for Don Macdonald, he had been **Paul Martin**'s parliamentary secretary. The people at DEA should have known him better.

Paul Martin did complain about the Non-Group paper because he could not identify its provenance. As for the halving of the Canadian Forces in NATO, that was probably just the old technique of compromise.

Head explicitly denied hitting back at DEA, as some alleged, because of his own frustrations, and implicitly half confirmed this. He liked a lot of FSOs, people such as André Bissonnette, his own chief in Malaysia, who was a plain, blunt guy, with no nonsense. He left DEA because he felt his future there would not be as challenging or as interesting as what he'd already done: Diefenbaker's office and Kuala Lumpur. It was true that he had management problems with the department, and he observed that one rule of thumb he used at the International Development Research Centre was to ask what DEA did and then do the opposite in administration ...

It wasn't Trudeau's idea to withdraw from NATO. He was certainly not a hawk on that. But his trip to Europe in January 1969 (after the London conference) helped form his opinions. He got the views of the old guard, who were all over Europe as ambassadors – Charles Ritchie, for example. During the trip, there were sessions on the **Robert Ford** perspective on things too (Ford was ambassador to Russia). Head was skeptical of the DEA view; his service in Malaysia helped him form a different impression from that of the Europe-centred old guard.

Head wanted Canada to retain membership in NATO. He wanted to keep a military contribution there, though when someone claimed that the Canadian Forces were a tripwire, he facetiously suggested that taking the soldiers out and leaving their dependants in place would be the best bet. If the Europeans wanted hostages whom the Canadians would try to retrieve, it was better to have women and children in the role.

He wanted more recognition of the worth of Canada's contribution to NATO. He resented people such as British defence secretary Denis Healey, who blustered on. After all, Canada and the United States were paying their way in Europe for their troops; the British troops were subsidized by the Germans.

What he wanted out of was the CF-104 nuclear strike role and to get rid of the Honest John missiles, which were useless anyway.

Commonwealth problems

President Idi Amin of Uganda had threatened to come to a Commonwealth conference in Ottawa.[39] In preparation for the conference, Head had gone to Kampala. In the end, Amin sent only a junior man, who begged the Canadians to let him read a prepared statement that had been drafted in Kampala. The rules prohibited this, but the young man would plainly be in danger back home if he didn't follow his instructions, so Trudeau convened a non-session; people sat around and conversed while the Ugandan read his speech. He didn't mind: he played the game too.

The same tactic was used in 1969, when the Nigerians allowed discussion of their civil war, not at a conference session, but over lunch. It happened again in Jamaica, when Prime Minister Michael Manley invited Abel Muzorewa of Rhodesia to address the conference. Because Muzorewa was not a government head, this was not possible, so they worked out an informal session to save Manley from embarrassment. This was Trudeau's suggestion.

Contrast this sensible and informal method with NATO. Head remembered Al Haig, a good NATO supreme commander, once complaining to him about his difficulties with Joseph Luns.[40] Head advised him to speak out, but in the NATO context this was difficult to accomplish.

....

39 Idi Amin was the notably brutal dictator of Uganda, 1971-79.
40 A US Army general, Al Haig was later secretary of state under Ronald Reagan. Joseph Luns (1911-2002), a Dutch politician, was secretary-general of NATO, 1971-84. Ponderous, formal, and unimaginative, Luns embodied everything that Trudeau thought was wrong with NATO.

Foreign Policy for Canadians

The results of the Foreign Policy Review were published as *Foreign Policy for Canadians (FPC)*, six booklets that were full of jargon.[41] This wasn't natural to Geoffrey Murray, who drafted them, but Murray was trying to please. He had read every published utterance of Trudeau, and he was trying hard. Probably because Head was still "an unknown quantity," he had not talked to him before publishing.

It was the atmosphere of the Age of Communication. Head remembered enthusing about his goals before the Council on Foreign Relations; he remembered the hexagon diagram that was to symbolize the goals. But the cabinet considered it ludicrous: too much like a stop sign, said one minister. The hexagon would have showed that there was no strict hierarchy of goals or policies; as it turned out, economics landed in first spot. Mitchell Sharp never said that this was incidental or accidental, even though Head put the denial in Trudeau's speeches time and again.

On personalities

Head insisted that he wasn't trying to interfere in the bureaucracy, merely acting as servant to the prime minister. He never attended cabinet committee meetings, though he was bidden to the cabinet once or twice. Mike Kirby and Jim Davey of Trudeau's political staff acted differently: "I think they were wrong."

What was **Michael Pitfield**'s role? It must have been substantial, but Head chose not to expand on this.

And Gordon Robertson's role? It was not great, except on Arctic sovereignty. That was Robertson's baby. Because Robertson was still in charge, however, Pitfield was not allowed to play as fast and loose as the media claim he did.

Lalonde, however, was different from Robertson. He was into everything; his perspective was Canada-first. "My guess is Lalonde probably thought Pearson had wasted his political arsenal on international affairs, and he believed that Trudeau had many political fires to fight at home," Head remarked. By the way, the phrase "no more helpful fixers" came from Murray, not Trudeau and Head. And "Viva Cuba," which Trudeau uttered during his

---

41 *Foreign Policy for Canadians* (Ottawa: Department of External Affairs, 1970), http://gac.canadiana.ca/view/ooe.b1603784E/1?r=0&s=2.

1976 visit to Cuba, was concocted or advised by the ranking DEA officer on Latin America ...[42]

Head concluded by noting that Trudeau did have some memories of how he was treated by DEA in the late 1940s. It was a francophone (decent treatment)-anglophone split (not well treated). The exception among the anglophones was Chester Ronning in Nanking,[43] who welcomed him and treated him very well.

INTERVIEW | 31 AUGUST 1987

Trudeau and separatism, international and domestic
Head began with a discussion of "national unity" as a factor in Trudeau's foreign policy. It could be taken in two senses, federal-provincial or specifically in connection with Quebec. Trudeau decided to resign as Liberal leader in December 1979 because of his conviction that the provincial premiers were impossible to deal with. His return in 1980 was therefore characterized by the decision to go full steam ahead.

In the Quebec sense, Trudeau fully supported Pearson's initiatives in extending recognition to francophone Africa. In the area of what became La Francophonie, Trudeau had a document prepared on educational conferences and federalism while he was minister of justice. His later remark, "Where's Biafra?" arose from his determination not to recognize a breakaway state. When Bangladesh seceded from Pakistan, Trudeau was very reluctant to recognize it, to the extent that Commonwealth secretary-general Arnold Smith flew over to urge him to do so. Unless the Bangladeshis got support from their friends, Smith argued, the Chinese would extend their influence

....

42 When Trudeau visited Fidel Castro's Cuba in 1976, Gerald Ford was president of the United States. The visit had to be balanced against the necessity for good relations with Washington, but fortunately the Ford administration was generally friendly and supportive, and did not link the visit to other important Canadian-American questions. Ford supported Canada's G7 membership despite irritation that Canada had banned Taiwan from competing in the 1976 Montreal Olympics. American documents show that Ford was less concerned about Trudeau's Cuban visit despite its chummy atmospherics. See John Dirks, "Managing a Cooperative Disagreement: Canada, the United States and Revolutionary Cuba, 1959-1980" (PhD thesis, University of Toronto, 2014), Chapter 10, especially 398, 412-26.
43 Chester Ronning was chargé d'affaires in the Canadian embassy in Nanking, which was then the capital of China.

there.[44] Trudeau did eventually recognize Bangladesh, but he explicitly drew the Quebec parallel in conversation with Head.

He had an interest in seeing divided countries united, greater than Head expected, and that included the two Germanys. He didn't precisely want their unification, but he understood Chancellor Willy Brandt's desire for *Ostpolitik* and sympathized with it. On the other hand, he understood the Soviet fear of a reunited Germany. He thought that the recognition by Canada of East Germany might help. The two Vietnams he thought a tragic accident of history; luckily, the United States had decided to end the Vietnam War, so Ottawa and Washington were not out of phase in this matter, as they had been under Pearson. But he never showed the slightest interest in the two Koreas.

Head moved on to Trudeau's western Pacific trip in 1970. As an Albertan, Head hoped that the interests of Western Canada would receive greater recognition in foreign policy. This he got, as witness Trudeau's remark in Osaka that Japan was "not our Far East but really our new west."

Trudeau and the USSR

Trudeau's trip to the USSR was postponed from October 1970 (the Russians were gracious about it). His visit occurred because Trudeau believed that he could not write off the Soviets as a constructive force in international politics. Nor did he wish to write off Canada's influence on them. He knew that the Russians would wish to appear accommodating during his trip.

Head implied that he had something to do with making Trudeau's speeches less accommodating toward East European ethnics, but this also reflected Trudeau's convictions. Diefenbaker had been the worst panderer to the ethnics, but even Pearson did his bit. When Trudeau refused to follow suit, this produced testy confrontations with ethnic groups; but he refused to be swayed. He didn't wish to take cheap shots, words without substance.

Head believed that the Russia visit was valuable, that the Canadians got to see a great deal, such as at Norilsk. At the press conference, Trudeau made the error in getting off topic and wandering into Canadian-American relations. Head took responsibility for Trudeau's speech in Kiev, which compared the Canadian and Soviet federations. The notes for the speech were composed in advance and handed out to the press. But when staff studied them, they could

---

44 A senior Canadian diplomat, Arnold Smith was an ambassador to Egypt and the Soviet Union before being appointed Commonwealth secretary-general.

see that they were inappropriate (especially Marshall Crowe, who blew up), and Trudeau changed the speech. That made no difference to journalist Charles Lynch, who filed the original version, not the speech as actually given.

Trudeau believed that we had to know the Soviet leadership better; Head also thought that the Soviets wanted a taste of responsibility in the Middle East, an argument he tried out on Kissinger,[45] who didn't buy it.

Trudeau was definitely not worried by the domestic fallout from his policies. Neither was Sharp, with his large number of Jewish voters in his riding in Toronto. He was consulted and said don't worry. Head had consultations with Herbert Levy of B'nai Brith, arguing that there was a need for conversations with the USSR, that they might help with family reunions. Levy visited the USSR and also advised Head on ways and means to avoid offending the Canadian Jewish Congress. He dealt as well with Walter Tarnopolsky on Ukrainian Canadian issues.[46]

The Canadian attitude to the USSR was not the same as the American. Securing the release of one or another important personality from the Soviet Union would just stimulate demand for more – an endless process. The Canadians preferred to place discussions on a different plane. But as for the ethnics, he preferred to deal with them vigorously, openly, honestly, and unyieldingly. He did not believe that Trudeau lost much ethnic support.

On the issue of Jews and the Middle East, Trudeau was always very careful. MacEachen and DEA had a tendency to distance Canada from Israel, feeling that we were unfair in the broadest sense to the Arab cause, and Trudeau shared this view. "My feeling strongly was that this is an area where Canada has no muscle," Head said. "This is the last place where you start venturing in."

He had met Prime Minister Golda Meir, who had a trick with the ash of her cigarette – mesmerizing. He was very impressed by Shimon Peres. King Hussein of Jordan saw Trudeau as both sympathetic and fair. Head's advice throughout to Trudeau was to stay out of the game of speaking at Jewish fundraisers and away from accepting this award or that prize. Once you began, it would never end. Head started to claim that this had no political effect, but conceded that in 1979, Joe Clark was able to move into the gap that Trudeau left.[47] On one occasion, though, Trudeau spoke to a Jewish function

---

45 Henry Kissinger, then Richard Nixon's national security adviser and later secretary of state.
46 Walter Tarnopolsky was a prominent Canadian legal scholar and judge.
47 Joe Clark was Progressive Conservative prime minister of Canada, 1979-80.

shortly after a terrorist attack, something he abhorred, and made a very effective speech.

Arctic waters

The USSR had been very friendly about the Arctic waters issue. The Soviets had an international law expert, Grigory Tunkin, who specialized in the field, and the Canadian lawyers read him. When the Americans reacted badly to the Canadians' Arctic ideas, Canada embarked on a campaign to propagandize its point of view round the world. Whenever the US emissary left or arrived, there was the Canadian. The Canadian legislation establishing the Arctic Waters Pollution Prevention Act (which produced the wonderful acronym AWPPA) was drafted very carefully to show that this was an emerging international law regime. Then we amended our submission to the International Court by establishing the Arctic exception.[48]

It was to this amendment that **Paul Martin** took such violent exception. To him, withdrawing anything from the World Court was a retrograde step in international law. Head dismissed this position as "academic"; he admired Donald Macdonald for pushing the matter through the cabinet ...

Head thought it was important not to go for national sectors, defined by lines leading up to the North Pole in a pie shape, on a map, which would appear to be land grabbing, but also not to limit by sector boundary the claims that Canada might eventually put. Sharp wanted baselines in, Head did not. Mulroney's eventual acceptance of sector lines was a defeat, not a victory.

Where did the government's other international lawyers stand on the amendment? **Gotlieb,** he thought, agreed, and **Alan Beesley** didn't.

Recognizing China

Head discussed China next. This, he said, was covered by the China team. Trudeau felt that failing to recognize China was a major aberration. Head was sure that, in this, dollars and cents were not foremost in Trudeau's mind. Let the political link be first, and the commercial link would follow. Canada did enjoy a warm spot in the affections of the current leadership in Beijing.

....

[48] The exception established a provision recognizing the jurisdiction of states in ice-covered areas to take measures affecting shipping – for the purpose of preventing, reducing, and controlling marine pollution – that go far beyond those they could take in other ocean areas off their coasts.

There was no opposition in Ottawa to the recognition – some background moaning from Paul Martin aside – but there was some, at a lower level, from the Americans. No, Canada knew nothing of US plans to move toward recognition.

Head told anecdotes of Zhou Enlai and his humility; and he mentioned the "water torture" at meetings with the Chinese – being plied with endless cups of tea without being able to relieve himself. The trade agreement of 1973 was a response almost as much to the memory of Bethune as to Trudeau, whom nevertheless the Chinese liked very much. He couldn't say what Trudeau's reaction was to the Cultural Revolution ...

The G7 summits

Head saw the G7 summits as very important indeed. After the November 1975 summit meeting in Rambouillet, France, it appeared that the meetings would become permanent, and Canada began to agitate to be included. We had not been invited to Rambouillet, even though the Italians, whose GNP was smaller than ours, had been asked. Head worked with **Peter Towe** and Bill Hood on this effort.[49] DEA dragged its heels, arguing that we should not try for something we could not get, so we put Pierre Trudeau onto Gerald Ford.[50] And Trudeau had clout. He used it with British prime minister James Callaghan, and Paul Martin in London took the bit in his teeth and ran with it. Callaghan and David Owen were good about it.[51] Head got the support of Kissinger and Brent Scowcroft.[52]

But the French opposed our inclusion because they felt that Canada was not in the right league and because they thought we would vote with the United States. The issue of Quebec independence didn't enter into it at all. "I was always very proud of the exercise," Head said. "It got us into the major leagues."

The summits under Ford and Carter were very different from what they became under Reagan.[53] In the June 1976 summit at Puerto Rico, Ford was

....

49 Hood (1921-2014) was a long-time senior official in the Department of Finance, rising to be deputy minister.
50 Ford was American president, 1974-77.
51 A Labour prime minister, James Callaghan was known as "Sunny Jim." David Owen was British foreign secretary at the time.
52 General Brent Scowcroft was US national security adviser, 1975-77. He enjoyed a distinguished career as adviser to three US presidents.
53 Jimmy Carter was US president from 1977 to 1981.

in the chair and obviously out of his league. But nobody criticized him for it; presumably Kissinger was right beside him. Real issues were discussed, and there was a genuine meeting of minds. They believed in clearing an agenda. The Downing Street summit was marvellous; everybody was thoroughly briefed, and everybody in the room was able to speak English. "Our man did well," Head commented. Callaghan ("the old lubricator"), Helmut Schmidt,[54] and Trudeau had the most influence. Carter showed that he was a good team player. The Canadian and American teams got along well, and you had the feeling that the Americans really thought we could be helpful.

Quebec
As for Quebec, Head disclaimed direct knowledge of the topic. The French Canadians around Trudeau reserved this area to themselves, and he felt that his views would not be very well regarded, even if they were politely received. He knew Premiers Manning and Lougheed but not nearly as well as the Quebec people knew their adversaries in the PQ. "On Quebec," he said, "I was just not one of the players ..."

The Contractual Links
Asked about the Contractual Link between Canada and the European Common Market,[55] Head said that the press had missed the boat. They ran around to foreign offices in Europe, talking to desk officers about the link, only to be told there was nothing there. The link was a top-down project, something to which Trudeau devoted much time and, he said, three trips to Europe. The idea was **John Halstead**'s, and the time seemed right. The European Community opened a big liaison office in Canada (only its American counterpart was bigger), and all the words were right. As for the Japan Contractual Link, **Ross Campbell** as ambassador had called Head and told him he must come to Tokyo to talk to Prime Minister Tanaka about it. When Head complied, he was denounced in the press for going over DEA's head. Still, he conceded that the links had not amounted to much.

....

54 German chancellor Helmut Schmidt was a particular friend of Trudeau's.
55 The Contractual Link was an extension of the Trudeau government's Third Option, which was to seek closer ties with Asia and Europe so as to counterbalance the overwhelming presence of the United States. Signed in 1976, the link was the rather feeble result of persistent and time-consuming diplomacy with Europe.

Leaving the PMO

Head left the PMO in 1976-77, with the PQ in power and matters heating up, because he was tired, had spent ten years there with Trudeau, and had lost the capacity, if he ever had it, to offer a fresh outlook. Then, "to be frank," the PMO had become so political under Jim Coutts.[56] At one time, the merits of an idea could be considered at the PMO, but under Coutts the political calculus was all that mattered. That was not for him.

RT. HON. PAUL MARTIN (1903-92)
INTERVIEW | WINDSOR, ONTARIO, 10-11 FEBRUARY 1987

> *First elected to the House of Commons in 1935, Martin served in the cabinet under four prime ministers. He was SSEA under Lester Pearson and a minister without portfolio and leader in the Senate under Trudeau. He went to London as high commissioner in 1974 and stayed in that post to 1979.*[57]

Ivan Head's influence

Ivan Head was much in evidence, Martin said. He was a lawyer with previous DEA experience, and he was a good speech writer. Through his previous experience, he saw DEA as slow and ponderous; he wasn't prepared to wait for it. Though he had no official role, he was an assistant to the prime minister. He could and did get close to **Trudeau**. DEA was not pleased, but **Mitchell Sharp** did not object. Martin considered Sharp efficient but thought MacEachen slow and lazy. MacEachen sometimes disappeared for days at a time in Ottawa, and nobody really knew where he was. It was MacEachen who later objected to Head.

Head's effect was to move Trudeau along and to get his input on foreign affairs. Sometimes, he did things that Trudeau would or should have done – took initiatives. On matters such as Trudeau's speech before Congress in 1977 after the PQ won power in Quebec, Martin advised Head to take up the

....

56 Jim Coutts (1938-2013) was principal secretary to Trudeau.
57 See Greg Donaghy, *Grit: The Life and Politics of Paul Martin Sr.* (Vancouver: UBC Press, 2015); Paul Martin, *A Very Public Life*, 2 vols. (Ottawa: Deneau, 1983, 1985); and William Young, ed., *Paul Martin: The London Diaries, 1975-1979* (Ottawa: University of Ottawa Press, 1988).

subject with Zbigniew Brzezinski, Jimmy Carter's national security adviser. Head did, and the speech occurred.

Head was careful to keep Martin informed while Martin was in London as high commissioner. And in Martin's view, Ivan was generally a good thing – he had links to Kissinger and Brzezinski; Trudeau owed him a great deal. As a general rule, what Ivan wanted, Ivan got; and if Trudeau really wanted something, hook, line, and sinker, only a miracle would stop it. But Trudeau seldom wanted anything that badly.

The Arctic
Martin turned to the Arctic sovereignty question and the cabinet discussion. **Donald Macdonald,** who had trained as an international lawyer and should have known better, said that Canada should take action in the Arctic to stop the USS *Manhattan*.[58] He wanted us to reserve our position before the International Court of Justice (that is, to withdraw the matter from its jurisdiction) in the event the United States complained. Martin added that the issue was far from clear in international law.

During the cabinet discussion, Martin objected violently to Macdonald's suggestion. He asked Macdonald if he feared the judgment of the court, and Macdonald said yes. Martin went on and on; Trudeau, who was present, tapped his leg with his foot to show his approval. Macdonald had got his idea from Head's own thesis. How could the Americans go for the Canadian position if we had reserved our position?

During the discussion, Martin had to leave the room to go to the bathroom; Trudeau actually thought that he was walking out and mentioned it to him later. But though Trudeau agreed with Martin, the majority of the cabinet agreed with Macdonald.

The NATO cuts
NATO was a different matter. On this, Trudeau reserved his position: "Trudeau did not fight for action on NATO as he had publicly indicated," Martin stated. During the 1968 election campaign, Trudeau had spoken

---

58 Without first seeking Canadian permission, the American ship *Manhattan* crossed the Northwest Passage in 1969 through what Canada claimed as its territorial waters. The issue generated a huge controversy at the time, and the principle of free passage through Arctic waters remains in dispute.

disparagingly of NATO, but he never did say we should get out, though Walter Gordon and Jean Marchand did.[59] The cabinet committee was split on cuts, but Martin and Sharp were opposed to them. Nevertheless, the idea for the cuts did come from **Léo Cadieux**, backed by Sharp. Perhaps this was because the cuts weren't fundamental, "and we eventually undid the whole thing." **Paul Hellyer** would have opposed them had he been on the committee; so would MacEachen, but it didn't come to a vote in the cabinet. "I had written a memo on it," Martin said. When Cadieux raised hell, Trudeau simply didn't reply. As for Jean Chrétien, he was basically on Sharp's side, as was John Turner.[60]

"I don't think the cuts would ever have taken place if Cadieux had kept fighting and not thrown in the towel – but then there might have been a real schism in cabinet," Martin recalled. Outside the cabinet too: Walter Gordon came up to Ottawa and saw Trudeau on the issue.

On DEA

Martin discussed DEA and its skills or lack of them. The department wasn't strong on Russia or Latin America: we usually didn't send our best people to Latin America. Nothing like our top men went to Brazil or Chile. DEA representatives didn't have the skills that their counterparts from other countries had; for example, John Starnes in Germany couldn't speak German. Neither could G.G. Crean. In Scandinavia, we didn't have people who spoke the language, which was also true for our reps in Russia, excepting our ambassador **Robert Ford**. It was the same at NATO: **Ross Campbell**'s French was very shaky, and some couldn't speak it at all. But there were remarkable people: Arthur Menzies, John Holmes, Klaus Goldschlag, **Ed Ritchie**, Jules Léger.

Then there was **Allan Gotlieb**. There was plainly no love lost here. In Martin's day, he was head of Legal Division, able and brilliant but quite ambitious. "He'd run over people" and seek to dominate them. He started building his empire when he was deputy minister of immigration; he and **Michael Pitfield** collaborated quite a lot, and he moved into the Trudeau circle. His

....

59   Gordon had been finance minister and president of the privy council under Pearson and was the leading Liberal dove on foreign and defence policy. See Stephen Azzi, *Walter Gordon and the Rise of Canadian Nationalism* (Montreal and Kingston: McGill-Queen's University Press, 1999).
60   Turner was a minister in the Pearson and Trudeau governments, leader of the Liberal Party (1984-90), and briefly prime minister in 1984.

ambition or arrogance was such that he even concocted his own plan for Senate reform, quite without authority. He was "not a popular fellow."

Pitfield sat right next to the throne: he had access to Trudeau, who was not close to DEA and who strongly believed that ministers should run their own departments. Very early on, perhaps in April 1968, Sharp asked Trudeau and Martin to meet a delegation of Czechs with him, and Trudeau blew up. Sharp had been appointed minister, so he should run the department.

Martin then said something cryptic about Trudeau's existing foreign policy views, which might have been formed sixteen years earlier, when he worked in the PCO. He indicated, rather than suggested, that there might have been some friction between Trudeau and the younger men of the day, such as **Gordon Robertson** and **Basil Robinson**. He elided into Trudeau's view of the foreign service, which was demoralized. Martin relayed this to Gotlieb when Gotlieb visited London in 1975 and told him too of the negative impact of his departmental reforms.

Gotlieb was not popular at all. Under him, the foreign service was demoralized. He brought all kinds of people into the department, promoted them, and undermined the department's political specialists.

Nobody at DEA was close to Trudeau, except for Gotlieb – certainly not Marcel Cadieux, who was a very different kind of person from Trudeau. Marcel had a firm grip on the department; he knew it well and sought to exercise leadership in almost every area. He was into everything, really; his administration was dynamic, and he was well respected.

Cadieux, like most DEA people who had served in Vietnam – a good third of the whole department – was very pro-American. There had been differences between himself and Martin on the subject.

Everybody thought that Basil Robinson would be first-rate as USSEA, but he just couldn't stand the great pressure of the job. He couldn't stand the criticism, even though people liked him. By the time he left, he was completely disorganized.

In Martin's time, Robinson was in charge of defence matters, and he also worked with Martin on China. He was given the latter assignment because of his general ability and knowledge of the US State Department. He had a fairly intimate impression of Secretary of State Dean Rusk's work habits. "But Basil was really a stereotype," a caricature of DEA professionalism. For example, when Martin met with Rusk in 1967, he asked Basil to intervene if he had something to say. Robinson did; Martin appreciated it and mentioned his contribution in his report. To his surprise, Robinson was furious. The civil service was supposed to be anonymous; the ministers were supposed to be the ones named in reports. "You're the minister," he said, and "our views should not be quoted." That was Basil's problem as an administrator; he couldn't criticize people, and he couldn't discipline them.

He was the opposite of Ross Campbell. Martin well remembered Campbell at a Brussels cocktail party, airing his views on Trudeau's NATO cutbacks; his comments were reported in the *Globe and Mail*. Strangely, Trudeau respected Campbell for it: "He must be quite a man," he said to Martin. There was another occasion with Campbell, when the Japanese prime minister, Tanaka, was making a speech. Campbell kept saying, "Balls, that's balls ..."

Ed Ritchie was a good deputy and a strong one. Everybody liked him; he was able and a good administrator. Ironically, he looked so powerful physically. He seemed more solid and more powerful than Marcel Cadieux.

The Foreign Policy Review

There were actually three Foreign Policy Reviews: Norman Robertson's, Basil Robinson's, and Geoff Murray's. At first, Martin thought of a review from outside, but Pearson was firm that it be internal. All that he wanted was to be able to tell Walter Gordon that our policy had met the test of a careful review. And Martin still thought that if you wanted it to be well done, you had to have it done by somebody inside the department.

Trudeau made the review an issue in his election campaign, and Donald Macdonald also thought it should be done. But when Geoff Murray wrote the new review, Trudeau wasn't too pleased. Then Murray was advised to put in maps and diagrams and contemporary stuff: he did so and Trudeau swallowed it whole. "I just don't think Trudeau read it. In any case," Martin said flatly, "Trudeau knew you couldn't vary the policy that much."

A few months before our interview, Martin had discussed this over dinner with Trudeau in Montreal. Martin told him that he thought there wasn't much variation, pre- and post-1968. "What did you do that we didn't do?" Trudeau said. "But wait, didn't we cut NATO?" Yes, said Martin, "but that really wasn't a change in basic policy." Martin remarked, "I don't think he liked the suggestion."

Trudeau and foreign policy

In fact, Trudeau had no real interest in foreign policy. He liked to make speeches on the Third World on great occasions, but he knew only a few diplomats at the top. For example, he had no real interest in the United Nations. When Martin sent him down there in 1966 or 1967, he left early. But he liked the summits, Commonwealth or whatever. In fact, he organized the best heads of government meeting ever, encouraging discussion and discouraging speech making ...

In Trudeau's time, there was never any foreign policy discussion except on those very rare occasions when he asked for further discussion after cabinet committee. As for Sharp, Martin considered him a good minister though an odd fellow. He didn't know how well Sharp got on with Trudeau. Near the opening of one Parliament, Trudeau asked whether Sharp had told a Western audience that he was leaving the cabinet. What should he make of it? At about the same time, Sharp told Martin that he thought Trudeau was considering moving him. But Sharp knew a lot about trade issues, and he knew Ed Ritchie very well.

SSEAs
Sharp was succeeded by MacEachen, a good minister when you could get him moving. He was "a slow mover." And though MacEachen and Martin were good friends, he never called. He used to exasperate Trudeau. He would set up a meeting, and MacEachen wouldn't arrive until it was half over. Yet he was a very good House leader for the Liberals.

Don Jamieson as SSEA was a very free-and-easy fellow, with a great gift of the gab whether he knew a subject or not. He got on very well with British foreign secretary David Owen, whom nobody else liked. Owen used to call him "Donnie," his way of showing approval. Incidentally, Owen didn't like seeing ambassadors and told Martin so when he was high commissioner in London. Martin immediately replied that Owen would be seeing him; he used to be over in the Foreign Office once a week.

Chrétien? "I don't know much about what he did as external affairs minister," said Martin. "I can't imagine that Jean was a very good foreign minister. I remember asking Gotlieb, but I'm sure that they wouldn't have got along. It was a case of careful science versus spurt it out." And yet Chrétien was very friendly. Trudeau mistakenly had **Marc Lalonde** handle contact with René Lévesque and company, when he should have given Chrétien the job. Lalonde was like a father superior who wouldn't suffer fools gladly. This used to enrage the Péquistes, and René Lévesque hated him.

Ministers

Léo Cadieux was a good minister. He was a very well-organized man, a very hard worker who got on well with the officers and others in DND. He was firm in resisting any attempt to impair Pearson's NATO policy. He accepted Trudeau's cuts, probably after long argument; later he was a good ambassador in Paris, always working at something.

Don Macdonald was very bright, able, and nice. But when he came to Ottawa, he was one of Walter Gordon's nationalist flock and definitely shared Gordon's economic views. He had strong opinions and could be pigheaded; he could also resist authority. For example, he insisted on coming to Martin's London banquet for Trudeau, even though Trudeau specifically didn't want the Macdonalds to attend. Trudeau was coming to London, and the Macdonalds just happened to be there. Martin phoned Head about the guest list, and Head gave the go-ahead for a standard list, from Prime Minister Callaghan down. As Macdonald was a senior minister, he could hardly be excluded. However, Trudeau threw a fit when Martin met him at Heathrow. He didn't want a boring banquet, and he regularly saw Macdonald in Ottawa. He wanted Ralf Dahrendorf and similar people.[61] The result was a very puzzled Callaghan, who had seldom if ever met the people whom Trudeau had to dinner with him, and the Macdonalds. There was quite a set-to between Trudeau and Ruth Macdonald ...

Martin's 1968 departure from DEA

Martin's departure from DEA was straightforward. Trudeau owed Sharp, and he had also promised Finance to Edgar Benson. Sharp had to be given a senior portfolio, and it had to be External Affairs (after all, he wasn't a lawyer). Martin, being a lawyer, was offered Justice. He was taken aback. On reflection, he thought he might well have accepted it, or should have accepted it. But he didn't really reflect at the time. He remained adamant that he had fought his last election. So Trudeau offered him government leader in the Senate, and Martin took it, though "after two or three days."

---

61 Ralf Dahrendorf was a German sociologist and liberal politician who had become warden of St. Antony's College, Oxford. He later became Lord Dahrendorf.

HON. MITCHELL SHARP (1911-2004)
INTERVIEW | OTTAWA, 8 DECEMBER 1987

A former senior public servant and minister in the Pearson government, Sharp served as SSEA in Trudeau's cabinet from 1968 to 1974. He was then president of the privy council until retiring from politics in 1978.[62]

The FLQ crisis of October 1970
The cabinet knew nothing about what was happening. In Sharp's view, the government acted to restore public confidence, to reassure the mother walking her kids to school. If the cabinet had known how small the FLQ was, it would never have acted as it did in deploying troops and invoking the War Measures Act.

Becoming SSEA
Sharp had asked to be SSEA. Trudeau had talked to him first among the ministers. Sharp didn't want to stay in Finance and said he could handle DEA. Trudeau said he'd talk to **Martin**, who was unhappy. Some years later, after Sharp had left the cabinet, he went to Paris for a meeting and stopped in London to see Martin. Had Martin really told Trudeau that he didn't want to be SSEA any longer? "Yes," Martin replied. "I don't believe you," Sharp said.

DEA was in good shape in 1968, a department with very high competence. The leading members were very able – **Ed Ritchie**, Klaus Goldschlag, **Si Taylor, John Halstead**, and Blair Seaborn.[63] Marcel Cadieux was Sharp's first USSEA – a brilliant international lawyer with good control over the department, although his interests were more legal than economic. DEA became more relevant to the issues when Ed Ritchie took over. What could have been more relevant than Quebec-France and defence, the questions that concerned Cadieux? Those were Trudeau issues, Sharp said, not department issues of relevance to Canadians.

Trudeau also named DEA people to other posts. This was a compliment to the department, though it weakened it. Sharp added that this period, when

---

62 Sharp's memoir is *Which Reminds Me ... A Memoir* (Toronto: University of Toronto Press, 1995).
63 A senior diplomat, Seaborn (1924-) was deputy minister of consumer and corporate affairs in the early 1970s.

cuts were made and missions closed, wasn't all to DEA's detriment. A number of FSOs who weren't useful were let go, and DEA emerged leaner. In his view, the department had been overstaffed for the problems it had to deal with. That he failed to resist these cuts did not cause problems with Cadieux.

The Soviet Union's 1968 invasion of Czechoslovakia had no impact on Trudeau.[64] Sharp, however, was relieved that the Soviet troops had not progressed beyond the Czech border and felt embarrassed that Trudeau had said so little and spoke so weakly on the topic.

However, on federal-provincial questions, Trudeau dominated discussion, though Quebec politics were never dealt with. That subject belonged to the Quebec ministers. In other words, there was never discussion of what was going on federally in Quebec.

Trudeau understood economics and had studied it, but it didn't interest him. He didn't usually intervene in cabinet discussions that dealt with economic issues, except in 1974 on price controls. Before the election, the data did not support controls; after the election, they did. The officials advocated a more comprehensive system of controls, but Trudeau stopped this, and he was right ...

US representation in Canada, except for Ambassador **Tom Enders**, was weak. Enders was critical but had a better understanding of Canada than most Americans.

Sharp thought the French had acted improperly in Canada, a "real conspiracy." He remembered that **Gérard Pelletier** went to a conference of La Francophonie's Agence de coopération culturelle et technique and had a hard time over flags, etc.[65] The next time, Jean Marchand went, saying he wouldn't stand for any nonsense. But Jean returned furious ...

Biafra
On the Nigerian civil war and Biafra, Trudeau started off badly, with his "Where's Biafra?" comment. The fear of creating a precedent for Quebec by recognizing the splinter republic of Biafra was "very important." So also were reports from the high commissioner in Nigeria and talks with neighbouring African states. Sharp came to the conclusion that children had been

....

64 In August 1968, the Soviet and satellite armies occupied Czechoslovakia and removed what was to them an unreliable, though still communist, government.
65 La Francophonie is the French version of the British Commonwealth.

deliberately starved to manipulate public opinion and that if Canada broke the rules by sending aid directly to Biafra, it would do no good anywhere. Near the end of the war, church leaders requested a meeting with Sharp. Before he saw them, the war ended. They told him that they'd blundered, that agitators had taken over the church in Canada, and that Anglicans in Nigeria had suffered as a result. Sharp added that Ottawa was close to giving in and sending direct aid to Biafra when the war ended.

Dealing with Canadian Jews
As for the Arabs and Jews, his primary principle in dealing with the Jews in his own constituency was not to mislead them and to be as clear as possible. He also insisted that Canada remain neutral, which the Jews disliked. In 1972, he hung on in his Eglinton riding by 1,500 votes. In 1974, his Tory opponent targeted the Jewish vote (35 percent) and attacked Sharp for offering insufficient support to Israel. Sharp refused to reply to that – to do so would be the worst thing he could do to Israel and for Canadian Jews. He added that Trudeau's relations with the Jewish community were awful. In 1979, Sol Kanee of the Canadian Jewish Congress saw Sharp to ask for his help. Trudeau wouldn't see representatives from the congress and was blaming them for the controversy that arose over the suggestion that the Canadian embassy should move from Tel Aviv to Jerusalem. Denying that the congress was responsible, Kanee asked Sharp to see Trudeau and tell him so, and to get contacts resumed. When Sharp complied, Trudeau's response was "They want it both ways, don't they?" In due course, relations were patched up.

Sharp talked about the United Nations Crime Conference that was scheduled for Toronto when he was president of the privy council. The question was how far Jewish opinion could influence Canadian policy to not allow Palestinian representatives to attend. Certainly, this was a big issue in the cabinet, as MacEachen wanted to support the UN and proceed with the invitation for the conference. Sharp led the opposition, feeling it unwise to go ahead with the Province of Ontario, the City of Toronto, and the Metropolitan Toronto chair against. If the conference could be held only under tight security, was it worth going on with? After a long discussion, the opposition prevailed, greatly upsetting MacEachen, who felt that his authority as SSEA had been questioned. A few months later, the similar Habitat Conference in Vancouver went ahead without difficulty, the Jewish community there being less organized.

REEVES HAGGAN (DIED C. 1997)
INTERVIEW | OTTAWA, 4 FEBRUARY 1988

A British-born barrister, Haggan worked for the CBC, went to DEA in Mitchell Sharp's office, worked in the PCO (twice), in the Department of the Solicitor-General, and in the London High Commission during the patriation controversy.

Haggan began by giving his background
He trained as a barrister at the Middle Temple in London, emigrated to Canada at some indeterminate point, and became supervisor for public affairs in Ottawa CBC sometime during the 1950s. By 1968, he was in DEA, where the new minister, **Mitchell Sharp**, remembered his public affairs background. Sharp was having troubles over Biafra and seemed to have decided that he needed help with the public side of his office. So he asked USSEA Marcel Cadieux to send Haggan in as his departmental assistant. This could have been better handled, as Cadieux thought such assignments were his prerogative, and it would have been as easy to describe the right qualifications and then let Cadieux discover that only one man fitted. So, where Cadieux was concerned, Haggan had a legacy of suspicion to overcome.

He served in Sharp's office from 1968 to 1972, when he was posted to the PCO. The main topics of the time were China, Nixonomics, "the NATO caper," and Biafra.

On Marcel Cadieux and A.E. Ritchie
Haggan greatly admired Marcel Cadieux. Fortunately, he got to know him better and could boast that he was one of the few people about whom Cadieux ever changed his mind. Sharp and Cadieux were not natural soulmates, but they worked together very well. Cadieux was a solitary man who had no close relationships and a relationship to Trudeau that was best defined as "wary respect" (a favourite). Cadieux was not a man of calm temperament, and he took his policies seriously. In relation to Charles de Gaulle, he was as Captain Ahab to the great white whale. During one exchange of telegrams between Cadieux and Léger in Paris on Canada's "French" policy, Cadieux fired off rockets while Léger remained perfectly calm, taking a "see-here-Marcel" tone. Haggan didn't like the exportation of our domestic problems to places such as Gabon – ridiculous and rather demeaning.

Nevertheless, when Marcel was replaced by **Ed Ritchie** (for whom Haggan professed affection and respect), "the intellectual tone of the place dropped precipitately." Ritchie was a skilled manager (the first thing he did was establish a senior management committee or group), but he just didn't have the knowledge or breadth of Marcel.

Cadieux saw himself as the government's principal adviser on foreign affairs. He was not a good manager, but that didn't matter too much since **Basil Robinson** actually ran the department. (A good manager, in Haggan's opinion, was someone with a knack for keeping the inkwells full.) Occasionally, Cadieux would erupt into some management issue, almost always unhelpfully. In sum, there was a high standard of discussion under Marcel, but under Ritchie it became endless talk about parking and typists.

Ritchie was probably over-specialized on the United States, and he believed (perhaps rightly) that he was brought into DEA to manage it. What was striking, however, about Ritchie and the senior DEA management was that they became practically unhinged when they discovered that their department was actually under attack. They were completely incapable of saying "no" to the silly demands and analyses that the Treasury Board sent their way. Haggan would have preferred to say, "No, I won't do it." After all, who is Treasury Board? Just another bunch of officials, like the DEA people. DEA should have said, "stuff it," but none of them had the guts.

So, there was less to Ritchie than met the eye, but as for Marcel, "I always wanted to hear what Marcel had to say."

Mitchell Sharp

Sharp was a splendid man, with a real knack for knowing instinctively what the country was thinking. He had an understanding of Canada and of Canadians that **Trudeau** never had; he just knew – he didn't have to be told. He had two weaknesses. One was systemic. The prime minister in Canada always has the capacity to be his own SSEA. Mackenzie King was, Diefenbaker was, and so was Trudeau. Only St. Laurent withheld his hand from Pearson, though Pearson did not reciprocate with **Martin**.

Sharp's second limitation was his consciousness of the fact that he had once sat on the other side of the desk, and as a result he bent over backward not to give direction to Cadieux. Haggan thought that a minister ought to say to his deputy, do a study on such-and-such; but Sharp was "overly pure" and wouldn't do it ...

Sharp would say that the function of an SSEA was to take the blame when things went wrong and let the prime minister take the credit when they went well. And, Haggan said, he lived up to his maxim.

HON. MARK MacGUIGAN (1931-98)
INTERVIEW | OTTAWA, 19 JANUARY 1988

A lawyer, MacGuigan was first elected to Parliament in 1968. He became SSEA in 1980 and was minister of justice from 1982 to 1984. He ended his career as a federal court judge.[66]

Becoming SSEA
Foreign affairs was a particularly congenial area to MacGuigan, but he never aspired to the job of SSEA. He thought he would get Solicitor-General or Justice. It was true that he had taught international law, but he had never even been a member of the parliamentary Standing Committee on External Affairs and National Defence.

Other MPs wanted the job as well: Roméo LeBlanc, André Ouellet, Jean Chrétien – who was desperate for it – and **Marc Lalonde** too. When MacGuigan got it, Chrétien wouldn't speak to him for months. So he carefully crafted a tactic to persuade Chrétien that he, MacGuigan, was indebted to him for his altruism in passing it over. And really, it was because Chrétien wanted it so badly that **Trudeau** decided to choose an anglophone: if a French Canadian had been picked, Chrétien would have been even more irritated.

MacGuigan believed he was selected because Trudeau thought he would be cool under fire and was probably a compatible personality. MacGuigan was bilingual, and he represented a border city, Windsor. But, MacGuigan added, he and Trudeau disagreed from the first on such matters as the American threat to boycott the 1980 Moscow Olympics after the USSR invaded Afghanistan. He was "outraged" by Trudeau's comments on the subject. The matter was crucial to the Americans. He complained vigorously about it to one of Trudeau's entourage, who never passed it on, which may have

....

66 MacGuigan's memoir, edited by Whitney Lackenbauer, is *An Inside Look at External Affairs during the Trudeau Years: The Memoirs of Mark MacGuigan* (Calgary: University of Calgary Press, 2002).

been just as well. If angered, Trudeau was quite capable of pursuing a course that was entirely different from the one you wanted.

On the boycott, Trudeau eventually followed the American line, and Canada joined the countries that did not participate in the Olympics. In MacGuigan's opinion, he was trying to make the Americans sweat a bit, trying to get something in exchange for his co-operation. But though MacGuigan had to persuade him, he finally did what was asked. Trudeau was not showing his power; he was always very petulant toward the United States and eventually toward Reagan. He liked to be cajoled back to a reasonable position. This occurred so often that MacGuigan concluded it was a deliberate technique.

When Trudeau told MacGuigan that he was to be SSEA, it was a Saturday night, and though such offers were supposed to be strictly secret, he did allow him to tell **Paul Martin** what was up. So Martin gave him lots of background and helped him prep for Monday's announcement. In the 1980 cabinet, DEA was effectively the number four position, not number two. The Energy portfolio had more standing, and so did Finance.

Aims as SSEA

MacGuigan had three goals as SSEA, and they were not always the same as Trudeau's.

The first was not to force the Third World into a Cold War mould: treat it independently on the basis of its own interests. The second was to view the USSR and Cuba with skepticism. He and Trudeau were most at odds here, he recollected. The prime minister liked to be against whatever the majority favoured, to *épater les bourgeois*. At an earlier stage, he had gone against the weight of public opinion in cultivating the USSR and Cuba. No, Trudeau had no personal attraction to Leonid Brezhnev, though he liked Alexei Kosygin.[67] He was also close to Ambassador Alexander Yakovlev and was determined to see Yakovlev on his own, though he did allow a note-taker from DEA to accompany him. That, plus a meeting with the pro-Arabists led by Professor Peyton Lyon, was the only time he insisted on being on his own. Though MacGuigan could not say that Trudeau was blind to the USSR, he took a

---

67 Leonid Brezhnev (1906-82), general secretary of the Soviet Communist Party, 1964-82, and president of the Soviet Union, 1977-82; Alexei Kosygin (1904-1980), premier of the Soviet Union, 1964-80.

consistently softer line than MacGuigan himself, which resulted in a clash between them over Poland.

Third was relations with the United States. Trudeau also differed there, but at least he was aware of the need to get along with the Americans. In MacGuigan's opinion, Canada must clearly side with the United States on everything to do with the USSR. That would create leeway for differences over NATO and the Third World. To Trudeau, this was paying an unwelcome price; to MacGuigan, it was just reality, our policy, and in our interest too.

Trudeau's foreign policy views
Despite the attitudinal differences between them, MacGuigan and Trudeau never quarrelled over anything fundamental. Yet, MacGuigan added, "I felt Trudeau was irrationally aggressive, suspicious, towards the Americans." On every issue, he continued, "I got the better of him," mostly over Poland, where the cabinet, very much including Marc Lalonde, "agreed with me" in opposing the attack on the Solidarity movement. Trudeau respected the majority even though it was clear that he did not want to impose sanctions. Very much to MacGuigan's surprise, and despite the cabinet, Trudeau phoned him the next day and begged him not to put the agreed policy into effect. The agreed-upon sanctions were duly implemented, but to Trudeau anything was too much.

Trudeau ran the cabinet like a chairman, not like a dictator. When he was determined on something, he'd just do it with only two or three ministers involved. But he would not confront the cabinet, one against many.

On Cuba, MacGuigan said, "I cut off the last vestiges of aid." Although Trudeau let it be known in the cabinet that he was opposed to this, MacGuigan "did it because of Cuba's militarism abroad: if Cuba could afford such adventures, it was not suitable for aid."

He felt that Trudeau did not believe in the balance of power. That was really a rationalization. The prime minister was impetuous and headstrong. And he was not consistent. At one point, he told Jim Callaghan that if Cuba got out of line, "we" would pulverize it. That contrasted with his usual pro-Cuba line. Nor was Trudeau really a civil libertarian: "He had a mind of astounding brilliance in the service of very unworthy passions."

As for the relations between MacGuigan and Trudeau, "I didn't have the access to Trudeau that Paul Martin did to Pearson." On foreign policy, "Trudeau was only interstitially interested," so you had to save things up. "I would often drop down to a seat beside the prime minister in the House and inform him" of what was up and get his reactions. Trudeau didn't like surprises; he didn't really care what the issue was, as long as he knew. Early on, Trudeau told MacGuigan that he expected ministers to be making up their own minds. But most didn't treat him that way, though Lalonde and MacGuigan went their own way. Herb Gray had irritated Trudeau very much in the early 1970s by constantly looking to him for direction.

On the Middle East, Trudeau "decisively affected my policy." He was a factor in the adoption of a more pro-Arab policy. MacGuigan was determined to be neutral; he was set at odds with the Jewish community by some of his radio comments, such as on the 1982 Israeli invasion of Lebanon. He thought of starting an aid program for the West Bank, but though the matter was online when he left the department in 1982, it never happened. It was connected to the proposed visit of the mayor of Bethlehem.

On DEA

MacGuigan said that **Allan Gotlieb** was "very solicitous for my education. He gave me a departmental assistant who led me over." Gotlieb was superb, one of the great minds in government, and he and MacGuigan thought "almost identically." They differed only once, on a multilateral force for the Middle East. When MacGuigan refused, Gotlieb with his permission took the issue to Trudeau. That was an easy step to take because MacGuigan knew Trudeau would send Gotlieb packing, which he did. But it was also a good thing to do because of Gotlieb's standing. On the whole, he couldn't "think of a better relationship" than he had with Gotlieb.

Interestingly, MacGuigan found one of Flora MacDonald's changes in DEA very good: that anyone who wrote a memorandum should sign it.[68] When the deputy minister came to MacGuigan on an issue, he had to bring all the people concerned. MacGuigan would hear what they had to say, even though Gotlieb always summed up the discussion. Of the officers, **Si Taylor** (deputy USSEA and then ambassador to NATO) was outstanding, and Klaus Goldschlag was "spectacular," surely Gotlieb's equal.

Middle East morass

Except on the Middle East and Latin America, DEA was strong. On Latin America, it had appointed a Japanese specialist as head of division. Performance on the Middle East may have been affected because Gotlieb

---

68 MacDonald was External Affairs minister in the Joe Clark government, 1979-80.

and Goldschlag were both Jewish, and Gotlieb certainly had problems on the issue. Everybody else (though not MacGuigan) was pro-Arab, and that included Trudeau and **Michael Pitfield**. Because Pitfield was the conduit, MacGuigan was never certain whether the word he got was Trudeau's or not. Pitfield even told Gotlieb that unless MacGuigan produced a better policy, Trudeau would find another minister.

The only area where they really had trouble on the Middle East was in caucus. Trudeau had a passionate hatred of Israeli prime minister Menachem Begin: that was the greatest source of his animus toward the Israelis. Practically the whole of the Quebec caucus was "anti-Jewish" and pro-Arab, except for Lalonde. The strongest on the pro-Arab side were Ian Watson (Liberal-Chateauguay) and Marcel Prud'homme (Liberal-St-Denis). Prud'homme was a particular recipient of the free trips that the Arabs used to give.

The Quebec caucus became agitated about the Middle East in the summer of 1982. There was a "drag-out fight," but at the end MacGuigan spoke and carried the balance ...

Dealing with Pitfield

Michael Pitfield did not have much contact with DEA. Security and intelligence were his baby. But he was the G7 summit co-ordinator in 1982. He was obviously very close to the prime minister, and "the person he used to terrorize with this fact was Gotlieb." Gotlieb became very upset when Pitfield failed to return his phone calls. He characterized Pitfield as "devious."

The prime minister exploited Pitfield's role, with the result that Pitfield was both visible and responsible. Departmental reorganization was a Pitfield preoccupation. "Trudeau told me at the outset in 1980 that he'd decided on departmental reorganization" and that MacGuigan was not to oppose it. Ed Lumley, the minister of state for trade, was in fact "very opposed," though Herb Gray in his day, 1980-82, was even more so. Pitfield was very, very interested, and he and Lumley argued fiercely all the way. But in MacGuigan's opinion, possibly because his department won out, the reorganization was very, very right. "I thought there should have been even more rationalization," he remarked. **Osbaldeston** (whom Gotlieb once called "a process freak") said it was as far as they could go at that point.

The Pitfield influence showed, however, in "endless, time-wasting reorganization." Marcel Massé as USSEA went farther: he ran roughshod and eventually was ousted as deputy minister. In fact, he was treated "rather poorly" when he was sent to the International Monetary Fund.

Operating at DEA

As for the quality of the foreign service, MacGuigan claimed that he read every telegram from the embassies and was generally very impressed. The quality was at a very high level. Yet DEA was lacking in language skills, and it was true that there was friction between DEA, Trade, and Immigration. Since he travelled a great deal, he met a lot of FSOs. **Bob Ford**, for example, was a man with a world reputation. MacGuigan tapped the abilities of Ford, Goldschlag, Gotlieb, and Taylor. For instance, when there was a problem on nukes, he gathered them together as a brains trust. Goldschlag was not present at the time, but he wrote up the conclusions as MacGuigan gave them. MacGuigan was very much a hands-on minister and was with departmental people at all times.

"If I had a relatively simple question, I would telephone the desk officer," he said. If a meeting were required, he had his departmental assistant (first Alan Sullivan and then Mike Phillips) arrange it; presumably, Sullivan or Phillips would then report to the USSEA. He never tried to do anything behind the back of his deputy or to circumvent his assistant.

No, there was no **Ivan Head** figure in the PMO at that time. But he liked Head – "so superb" – equal to Ford or Goldschlag or Gotlieb. He often talked to Ivan during the 1980s; they consulted on a friendly basis, and at MacGuigan's invitation he attended, for example, the meeting on nukes.

Outside the government, Montreal human rights lawyer Irwin Cotler influenced him the most.[69] MacGuigan thought him very able, with a great understanding of the USSR. He was more aggressive than DEA in playing up the issue of Russian dissidents. Actually, MacGuigan considered Cotler the most moderate Jew in Canada. Irwin had a dialogue inside his own house, with his wife, who was a Begin-ite. Once Cotler challenged the Canada-Israel committee to make representations to Israel, which resulted in a great hassle – the worst of MacGuigan's time as minister.

Dealing with the Americans

Relations with the Americans were much better under Carter than under Reagan. MacGuigan inadvertently gave Cyrus Vance his farewell dinner as secretary of state, as the Iranian operation was simultaneously going on, over

---

69 Cotler (1940-) later became a Liberal MP (1999-2015) and minister of justice (2003-06).

which Vance resigned.[70] Then there was Ed Muskie.[71] He was no expert in foreign policy, not first-class, and though he was a very pleasant man, he wasn't really on top of the issues. US ambassador Kenneth Curtis was "very nice but not strong."

The main problem was probably the Atlantic fisheries. MacGuigan made strong speeches on it, hoping to stir the Democrats to some action in getting the treaty ratified. Senator Claiborne Pell of Rhode Island was passing through on another invitation and the two had dinner. Pell made it quite clear that he would oppose the treaty. He had no sense of its national or international merits; what concerned him was that some of his constituents were opposed to it. Only by international arbitration, Pell said, would the treaty or its provisions be put through. "I learned my lesson," MacGuigan said, and he changed his speeches. So the next year, when Al Haig, Reagan's secretary of state, announced that the treaty had been abandoned and the dispute was going to arbitration, "I didn't say much," and in fact thought it the best solution.

The US administration didn't ask for Canadian help or input in pulling the treaty from the American Senate, though MacGuigan had made representations to Haig on the issue. Before he ever came to Ottawa in March 1981, the treaty was no longer a subject for discussion.

Unlike most Americans, Al Haig was an Atlanticist. He was dedicated to the Atlantic alliance, and that was "the heart of our relationship" in dealing with the USSR. He was admittedly not so good on other issues. He had "what seemed to me to be a fondness for Canadians," though MacGuigan acknowledged that he could be "quite bristly though never with me." He had some reason for being bristly, given the state of his relations with the White House.

MacGuigan confessed that he liked Haig and thought we could do business with him; in retrospect, however, he probably appeared to go too far in that direction, giving the impression that he was a patsy for the Americans, an easy mark. This may have been his biggest political mistake. "My influence in the country would have been greater if I'd made more anti-American statements," he said. Certainly, the pro-American statements that he did make never got him anywhere.

....

70 Cyrus Vance was Jimmy Carter's secretary of state, 1977-80. He resigned over Carter's decision to attempt a military rescue of US hostages in Iran.
71 Democratic Senator from Maine and subsequently secretary of state, 1980-81.

There was, he said, no pressure from the Americans on Argentina's invasion of the Falklands or other issues, even Poland. They implied what they wanted, but they never said so.

The Cruise missile was part of Carter's two-track policy, and we adopted the policy earlier than might appear. The prime minister dissented on the issue. We permitted the Cruise to be tested on our soil because it was in our interest and very much in keeping with our foreign policy. It was not a concession to the Americans. In the cabinet, MacGuigan was sure that John Roberts did not oppose it. Otherwise, the missile was overwhelmingly favoured. Lloyd Axworthy made it clear that he was not convinced, but MacGuigan was not sure that he stated his opposition as such.

He saw Trudeau and Carter together at the Venice Summit and felt that their relations were good but not close.

Trudeau and Reagan

Reagan was very much more personable than Carter, very gracious, always ready with a quip or a story without any point to it. We would laugh politely if we knew that laughter was the proper response. Soon, when Trudeau and Reagan were at meetings, Trudeau got into the habit of speaking shortly after the president and contradicting everything he said. Haig bitterly resented this. Relations between Haig and Trudeau suffered as a consequence, as shown by Trudeau's NATO speech. It was a good speech, which Trudeau delivered on the wrong occasion. MacGuigan remembered Haig clapping two fingers together. MacGuigan knew about the speech in advance and was aware that it was a mistake; but it did not deal with a treaty or anything permanent, so he did not press his opposition.

Summitry

Trudeau was not dominant at G7 summits. The "great figure at my three was Helmut Schmidt." Though MacGuigan was told that Trudeau had good relations with Schmidt, he never personally witnessed them. He tried but failed to get Trudeau to call Schmidt in February 1980, when the Liberals were returned to office. Schmidt was very much the master statesman, too clever to say what he meant, though on occasion he could speak bluntly in irritation at something. He never said anything personal, whereas Trudeau would make personal remarks in his nasty comments. On such occasions, Trudeau often voiced what Schmidt was thinking. He was really "an innocent compared to Schmidt."

At summits, Canada was a player, though not a major one. If Canada was listened to, it was on Third World issues. The Big Four had a relationship to which Italy, Canada, and even Japan were somewhat peripheral.[72] What we said didn't matter as much as what others said.

He thought that Margaret Thatcher probably didn't have much respect for Trudeau, though Trudeau respected her. He said as much at Venice, and indeed in MacGuigan's opinion, her mind and expression were admirable. "Isn't she magnificent?" said Trudeau to him.

Trudeau's personal relations with French president François Mitterrand were better than with Valéry Giscard d'Estaing, though his policies were closer to Giscard's ...

Canadians and foreign policy
The press – with very rare exceptions – were not interested in foreign policy. They were always looking for sensation, and that was not DEA. Canadian newsmen were totally naive about foreign affairs and were not capable of more than an either-or philosophy. If you were anti-communist, you must therefore favour fascism, or so they believed; they could not see the middle way. "I used to become even angrier with the clergy" – the bishops who thought they knew more about Central America than the Central American bishops. Fairness on Central America meant that you were appalled by the behaviour of both sides. This was the greatest problem in foreign policy.

The Opposition in the House he did not rate highly. There was not a great deal of co-operation. It was hard to have a rational conversation with NDP MP Pauline Jewett, let alone work with her. The Conservatives were split. Some you could work with, but some always wanted to oppose for political reasons. On the Constitution and Thatcher, Joe Clark handled it. MacGuigan liked Joe, but there was no possibility of co-operation on that issue. MPs Doug Roche, John Fraser, and Walter Maclean were fine. John Crosbie was the external affairs critic "for a while; he refused even to speak on the subject for ten months." His ambition was to be the financial critic. So Pauline Jewett of the NDP was out in left field, and Crosbie was uninterested.

MacGuigan mentioned Allan MacEachen in passing, possibly unfavourably, as one who was not awake very much. MacEachen was, of course, his successor. It happened as follows: Trudeau told MacGuigan that he had to

---

72 The Big Four were the United States, the United Kingdom, Germany, and France.

move Finance Minister MacEachen; afterward, he called MacEachen and said that he, MacGuigan, accepted the move and would support it. MacEachen was astounded that Trudeau was thinking of moving him, and so soon. This was on a Monday; the swearing-in was scheduled for Friday. MacEachen was so upset that he almost didn't come to the swearing-in. Trudeau had to cajole him. That Friday he refused to do any of the work in the department, so MacGuigan, though no longer the minister, had to host a lunch.

As SSEA, MacEachen refused to see ambassadors. MacGuigan's scholarship program for the Commonwealth was lost, and there were no initiatives on the Middle East. "Allan rises to occasions," he quipped, "but when there's no occasion, he won't."

II
Deputy Ministers and Senior Diplomats

PIERRE TRUDEAU HAD A FRAUGHT relationship with civil servants and with diplomats in particular. It was a case of familiarity breeding skepticism. As a young man on his travels in Europe and Asia, Trudeau encountered Canada's fledgling embassies abroad and later wrote unappreciatively of some of his experiences. His diplomatic hosts returned the favour, though usually not in print. The experience was apparently not utterly traumatic, for Trudeau shortly afterward applied to join the foreign service, only to be rejected by an interview panel that included Marcel Cadieux, a rising star in the Department of External Affairs. Cadieux, according to a believable story, found Trudeau insouciant and arrogant – spoiled, in his opinion. After all, Trudeau came from riches and Outremont; Cadieux rose from poverty and east-end Montreal.

Cadieux would become legal adviser and then under secretary for external affairs (USSEA), after rising through the ranks of the diplomatic service. A protégé of Norman Robertson, he became deputy minister in 1964 on Robertson's very strong recommendation. A fervent federalist, he battled separatism and French meddling in Canadian affairs, and objectively he became an ally of the new minister of justice, Pierre Trudeau.

Allies on Quebec and separatism, the two men agreed on little else. The problem was not so much Cadieux's lingering resentment of Trudeau as the child of privilege, as a fundamental disagreement about the governance of the diplomatic service. As with so much during Trudeau's period in government, the roots of the problem lay with Pearson. A former diplomat and under secretary himself, Pearson was too wise and too experienced to assume that ministers could simply press a button and see their wishes implemented to the letter. Sometimes, Pearson knew, it was necessary to dig new channels for policy and to bypass immovable objects and protocol. As prime minister, Pearson created several new departments to implement his policies, judging the old ones insufficient.

Observing the cabinet as justice minister, Trudeau viewed Pearson's style of government as chaotic and sometimes contradictory. He decided to bring order to cabinet business, to manage public business efficiently and systematically. That meant bringing the cabinet to a sense of collective responsibility, but it also meant getting the bureaucrats to follow policies designed and determined by the politicians.

External Affairs, however, was different. There the problem was not too little order, or system, but too much. What he was really confronting was professionalism, and the incarnation of professionalism was Marcel Cadieux. Diplomacy, Cadieux believed, was more than a specialty: it was a profession. Like any profession, it was arduous, and it was arduous because there were so many nuances to be grasped, so many techniques to be mastered. The deputy minister had a broad mandate to keep his department in order, and his tools included the power to assign jobs and promote the worthy. And, of course, not to promote those who did not meet proper standards.

Trudeau was no stranger to organization and form. Systematic study and rationality were ideas close to his heart. Yet at the same time, he appreciated novelty and authenticity – essentially romantic values, as the poets of the nineteenth century saw them. He did not see novelty and authenticity in Canadian foreign policy or in the people who conceived it, promoted it, and enforced it.

The problem began with policy, or rather, the orthodoxy of policy. Trudeau came to the Prime Minister's Office equipped with a collection of fashionable nostrums that had as their laudable object the decompression of the tensions of the Cold War and had as their backdrop an entirely justified dread of nuclear war. East and West were frozen in confrontation, Trudeau believed: it was time for a thaw, to demonstrate optimism and reasonableness.

Cadieux, and with him most of Canada's foreign service, believed the opposite: peace had been achieved and would be maintained through strength and firmness. Practically, this meant that Canada's existing commitments, diplomatic and military, must be maintained. Though Trudeau seemed not to have known it, Prime Minister Pearson had his doubts about the rigidity of Canadian policy and questioned whether policies made in the 1940s still had the same relevance, or relation to reality, in the 1960s. But Pearson and his doubts were out of office, and Trudeau and his much more forceful reservations were in.

The bureaucratic reaction was to dig in, a tactic that usually worked, and not just in Canada. Trudeau's solution drew on his perception of another problem, and here he relied on the advice of the deputy clerk of the privy council, Michael Pitfield. It was a question of personnel – a surplus of personnel. External Affairs had a systemic problem: too many bright, talented people chasing too few jobs. In other departments, especially the newly founded ones, there was need of talent. The solution was obvious: draw on the old to reinforce the new. Marcel Cadieux, who regarded the foreign service the way the Master of the Templars might have seen his knights in the Middle Ages, was apoplectic – which, admittedly, and given his temperament, was not unusual.

A. EDGAR RITCHIE (1916-2002)
INTERVIEW | OTTAWA, 15 MARCH 1988

Edgar Ritchie joined DEA in 1944. He served in Washington, London, and Ottawa, became ambassador to the United States in 1966, and was then USSEA from 1970 to 1974. After he suffered a stroke, he was made ambassador in Dublin from 1976 to 1980.

Trudeau and DEA
He and **Trudeau** were never "buddy-buddy," Ritchie said, "but he treated me reasonably well," then and later. Though not a warm and caring personality, and apparently indifferent to human considerations, Trudeau nevertheless gave Ritchie the job in Ireland after his stroke ...

Ritchie never knew the ins and outs of the Ottawa background to his appointment as USSEA in 1970. Trudeau wanted somebody who was not wholly preoccupied with Quebec and France, and who had an economic background. No doubt Marcel Cadieux's wishes (to be ambassador in Washington) were a factor too. Did he see Cadieux? They passed in transit – somewhere on the highway, possibly around Syracuse. Ritchie respected Cadieux as a good lawyer, "and he respected me as one who'd dabbled in economics." They did not have a long discussion about the changeover.

He did not arrive back in Ottawa with any great agenda: he was not so naive. He had felt too great an inclination in the department to go for the European connection and not the multilateral one. He saw our role in Europe more in terms of our relations with the Americans than of anything else. By the way, **Paul Martin** had more understanding of these issues than most people did. And if you are looking for a clear, independent Canadian voice, take Howard Green, Diefenbaker's SSEA.[1] However naive and innocent, his was a clear Canadian position.

Ritchie and Trudeau met for the third time after he returned to Ottawa. He did not consider Trudeau's views to be particularly left-wing, though admittedly Trudeau had attended that Moscow economic conference in 1952. It is always possible that when Trudeau presented an argument, it did not reflect his real views. He was a very stimulating man to serve, though not perhaps the most humane. But then, neither was Mackenzie King.

Ritchie got on reasonably well with **Ivan Head**. They gave Trudeau what he wanted, on Europe with Ralph Collins, and on economics, where Ritchie could make his own contribution.

Sharp and October 1970

As DEA minister, **Mitchell Sharp** was a very competent, honest, conscientious person – as far as a politician could be, of course. Ritchie could not imagine a minister more calm or more professional, as his actions showed throughout the FLQ crisis of October 1970. As for the crisis itself, it had a profound impact on the department. It enabled the department to show that its operations centre could function throughout: all those stories are true.[2] "I think Trudeau developed more respect [for us] because of the competent way things were handled and because we were pretty hard-headed when we had to be," Ritchie said.

As to Transport Minister Don Jamieson's October 1970 diary, published in *Saturday Night* magazine in 1988, it was the work of a peripheral minister; it showed how ill-informed he was during the FLQ crisis. There may be evidence of a conspiracy, but Ritchie said he didn't see it at the time: don't forget that the War Measures proclamation depended on Quebec premier Robert Bourassa's advice, which was definite.

"Here I was, an old anglophone Protestant presiding over a department that had a key role in this francophone crisis," Ritchie commented. He remembered the concerns of André Bissonnette, Paul Tremblay, and Christian Roquet. "It strained a lot of the French Canadians, though of course all of

....

1 A veteran Progressive Conservative MP, Green was SSEA from 1959 to 1963. He was at one and the same time thought by his diplomats to be both naive and authentic, and was greatly liked by many.
2 "The Operations Centre of the Department of External Affairs," *External Affairs* 23 (January 1971): 3-5.

them were completely loyal to Canada in its entirety," he recalled. Bissonnette was very calm, very balanced, but Roquet's reaction was "more difficult to judge."[3] Of course, he later left for Quebec's service; he was a very able man, one of Marcel Cadieux's most trusted lieutenants. **Gérard Pelletier** was very cool and balanced throughout. Trudeau and Jean Marchand were fascinated by the question of who had written the FLQ Manifesto, with all its insulting references. Was it a genuine product of a working-class hand, or had it been written by somebody pretending to a working-class approach? Trudeau never let its tone bother him; he was intrigued by the detective work of discovering its authorship.

It was a strange time. Now it is "so damn easy" to say there was no justification for what was done at that stage. After all, where would the conclusive evidence have been for Kerensky in Russia in September-October 1917? The police effort was scattered, and John Starnes had pneumonia.[4] Mitchell Sharp did a good job, and Trudeau trusted him to do it.

The United Kingdom was very supportive throughout. High Commissioner Sir Peter Hayman naturally dropped by to enquire about the fate of British trade commissioner James Cross, whom the FLQ had kidnapped, but in their public statements the British were supportive of the "no concessions to terrorists" line. Cross's wife and the UK staff association took a rather more anxious approach. With Cuba, we fortunately had a special relationship that could be used. When the FLQ terrorists were flown to Cuba, they were shunned rather than treated as heroes.

Though Trudeau was more appreciative of DEA, there were still cuts, nonetheless. "Trudeau gave me a little lecture not to be misled by his attitude," Ritchie said. He appreciated people in the department. That was why he believed they had to be used in important jobs of higher priority.

The Foreign Policy Review
Was the purpose of the review to do down Lester B. Pearson or to bring some rhyme or reason into our international activity? Pearson was angry about it, Ritchie recalled. In fact, some of the rhetoric he particularly objected to ("helpful fixers" and so on) was contributed by his son, **Geoffrey Pearson**, to Norman Robertson's ill-fated review.

....

3   Tremblay, Bissonnette, and Roquet were senior foreign service officers.
4   Starnes was then the civilian head of the RCMP's Security Service Directorate.

Ritchie knew that the Foreign Policy Review and the Special Task Force on Europe were on, but he never got excited about them. As to DEA and PCO official Hume Wright's Non-Group review, he had never pursued it. He knew Hume well and talked with him about the report. Ivan Head claimed credit for it, as he did with a lot of things if they could be useful to him.

Nobody now remembers the session with theorist Buckminster Fuller on the Foreign Policy Review; it was never written up. It took place in Kingston: the role of foreign policy in a modern society. It was stimulating though not concrete; it was reflected a bit in the idea of broadening our foreign relations.

At that time, Ritchie was unsure whether Trudeau was a friend or an enemy. To what extent was he putting the department in its place? Ritchie was now more inclined to give Trudeau the benefit of the doubt.

When Ritchie arrived in Ottawa, Marcel Cadieux and **Basil Robinson** had already worked out some proposals. One aspect of the cuts was Simon Reisman's attempt from the Treasury Board to show Trudeau what a good cost-cutter he was. It was pure cost-reduction. The impact of the cuts was out of all proportion to the economies achieved. They were "not painful to me," but they were to those axed. This achievement was followed by "the integration nonsense."

ICER, Pitfield, and Head

It was argued whether the Interdepartmental Committee on External Relations (ICER) was to co-ordinate policy or to harmonize administration. In the event it was the latter, **Michael Pitfield**, of course, wanted more. Pitfield's attitude to the department was not at all helpful. "I didn't forgive him for it," Ritchie said.

There were two factors. One was Pitfield's attitude, as above; the other was the struggle between Pitfield and Ivan Head. Ritchie didn't have enough knowledge about that part. There's still a fair bit of feeling on the subject ...

There was no consistent theme to Ivan's efforts. He was not specially preoccupied with the Third World. It is true that he had some hang-ups about DEA and let that influence his attitude on major questions, but the prime minister was no fool about that kind of thing. There was no major policy that Ivan misdirected.

Ivan would go and see Prime Minister John Gorton in Australia because he felt like taking a trip in that direction. He attended a prime ministerial funeral in New Zealand. But he did no major concerting of policy. On the

Commonwealth, he was used, but **Gordon Robertson** was used much more because of his connections with Burke Trend, the head of the British public service, or with the Nigerian cabinet secretary.

Ivan's main positive contribution was to adapt Aesop's fable of the elephant and the mouse for Trudeau to use in his 1969 speech in Washington.

The USSR, 1971
Trudeau's 1971 visit to Russia was good and useful, though in part because it produced something that we didn't want: the Protocol on Consultations. But we knew that it might be raised, and that it might be difficult to escape, so we had **John Halstead** prepare a draft similar to, but superior to, the one the French had already signed. "I used that for my consultations at the time of the 1972 hockey series," Ritchie said, and it should also have been used when the Soviets invaded Afghanistan in 1979.

"The visit was an education for all of us," Ritchie recalled. The discussion with Brezhnev and Kosygin was pretty set-piece, but Brezhnev was impressive. President Lyndon Johnson could have handled Brezhnev in his best days. Kosygin was easier, more rational, but Brezhnev was a pretty balanced sort. Trudeau didn't give away any of NATO's main debating position in the discussion.

ALLAN GOTLIEB (1928-)
INTERVIEWS | WASHINGTON, DC, 15 JANUARY 1988 AND
14 NOVEMBER 1988

> *Gotlieb joined DEA in 1957 and served in the Legal Division. He was assistant USSEA in 1967-68 and then deputy minister of communications and deputy minister of manpower and immigration. He became USSEA in 1977 and was ambassador to the United States from 1981 to 1989.*

INTERVIEW | 15 JANUARY 1988

Trudeau and Quebec's powers
Gotlieb knew **Trudeau** fairly well back in the 1960s. They were introduced over before-dinner drinks at the Rideau Club by **Pitfield** at the end of 1965. Trudeau was functioning in the political-constitutional field and later acted as the informal political director in the fight to stymie Quebec's international

pretensions. Gotlieb could be of use to him. In 1967-68, the two interacted on two levels in two committees. He wrote a foreign policy paper for Trudeau. One level became more formal, and "on the conceptual level it was all mine." Gotlieb was motivated by the belief that internationalism for its own sake had gone too far, and, as interpreted by **Paul Martin**, was a burden on national unity ...

In 1967, Trudeau as justice minister offered to create a second and equal deputy minister of justice for public policy and constitutional questions, and he offered the position to Gotlieb. Though Gotlieb believed in Trudeau and thought he would eventually be prime minister, he declined. He discussed the offer with Marcel Cadieux, his mentor, who had promoted him far and fast, and Cadieux persuaded him that his interests really lay in staying in DEA.

Cadieux was "a tank," who ran his department in "a wilful and personal way." Gotlieb and Cadieux were in basic agreement that it was necessary to stand up to Quebec in connection with the Constitution. Very few agreed with them in Ottawa in 1965 ... Cadieux prepared for the coming storm. "He did a number of things: he made me head of Legal Division in 1965, made me head of federal-provincial matters," and directed that all documents and papers with a federal-provincial aspect be routed through Gotlieb.

Cadieux also realized that if one denied the legitimacy of Quebec's demands, one was into projecting a bilingual and bicultural foreign policy. Having inherited a totally anglicized department, he set out to create francophone enclaves. Many of the French Canadians who were already in the department hadn't worked in Ottawa for years, and many were totally incompetent; Cadieux was harder on them than he would have been on equally incompetent anglophones. Anyway, he opened missions in French-speaking Africa, and he pushed an aid program to francophone Africa, and he created divisions in Ottawa to back them up.

Federalism and international conferences was an interesting issue. DEA was to some degree forthcoming. It allowed that some provincial delegates be chosen to attend as part of a Canadian delegation, such as for UNESCO. The whole process was working with lightning speed.

All this was resented by the old guard, the **Basil Robinsons**, the **Ed Ritchies**. They felt it was not serious, that things would work out as they always had. Besides, all this stuff was "chickenshit": foreign policy was NATO and the like. These people knew nothing at all about economic or cultural issues. It was Cadieux who created the cultural affairs program so that we had an instrument comparable to what the Quai d'Orsay wielded – or Quebec. Still, Gotlieb remembered Douglas LePan saying to him, "Culture is not a word that a gentleman uses in foreign policy."[5] But when Trudeau came in, he understood the importance of all of this.

In fact, the war over culture involved Trudeau very early on. An invitation arrived for Trudeau, as minister of justice, from L'Institut International de droit d'expression et d'inspiration françaises, the aggregation of French-speaking lawyers. It had been sent by mistake since it had really been intended for Quebec, but Trudeau insisted on going anyway. It was Ottawa that represented French Canada, Trudeau said. Later, he would look for causes and grabbed Gabon, but for the moment one should bear in mind that he was behaving differently from the Pearsonian norm ...

Trudeau's arrival in Ottawa should have pleased Cadieux, but it didn't. Cadieux was a man of the people; Trudeau was a playboy. Cadieux couldn't believe that Trudeau was serious. As important, Trudeau's presence undermined Cadieux's own pre-eminence as the principal French Canadian in the federal capital. Emotionally, Cadieux didn't trust Trudeau ...

Anyway, Gotlieb continued, when Trudeau was justice minister there were two committees, an informal one and a more formal one, where **Pitfield** was the master hand. Thanks to a letter from Pearson, Martin formally seconded Gotlieb to it. It was chaired by **Gordon Robertson** and had as members Pitfield, **Head**, Beetz,[6] **Lalonde**, and Carl Goldenberg; its mandate was to develop positions for Trudeau and Justice. From it emerged the two foreign policy documents: one written by Gotlieb, the other by Gotlieb and **Max Yalden** together. By way of this committee, a lot of foreign policy content went to Trudeau.

The other informal committee met in Trudeau's office once a week. "There very often we discussed federal-provincial matters," Gotlieb said. Yet apart from the constitutional aspect, it was entirely personal to Trudeau.

Gotlieb did not favour Canadian foreign policy as it was expressed by the "extremes" of Paul Martin. Martin's idea was like "the Danes are good at furniture; the Dutch at cheese; the Canadians at foreign policy." Gotlieb prepared a paper for Trudeau at the beginning of 1968, and many of its themes found

....

5   A poet and novelist, LePan was a senior Canadian diplomat, renowned for his skill in drafting.
6   Jean Beetz had been a colleague of Trudeau's in the law faculty of the Université de Montréal. Trudeau appointed him a justice of the Supreme Court in 1974.

their way into Trudeau's speeches and later into the Foreign Policy Review. The theme of the paper was that foreign policy should be based on national interest. It went to Trudeau in January 1968, and it dealt with all the critical issues, such as China and NATO. It was a rationalization of foreign policy through the prisms of national interest, through economics, and it looked away from "hollow multilateralism." History will show that it had its ramifications. Martin would not have been pleased had he known that Gotlieb was advising Trudeau, but Gotlieb himself saw nothing wrong with what he did.

During the campaign of 1968, Trudeau used to drop by the house for a chat. He was quick to pick up points, and very general themes of foreign policy emerged in the discussions. Ultimately, *Foreign Policy for Canadians*, drafted by Geoff Murray, derived from this process. It was the purest expression of what Trudeau said about foreign policy in 1968.

There were a number of differences between what "we" thought and all of the mainstream department opinion – that it was wrong to annoy the French. They, and especially the francophone diplomats, thought the approach to Paris was wrong. That was true of every francophone, except Cadieux and Paul Tremblay. The Jules Léger school just hated it. The department thought it "voodoo foreign policy." Even Norman Robertson thought it wrong to be upset with the French.

After Trudeau became prime minister, Pearson was "a dead duck" around Ottawa, and sometimes the language used was rather cruel and hard. Gotlieb found that there was substantial resentment in the department for what he himself had done and was doing. He was only forty and was holding down a position, assistant deputy minister, that was four grades above his personal rank. Pitfield, "my evil genius," said that Cadieux was destroying Gotlieb by not giving him the appropriate rank for his responsibilities. Gotlieb was used to vetoing papers by seniors, and Cadieux concluded that he had to be promoted to SX-1.[7]

In early 1968, Cadieux told Gotlieb that Basil Robinson was going and that he would make Gotlieb deputy USSEA. But two or three months later, he said he couldn't do it. Perhaps Gotlieb should go abroad, Cadieux suggested. How about the UN, which was coming vacant? That was fine, but a month later he told Gotlieb that he couldn't appoint him, because he was Jewish. "It was the only time I was ever disappointed in Marcel," Gotlieb said.

....

7   SX-1 through SX-4 are senior civil service ranks.

"By then, I had the choice of three deputy ministerships or the PMO." He chose one and went ...

On Ivan Head
After 1968, Gotlieb was off in a different sphere in the PMO, and Head moved into the gap. (Gotlieb did remain on Gordon Robertson's constitutional committee.) At the end of 1968, Gotlieb had a terrible falling out with Pitfield, to the point where they would barely speak to each other and only on business. The chill lasted five or six years, and it occurred because Pitfield had not, in Gotlieb's opinion, played fair on some issue.

Ivan Head was effective in his job. He was quick and decisive, though one of the most secretive people Gotlieb had ever met. Nobody in the PMO saw his memoranda. He established contacts with virtually every embassy in Ottawa. Except on the issue of Arctic waters, Head did not invite Gotlieb's participation.

Interestingly, Gotlieb thought that Head was much more in the traditional multilateral mode than he himself was, though people point to Trudeau's Mansion House speech in 1975 on Third World poverty as evidence of his conversion to that direction. One result was that the second Trudeau era, mid- and late 1970s, was *"tiers mondial."* "What I'd argued in 1968" on national interests was not that way. Connections to the Third World made sense only if they were in our interest. A sign was that Trudeau made his first appearance at the UN only in 1978, but thereafter he was interested.

Another change was consequent on Trudeau's anger at Menachem Begin's intervention in the 1979 election campaign.[8] He felt betrayed by the Jews that year and became more sympathetic to the Palestinian cause.

In Gotlieb's later years, Trudeau liked glamour and travel ... though he was not at home in the United States. He just didn't have the intellectual interest in how the United States worked.

Trudeau had a natural empathy – sympathy – for the Third World leaders, but at the end there was a lot of self-indulgence in his foreign policy. Perhaps some of it was in tune with the country, but a lot of it was actuated by his desire to be applauded on the world stage ...

---

8   Begin was the right-wing prime minister of Israel, 1977-82. He openly intervened in Canadian politics by supporting Joe Clark's pledge to move the Canadian embassy from Tel Aviv to Jerusalem.

As USSEA, 1977-81
Despite his bonhomie, Gotlieb said, SSEA Don Jamieson was very suspicious of civil servants, particularly DEA types. He didn't want Gotlieb as his USSEA, though he didn't object to Gotlieb's personal relations with Trudeau; his preference was for **Peter Towe**. Trudeau phoned Gotlieb and said, "We've got a problem, and the problem is Don Jamieson." Gotlieb, on the other hand, was encouraged when he learned that Ivan Head was leaving the PMO. Head's modus operandi would have irritated Gotlieb as USSEA.

Again, there had been a shift in Pitfield's feelings. The "Metternich of the Canadian public service" liked having balance, in this case balancing centres to assist the PCO. Pitfield had started off hating DEA, wanting to humble it (he had been turned down for a position there). A lot of his feelings weren't grounded in anything real, but a lot were right too. He was trying to give the power back to the politicians through all his cabinet restructuring. But if power had to go back, it was power away from the departments and from their ministers.

"By 1976, when he broached with me a return to the department, DEA was so low it had had no damn power for at least six or seven years," Gotlieb claimed. Of course, it had no power of the purse. Even on the administrative side, it couldn't recommend an ambassador by itself. Maurice Strong had created ICER-DC (Developing Countries) and had carved aid out of DEA; **Donald Macdonald** had demanded that Energy, Mines and Resources control all external energy policy. So, with DEA so low, Pitfield recommended a buildup.

Gotlieb established a deputy ministers' committee for foreign relations with developing countries; the deputy ministers of Energy and Finance were on it, and he himself was chairman. Michael got behind integration of the various foreign services (trade, immigration, and the existing DEA) and the abolition of the separate services. It was not a good thing to have a separate, but weak, foreign service.

The resentment he had detected at DEA a decade earlier had vanished by the time he returned: "I believe people were very happy." Articles began to appear in the newspaper that DEA was resuming its old authority. The FSOs wanted a deputy minister who was winning his (and their) battles, one who was relevant. Intellectually, there was rebellion from some people about the idea that DEA should be a central agency.

But Gotlieb got it recognized that an ambassador abroad represented all ministers and departments. At the same time, the ambassador had the right and duty to communicate with heads of departments at home. That followed if you abolish the separate foreign services.

The agitation got to the point of meetings at homes. **Geoffrey Pearson** represented the idea that this was an insidious notion, undermining the elitist foreign service. Nevertheless, in Gotlieb's view, if you're to represent the country, you must represent the country as a whole.

There was a debate as to whether the foreign service's job was to "represent Canadian interests" or to "promote peace." "Some thought I was distorting what the department was about," Gotlieb recalled. Pitfield continued his support and pushed hard at the end of Gotlieb's days. The ultimate act was the integration of the foreign services. As a result, the architecture of the Canadian foreign service is conceptually sound: it's like the British version, not like that of Australia. A lot of blood was spilled en route to this state, but today DEA has a substantial ("good") influence ...

As USSEA after the Trudeau return
When the Liberals returned to power in 1980, matters did not improve. Gotlieb, who felt excluded and betrayed, described himself as "very, very deeply resentful" that he was "not in the picture."

Pitfield ran the National Energy Programme (NEP) through a cabinet meeting at Lake Louise, to which Gotlieb was not invited. "I knew something was going on, but not what," he said. The NEP was devised by Mickey Cohen, Ed Clark, Robert Rabinovitch,[9] Pitfield, Lalonde, and Trudeau. It was treated as a budgetary matter, and he himself was briefed, not consulted, only the night before, along with the other deputy ministers, by Cohen.

But it was a very important topic for foreign relations. Cohen insisted that Gotlieb had no right to complain, because **MacGuigan**, his minister, had been briefed. Since MacGuigan was a new minister, Gotlieb thought this was not a fair comment.

In any case, by the summer of 1980 he wanted to move on, possibly to Washington. He felt that he "should be a sherpa for the Ottawa summit." Pitfield reluctantly agreed, and Gotlieb spent a good deal of his last year in Ottawa doing preparatory work. He expected to leave in July 1981, but he left in December, after long arguments with Pitfield about his successor.

During this period, he still saw Trudeau, but they were inclined to argue rather than agree – all in an impersonal, intellectual manner. For example,

9   Cohen, Clark, and Rabinovitch were all senior public servants, not politicians.

in 1968 Gotlieb had thought less of NATO than he did today, approving the political, rather than military, French way. He thought the NEP extremely crude, and he thought that Trudeau had become anti-Israel. In 1976, by way of contrast, Trudeau had personally ordered the cancellation of the UN Toronto Crime conference because of the presence of the PLO. (Because it was a UN conference, Canada was bound to accept whomever the UN approved.) What moved Trudeau in 1976 was the terrorist analogy to the FLQ. But he developed a sense of betrayal, especially with Menachem Begin. At first, Trudeau rather admired Begin's blunt, plain-spoken manner, and he was intrigued as an intellectual by Begin's mental acuity. The issue of moving the Canadian embassy from Tel Aviv to Jerusalem had gotten to Trudeau's principal secretary, Jim Coutts, who pressed for action on it. (And it was not just Canada, and indeed Canada was not the principal target: Carter had had Jerusalem as Israel's capital in the Democratic platform in 1976, and American action was truly desirable.) It was around then, 1978, that Trudeau warned Begin to keep out of Canada's election.

The Trudeau position was congruent with that of the older heads of the Canadian Jewish Congress, who thought moving the embassy dangerous, reckless; only a small minority thought it double-cross, and he proved to be very vengeful but not anti-Semitic at all. Still, after the 1980 election, Gotlieb got complaints that Trudeau refused to see Jewish representatives, and he knew that Trudeau was unwilling to co-operate with the Sinai peacekeeping force, which was a major part of the Sadat-Begin peace agreement. To Gotlieb, obliging the United States and Israel made absolute sense, but Trudeau was unmoved; he finally said via Pitfield that he would join the force if the PLO got recognition, and that ended the matter.

By 1981, Gotlieb said, "I felt that Trudeau was too absorbed in North-South" issues. By then, he had become "the Prince," and he allowed "his tastes, his impulses" to dominate. It was still true that those around him could bring out a latent side of his nature, but most of the time he had become a man of impulse, a complete contrast to the rational being of 1968.

INTERVIEW | 14 NOVEMBER 1988

On Basil Robinson
Basil Robinson didn't have a breakdown exactly; it was better described as a burnout. He didn't enjoy the social life, didn't like the pressure. He even sent a memo to the diplomatic corps, saying he was dropping out of the

hospitality circuit, giving his teeth as a reason. From 1976 on, it was known that Basil wanted out. But he wasn't seen as disabled, and he was considered for Washington, but he didn't want the socializing. (Another possibility for Washington was Ivan Head, but he'd broken up with his wife, and it was impossible to have him there with his mistress. **Gordon Robertson** also refused the post.)

Jake Warren's departure from Washington was due to several factors, Gotlieb continued.[10] First, he was annoyed at losing the post in London, booted out halfway to make room for Paul Martin. Once "mini-Kissinger" Ivan Head and his conduct over Trudeau's visit to Washington were added to the mix, that must have been the final straw. When Marcel Cadieux was ambassador in Washington, he used to complain that Head intervened on his dinner menus.

Basil got the job of Northern Pipeline commissioner, and it was not, as it later became, a nothing job. He was seen as competent, intellectually alright. He was to preside over a vast megaproject, and the position relied on his northern expertise.

Becoming USSEA

When Gotlieb agreed to become USSEA in 1977, it was assumed that Ivan Head would be gone. He liked Ivan but didn't want to work for him. Head had started to look around, and he let it be known that he wanted the International Development Research Centre. So Gotlieb in effect replaced Head. Trudeau always preferred to travel with an official rather than a minister. Gotlieb said he got a personal call from Trudeau while on vacation in Venice. Michael Pitfield had decided that DEA had to be reconstructed. He'd made it marginal and destroyed its morale. The tradition of running the state had disappeared. Some officers liked it that way – less strenuous, Gotlieb claimed. He organized a committee of deputy ministers, over which he presided, including the heavyweights in Finance and Energy. He reconstituted ICER-DC (the DC dealt with developing countries).

Pitfield never – well, hardly ever – interfered. He didn't want to take calls from foreign capitals. Only once, in July 1981, did he pull a fast one, getting Gotlieb and company to give a press conference at exactly the same time that he and Tom Axworthy met with President Reagan's White House team ...

....

10 Warren (1921-2008) served in DEA, as deputy minister in Trade and Commerce, high commissioner in London, ambassador in Washington, and as a trade negotiator.

WILLIAM BARTON (1917-2013)
INTERVIEW | OTTAWA, 22 APRIL 1988

Barton joined DEA in 1952 and served in Vienna, Geneva, and at the United Nations, where he was ambassador and permanent representative from 1976 to 1979.

Barton began with Canada and the United Nations
The turning point in Canada's relations with the UN went back to 1967, when Canadian peacekeeping troops were thrown out of the Sinai by Egypt's president Nasser. In his view, SSEA **Paul Martin**'s scenario was unreal: the logic that governed the UN was different from Martin's. Perhaps if Ralph Bunche had been in better health and had tackled the issue, it would have made a difference. "I guess in a way it affected our thinking," Barton said. "We'd had an unreal assessment of what peacekeeping could do; it only worked in specialized circumstances," such as Cyprus or in the Sinai in 1973.

"We were right in thinking that peacekeeping in Lebanon in 1978 was a turkey," he went on. That was because of the kind of contribution the UN wanted: communications specialists. Our supply of these was too limited, particularly in signals. We could rotate infantry easily enough, but specialist troops would be spending every other assignment in the Middle East. We went into Lebanon only for six months after UN secretary-general Kurt Waldheim twisted Trudeau's arm.

"The more I look at the problems of the UN," he said, "the more it reflects the problems of the world. The members can vote through great budgets they don't have to pay for. The current budgetary crisis might have been salutary in rescuing the secretariat from elephantiasis." But it hadn't. Third World critics had reacted against Western economic imperialism, and in many cases the irresponsibility of delegations to the UN headquarters in New York didn't even reflect policy at home. One Third World ambassador in New York said to him that he was told it was the UN or jail. Barton's sense of communication with his head office was not strong.

The other great source of damage to the UN was the "Zionism is racism" resolution.[11] This did harm for the UN among American Jews; it did harm

---

11   This refers to a 1975 UN resolution in which Zionism was declared a form of racism. The resolution was repealed in 1991.

here in Canada too, but our weight in New York wasn't as important. There was, too, the Vietnam War, which led some Americans to declare, "The hell with the UN, we'll just proceed without it." During Jimmy Carter's time in office, Andy Young and Cy Vance tried to repair the damage, but when Reagan came in, with Jeanne Kirkpatrick as US ambassador, it was difficult again ...

Barton had put **Trudeau** on the UN delegation back in 1966. He sat for us on the Special Political Committee, which was dealing with the South African issue among others. Trudeau became convinced that the policies we were pursuing were not responsive to the needs of the Africans and that officials, not politicians, ran the policy. Barton himself came back from that session "convinced that we needed a major policy review" in DEA of our South African policy.

This took place despite the resistance of the Trade people. We looked at every option, from co-operation with the African National Congress to co-operation with the Republic of South Africa, and we ended where we started, except that we told the Crown corporation Polysar to drop its South African subsidiary.

DEA and Trudeau

In 1968, Trudeau was elected prime minister and we became much more concerned with the larger problems that he posed. These were his skepticism about the utility of diplomacy and the function of the department. As an assistant USSEA, Barton had to deal with some of the cuts of the period. Though **Ed Ritchie** was an effective USSEA, he and Barton were both bothered by the fact that "we were busting our asses to run a good operation and we were completely unable to penetrate the prime minister's consciousness."

When the Treasury Board issued the instructions to make cuts, we did as we were told "and were blamed for it." In this case and others, you could say that administration was not DEA's strong suit. He could see this from his perch with the rest of DEA's senior officers on Killers' Row.

As for the UN, Barton and **Ivan Head** would plot every year to get Trudeau to go down to New York, and every year Trudeau would refuse. He used to say to Head, "Have I got a message worth saying? What purpose would I serve?" **Sharp** would come down, of course, and make the traditional Canadian appeal for more efficiency in the organization. Barton remembered telling the Norwegians at the time that the best contribution they could make was to give every Canadian foreign minister the Nobel Peace Prize at the outset of his term of office.

Between 1968 and 1970, Mitchell Sharp was a typical minister. He was very efficient and very effective, and as for the UN, "I have to plead responsibility for his remark that the UN was drowning in a sea of paper." His effort to help DEA get over its slough of despond in 1969-70 was useful, as was his outreach program to the universities, the establishment of those university visitors.

Barton never had any problems with Ivan Head, who was very supportive of Barton's issues, though of course they disagreed about NATO. He could get through to the prime minister, no doubt about it, except on the UN.

Ed Ritchie was "creative, imaginative, bubbling with energy," though he wasn't strong on the bureaucratic side. He was not the last of the generalists: look at **Basil Robinson** and **Si Taylor** ...

The Pitfield effect
Michael Pitfield did more harm to the Canadian public service than any other single individual in the last hundred years, Barton maintained. His impact on the service was tremendous. When Pitfield served on the Canadian delegation to the UN, he played the same airy-fairy conceptual game. He wanted to link the economic with the political. "I wouldn't argue that economics is not important," Barton said, "but the world subordinates the economic to the political." Look at the stupid things our own Parliament does from time to time ...

On the UN Security Council
Barton went to New York as ambassador to the UN in the summer of 1976, with the expectation that Canada would become a non-permanent member of the Security Council in January 1977, which it did, uncontested. There can be no doubt that going on the Security Council improved your standing around the UN. "I thought our main problems would be in the Middle East, but it was not really so," he recalled. Even Lebanon in 1978 didn't raise any real problems for us. The main issues were South Africa and Namibia.[12] On that, we formed the Western consultative group, which they initially called the Gang of Five, though the Chinese suggested that really it should be "the Gang of Four plus One." It tended to meet at the handily located Canadian

------

12 This refers to the Israeli invasion of Lebanon in 1978, the continuing issue of South African apartheid, and the Namibian war for independence from South Africa.

mission, with its useful facilities, such as a good conference room. The Namibian negotiations produced all kinds of peculiar nuances. For one thing, the General Assembly view was that the situation didn't exist; that was all described in a General Assembly resolution. But it existed all the same.

In these discussions, the US ambassador Andy Young was very concerned about his position and the American position in general. He laid down a two-track strategy. We knew that the developing countries were putting together an initiative on South Africa, which the big boys would have to veto. Andy decided to seek maximum agreement between us and them; in return we would use our economic influence to seek a solution in Namibia. Andy got the British, French, and Germans to pledge that if the South Africans didn't co-operate, we'd come down on them hard.

So we started two-prong negotiations. In connection with South Africa, we negotiated all spring and summer, but by fall it had become evident that South Africa's bottom line on apartheid was still above our top line. This led to a confrontation in the Security Council that was perhaps nastier than it would otherwise have been.

On Namibia, we worked out a plan that SSEA Don Jamieson, incidentally a good advocate, supported. The context was that he was looking forward to presiding over the Security Council. Unfortunately for his dream, the Queen was visiting Newfoundland on the great day, and he had to be there. So Barton presided instead ...

ALAN BEESLEY (1927-2009)
INTERVIEW | VANCOUVER, 7 MARCH 1988

Beesley joined DEA in 1956 and served as legal adviser, as ambassador to Austria, for disarmament, and to the UN in Geneva. He was also high commissioner in Canberra.

Law of the Sea
In international law, Beesley said, we tried to meet objectives of direct and indirect interest to Canada, and the Law of the Sea (LOS) was an example. We proceeded in a very methodical way. We brought together representatives of all interests, including industry, got our fish experts researching, and hounded geographers. As a result of all this consultation, we eventually settled

on a two-hundred-mile limit. Of course, we had to balance our national objectives with what the traffic would bear, but we arrived at the concept of our economic zone and the seabed beneath. In conference, our tactic was to seek out allies who hadn't done their homework, who needed help. We could offer it, sometimes on issues that didn't concern us, and we would give it straightforwardly; but we anticipated a pay-off, even if it took years. In the case of India, we worked on them for years, and eventually they rallied to our position. Apart from the law of outer space, the negotiation was the first attempt to define a common regime for areas beyond our – or indeed any – jurisdiction.

Our policy making began in an interdepartmental committee, which Beesley took over from Marcel Cadieux. The committee was central to our methodology; we got officials sensitized to domestic political realities, as seen by the government. It was a good way to get instructions. Apparently, a similar system was used in the free trade negotiations with the United States. Beesley also got ministers knowledgeable about the LOS and ended up taking pride in their mastery of this or that detail. It was also at work in the Uruguay trade round.

In negotiation, he found it was not desirable to take a black-and-white, hard-and-fast role. We would work with anybody who was willing to share our interests. The trade policy committee in Ottawa couldn't see why we were messing around with all these little Third World countries in Uruguay, as in UN negotiations, but it was mutual help. Beesley once explained this to a disbelieving Professor Peyton Lyon,[13] who did not think that we could possibly get much use from our efforts; but as it turned out, it was so, and Lyon's research in New York confirmed it circa 1982. It built up solidarity and established links of personal trust. Don't forget that from these countries many of the same people turn up at Geneva, in connection with the General Agreement on Tariffs and Trade, and elsewhere. They can and do play the same game they play elsewhere. Incidentally, at the UN or in such negotiations, the positions of the Trudeau and Mulroney governments were virtually identical. (The Uruguay position was really all worked out beforehand in Geneva.) We worked with apparent rivals, with the European Free Trade Association, and found more support among developing countries.

....

13 A political science professor at Carleton University, Lyon was a former foreign service officer.

In legal negotiations, such as the LOS, we found it useful to develop and document a claim before asserting it formally. A civil servant can use every means at his disposal in projecting the Canadian position. Beesley recounted how he managed to cook a TV documentary, getting the producer to downplay the opposition and to talk up the Canadian view, even to the extent of having an announcer read the US position that the Arctic waters were like those elsewhere, while on the screen an icebreaker struggled unsuccessfully to crush its way through the ice pack. A picture was worth a thousand words.

In negotiations, the bureaucrats have to work with ministers; eventually, only ministers can go beyond their own brief. For their part, ministers must work with the pre-existing civil service. The Trudeau people were said to be nationalists, but in the LOS talks they were not that way so much ...

Arctic sovereignty
On Arctic sovereignty, Legal Division advocated some bold policies, Beesley stated. In 1968, international law got a relatively good hearing from the Trudeau people, despite all their musings about practicality. For one thing, **Ivan Head** was an international lawyer, and **Mitchell Sharp** took pride in becoming an expert on such occasions. Indeed, of all the ministers whom Beesley served, only Don Jamieson was unsympathetic. Jamieson believed that lawyers made things wasteful and unproductive, that they complicated matters, rather than smoothing the path to agreement. "Don had a kind of anti-legal, anti-intellectual bias," Beesley remarked. Jamieson claimed that he could straighten out the Gulf of Maine dispute with Henry Kissinger in twenty minutes. He did, and it took us years to get out from under his "solution." When Geoffrey Stevens said as much in his *Globe and Mail* column, Jamieson was furious, especially at its call to unleash Beesley. Jamieson was accused of screwing up, which he had; take note that he never dared bring his Gulf of Maine solution before a cabinet committee. Jamieson also got an agreement over St. Pierre and Miquelon thrown out.

Paul Martin probably thought of himself as a man with credentials in international law, Beesley said. Though this caused difficulty in the Arctic sovereignty case, it was a good thing in general. Except for Jamieson, Martin and the other SSEAs were problem solvers.

Canada refused to accept International Court of Justice jurisdiction on some quite specific aspects. The reservation applied to the Arctic and the fisheries. We had good reasons, for we might well not have succeeded in the court. Yet at the same time, we established a twelve-mile territorial limit without the reservation. Interestingly, the Americans had yet to take us to court on that.

On Arctic waters, there was the usual memo to the cabinet. Beesley handled the presentation to the cabinet committee, to ministers who had had the chance to be thoroughly briefed by their officials. The trouble was more from the officials than the ministers. Gotlieb, then at Communications, nailed Sharp on the street and got him exercised about the possibility that the United States would object to the twelve-mile limit. Legal scholar Max Cohen claimed that we had reversed our position on the twelve-mile limit and got upset about it, but unfortunately for him that was something we hadn't done. **Gordon Robertson** eventually had to intervene and tell the officials to stop fighting. A committee of officials, Robertson, **Gotlieb**, Head, and **Pitfield**, became concerned with the issue. Some Canadian officials thought that the claim to environmental jurisdiction would avert American objections, but Beesley never believed that. The Americans would see it as just another Canadian assertion of sovereignty, and they did.

Trudeau was onside regarding the environmental issue. It was, however, one of the two occasions on which Beesley threatened to resign. He needed a resolution to the environmental question.

There was actually a revolt in caucus, as well as a change in the government policy. During all this, Beesley had to hold midnight briefing sessions for MPs. For some, it was just fish and fishermen; for BC MPs Paul St. Pierre and David Anderson,[14] it was a real matter of interest and concern. The Department of Transport saw itself as defender of the freedom of the high seas. There were other critics in Justice and some in Trade. The political diplomats were also worried because of pressure from our Western European allies.

LOS again

Later, on LOS, Finance Minister **Donald Macdonald** was very influential. He would make no concession on sovereignty, but he was amenable to revenue sharing with other states, a concession that greatly bothered his officials when they learned of it.

---

14 St. Pierre and Anderson were both BC Liberals. Anderson was a former foreign service officer, former leader of the BC Liberal Party, and a future federal minister.

On LOS, Beesley would match our experts against anyone's. We had provincial experts, industry representatives, and politicians from all parties. His people were working hard on their opposite numbers, and Leonard Legault, Paul Lapointe, and Jane Gaskell in DEA were outstanding. We were not just expert; we could sit down with anybody and negotiate. And no, there was no rivalry with Energy, Mines and Resources on such issues.

JOHN HALSTEAD (1922-98)
INTERVIEW | GRAINAU AND AUGSBURG, GERMANY, 20 AND 23 FEBRUARY 1988

Halstead joined DEA in 1946 after wartime service in the Royal Canadian Navy. He had posts in London, Tokyo, at the UN, Paris, Germany, and NATO. He served in Ottawa in a variety of positions, including director of European division, assistant under secretary, and deputy USSEA.

Trudeau, youth, and NATO
Halstead noted that **Trudeau** had called him on the phone when he was thinking of running for the Liberal leadership. He doubted that **Allan Gotlieb** had put him up to this. Halstead had met Trudeau when he came to Paris, and he was in the embassy. The talk was general, not just foreign policy, and what struck Halstead was Trudeau's desire for things that would appeal to youth, to the trendies. Halstead had said the flag dispute had been generational, and Trudeau turned that instantly into an appeal to youth. Halstead thought this typical of him.

Halstead said that if NATO were extracted from the Defence Review, Trudeau was quite prepared to accept his thesis that Canada should strengthen relations with Europe. Trudeau didn't see this as a paradox. In fact, he used Halstead's phrases from his 1967 paper on relations with Europe in his April 1968 statement on foreign policy. In essence, Trudeau thought he could de-emphasize the military side and keep other links with Europe. To Halstead, the intention of the review wasn't to downgrade Europe; after all, *Foreign Policy for Canadians* advised that the ties should be strengthened. In other words, before Trudeau, the policy was NATO, not Europe; after Trudeau, it was Europe, not NATO ...

Although Trudeau was well travelled and well informed, he was naive and not knowledgeable about foreign policy; he was totally ignorant about diplomacy. His line about diplomats in 1968 wasn't a joke but was the way he acted to DEA ...

Trudeau, Helmut Schmidt, and tanks
The Trudeau-Schmidt "no tanks, no trade" story wasn't true.[15] Halstead was at the first meeting of the two in 1975, where Helmut Schmidt said he was a social democrat and no militarist, but Germany had a serious problem with the USSR. Trudeau just sat and got a primer on European security. To Schmidt, security was necessary, and he wanted Canada to contribute, as in the past. He wanted more than one North American partner. He left Trudeau to draw his own conclusions. Schmidt and Trudeau became friends, but Halstead thought there was little policy implication there, because Trudeau never followed up on foreign policy. He liked exchanging ideas but only for dabbling. He made no connection between ideas and action. When Trudeau went to Bonn for the 1978 G7 summit and was about to go sailing with Schmidt, Halstead jotted down a number of points for him to make to Schmidt on bilateral questions and stuck the paper in Trudeau's hand. When Trudeau returned, he said, "I've carried out your instructions," sounding like an errant schoolboy ...

The Conference on Security and Cooperation in Europe
The 1973 Conference on Security and Cooperation in Europe (CSCE) took place in Helsinki. On its critics, Halstead said that Carleton professor Peyton Lyon had directed a graduate thesis on the subject, and it was all wrong. The conference did not take a hard line toward the Soviets, and Canada used it to get what could be got, an effort that succeeded. Halstead handled the pre-Helsinki stuff from DEA. He had **Sharp**'s okay (he was a good SSEA, who understood how the civil service worked). Trudeau had little understanding or interest until the end when the issue blew up in the United States, and he wanted to be sure before Helsinki that ethnics wouldn't attack him for selling out to the USSR. Halstead wasn't sure why there were no kudos in public for the Canadian role, perhaps because the Canadian press didn't notice things until the US media played them up. He added that Canadian Balts had called

---

15 "No tanks no trade" was a common summary of Schmidt's message to Trudeau, which Halstead was disputing.

on him before the CSCE negotiations. He had listened but did nothing for them; in this Sharp backed him fully ...

Trudeau and the Contractual Link

Trudeau's Mansion House speech of 1975 was delivered during his trip to sell the Contractual Link. The speech was written by **Ivan Head** (who didn't understand Europe), and his draft dealt only with the Third World. Halstead did a rewrite in Rome, dictating for three hours, and put it directly into Trudeau's hands. The prime minister never gave a straight response to Halstead, except to say that it was a good speech for another occasion. Nonetheless, it served its purpose, and Europe was written into it, with material from Halstead's text. Halstead also pointed out that Trudeau's public criticism of the Canadian Contractual Link proposals in Brussels was typical of him and a reflection on Trudeau himself for not looking over the proposals before leaving for Europe to sell the link. He should have criticized himself. Trudeau's remark – to **Paul Martin** on 14 March 1975 – about his initial hesitancy over the link was correct. Halstead also noted that when SSEA Jamieson spoke on the link to the Canadian ambassadors in Brussels in December 1976, his tone was critical. Halstead called him on it, and the minutes notwithstanding, their exchange was very sharp. None of the ambassadors came to Halstead's aid, but afterward several said "good for you."

Geoffrey Pearson as ambassador in the USSR was in a difficult spot, with **Robert Ford** acting as special representative on East-West relations. If Halstead had been there, he would have insisted that the hard-liner Ford be dumped, as this was just impossible for any ambassador.

Trudeau and foreign policy

At a NATO Heads of Government meeting in 1982, Halstead tried three times to speak during the discussion, but Trudeau refused him, the last time angrily. During a later press conference, Trudeau denounced NATO as boring and organizationally stultifying. Then he said to Halstead that he hoped he hadn't minded this. Halstead (with four months to go before retiring) said he didn't mind, but if Trudeau wanted to change NATO he should have responded to the telegrams he'd been sending him during the previous six months. That comment left Trudeau nonplussed.

To Halstead, all of this was typical Trudeau. He was never well briefed, didn't read papers, and wanted a thirty-minute briefing on complex subjects. He relied on his quickness to cope – and usually that was enough.

Pitfield's influence

Halstead discussed **Michael Pitfield** and his byzantine ways. He would offer Halstead advice on how to phrase cabinet memos, dissecting them and pointing out how best to deal with Trudeau. He was bright but essentially an evil influence, especially on DEA, where his administrative changes had a disastrous effect. He created a system in which DEA and the Department of Industry, Trade and Commerce were joined together, but each reported separately to the USSEA. And Pitfield's PCO, with its division into planning and operations, had dreadful planning.

At the end of his interview, Halstead made a brilliant observation on the conflicting desires of Canadians: they want a multilateral foreign policy, a bilateral economic policy, and a nationalist defence policy.

GORDON SMITH (1941-)
INTERVIEW | BRUSSELS, 8 OCTOBER 1987

Smith joined the Department of National Defence after completing his PhD, served in NATO, and was the principal drafter of the 1971 Defence White Paper. He went to the PCO, became deputy under secretary in External Affairs, and was then deputy minister. He was the permanent representative to NATO and ambassador to the European Union.

DEA and Pitfield

Smith didn't disagree with the judgment that DEA was losing its intellectual force and ability through the 1970s. It had been demoralized by **Trudeau's** statements and was in a collective depression by 1969-71. It had able people, but it was a strange institution, as it was not one organization managed from the top like other departments. Its administration and policy formation were bottom-up. The PCO and **Michael Pitfield** shared this view of DEA. Pitfield saw it as elitist, though he was an elitist himself.

When Smith went to the PCO, **Gordon Robertson** was cabinet secretary, and Pitfield was the associate secretary. Robertson was a consummate civil servant, quiet, clear on the roles, no public profile but not detached. He cared about the outcome of things. Pitfield had a personal connection with Trudeau, but he didn't use it or flaunt it. In the 1968-72 period, he related to Trudeau's desire that the approach to policy making should be more rational. To 1970,

Smith said, no one had full-time responsibility for the machinery of government, for keeping an overview on government organization: the paper flow, structure, relations, need for, and responsibilities of departments. With Treasury Board assistance, Pitfield installed a small unit in the PCO to do this, and that was where Smith worked. Trudeau wanted rationality, and management was Pitfield's, but Trudeau certainly marked up Smith's memos. Pitfield also improved priority setting and planning work. He wanted to force the cabinet to agree on the most important priorities, as this affected budgets and legislation. (Joe Clark, Smith said, liked all this; John Turner and Brian Mulroney didn't.) Pitfield believed that ministers were the ones to make decisions, and it was unfair to say that he wanted to centralize power in the PCO under him. That was not his object, even if it did occur. He saw the PCO as the prime minister's department, yes, but also as working for all ministers. He was shocked when Joe Clark fired him. He wasn't a Liberal, and he and Trudeau had an intellectual relationship, not a friendship. He was oblivious to the way that people perceived him and his connection to Trudeau.

Senior Appointments Secretariat
Smith spent time at the Senior Appointments Secretariat, especially during the early 1980s.[16] Prior to 1968, this function was very haphazard. With Robertson's support, Pitfield brought about systematic performance evaluation by ministers, the Treasury Board, and peers. Future planning was hard to do, but from the early 1970s a system was in place that put names by slots. This at least forced thinking about who should be the next deputy minister of finance, for example. He cited **Basil Robinson** as USSEA. The PCO feeling was that it was necessary to have a USSEA who had spent time in other departments to help integrate DEA into the civil service. **Gotlieb, Osbaldeston,** and Smith repeated the pattern. Taking people from DEA and putting them into other departments was also deliberate, as this gave international expertise to domestic departments. DEA had too many good people who had too little to do. It was the best recruiter of civilians, the department with the clearest career path. The rest of the bureaucracy was entrepreneurial, with people selling themselves.

16 By the early 1970s, there was a Senior Appointments Secretariat inside the PCO.

Trudeau

Smith liked the Richard Gwyn and George Radwanski biographies of Trudeau.[17] Trudeau was very demanding to work for. If he was sent a paper that had errors of spelling or math, he lost confidence in the whole paper. He listened. He might state a view, but he wanted arguments on the other side. He respected people who did argue, as he didn't like sycophants. Although he wasn't interested in machinery questions, he wanted logical, rational solutions from others. He had a clear idea of what he wanted to do, especially in 1980, and he set clear priorities. He was aloof personally, he didn't like people touching him, and ministers tried to avoid sitting next to him at the cabinet. He didn't have friends – Pitfield was an intellectual soulmate who debated with him, not a friend. Trudeau was very bad at small talk; he just couldn't be bothered. He had a Laser sailboat and he liked skiing, but he probably talked for only thirty minutes total on these subjects. He would listen to specific discussions but had no chit-chat. He was a good person to work for if you could relate to him in the world of ideas.

He had an enormous interest in what was happening in the world, and he liked travel, meeting people, and cultural experiences. He believed that Canada had a role in improving prospects for peace – a throwback to Pearson. DEA, however, felt that he carried the Peace Initiative too far and beyond credibility. Trudeau had a healthy skepticism of the United States and its behaviour, especially under President Ronald Reagan. Smith didn't know if Trudeau ever believed in neutrality as an option, but by the late 1970s, he had become quite comfortable in the NATO framework – expenditures on defence increased by 3 percent a year. Did Trudeau change? His pre-1968 knowledge of the world was a traveller's knowledge. He didn't really see international politics in the same terms as domestic ones, and he was alienated by his first experiences in the cabinet, which were negative. In 1968, he was a man highly developed in other areas but only informed in foreign policy. He saw concepts, relationships, and frameworks, and hadn't adopted anyone else's views. By the time of the 1971 Defence White Paper, much had happened. From then, Smith said, there was a steady onward progression. Trudeau wasn't a hawk at the end, but he understood the system. He was still naive but less so. His policy wasn't sporadic; it didn't turn on and off; it was just that there were

---

17 Richard Gwyn, *Northern Magus: Trudeau and Canada* (Toronto: McClelland and Stewart, 1980); George Radwanski, *Trudeau* (Toronto: Macmillan, 1978).

times when he was actively involved and times when he was not. Smith thought that Trudeau wanted to shake up DND and DEA more than he wanted to change policy, as this was something he was getting from Pitfield. Pitfield didn't like those departments, which he perceived as stuck and bereft of ideas; he saw DEA as airy.

HON. GORDON OSBALDESTON (1930-)
INTERVIEW | TORONTO, 15 APRIL 1988

Osbaldeston joined the Trade Commissioner Service in 1953 and served abroad and in senior positions in Ottawa, including secretary to the treasury board. He was Industry, Trade and Commerce deputy minister from 1976 to 1978, USSEA in 1982, and clerk of the privy council from 1982 to 1985.

Reorganizing DEA
Osbaldeston spoke of the DEA reorganization of 1982. The reality of the situation was that DEA had become irrelevant. The real issues were economic and trade for Canada, and since the time of **Ed Ritchie**, DEA had had little expertise and less clout in trade policy and promotion. Marcel Cadieux, **Basil Robinson**, and the early **Allan Gotlieb** were not heavyweights in these areas. The Departments of Finance and Industry, Trade and Commerce (ITC) dominated, and all DEA did was provide the glassware. Even Gotlieb had had to work hard to sell the idea of DEA as a central agency; he had to force his way to the table as a central agency. That was the right concept, as it at least gave DEA a co-ordinating role over all domestic departments. But in a telephone and jet age, it was very hard to get departments to accept this. And as late as 1980, Gotlieb had to plead with departments not to visit Washington without telling DEA.

Certainly, when Osbaldeston had been deputy minister at ITC, he would bypass DEA. He didn't talk much to DEA people; they were invited to the meetings, but they had little to say. They were invited essentially because "they ran the embassies where the Trade Commissioner Service (TCS) operated. Their substance on the economic side was nil. He mentioned Klaus Goldschlag as the best mind of the period but someone who was completely uninterested in the economic side. The result was battles with DEA over prestige. DEA wanted to chair the delegations abroad on, for example, tin.

He would insist that his ITC expert chair the meeting, as this role had to be filled by an expert, and would give DEA the position of vice chair, if it insisted. The problem was that DEA still thought generalists could operate in a specialized technical era. The department had to bring more to the party.

Pitfield's power
He and **Pitfield** had long agreed that DEA was weak. Osbaldeston had been Treasury Board secretary when Pitfield was cabinet secretary, and they'd long been friends and confidants. But from the 1960s on, Osbaldeston had resisted DEA efforts to absorb the TCS. The motivation for those attempts was wrong. He had also lived through the reorganization in 1969-70, and he knew that reorganization was hell. But by 1982, DEA had to be changed and made a player once more. Integrating the TCS with DEA was a Pitfield move – only the cabinet secretary could have decided to do this ...

Pitfield could do what he wanted. The reorganization of departments, like the appointment of deputies, was a prime ministerial right. The ITC and DEA ministers were told. Ed Lumley was unhappy. **Mark MacGuigan** was unhappy but pliant, someone who didn't meddle in running the department's foreign policy. Still, MacGuigan was a bit petulant, though he knew he couldn't take on Osbaldeston and Pitfield. In other words, Pitfield and he did what they thought was necessary.

The integration of the TCS and DEA was done by force. However, there was a lot of talk, and logic won out. The key session took place at the Donald Gordon Centre at Queen's University, where Osbaldeston threw together senior management of both departments for a several-day period. An important player was Glen Shortliffe, who pushed the organizational boxes around. Others were Bob Johnstone, **Si Taylor, de Montigny Marchand**, and all the assistant deputy ministers (ADMs), to about twenty in total. They began by covering the walls with flipcharts of complaints about ITC and DEA, a flood of complaints. In a helluva session, Osbaldeston told them that integration was a fait accompli and that they'd better start to enjoy it. Then he let them argue until they saw the logic of it. The point of this process was to provide a forum for talk until the views began to change, and they could see the opportunity they'd been given.

Making it work
Osbaldeston said he was resented, and DEA was infuriated. DEA people doubted his intellectual capacity to do the job. He was from the wrong side

of the tracks and didn't have a hankie up his sleeve. They were also threatened by the emphasis on management and the fact that economics was back. D'Iberville Fortier and others who'd grown up under Pearson thought the business of foreign policy was peace and that everything else was crass economics. But to Osbaldeston, DEA had too many pseudo-Goldschlags who lacked Klaus's intelligence.

Of course, ITC was also unhappy. The TCS felt like kids who'd lost their parents. They were dependent on Osbaldeston to protect them and feared he couldn't do it. The arrogance of DEA frightened them. The business community was also unhappy at the disappearance of the TCS, and the TCS feared that its connection to this community would be cut. But the TCS people gained confidence when they saw they were getting posts and ADMs; they saw that trade policy wasn't lost; and they saw they were winning.

Osbaldeston and Pitfield knew that full integration would take a decade. When Osbaldeston became USSEA, he tried to calm DEA by saying that he wouldn't mess in foreign policy. He said they wouldn't see him for the first year while he did reorganization. But he also served notice that no USSEA could keep his hands off foreign policy forever. Although he'd expected to be at DEA for three years, Marcel Massé replaced him after nine months, did the second reorganization, and proceeded to get involved in policy. DEA forgot Osbaldeston's warning. In any case, he didn't frighten them, as they realized that his love was management.

He had an understood mandate, understood by himself and Pitfield ... He was seen as someone who wouldn't cause problems, was respected as a workman, in other words. The aim was to make DEA relevant and restore it to prominence.

In this period, foreign policy was run by Si Taylor, not de Montigny Marchand. Taylor had the best mind next to Goldschlag. And he and Osbaldeston had entered the foreign service at the same time. Osbaldeston thought that Taylor's attitude regarding the reorganization was neutral tending to positive, but he worried that Taylor might not understand the importance of the Trade side relating to the support of business. Business, in other words, had to be kept off the department's back. And it was.

There was chaos in the reorganization. Osbaldeston worried whether the sheer application of intellect could override the absence of systems while the organization changed. Would people consult enough? Would Taylor have the energy? By the tips of their fingers, things worked, although it wasn't easy until the desks merged. He had two prima donna deputies – de Montigny

Marchand, who thought he should have been USSEA, and Bob Johnstone, who wanted to be anywhere else. Osbaldeston feared a big crisis, and the only one was the American invasion of Grenada in 1983, where DEA's response was a bit slow.

Osbaldeston had set up two wings in the reorganization, and although he knew that integration had to be complete (which would have occurred if he'd stayed for three years), he used to calm the troops by disparaging the idea of a great integrated desk in the sky.

Massé takes over
In 1982, Osbaldeston went to the PCO to replace Pitfield. He hadn't expected to move, and Pitfield resigned only because he thought Trudeau would be leaving at Christmas 1983 ... Osbaldeston was involved in the selection of Massé as USSEA. It had to be someone from outside – the position couldn't be given to a DEA person, as they could not leave the reorganization half done. He thought that Massé went too fast at DEA but not too far in integrating. Massé was a more authoritarian manager than he was. Certainly, however, he and Massé talked about what Massé was doing – they had to, as Massé needed the cabinet secretary's okay. Massé's worst period was after one-and-a-half years when, the reorganization work largely finished, he did begin to meddle in policy. He wasn't a Goldschlag. Osbaldeston himself would have played chairman, not practitioner, feeling that the people with the expertise should make the policy. Massé tried to be the chief operating officer, which was a mistake. He also caused interpersonal difficulties, unlike Taylor ...

DE MONTIGNY MARCHAND (1936-)
INTERVIEW | GENEVA, 11 JULY 1988 AND 6 FEBRUARY 1989

Trained as a lawyer, Marchand went to Ottawa in the late 1960s after a detour in university administration. He served in the Communications department and then in the Privy Council Office as deputy secretary until 1979. He studied the Third Option's failure in Europe, returned to Ottawa to work on the 1980 Quebec referendum, and was associate USSEA from 1980 to 1985. He served as Trudeau's "sherpa" for the Williamsburg G7 summit in 1983.

Organization of the PCO in foreign and defence policy
This organization gives the prime minister an advantage, Marchand said, but he needs it to govern. And remember that the PCO's independent brief to the prime minister must draw heavily on information that DND furnishes. True, Defence Minister Jim Richardson was not effective, being lazy among other things.

In the PCO as deputy secretary to the cabinet
In the PCO, Marchand had responsibility for defence and foreign policy. He thought it was very important that DND had an officer in the PCO, Colonel François Richard, to help water down the us-them syndrome. He knew and thought it normal that the officer would keep DND informed of everything that took place. After all, the same thing occurred when an officer from National Health and Welfare was in the PCO. The officer's presence also gave military input into decision making, when hitherto only the DND civilians had enjoyed this role. On the defence side, the key figure was General **Jacques Dextraze**, the CDS, who got on well with **Trudeau** – the prime minister admired him.

The Cabinet Committee on External Affairs and National Defence was not unimportant. DND funds were enormous, after all. But he admitted that much depended on the SSEA who chaired it. Personality mattered. Allan MacEachen, for example, didn't like committees and preferred to resolve things with the prime minister. He was the kind of man who thought that no issue was important if it couldn't be resolved privately with another minister.

Marchand agreed generally with the story of Schmidt's role in the purchase of new tanks during the mid-1970s, but he said that Trudeau was coming to feel the need to boost Canadian defences so he could get some credit with our allies. **Don Macdonald** opposed the expenditure, but the idea of tanks had been canvassed in the PCO, and the dollar figures had been run past Finance and the Treasury Board first. Macdonald lost in the cabinet on that one. Trudeau wasn't an advocate on that decision in the cabinet. The DND budget had to be increased because equipment had to be replaced, and decisions couldn't be put off. There was also a clear connection to the Contractual Link.

Ivan Head's departure from the PMO occurred while Marchand was at the PCO. He didn't much like Head's earlier role. Head's special links with

Julius Nyerere in Tanzania and Michael Manley in Jamaica were dropped, though he "purported" to continue to carry messages back and forth. Ivan was a consummate backroom performer and a very proactive fellow. He was highly skilled as a manipulator and as a writer, but the world seen through Ivan's eyes was a very Pearsonian one, not the real world of the mid-1970s.

"I preferred to base foreign policy on interests, however crass," Marchand said, rather than on ideals. The Canadian broker was an obsolete conception. The idea of the representative of any small country as broker or oracle is foolish. Look at Carlos Romulo of the Philippines. For years, he was the stuff of congratulatory after-dinner speeches. So many years, so much wisdom ... But in the end, he merely represented the Philippines, and who cared?

Yes, the PCO took up some of the slack from Ivan's job, but remember that his departure must also be assessed against the background of changes at the top in DEA. Jim Coutts in the PMO did not attempt to interfere. He was concerned about the domestic impacts of foreign policy, and that was all. He did not play a role in formulating it.

At DEA
In 1980, when Marchand moved to DEA headquarters in the Pearson Building, he encountered some initial mistrust. Naturally, there was skepticism and apprehension. But he brought advantages, as one who knew "the interdepartmental sniffing games." He had help from **Allan Gotlieb** and **Pitfield**; and **Mark MacGuigan**, the SSEA, had confidence in him.

He played a role in the great constitutional pursuit in the United Kingdom, co-ordinating the DEA end of things. He confirmed that Trudeau and Margaret Thatcher didn't like each another, in her case "from square one." But in his view, Thatcher was trying to demonstrate that the UK government was a most unwilling agent. The demonstration, not the position, was the important point. They did not like our argument that our legal rectitude supported our political objects. As to the opposition outside the UK government, it would not have prevailed. Gilles Loiselle, Quebec's representative, complicated matters. Starting from a very small base, he, as a real pro, got maximum attention. But in the end, he would not have succeeded in derailing repatriation.

Trudeau at the G7 summits
Marchand saw Trudeau in three or four G7 summits and could say that he was not at his best on those occasions. The most important reason for that

was the "chemistry" of the summits. They were really G5, plus Canada and Italy. The "plus" expresses a gap. We and the Italians were the juniors.

The other reason was that Trudeau's priorities – his agenda – were not shared by other players. The first theme in his approach was his desire to expand the agenda beyond the economic to include political topics. This was heresy, but it was also "natural for a junior member who considered himself lucky to be there."

As a sherpa, Marchand "incarnated the political side," but he also had to be very careful to pay attention to the economic advisers. Among the sherpas, everybody but himself and Jacques Attali, who was François Mitterrand's sherpa, were economists, and Attali had trained as one. Marchand "had to tone down Trudeau" because he knew his crusade would be futile; but time and again, Trudeau would return to his preoccupation. Trudeau's second theme, related to the first, was his idea that the summits were a kind of board of directors of the rich Western nations, who should use them to get their act together to deal with the impoverished South. On that tack, only France, with Mitterrand, was our ally, though latterly the Japanese joined in.

As to substance at the G7 summits, Trudeau wanted some discussion of replenishment of capital flows from private banks, encouragement of International Monetary Fund loans, and so on. The whole thrust was liberal, left of centre, in many ways Pearsonian. Thatcher and Reagan were not receptive. Helmut Schmidt more often than not told Trudeau to restrain his enthusiasms.

The result was that, being in a minority, and in a position of contradiction, Trudeau could be, and was, both preachy and flip. But even when he mounted a very good argument, as he did in the 1984 London G7 conference, with his five points, and got into a tremendous fight with Thatcher, he would not prevail. In that case, the manner in which he defended his case was admirable. He performed well and was very impressive in terms of his passionate presentation. But he was using up a lot of credit ... The summit was very sharp-tongued, with Trudeau versus Thatcher and Reagan. He and Margaret didn't like each other. At one meeting, she read her brief and Trudeau gave his view, which differed. After listening politely, she returned unchecked to her text. That left Trudeau discouraged, not angry.

Trudeau was at his best in international meetings at the Commonwealth summits or in things like Caribbean conferences. There Canada was a significant player, and what we said mattered. Trudeau could take the intellectual leadership of the group. When he was not in that situation in meetings, he tended to be turbulent ...

Reorganization of DEA
Marchand traced the DEA reorganization back to Norman Robertson, who had played the co-ordinating role on international economics. The central agency idea was Gotlieb's, and he pushed until he got Trudeau and Pitfield to buy it. But although the cabinet went along, there was little follow-through, and nothing much came of it, exactly as with the Contractual Link.

At DEA, the reorganization was pressed by **Gordon Osbaldeston** – Marchand said he "loved" him and had no problem working with him. But before Osbaldeston left DEA, he was beginning to wonder about the place of the USSEA in a system that divided power between the two deputies in charge of trade and external policy. When Marcel Massé replaced Osbaldeston, he was proceeding in a vacuum. He may have cleared moves with the clerk of the privy council, but attention was fixed elsewhere. Moreover, he tried to horn in on foreign policy, and his talk of process plus substance offended many. Marchand liked Massé – before he came to DEA. When Marchand's appointment to DEA was made in 1980, there was an understanding that he would succeed Gotlieb. But first Osbaldeston and then Massé were put in at the top. When Massé was named, Pitfield called Marchand in to ask if he wanted the CBC – he didn't – or at least to see if he wasn't unhappy at being passed over. He wasn't too unhappy, and he liked DEA, so he stayed.

The model of an all-embracing foreign service was basically a good one, Marchand said. It made sense to centralize initiatives abroad under the head of post, the ambassador. And why should that not occur at home? The model made sense and should work, provided a number of things were connected.

Now, you do not appoint a minister for trade who can rival the SSEA; it should always be clear that the SSEA is senior. Otherwise, things become confused. And your central machinery in the department, the control mechanisms such as personnel, must be staffed by good people ...

Some of the political officers at DEA felt aggrieved, Marchand agreed, but such people needed their heads bashed, their position being so contrary to common sense. So what if they resented it? Now they had to associate with trade commissioners, "people with dirty fingers." He thought their real grievance had to do with the promotion system. The current system was designed for another era, and if it was maintained, "they're going to lose our good young people."

Generally, he said, he was satisfied with reports from our missions abroad, but he had to admit that the economic reportage was quite inferior to the political stuff. In fact, the best analysis of economic trends he ever got was from a political officer, Klaus Goldschlag in Bonn ...

On Trudeau

Trudeau worked very hard himself and got the very best from his staff, even though he never said thanks, because all knew that he worked harder than they did. His vanity was enormous, and he had no management skills. Marchand admired the way Trudeau operated in the cabinet, but he recognized that his style bruised some of the egos around the table. When Marchand arrived in the PCO, ministers offered judgments on policies without knowing the financial implications. At his insistence, procedure was altered so that the Treasury Board saw proposals first and put dollar figures on them.

Marchand was never bothered by Jewish representations on the Middle East. DEA factored the representations into its policy, but he recognized that politicians felt they had to hold back because of the lobby. Trudeau was furious after Menachem Begin's attempt to intervene in the federal election, and intermediaries had to be used to restore his relations with the Jewish community after the 1980 election ...

THOMAS DELWORTH (1929-2012)
INTERVIEW | UPPSALA, SWEDEN, 26 OCTOBER 1987

After joining DEA, Delworth served in Stockholm to 1963, in Vietnam from 1963 to 1964, and on the Vietnam desk in Ottawa from 1964 to 1970. Then he went to Indonesia as ambassador and took over managing the Conference on Security and Cooperation in Europe file in 1974. He was successively ambassador to Hungary, Yugoslavia, and Sweden. He was known for his incisive and eloquent dispatches.

DEA's problems

Marcel Massé had said to Delworth that "if the systems were right, then policy would follow," but Delworth dismissed this approach with scorn.

Gotlieb, as a professional, was not responsible for the integration of DEA, ITC, and Immigration. He had seen it coming and had left. **Osbaldeston** had done it. He had started in the TCS, done one overseas posting and not liked it (Delworth's implication was that he didn't understand DEA), and in his one year as USSEA, he brought the departments together. Then, when the unpopular **Michael Pitfield** left, he became cabinet secretary. In Delworth's view, Pitfield was the villain, an elitist who disliked DEA elitism. He had enormous influence and was concerned with power.

Pitfield had views on foreign policy, although Delworth could not disagree with the argument that Pitfield simply carried out **Trudeau**'s policy. To him, Pitfield was interested in the process, not content. He was concerned with the machinery of government and wanted a symmetrical process, with everything funnelling upward to one level below Trudeau – that is, to him. He had no strong views. **Ivan Head** cared, but Pitfield didn't. Delworth didn't believe that there was a DEA analogue to Colonel François Richard posted by DND to the PCO. But when Delworth wanted something, he would write to Head, although with **Ritchie** and Gotlieb as USSEAs, he had to be careful doing this. They saw themselves as the channel to Prime Minister Trudeau, who had named them.

Delworth suggested that there was a tacit agreement between Gotlieb, Pitfield, and Trudeau (after Head left) that the role of the PMO on DEA would change. Jacques Roy was to be the channel to the prime minister, not an adviser to him.[18] Gotlieb and Pitfield weren't personal friends, but they understood each other, and each knew what the other was talking about. They sometimes fought like cat and dog.

On Trudeau

Trudeau was unlike any other leader. Goldschlag had described him as not serious, an adventurer in ideas. Delworth added, one with great articulation and little commitment. Trudeau understood the outside world and was one of the few Canadians who did, but he was vain. His relationship with DEA was bad because he thought he knew more than DEA. He had no commitment to anything but his own amusement. He had whims and he changed year by year; each year had little connection to the last. But he was more brilliant than Pearson, though unlike Pearson, he believed that policy could

---

18　Roy joined DEA in 1960 and served in numerous posts. In the PCO, he became assistant secretary to cabinet for foreign and defence policy.

be changed like a hem length. His views of the national interest were based on his own perceptions rather than a carefully thought-out position. He was afraid of being grey and dull, and he wanted to be relevant. Above all, he was a man who had to win.

Trudeau hated NATO secretary-general Joseph Luns and his NATO meetings, which were so formal. He would speak, and Luns would say, "Thank you, Mr. Trudeau. Now let us turn to the communiqué." Trudeau called him General Luns.

Trudeau admired the way Commonwealth conferences worked. They were the only free and open discussions, very critical and sharp (as Singapore's Lee could be on Robert Mugabe, for example). Delworth saw these as great fora for the exchange of views.

Personalities
On Marcel Massé, Delworth said that Pitfield couldn't stand that DEA didn't perform according to rules laid down for other departments. Delworth doubted that Massé got a reorganization mandate from Trudeau and thought that Pitfield simply wanted to make DEA a department like the others. Massé (who downgraded foreign policy expertise) was a "mad organist," rearranging pieces, but the organ played so loud that everyone was deaf at the end. It was crap that process was more important than policy. Policy has quality and process doesn't, something that Pitfield and Massé didn't understand, though Pitfield, unlike Massé, was a man of quality and intelligence. Pitfield felt that elitism in government couldn't be swallowed, though he was an elitist. He also blamed DEA for things even when it had nothing to do with them. This, plus Trudeau's belief that he was always smarter, hurt severely.

Marcel Cadieux was a great intellect, a great Canadian. He was the only public servant who could put lead in Pearson's pencil where Quebec was concerned. He came from humble Montreal stock (his father was a streetcar conductor). Massé's background was privileged, and he was pissed that early on when he was at the World Bank, Cadieux didn't invite him to the embassy in Washington. He was hung up on the old DEA and couldn't see around it. Small-minded and vindictive, he wanted to humiliate the aspects of a system that he wasn't part of. He also had a remarkable view of his ability to control ministers. He had power, and ministers had none. He could divide up the pie and tell ministers that if they spent X, they'd have nothing for Y. And he did intervene in policy questions, demonstrating to ministers (such as Joe Clark) that he knew nothing about foreign policy. He was messianic, and he made DEA sick.

Osbaldeston was okay and had no kinks about the foreign service. He was a technician without a mission. He came to see that the TCS could be put together with DEA in a way that increased the clout of both. He never interfered in policy ...

Mark MacGuigan was very good. Once he trusted your judgment, he'd listen to you. He made things happen, and there couldn't have been a better minister. Delworth recalled no fights between Trudeau and MacGuigan, although there were difficulties between MacGuigan and Ed Lumley, who was ITC minister in 1982-83.

Delworth had known Gotlieb forever and loved him dearly, but he wasn't a great USSEA. He came to DEA after a period of stagnation and traditionalism. His mandate from Trudeau and Pitfield (with whom he was close but not friendly) was to modernize Sleepy Hollow. He told Delworth that he wanted to be known as "a reforming USSEA." He was bold and courageous (once he briefed Trudeau prior to a visit to Melbourne, telling him to read something, which Trudeau did) ... Gotlieb left little behind in DEA, as he confused noise with purposefulness. He was like Trudeau in that he had interests and emphases that were all-encompassing. He held staff meetings twice a week that drove everyone crazy as he pushed his views. He got hot on Mexico after a trip there. He drafted a paper on bilateralism in foreign policy after our long road with multilateralism, and this resulted in the department carving up the world. His paper was interesting on the way that multilateralism had obscured the importance of bilateralism, but, like Trudeau, he didn't follow up.

The Policy Analysis Group (PAG) wasn't a den of fools. Some very good people served there. **Geoffrey Pearson** operated in left field, but that gave him impact. He was like his mother, Maryon; he knew he could make waves by being difficult, and he was an effective counterpoise to kneejerk hardliners. He was no fool.

Ed Ritchie was the last of the greats, though he wasn't in Marcel Cadieux's league. He was responsible and loved (unlike Gotlieb, who was feared and hated), but he couldn't manage, though he was big, generous, fair, and persuasive. He sent Delworth to the Banff School of Management to see if he could learn anything that was worthwhile for DEA. But he had no bullshit in him. His weakness was that his specialty was international economics; elsewhere, he had to take advice.

Basil Robinson was a disaster with Trudeau, not a good manager, and not a good USSEA. He had decided when deputy USSEA to resist Trudeau, and he spent time building defences. He was committed to the traditional wisdom. Delworth didn't know if he had a breakdown.

MacEachen was a strange man. His silences could make officials babble to fill the air space, and this sometimes got them into trouble.

III
The Defence and Foreign Policy Reviews and After

THE FIRST GREAT ISSUE of Pierre Trudeau's time as prime minister had to do with defence and foreign policy. Trudeau had travelled widely and written newspaper and magazine pieces on foreign policy, but he had little real expertise on the subject. He held not atypical francophone views on defence, and he had little real interest in the military. Certainly, he had no experience of it beyond a limited and abortive exposure to the Canadian Officers Training Corps at the Université de Montréal during the Second World War. But Trudeau had a tough, focused mind, and he had become convinced that Canadian policy concentrated too much on being the "helpful fixer" of problems abroad, paid too little attention to the country's national interests, and gave far too much weight to the interests of the NATO and NORAD alliances that drove its defence and foreign policy.[1] Should Canada not focus on its own internal troubles and the possibility that unrest might spill north over the American border? Was NATO the best way to achieve peace? When would we arrive at a plan to achieve peace by not getting stronger militarily? Could we assume that the Soviet Union wanted war? Was the North Atlantic Treaty Organization really any longer necessary? Did it serve Canadian interests? Why didn't the Europeans, now wealthy, defend themselves? How could Canada justify having nuclear weapons? Should it be a neutral in the Cold War world? Such were the questions that Trudeau began to ask of officials and ministers when he came to power in the spring of 1968.[2] Such questions produced much eye rolling from most of those who heard them.

---

1   See John English's account of the 1968-69 Foreign and Defence Policy Reviews in *Just Watch Me: The Life of Pierre Elliott Trudeau, 1968-2000* (Toronto: Knopf, 2009), 57-69.
2   For a list of the questions that Trudeau asked officials in December 1968, see J.L. Granatstein and Robert Bothwell, *Pirouette: Pierre Trudeau and Canadian Foreign Policy* (Toronto: University of Toronto Press, 1990), 18-19.

Trudeau, however, was not alone in his concerns. Some ministers – Donald Macdonald, Eric Kierans, Gérard Pelletier, and others – shared his skepticism. Mitchell Sharp, Léo Cadieux, Paul Hellyer, and others did not, seeing Canadian alliances as being very much in Canada's national interests in a world where the USSR and China were hostile, and where Canada shared a continent with a superpower.

In the federal bureaucracy as well, the lines were sometimes sharply drawn. The Department of External Affairs had shaped Canada's alliances when it was led by Lester Pearson as USSEA, SSEA, and prime minister; the key figures in DEA believed that nothing major in the nation's alliance policies needed changing. But many younger foreign service officers, more nationalistic and aware of the growing academic and public criticism of American and NATO policy, were more receptive to Trudeau's incisive questions. In the Department of National Defence, much less policy-oriented than DEA, there was certainly less receptivity among uniformed officers, but there was some.

The battle over defence and foreign policy came into crisp focus with the reviews that Trudeau launched within weeks of taking power in April 1968. For the next ten months, officials in DND and DEA tried to divine his true intentions and to offer up a policy that met his wishes. Essentially, they failed, and when departmental reviews produced what the prime minister saw as a reiteration of the "same old, same old," Trudeau turned to his PCO and to a "Non-Group" of bureaucrats led by Ivan Head. A former junior DEA officer and law professor now seconded to the PCO, Head and his small team drafted a radical proposal that, if implemented, would effectively reduce the Canadian Forces to a quasi-paramilitary body and take Canada out of NATO's military apparatus. The Non-Group paper, sent to ministers at the end of March 1969, sparked threats of resignation from Defence Minister Léo Cadieux and bitter words from SSEA Mitchell Sharp. Trudeau duly withdrew it from cabinet consideration but not before all ministers had read it.

At the subsequent extraordinary two-day cabinet meeting over the last weekend in March 1969, ministers debated Canada's role. Trudeau himself eventually came down for remaining aligned with the West, though he did argue that "Canada's present military establishment was determined not to impress our enemies but rather to impress our friends." Given that, it was logical "to think in terms of other domestic or international contributions that could be made which would carry with them the same degree of political persuasion." In the end, Trudeau told his cabinet that Canada would remain in NATO "but on different terms and with increased control over our own contribution."[3]

What those terms should be now became the issue. After a tense meeting between the prime minister and Defence Minister Cadieux on 2 April, the two reached agreement on "a planned and phased reduction" of Canada's NATO force. That took time to work out, amidst very harsh words from British, Dutch, Belgian, and American officials, but ultimately, Canada's troops in Europe were halved to five thousand and no longer played a nuclear role.

By the fall of 1970, Donald Macdonald had been named defence minister, charged with creating a new defence policy. Macdonald had been one of the most vigorous critics of the nation's pre-Trudeau alliance policy, he was a strong minister, and now he had charge of DND. To draft a Defence White Paper, he recruited Gordon Smith, a young DEA officer who had been posted to NATO. With a fresh PhD from the Massachusetts Institute of Technology, Smith believed in national interests and in Canada's alliances, and he persuaded Macdonald of the rightness of that course. The White Paper he drafted married the two, adding a heavy emphasis on domestic security, something obviously important after the October Crisis of 1970. The paper called for the protection of sovereignty, a continuation of the NORAD role (including retaining the nuclear warheads on air force fighters), maintenance of the five-thousand-man NATO force, and an end to the nuclear role for the three remaining air force CF-104 squadrons in Europe. Peacekeeping remained a policy priority, though the tone was somewhat more skeptical than it had been in the past fifteen years. Peacekeeping, the White Paper stated, had "too often been frustrating and disillusioning," many conflicts having "their roots in subversion and insurgency, and therefore ... not lend[ing] themselves easily to resolution through the use of internationally constituted peacekeeping bodies."[4] The document also called for, and Macdonald soon set up, a committee to review DND's structure. It fell to Sylvain Cloutier, the new DND deputy minister, and General Jacques Dextraze, the CDS, to implement the reorganization in the mid-1970s.

---

3   Ibid., 23-24.
4   D.S. Macdonald, *Defence in the 70s: White Paper on Defence* (Ottawa: Information Canada, 1971), 39-40.

While the Canadian Forces and DND began to march in the Trudeau government's new direction, work in DEA continued on what was called STAFEUR, the Special Task Force on Europe, and on the drafting of a new foreign policy. This was published as *Foreign Policy for Canadians* in six booklets in June 1970, which curiously omitted detailed consideration of the United States but favoured greater Canadian efforts to connect with Europe, Latin America, Asia, and the Third World. The booklets pointed to new directions. Foreign policy was an extension of internal policies and interests, and must be looked at in its totality, argued one December 1969 memorandum accepted by the cabinet. Canada in the 1970s would be active abroad but "in different, perhaps more modest ways"[5] ...

In this chapter, we have interviews with five of Trudeau's ministers (Mitchell Sharp, Léo Cadieux, Paul Hellyer, Donald Macdonald, and Otto Lang), five senior DEA officers (Ross Campbell, Basil Robinson, John Halstead, Michael Shenstone, and Gordon Smith), and four top officials from DND (Jacques Dextraze, Robert Murdoch, John Anderson, and Sylvain Cloutier). From their accounts, readers can put together the way that Trudeau shaped Canadian foreign and defence policy after his ascension to power in April 1968. The immediate shock imposed by the new regime had the effect of an earthquake on the policy establishment, but the longer-term results, as the following chapters will demonstrate, turned out to be relatively minor.

HON. MITCHELL SHARP (1911-2004)
INTERVIEW | OTTAWA, 8 DECEMBER 1987

Trudeau and the Foreign Policy Review
Trudeau wanted the Foreign Policy Review. He and Sharp had talked about it before the election, and Sharp had agreed, but their purposes turned out to differ. Sharp thought the review would confirm the present policy; Trudeau thought he could make major changes. Sharp was always a bit uncertain about Trudeau's views on the NATO review. He recalled a dinner with Trudeau and Japanese ambassador Michiaki Suma sometime after he himself left the cabinet in 1978. Suma attacked the premier of Japan, looked at Trudeau,

....

5   Granatstein and Bothwell, *Pirouette*, 31.

and said he had no such problems as dissenting ministers and diplomats. Trudeau stopped him there and said there was a prime minister who was a dove and a foreign minister (Don Jamieson) who was a hawk, and he had a diplomat (**Ross Campbell,** who was there too) who was not careful in what he said. Campbell said later that Trudeau never forgot anything. Trudeau said to Sharp that one of the most remarkable things about the NATO review was the way the issue vanished from public opinion once the decision was made. Sharp agreed, and added that opinion polls before and after the cuts indicated that Canada had the right number of troops in NATO. All of this heightened Sharp's uncertainty as to what Trudeau had wanted. In the end, he decided that Trudeau had wanted to shake up the establishment.

Ivan Head did not cause Sharp any problems, except at the beginning before the modalities were clear. He scrupulously kept Sharp informed of what he was doing. Head was used mainly to keep up the personal contacts that Trudeau had established abroad.

The Defence Review
The one place that Head hadn't informed him was the Defence Review, Sharp observed. How had DEA and DND so misjudged what Trudeau had wanted? To Sharp, the departments took the view that foreign and defence policy had developed over a long time under both parties. The fundamentals couldn't be changed. They knew nothing about Trudeau and couldn't believe, for example, that he'd want to look seriously at neutrality. The mandarins believed that they represented the national interest. Thus, the first draft of the review was traditional, and Trudeau said it wasn't what he wanted. Sharp agreed that DEA looked on DND people as technicians who couldn't be allowed to handle policy. He didn't know how Geoffrey Murray at DEA had landed the job of heading the review and was clearly no admirer of Murray. Later, Murray wrote a piece on the review for a DEA administrative history in which he said that the Third Option paper had fallen with a thud. To Sharp, this was the only part of the review that was remembered and had influence.

Foreign policy rarely aroused the cabinet. Sharp tried and failed at getting regular discussion. The Cabinet Committee on External Affairs and National Defence just talked shop. The situation was worse under Pearson, however, where no questions of foreign policy ever got to the cabinet.

Léo Cadieux strongly supported DND. His relations with Trudeau deteriorated – he'd not been a Trudeau supporter at the 1968 leadership convention. To Cadieux, Trudeau was a disaster.

In January 1969, when Eric Kierans made a speech that advocated withdrawal from NATO, Trudeau's understanding of cabinet government was imperfect. He then thought it okay for ministers to advocate policies that were not subject to cabinet decision; once a decision was made, ministers had to abide by it. Certainly, Kierans thought that Trudeau would okay what he'd said, but Sharp had to make a speech to explain that his views weren't Canadian policy. Kierans said he wouldn't do it again.

The Defence Review took place at a time of real skepticism about NATO and East-West relations. Trudeau saw holes in the accepted doctrine. But in the end (and later), he realized that it was the relationship with Europe that was at stake. However, he never admitted making a mistake over NATO.

Sharp recounted the phone conversation with Trudeau prior to the weekend cabinet meeting on the Defence Review. He had just seen the Non-Group paper.

"Have you lost confidence in the minister of national defence?" he asked Trudeau.

"No," Trudeau replied. "I attacked Jean Marchand's paper on immigration."

"But you didn't issue a paper to the cabinet."

"Oh, I will withdraw it. I didn't mean this."

"I hope so," Sharp said, "as I've asked Léo not to submit his resignation immediately."

The Head paper was withdrawn and never discussed at the cabinet. Sharp said he thought it had little effect. He added that neutrality had been rejected earlier, and it had no substantial support at the cabinet meeting (except by inference from **Gérard Pelletier** and Kierans). Non-alignment was also dismissed. To Sharp, there were three groups in the cabinet: those who wanted out of NATO (Kierans, Pelletier, **Don Macdonald,** and Jean Marchand); those who wanted to stay in NATO but without troops; and those who wanted to stay in with troops. The first position was rejected overwhelmingly without a vote. Then the possibility of staying but without troops was rejected more heavily still. The question then was the number of troops. Other ministers let Sharp and Cadieux make the running, and they had earlier reached the conclusion that the status quo could not be maintained. They couldn't get an increase in the defence budget to re-equip the troops and so were reconciled to a cut.

Sharp had no recollection of Trudeau seeing the cabinet decision as meaning total troop withdrawal. But he remembered that he and Cadieux opposed the 3 April 1969 statement announcing the new policy, which, they thought, would be interpreted as a sign that Canada was losing interest in Europe. There had been quite a row over this statement on 1 April. Sharp suggested, "Why not announce the review was over and we're staying in NATO?" and then talk to the allies about the size of the force. The opposition in cabinet asked if this meant no change. Sharp replied that cuts didn't need to be done at once, and there had to be consultation to minimize the effects on NATO. Trudeau finally insisted on making the statement himself. Sharp thought he did so because he wanted to appear to the anti-NATO ministers as having made a change.

The NATO response
There were no terrible shrieks from the allies about the cuts, except at the NATO Foreign Ministers meeting in April 1969. Sharp took a rough ride there, being asked why Canada had done it this way. Some saw it as a "fundamental revision in your representation," though he realized the real problem was the United States and fears about Senator Mike Mansfield's intentions to reduce the US commitment to the alliance. Certainly, the United States didn't object strenuously, Sharp maintained ...

When Trudeau had an interest in a subject, as on foreign policy between 1968 and 1970, he had real interest, but once the issue was settled, he moved away. In Sharp's view, Trudeau wanted only a settlement and to shake up the bureaucrats; then it was fine.

HON. LÉO CADIEUX (1908-2005)
INTERVIEW | OTTAWA, 9 DECEMBER 1987

A journalist, Cadieux was elected to Parliament as a Liberal in 1962, became associate minister of national defence in 1965, then minister in 1967. In 1970, he became ambassador to France, holding this post to 1975.

On DND
When Trudeau formed the government, he asked Cadieux what post he wanted, and Léo said he wanted to stay in DND as he had not finished his projects there. These largely related to making French a military language, a task in which he had the "good fortune" to have General Jean Allard as CDS. He didn't want two languages separate, one from the other, but a system in which both could merge. And he had good results in this.

Trudeau's Defence Review

Cadieux then gave a long and jumbled account of the Defence Review. The PMO would cannibalize DND papers and use one part to prove a point against another paper, he claimed.

On the day that he got **Ivan Head**'s Non-Group paper withdrawn from the cabinet papers, he and **Sharp** talked. They agreed that they could tear the Head paper apart but felt that to present it in this manner was simply dishonest. They phoned the prime minister, who withdrew it.

At the Cabinet Committee on External Affairs and National Defence, they were always outnumbered. He had the deputy minister and the chief of the defence staff, but there were twenty-five people at the table. **Don Macdonald** favoured neutrality but couldn't define what kind of neutrality – active or passive. To Cadieux, other ministers were trying to get DND funds for their own projects. He argued that neutrality would translate to higher defence costs. Trudeau never told him what he wanted – out of NATO or reduced troops. But Cadieux was sure that he leaned to complete withdrawal of troops. And he was certain that Eric Kierans had Trudeau's okay when he made his January 1969 speech in which he called for withdrawal from NATO.

At the cabinet, the showdown came. Cadieux threatened to resign on 1 April 1969, when the total troop withdrawal was proposed. If the troops were withdrawn, he said, it would be without him. Trudeau had him to lunch the next day and said, "If you feel you must resign, do so, but is there no common ground?" So Cadieux wrote out a formula for "a planned and phased reduction," which Trudeau accepted. Cadieux agreed to try to sell the cuts to NATO, but he strongly objected to reaching such decisions without consulting our allies (although it was clear to him that any planned and phased reduction would entail consultation ...).

The defence cuts at NATO

At Brussels, he worked out a plan to avoid questions at the meeting. Instead, he held a lunch at Ambassador **Ross Campbell**'s residence to explain what Canada was doing if the delegates promised not to raise it at the North Atlantic Council meeting. In his view, half of NATO's members didn't provide troops to NATO and so had no right to complain about Canada. Also, he didn't want the official meeting turning into an alley fight. The lunch was dramatic, the Belgian actually crying. But at the meeting, British defence minister Denis Healey raised questions about Canada, which fell on a dead silence from everyone else. After the meeting, the press wanted to see Cadieux, who said he was scandalized that the United Kingdom would say such things, after all the help it had received from Canada. He worried how the cuts would turn out and said that resignation was still on his mind. But he was reassured by General Don Laubman, commander of the CF in Europe.

Later, after the cuts, Cadieux insisted on going to Germany to close the army base in the north. It was a rainy day, but everyone stood straight. He had told Trudeau that he was loyal; he hated the chore, but he'd do it.

HON. PAUL HELLYER (1923-)
INTERVIEW | TORONTO, 6 NOVEMBER 1987

Hellyer served briefly in the St. Laurent government as associate minister of national defence and was defence minister in the Pearson government, where he unified the armed forces.[6] *He lost the leadership race to Trudeau at the Liberal convention in 1968 and was briefly transport and housing minister before resigning from the cabinet in April 1969.*

Hellyer began with the Defence Review
Hellyer was convinced that **Trudeau** wanted to get the troops out of NATO, though he was not sure whether he wanted to leave the alliance altogether. Trudeau had said to him at 24 Sussex that "if he had his heart's desire, he would pull all the troops out. But it might not be possible." Hellyer thought Trudeau had said this at a March 1969 dinner that he'd recorded in his diary (he'd brought the diary with him). There was no doubt what Trudeau wanted. Trudeau and **Gérard Pelletier** belonged to the "everything is fine if we love one another" school of foreign policy. This didn't apply to Jean Marchand, but only because Marchand was uninterested in foreign policy.

Trudeau's technique in the cabinet was to have his mind made up before he began but to conceal this by exercising what appeared to be participatory democracy there. He seemed to allow ministers total freedom to talk, but no decision would be taken until one by one they learned what he wanted and shifted their positions toward his. He had tremendous patience in allowing this process to occur.

------

[6] Hellyer's memoir of his time as defence minister is *Damn the Torpedoes: My Fight to Unify Canada's Armed Forces* (Toronto: McClelland and Stewart, 1990).

During the 28-29 March 1969 cabinet discussion on foreign policy, some ministers might not have realized how he operated. Perhaps they thought the dialogue was genuine, which could explain why so many still wanted to keep troops in Europe. Hellyer could not remember much about the 28-29 March cabinet meetings, even with his diary as a prompt. At that time, he was on the verge of leaving the cabinet and was not participating or following events as closely as before.

But he was sure that **Léo Cadieux** was the key in blocking total withdrawal; by threatening to resign, he put limits on the withdrawal. And after the 1 April 1969 cabinet meeting described in the diary, Cadieux was still in doubt about whether to stay in the cabinet. Hellyer hitched a flight back from Brussels with Cadieux and his deputy minister, Elgin Armstrong, after the May 1969 NATO meetings. They talked, and Cadieux was still in doubt about what to do. Armstrong argued that he had to stay, as DND could keep more troops in NATO if he did. Léo was leaning toward staying, and Hellyer saw the increase in troop strength up to five thousand as a ransom to keep him in the cabinet. His own resignation (in late April) gave Cadieux more clout in threatening to go; losing two ministers in a short period would be hard for Trudeau to bear. A popular defence minister, Cadieux implemented unification and made the forces more congenial to French Canadians.

Hellyer discounted the financial argument as a reason for the NATO cuts. This had been talked about in the past, but usually because of concern over foreign exchange. Nor were re-equipment costs of the NATO brigade high, most of the equipment having been purchased already during his time as minister: armoured personnel carriers, trucks, self-propelled guns. The big deal was to re-equip the remainder of the division to be sent over from Canada during a crisis. That was expensive, and Canada got out of the commitment to send the remainder.

Hellyer didn't know whether Trudeau was aware in advance of Eric Kierans's January 1969 NATO speech, although he thought he must have been. Certainly, he never indicated any sign of disapproval. The speech occurred during a brief period when Trudeau had allowed ministers to take public positions that were not in conformity with cabinet policy.

Hellyer believed that **Don Macdonald**'s closeness to Trudeau, the closest of any anglophone, might have explained his anti-NATO views. He thought that Macdonald and Trudeau had shared a room at the UN and got to know each other then. Macdonald was Trudeau's spear carrier in many areas.

Hellyer couldn't explain Minister without Portfolio James Richardson's anti-NATO views but thought he might have been compensating for his wealth by supporting the views of those from different socio-economic backgrounds.

There was, he said, no question that the Liberal caucus was overwhelmingly in favour of keeping troops in NATO, referencing his diary entry of 23 April 1969, but Trudeau used a strong emotional appeal to get the caucus behind him and drew a standing ovation at the end. He wasn't always good in caucus, but he was fantastic that day, as he often was on the issues that deeply concerned him: bilingualism and biculturalism, criminal law, the Constitution, and foreign policy. Foreign policy was of deep concern to Trudeau: China, NATO, and co-operation with the USSR. His goal was to change our foreign policy.

DND and DEA naturally supported the status quo; this was just the way the system operated. The individuals who rise are those who support the status quo, and implementing major change is hard. To get around this, Trudeau installed a quasi-US system, with **Ivan Head** in the PMO as his man who could inject different points of view and get the debate going.

HON. DONALD MACDONALD (1932-)
INTERVIEW | TORONTO, 5 APRIL 1988

First elected to Parliament from Toronto in 1962, Macdonald became Trudeau's president of the privy council in 1968 and was then successively defence minister, energy minister, and finance minister. He left government in 1977.

The Defence Review
Macdonald formed his views out of the more adventurous generation. On NATO, he had been on parliamentary delegations and had been briefed in Europe. He saw that the effort to put a military component in NATO distorted Canadian defence policy. He believed that the 1951 policy had been overtaken by events and wanted a fresh look.[7] His view, expressed in a 1968 memo to the Cabinet Committee on External Affairs and National Defence was that

---

7   The 1951 policy entailed sending an army brigade and an air division to Europe.

Canada should have no troop commitment but should remain in NATO unless NATO got too nasty, in which case we should leave.[8]

At the cabinet committee, there were some sharp tussles. He recalled **Ross Campbell**, the ambassador to NATO, bearding ministers, and he fought with him there. Macdonald clearly had affection for Campbell.

Trudeau didn't share Macdonald's NATO views very strenuously. And eventually, after stimulating the argument, Trudeau fashioned a compromise in the cabinet. He was chair of the board. Macdonald didn't recollect Trudeau being particularly supportive of his own position.

Léo Cadieux was strong for NATO, and Trudeau didn't want to lose him, even though Cadieux hadn't supported him at the 1968 Liberal leadership convention. Cadieux wasn't a heavyweight, but he was thoroughly decent. He got quite agitated with Macdonald on the NATO issue. Macdonald had almost no recollection of the 1969 events, couldn't recall Ivan Head's Non-Group paper, and was unclear on the players in the debate. He did remember that Eric Kierans was a trial generally. Eric could work himself into a rage, but he was never there at the crunch, didn't speak much, and could even switch positions. Kierans and **Paul Martin** lived in the same apartment building and drove to Parliament Hill together. Macdonald once asked Kierans if he worked on Martin during their drives. Eric's reply: "Have you ever driven with Paul?" – a reference to his inability to speak when in terror.

HON. OTTO LANG (1932-)
INTERVIEW | WINNIPEG, 13 JUNE 1988

A former dean of the law school at the University of Saskatchewan, Lang was elected to the House of Commons in 1968 and served in Trudeau's cabinet in a variety of portfolios from 1968 to 1979: Manpower and Immigration, Justice (twice), and Transport.

The Defence Policy Review in the cabinet
Contrary to popular belief, **Trudeau** was patient to a fault in cabinet discussions. "Certainly, I became impatient on occasion. He knew it and I knew it,"

....

8   See Macdonald's *Thumper: The Memoirs of the Hon. Donald S. Macdonald* (Montreal and Kingston: McGill-Queen's University Press, 2014).

Lang said. Yet in discussions, Trudeau was always ready to accept the possibility of a novelty that would turn the dialogue in a different direction.

Trudeau was well briefed in advance on issues and on where ministers stood. He always knew where the departmental minister stood. On issues such as NATO, he knew where the DEA and DND ministers stood. But he did not necessarily know where the other ministers were coming from. That was important, because in the 1968-72 cabinet, a lot of ministers took an interest in foreign policy topics. In the first circle of interest (in terms of intensity of interest) Lang put himself, **Donald Macdonald, Sharp, Pelletier,** and Jean-Luc Pepin. In the second circle he put John Turner, Ron Basford, and Charles "Bud" Drury.[9] "I believed that our overall viewpoint of Canada and its place in the world was quite consistent," he said. By this, he meant that there were no differences of principle. Perhaps **Paul Hellyer** was an exception, but he had the quality of becoming obsessed with whatever was directly in front of him. Fortunately, he was no longer defence minister and was wrapped up in housing. So he tended to speak on housing in the cabinet and not on much else; he caused no particular trouble in that regard. The other ministers already mentioned were much broader in interest.

By "consistent," Lang meant that no one in the group doubted that we should get closer to Russia and "Red China." He considered this approach justified in the later perspective of *perestroika*.

The briefing papers from DEA were quite good, Lang said, and they were given an appropriate reception. But DND's papers were considered to be self-serving. By nature, the denizens of DEA were more open-minded about their jobs and perspectives; those in DND had a definite mission, and it showed.

What about the Meech Lake cabinet meeting on NATO, held during a weekend at the end of March 1969? Lang had no quarrel with that scene, save one: the meeting was in Ottawa, not at Meech, and he remembered it particularly because he and a number of other ministers (including Trudeau) took two hours off that Sunday morning to go to Mass. He and Trudeau went on that occasion to the same church.

....

9   Jean-Luc Pepin was minister of industry and of trade and commerce (the two departments were merged on 31 March 1969). Turner was minister of justice; Basford minister of consumer and corporate affairs; and Drury Treasury Board president and a very senior and influential minister, as well as a former deputy minister of national defence.

He thought that nobody in the cabinet wanted to leave NATO. It was not so much a question of principle as a discussion first of strategy and then of tactics. Both Sharp and **Léo Cadieux** spoke up firmly for their departments, and there was a sense that the resignation of one or both was not impossible if the other side pressed too strongly. Perhaps only one would have gone, but it was obviously in the interest of both men for the feeling to get around that two positions were in jeopardy.

The government took the tone that NATO was not of such fantastic importance that it was worth getting into a mess over. The policy swing would go too far if we left, and leaving would attach too much importance to the issue and to NATO. As far as the political fallout was concerned, NATO was of no interest to his own constituents as long as it was not reduced to a single point of principle: who were our friends and who were not? Then there would have been reason to expect political danger.

If left to itself, the cabinet would have been inclined to cut our defence effort back to a combination of civil defence and peacekeeping, and to increase foreign aid. But politics required a different policy. He defined politics as the art of "doing what's right when you can get away with it." At no other time during his eleven years in the cabinet did things get to a breaking point, he said.

ROSS CAMPBELL (1918-2007)
INTERVIEW | OTTAWA, 29 SEPTEMBER 1987

Ross Campbell trained as a lawyer, served with distinction in the Royal Canadian Navy during the war, and then joined DEA. He held posts in Norway, Denmark, Turkey, and in Ottawa as assistant under secretary. After being ambassador in Belgrade, he went to NATO in 1967, where he remained until posted to Tokyo as ambassador in 1972. Campbell ended his career as president of Atomic Energy of Canada Limited.

Going to NATO
Campbell went to NATO in the spring of 1967, replacing Charles Ritchie as ambassador. De Gaulle had done "his little dirty at the end of 1966," when France withdrew its troops from NATO but remained a member of the alliance. NATO's North Atlantic Council was still headquartered in Paris. De Gaulle had pushed the Supreme Headquarters of the Allied Powers in Europe

(SHAPE) out of France but not the council. Leaving the council in what might be a neutral country made no sense. Really, de Gaulle had pulled a massive hoax on the French people. Except for the departure of SHAPE, everything remained as before. French "integrated" officers became liaison officers, for example. This was a spurious distinction, but he got away with it.

In 1967, **Paul Martin** brought Walter Gordon over to a NATO meeting. "He stayed very nicely in line," and Campbell had fond memories of a most marvellous dinner. Gordon's views changed when he saw that NATO was not merely an American instrument, Campbell claimed. Sensible Europeans wanted it as a tangible link to the power of the United States. Gordon realized that NATO was not just an American toy. Europeans did want it badly enough to ride out the French defection ...

The Trudeau cuts
During this period, **Trudeau** met regularly in Toronto with Jim Eayrs, the University of Toronto political scientist and media commentator.[10] At some point, Campbell bumped into Trudeau at the airport, presumably on his way to or from one of these meetings. Eayrs's advice was to pull Canada out of NATO. Anyway, withdrawing from NATO was interrupted by the Czech crisis in August 1968, when the USSR and its satellites invaded Czechoslovakia and suppressed its reformist government.

Campbell came to Ottawa two or three times to participate in the STAFEUR exercise. "So many of the premises they were operating on were false," he said, but he was so busy dealing with NATO and the European connection that he paid little attention. When the USSR was warned not to go into Romania or Yugoslavia, Canada had to be dragged to go along with it; we issued an ultimatum. The invasion of Czechoslovakia in 1968 had been a lesson to all the Soviet satellites as to who was master.

These were also dramatic lessons about détente. But what lesson did we absorb? What then happened? Canada's subsequent policy was one of bad timing and total insensitivity. **Mitchell Sharp** and Campbell had a bit of contact then, but Campbell had difficulty in perceiving Sharp's strength.

....

10   James Eayrs (1926-), a professor at the University of Toronto and later Dalhousie University, was an influential commentator on foreign affairs and, in the late 1960s and the 1970s, a strident proponent of neutrality.

Sharp's story of the defence cuts now differs from what Campbell thought then, Campbell maintained. During his six years as SSEA, Sharp never made a dramatic gaffe, but he never did any outstandingly good things either. His was "a pot-boiling stewardship."

On the day that the cabinet decided how much to cut the NATO force, Campbell had a "famous" conversation with Sharp. Trudeau wanted a 50 percent cut. Campbell had talked to **Basil Robinson** at 8:00 Ottawa time. At 8:30, he phoned the cabinet office and called Sharp out of the meeting. He tried to get him to stand firm, citing the military consequences of a 50 percent withdrawal, the political impact. Living it down would take forever. Sharp said, "So, what do you want me to do, resign?" Campbell said, "If necessary, yes." Sharp hung up.

Early in 1969, our allies in NATO became perturbed about the possible cutbacks. In May, **Léo Cadieux** came to Europe and told Campbell what was up – a 50 percent cut. At his own request, Campbell informed NATO secretary-general Manlio Brosio of the situation and asked his advice on how to handle it. Brosio feared that the cut would tear NATO apart. Campbell and Cadieux decided to hold a private lunch meeting with all the defence ministers. Present were Brosio and fourteen defence ministers, including the US defense secretary Melvin Laird and Denis Healey, the British defence minister.

When Léo made his announcement, Campbell said, "I've never seen such high drama in my life." The Belgian minister broke down and cried, stating that Canada had twice liberated Belgium. The Dutchman was equally strong. Laird was curiously silent; perhaps he understood. The Brits were "despicable." Of course, they had been cheating on their own commitments like mad. That day, they were patronizing. Then Healey leaked the story to the media. The difference between the Brits and us was that we told NATO; the Brits never did. There was a gradual decline in our influence from then on.

We mustered our people the next day and explained to them that we had to keep our morale high. We rationalized the decision to the best of our abilities. We redoubled our political efforts to compensate; it drove our people to distraction. But after the cut, there was no special Canadian problem. The Europeans did not organize to lobby Ottawa in 1969. Each government had a limit as to how far it would condemn sovereign actions.

JOHN F. ANDERSON (1923-2004)
INTERVIEW | OTTAWA, 7 AUGUST 1987

Anderson joined DND as a civil servant in 1951, worked in increasingly senior positions there in finance and on policy programming, and then became assistant deputy minister (policy) in 1978.

The Defence Review's context
In DND, Anderson lived by the pen – he was called in whenever a scribe was needed. That was the case with Deputy Minister Buzz Nixon in the early 1980s, and in 1968-69 it got him the post of chief scribe on Trudeau's Defence Policy Review. "I learned the power of being continuously the editor of a document," he stated. "You could do a lot with other people's inputs."

Anderson had his own views on the context of the Defence Review exercise. He argued that the real turning point in Canadian defence policy was not 1968 but 1962, with the Cuban missile crisis. The issue was not Prime Minister John Diefenbaker's awful snit about being left in the dark by the Americans, or even to a lesser degree the lack of consultation, but the impression that what Canada had to contribute had not mattered and would not matter. "Our fate would be determined by the US strategic arsenal and not by our own efforts," he said. "The government concluded that the armed forces were a piece of diplomatic baggage that had to be carried around but for that reason had to be kept as light as possible."

The Americans had not intended that we would form this impression, but it was a turning point just as surely as the buildup of the Soviet navy or the subsequent achievement of nuclear parity by the Russians, which the Americans allowed them to attain. At any rate, from 1962 onward, the defence budget began to decline in real terms. Under Pearson, the increases did not keep up with inflation, and force levels began to decline from their 1962 peak.

At the end of 1967 or the beginning of 1968, the military in DND took the bit in its teeth and sent up a paper to the cabinet, which demanded that funding be increased or the armed forces be cut. It was Trudeau who took up that gauntlet. The moral of the story, Anderson said, was never challenge a politician when you don't know you can win. Trudeau, therefore, rode a wave that had begun under Pearson and simply deepened the trough. Some argue that unification had already sapped the military. Anderson denied that it had a fundamental impact, though it had had some. Some sycophants had been promoted, and it was certainly a shock to the military system. Now the military was about to get another.

The Defence Reviews
Shortly into his term, Trudeau announced that foreign and defence policy would be reviewed. The bureaucracy in its wisdom decided to conduct two reviews, one of foreign policy and one of defence. The first Defence Policy Review was done during the summer and fall of 1968 by Anderson and Chuck Marshall of Defence Liaison 1 at DEA. A lot of people were involved and saw it, from **Basil Robinson** to General Fred Sharp, the CDS. There was not as much reciprocity in the Foreign Policy Review, which in any case got diverted into a review of our relations with Europe. Its code name was STAFEUR, and it was run by **Robert Ford**, the ambassador in Moscow. It took place while the second Defence Review was under way. The second review was necessary because the first one had been rejected when it went up to the cabinet in November 1968. In the cabinet's opinion, it was not fundamental enough; it merely defended the status quo. So Defence Minister **Léo Cadieux** had to bring it back to DND.

The paper produced by the second review dealt with all the options, from unarmed or lightly armed neutrality to maintaining the status quo. It offered a range of options. In the event, Anderson maintained, the wrong ones were chosen.

Take the neutrality question. There were two possible options: heavily or lightly armed neutrality. Maintaining the former would require three times the current defence budget, and it might be destabilizing because a large armed force would exist whose intentions were not tied down to those of either superpower. The lightly armed option was in that case better.

What the government really wanted was clear to Anderson. It wanted to reduce expenditure, which meant a reduction in the armed forces, which meant a reduction in commitments, which meant a reduction in Europe. "I think expenditures are the key," he said.

The amazing thing was that the Americans put up with it, but in fact the politicians could get away with cuts because of Canada's propinquity to the United States: Robert Sutherland's "involuntary guarantee."[11] By the late

....
11   See Robert J. Sutherland, "Canada's Long Term Strategic Situation," *International Journal* 17 (Summer 1962): 223. Sutherland served in the Defence Research Board and established a substantial reputation as an analyst.

1960s, the Americans needed us much less in North America. The bomber threat was receding, and the DEW line was not as important as it had been. They were almost prepared to guarantee us without our lifting a hand.

The ministers saw things strictly in terms of security, the unconscious lesson of Cuba. They couldn't see how our forces in Europe guaranteed our security, and they thereby missed the point. NATO was really needed because it "has got the European devil off our back," the generational wars of the Europeans.

Although the Americans didn't complain much about our role in North American defence, they were concerned with our behaviour in Europe. They thought we were a bad example, both to the Europeans and to Congress.

In the second draft of the Defence Review, Anderson made absolutely certain that the word "sovereignty" was never included. Unfortunately, it was slipped in, and it duly appeared in Trudeau's April 1969 speech in Calgary, the one written by **Head** ...[12]

The second draft of the Defence Review was ready in February 1969, and it was to be considered by the cabinet during the last weekend in March. Once again, it was just defence, no foreign policy. The day before the cabinet met, the two ministers, **Mitchell Sharp** and Léo Cadieux, met with their officials in the SSEA's office in the East Block. The DEA gang were all there, led by Sharp and Marcel Cadieux. Their team had all been in and out of Defence Liaison (Jim Nutt, **Michael Shenstone**, and **Basil Robinson**). Sharp had the briefing book for the cabinet in his hand and began to leaf through it. He came to a paper titled "Defence Review, 1969." It started with a quote from Barbara Ward and went on from there.

Who had written it? Was it John Roberts? Trudeau himself? At the time, nobody mentioned Ivan Head in the PMO as the possible author. Later, Anderson learned who was on Head's Non-Group team: the Treasury Board man was Henri de Puyjalon, but he did not know of a general or of any serving officer.

The Head paper was posed in the form of issues and questions, but the intended answers to the questions were obvious. Also, it gave armed forces levels for five to ten years hence, which added a certain predictive quality to

....

12 Trudeau himself told the authors that he ad libbed the Calgary speech and did not use Head's text (see page 377).

the document. The forces would be confined to domestic duties – civil duties, in effect, or policing: the CF would have a strength of 50,000; there would be a coast guard navy; 1,800 troops would remain in NATO to be in the Allied Command Europe mobile force; and Canada would stay in NORAD.

Anderson heard that Sharp telephoned Trudeau, asking who had drafted the document and why it didn't carry the signature of Cadieux, his defence minister. If Trudeau did not wish to receive advice from the appropriate minister, he should ask for his resignation. Sharp had done the telephoning, Anderson thought, because of his seniority and perhaps because his English was better than Cadieux's.

The DEA and DND people did not hear this phone conversation with Trudeau. Sharp had asked them to leave while he made a few calls. Anderson walked down Parliament Hill with the DND deputy minister, Elgin Armstrong, who told him how very unhappy Léo Cadieux was with the trend of events. Armstrong had talked him out of resigning on the grounds that he could do more good inside the cabinet than he could outside, limited though that might be.

Out of the end of the March debate came the 3 April 1969 statement announcing the new NATO policy. It really rotted his socks, Anderson said, because of its many references to the defence of sovereignty. But at least, he reiterated, the Head paper was not on the agenda on the famous weekend cabinet meeting. Because it had circulated, it might have done some damage but less than Basil Robinson believed.

Certainly, Sharp and Cadieux made a difference to the situation: without them, the reduction could have been larger. In Anderson's memory, some things stood out: scrapping the aircraft carrier HMCS *Bonaventure* because we couldn't afford it, for example.

As for the attitudes of cabinet ministers, the pro-NATO ministers were Cadieux, Sharp, **Martin,** and probably Drury, though the latter would not have been to the fore. Cadieux was totally opposed to the cuts, and Sharp was less so. Many cabinet members thought that ten thousand troops in Europe was an over-commitment; how they believed this, he could not see. And some, especially one francophone minister, regarded the military as a bunch of sacred cows. In the final analysis, Sharp was a realist.

The DND people had also hoped that the cabinet would choose one component or the other to be phased out in the NATO force. But the CDS, General Jean Allard, couldn't face up to it. Allard did not want a fight between the army and the air force, which would have ensued from a choice. So bits and pieces were chosen ...

H. BASIL ROBINSON (1919-2013)
INTERVIEW | OTTAWA, 5 AUGUST 1987

Robinson was deputy USSEA in 1964-70, deputy minister of northern affairs from 1970 to 1974, USSEA in 1974-77, Northern Pipeline commissioner in 1977-79, and special adviser to the USSEA from 1979 to 1981.

On the Defence and Foreign Policy Reviews
STAFEUR was to determine whether the CF should remain in NATO. The difficulty was that the DEA people proceeded very deliberately (and would still claim that the deliberation was justified). Their conclusion, however, was that the status quo was the best option; that, coupled with the delay, was a major factor in annoying the PCO. DEA couldn't produce fresh, quick policies at a time when they were wanted.

Geoffrey Murray was responsible for the political science jargon in *Foreign Policy for Canadians;* it wasn't characteristic of him, but he thought it was current and decided to try it out. Certainly, he was hurt by Pearson's very negative reaction to his efforts, because he had been closely identified with Pearson. Really, he was trying to give Trudeau and his people what he thought they wanted. He did the best he could, and they got what they wrought.

Neither **Ed Ritchie** nor Marcel Cadieux, his predecessor, were dedicated to the kind of review that was proceeding, Robinson maintained. They regarded it as a drain on scarce departmental resources.

There was very little ministerial goading. As far as Robinson could see, **Sharp** took the view that something had to be done to establish a distance between **Trudeau**'s government and Pearson's. The minimum was a fundamental review of relations with Europe, early progress on recognizing China, and in the long run, a more open-minded look at East-West relations. Trudeau thought that DEA minds were stuck in a Cold War mould on the latter issue.

In the review, Trudeau was determined not to be influenced by other people's views of Canada. (All this, he stressed, was Sharp's interpretation of what Trudeau thought.) "I don't think," Robinson continued, "that Sharp had any particular views, except that something had to be produced. There was interest in Latin America, some on arms control, and some on North-South," he said, "but Sharp and Trudeau didn't disagree on the fundamentals."

DEA was not monolithic. There was a restlessness in the department long before Trudeau came on the scene. This was partially due to its lack of promotion opportunities, which may have prompted **Ivan Head** to leave. There was restlessness about Pearson's relations with SSEA **Paul Martin**; and interestingly, Pearson was more inclined to question the status quo than was Martin. During some of his interviews with Martin, Pearson would say that relations with Europe had to be reappraised. Martin would be dreadfully upset and would react with horror: "I wish he wouldn't talk that way." Pearson sometimes remarked on the prosperity of the Europeans. In the department, there was also a consciousness of the views of **Gérard Pelletier**, Eric Kierans, and Walter Gordon; some of the junior people favoured a review of existing policies and believed that their seniors were being unreasonably defensive. In retrospect, if there were demoralization in DEA, it was because of sentiment for a foreign policy review, pushing for it and not getting it: "I would say the [existing] positions were wise, but it was unfortunate that we could not respond to the desire for novelty ..."

The younger people in DEA probably thought that the Foreign Policy Review was good. However, the people who were connected with NATO thought that we should stay in Europe. It started off with the question of neutrality. That was apparently discussed in the cabinet and ruled out. Then there was the next question: Should any Canadian troops stay in Europe? "There was a chance that we would leave totally," he said.

The question of staying or leaving was to be discussed at a cabinet meeting during a weekend at the end of March 1969. To prepare, Sharp and **Léo Cadieux** were meeting with their officials. They had before them the Defence Policy Review, which was to be discussed the next day. The review effectively committed Canada to staying in Europe, and it had been circulated in the usual way. As far as Cadieux and Sharp were concerned, reduction, not withdrawal, was the operative word; Cadieux was unhappy about this, but Sharp rationalized it by stressing the savings in money. Reduction, therefore, became necessary for budgetary rather than political reasons; the latter, Robinson observed, Sharp could not have made himself swallow, so he found another way. The pro-NATO group in the cabinet believed that the status quo was a non-starter, so they (Sharp, Cadieux, **Hellyer**, and Drury) had argued for a reduction: that was the pro-NATO position.

Their conference was interrupted by the arrival of a new paper from the PCO. It presented an alternative policy: the withdrawal of the CF from Europe, period. "We were quite shocked, you know," Robinson said, "because I don't remember any comparable situation. The two ministers were absolutely pole-axed. They went off by themselves for half an hour and had a talk on the phone with the prime minister." They were careful to keep the officials in the dark, but it was possible to reconstruct what had happened.

It was generally known that the Trudeau cabinet would soon be reconsidering its relations with Europe, and the European allies made representations through their embassies in Ottawa and our delegation in Brussels. **Ross Campbell** added his own very able advocacy of the case for NATO. Did these pleas reach Trudeau? It would be up to the minister to forward them, but whether he did or not, they had no impact. The European views were treated as not essential to Canada's national interest. Only a warning from the United States would have been treated differently, for warnings from the Americans were the real stuff, something that could quite possibly affect "the national interest," as Trudeau defined it.

The story of the Defence Policy Review was as follows. The review had, of course, arrived in the PCO. The officials there noticed what it implied. The key person was **Gordon Robertson**, the clerk. He was not especially interested in foreign policy and seldom intervened in it. His specialty was the Constitution, and getting Trudeau properly launched was his immediate concern. Gerry Stoner, later deputy minister of ITC, may not even have known what was afoot. He did not favour withdrawal from NATO, but was he asked? Then there was **Michael Pitfield,** assistant clerk or secretary in charge of plans. At first, he took the view that DEA could come up with a change in policy, but he eventually concluded that DEA and DND were in cahoots in frustrating the will of his master, the prime minister. Pitfield and Trudeau were close. Pitfield appealed to the prime minister because he wished to rationalize decision making. He had tried to achieve this under Pearson (some of the reforms dated from 1967), but Pearson kept kicking over the traces. If he wanted to talk to Martin about something, he did. System flew out the window. But Trudeau believed strongly in rational process, as did Pitfield. Then there was **Marshall Crowe**, who took the view that East-West accommodation deserved a higher priority than it was getting from DEA; his bent was toward withdrawal from Europe and détente. And then there was Ivan Head, who from his service with DEA in Malaysia had acquired a preference for North-South. He may not have been especially opinionated on the withdrawal (he did not have a "comprehensive view of his own," Robinson stated), but he recognized his master's wish, and "in any event, he wouldn't be on the pro-military side."

These people were quite correctly interpreting Trudeau's views: "I think he knew what he wanted." His acolytes, therefore, formed what they called the Non-Group. They met and worked in secret, and their purpose was to prepare an alternative policy for withdrawal that met their master's specifications.

What Robinson resented at the time, and still resented, was that this tactic was underhanded. They worked in secret and didn't bring their policy out in the open. They relied on surprise and stealth. He did not object to the PCO presenting views on foreign policy, as long as it was done in the open. The secrecy, not the provenance, was wrong.

When Sharp and Cadieux withdrew to confer with each another and then with Trudeau, Cadieux seemed the more upset, the one who had the greater difficulty in swallowing the paper. The paper was then "withdrawn." It did not appear on the cabinet agenda for the next day as a document to be considered. It became a kind of "non-paper." But of course it had already been circulated, and the damage was already done. It had influence.

"I felt sort of sick about it," Robinson recalled. He knew, because Trudeau had told him in October 1968, that the prime minister wanted to shock the department into a fundamental reappraisal. But there was so much happening: Czechoslovakia, Vietnam, long days; there was a "new world" of flow charts and planned program management. "It used to drive Marcel Cadieux wild," Robinson remembered. There was planning (which was fine, but nobody ever explained to him how it could be of practical use). There was nickel-and-diming with the Treasury Board. There was de Gaulle and Quebec, a major concern of Cadieux. And we had Sharp, a minister we didn't know, and on top of that a French tutorial in his office three times a week. "I felt beleaguered," said Robinson.

There was a cooling of relations as a result of the Non-Group paper episode. He did not so much blame Crowe. He was pretty frank; but Head wasn't. Though Robinson and Head continued to be civil, matters were never the same again. And Head had actually worked in Robinson's own office, back in 1961. "I never spoke to him about the paper," Robinson said.

Once reduction of the NATO commitment was chosen rather than withdrawal, it remained to work out what that entailed. The process took about a month, which meant that the result could not be announced at the twentieth anniversary meeting of NATO in Washington that April. The Europeans were curious, but they could learn nothing; there was nothing as yet to tell, though Trudeau did give a general hint in the House of Commons in April.

The next meeting was in May – of the NATO defence ministers in Brussels. At that meeting, Léo Cadieux became the bearer of a message that he had fought hard to avoid. The reaction in Brussels was sadness and distress, especially from those who believed in NATO and who saw the Canadian move as betraying the spirit of the alliance. "It was an emotional meeting," Robinson said. "I'll never forget the dignity of Cadieux or the extraordinary sensitivity with which he put across this news." Some of the smaller countries felt it keenly, especially the Belgians and the Dutch. "The British were very rough," Robinson noted. "The Americans were disapproving but not in any offensive way." The Germans had hoped that we wouldn't do it, but Robinson could not remember what they had to say on this occasion.

It was fashionable in DEA to argue that the consequences of the force cuts were many and unfavourable to Canada. Perhaps in atmospherics that was so. Some people felt let down. Denis Healey, Peter Carrington, and Joseph Luns continued to hold it against Canada.[13] The cuts may have added to a gathering impression, started under Diefenbaker and continued under Pearson (notably due to a Temple University speech that opposed the US bombing of Vietnam), that Canada was unreliable, leading in turn to a "screw-them attitude."

We knew what Trudeau wanted at that time, Robinson said, by his speeches, but also through departmental people, such as André Bissonnette, who had known Trudeau way back. They conveyed the message that he meant what he said.

USSEA Marcel Cadieux and Trudeau were not inclined to get on. This was a great disappointment to Cadieux, whose views on Quebec and the Constitution were so close to Trudeau's. But their personalities were incompatible. Cadieux liked to get your views out in the open for combat or discussion; Trudeau liked to toy with an interlocutor, to keep him off balance. He kept people at arm's length, and Cadieux just could not stand this.

....

13   Denis Healey was British defence secretary (1964-70). His bloviating about the Canadian reductions was particularly resented because the Canadians knew that Great Britain had repeatedly done the same thing. Peter Carrington, sixth Baron Carrington (1919-), was defence minister (1970-74) and foreign secretary (1979-82). He was later secretary general of NATO (1984-88).

Robinson was coy about Mitchell Sharp. In 1969, Sharp was going through the terrible personal tragedy of his wife Daisy's dementia, and every day he came to the office after horrific experiences at home. As a result, he was not himself, and he kept a mask over his emotions. Also, he had to learn his job since he had little or no background in the political side of foreign policy. He had to learn substance, and he had to learn fast. Robinson wouldn't say that he was a strong minister. We could infer what we liked. Later, however, he described Jean Chrétien in that period: one who didn't know Trudeau and kept out of his way, doing pretty well what he wanted and very successfully too. He wasn't busy scoring brownie points or intruding himself on the prime minister, this last being an unsuccessful tactic to use with Trudeau.

At DND, there was nobody who was really top class, no strategists since the death of Robert Sutherland. There were people who knew anti-ballistic missiles inside out, but they were technicians, not strategists. There was Elgin Armstrong and General Fred Sharp, both involved with the Defence Review. Armstrong was really a budgets man, allocating what spending money there was among the various components of DND. Sharp was the best of the lot and more likely to give a reasoned presentation of the defence point of view than General Allard. Rear Admiral **Bobby Murdoch** in the Canadian mission at NATO helped work up the military side of the Defence Policy Review. "I don't think our military were as good as their opposite numbers in Washington, but Sharp was the best," said Robinson. Of course, their reaction to Trudeau's cuts may well be imagined. But they accepted the government position because they were trained to accept it, whatever it was. Trudeau remained a total mystery to them.

Robinson commented briefly on whether DEA should have lobbied more strongly for its point of view. The DEA people did raise their positions socially, and they had tried, with Martin, to co-opt Walter Gordon by taking him along to a NATO meeting. Marcel Cadieux did his best with Jean Marchand and Pelletier. But it might have been resented if they had been any more forward. They had got the message loud and clear that Trudeau's government would not be run by the civil servants who prepared the background briefings.

But Trudeau, as a general rule, was deliberate and very cautious in taking decisions. Officials were always present in cabinet committee and would speak if their minister wanted them to. Sharp presided at the Cabinet Committee on External Affairs and National Defence, but he did not try to impose his views. That was characteristic: he gave his views but did not insist on them. And Pelletier and **Donald Macdonald** sat on that committee. They "gave us a pretty active session" prior to the Defence Review.

Perhaps, Robinson reflected, "the fact that we didn't jump to the tune from PCO affected the attitude towards us in terms of allocating resources." Certainly, the Treasury Board attitude toward DEA was hostile. Northern Affairs was a very different matter: it was fashionable. With Chrétien as its minister, it was supported by the PCO and the Treasury Board and everybody else.

As for the administrative fads of the period, they amounted to applying an administrative technique appropriate to Quaker Oats to the management of foreign policy. How, he asked, could you tell what de Gaulle would do next year, let alone tomorrow, and pretend to allocate your budget to meet it?

JOHN HALSTEAD (1922-98)
INTERVIEW | OTTAWA, 9 DECEMBER 1987

STAFEUR
The Contractual Link with the European Economic Community (EEC) began with the Foreign Policy Review's STAFEUR process. As deputy chair, he had effectively run the STAFEUR study with Paul Tremblay, ambassador to Belgium and the European Community, and Robert Ford, who were posted abroad and named as chairs to give it a high profile. Neither attended more than twice. All departments with interests abroad were invited to join. In the end, there were close to twenty members, although only ten or so regularly participated. STAFEUR was set up before the Foreign Policy Review was actually under way. It was the first of the regional studies, and its early creation came about because the most controversial ideas from the PMO centred on NATO.

Halstead couldn't remember if he had received a USSEA directive on the terms of reference for STAFEUR. But even before he became head of European Division, he himself had felt that it was high time for a new look at relations with Europe. Our ties to Europe were treated as traditional ones, but when he was posted to Paris, he was struck by how little substance there was in our bilateral links, except those with the United Kingdom and, to some extent, France. We dealt with Europe on a multilateral basis; with Eastern Europe, we dealt with the USSR but made little effort to differentiate among the others. This was a blind spot in our policy but one that had been masked by the success of our multilateral policy, especially at the UN. By the late 1960s, we were reaching the finite limits of multilateralism, and it was time to think about relations with Europe, especially in light of US power on, and influence over, Canadian policy and the increasing preoccupation of Canadians with this.

This was the philosophical background that Halstead brought to STAFEUR. He welcomed the opportunity to do the first thorough review of European policy, the first interdepartmental look at our relations. He tried to identify the domestic Canadian interests in these countries (which explains why there were country studies and why he tried to set out priorities among the countries and among functional areas).

The thrust of the STAFEUR conclusions was that relations with Europe, except for the United Kingdom and France, had been neglected, that there were opportunities to broaden and deepen relations and put more substance into them to serve Canadian interests and to help achieve better balance in our external relations. The word "counterweight" wasn't used, but the idea of balance was there, including the EC as offering the best possibility for trade diversification and a substantial source for investment and technology. As well, cultural and personal ties offered the opportunity to forge meaningful links. There was no recommendation to negotiate a link or agreement with the EC, but the language vaguely pointed that way.

The controversial part of STAFEUR dealt with NATO and Canadian security interests in Europe. DEA knew that **Trudeau** had made up his mind to alter the NATO commitment, but it was unclear whether that meant withdrawal or cuts. Trudeau had intentionally opened up the debate in public and in the cabinet on all options. But after looking at the options with an open mind, STAFEUR concluded that we should stay in Europe. **Basil Robinson** had chaired an informal group in DEA on this part of the preparation of the STAFEUR report. The argument made for staying in was consistent with the line above.

Halstead clearly remembered telling Marcel Cadieux when he submitted the STAFEUR report that, when discussing relations with Europe, we needed a review of US relations. You couldn't talk about one without the other. But Cadieux said that the subject of the United States was too big to cover in the available time as it touched on so many areas of domestic policy.

The next step was the *Foreign Policy for Canadians (FPC)* pamphlet on Europe, which he drafted on the basis of the STAFEUR report. In preparing the draft, he had to take into account the NATO decision, and the STAFEUR argument had to be altered there, weakening the case for special ties. But curiously, the message from the PMO was that after the NATO cuts, it was more important than ever to emphasize economic, political, and cultural ties. **Head** and Trudeau ("could you tell one from the other?") used this line in public too. To Halstead, the most important decision was not that we cut NATO forces, but that we chose to stay in NATO and keep reduced forces in Europe. In the long run, that made it possible to pursue the STAFEUR policy. Again, in *FPC,* the language pointed toward a link without directly saying so.

MICHAEL SHENSTONE (1928-)
INTERVIEW | VIENNA, 2 FEBRUARY 1989

A DEA officer, Shenstone was the department's premier Arabist, with service in Lebanon, Cairo, Washington, Saudi Arabia, and on the Middle East and Africa desk in Ottawa. He worked on the Defence Policy Review and in Austria, the disarmament negotiations, and the Conference on Security and Cooperation in Europe.

He began with the Defence Review
In 1968, Shenstone headed the NATO and North American Defence section in DEA under Jim Nutt. When **Trudeau** came in, he was DEA's man on the Defence Review, and he worked with **John Anderson** and in parallel with **John Halstead**'s team.

Referring to a personal memorandum that he had made at the time, Shenstone said he was present on 28 March 1969, when **Sharp** and **Léo Cadieux** saw the **Ivan Head** Non-Group paper. He himself had picked up the phone in the outer office and heard Cadieux blasting at Trudeau in "very cross, very *joual*" French. That meeting had been intended to draft a final statement for the cabinet, but in fact it had spent the first few minutes dealing with a Diefenbaker request that he go to former president Eisenhower's funeral! Sharp had taken out the Head report, Cabinet Document 310/69, and asked what it was. Shenstone read it to the group, and there was great shock when everyone realized that it varied from the DND/DEA line and, more, that it was under cover of a note from the prime minister. The paper included an anti-NATO comment from **Robert Ford** that was out of context.

The upshot of the Cadieux-Sharp telephone calls was that Trudeau withdrew the paper as a cabinet document. It was written under the direction of **Marshall Crowe** at the PCO.

As far as Shenstone was concerned, Trudeau was operating out of his isolationist past. He saw NATO as outmoded and felt that defence policy pulled foreign policy after it. His policy was a gesture of contempt for Europe. He retained some of this in the Peace Initiative, which was another attack on old policies, the old DEA, the old structures in the old modes. He, Trudeau, was the man to apply logic and new thinking, and to move on.

The decision to cut NATO forces by half took a long time to reach in meetings at DND. Talk of cutbacks ended only when the Contractual Link idea with Europe emerged. Trudeau probably never saw the 1969-70 cuts as a mistake, though to Shenstone, Halstead, and others, the link proved that DEA had been right at the time.

There was close connection between the officials working on the Defence Review and STAFEUR. Hume Wright of the PCO was on the STAFEUR group, but he made it clear that his participation could not bind him to agreeing with any recommendations. (Shenstone later added that Wright had seemed willing to consider withdrawal of the troops to zero.) The Defence Review was stand-pat stuff, all done in co-operation with Halstead. At one point, it was stopped to allow STAFEUR to catch up; the papers were intended as companion pieces.

DEA and DND had misread Trudeau because they were encouraged by their ministers to produce what they did and genuinely thought it the right policy. Over time, they came to feel like a band of warriors under attack for defending Canadian interests. They were DEA-oriented, and they thought Trudeau wanted their honest opinions. He didn't. In any case, the CDS, General Allard, was unpredictable because at some points he seemed to be willing to accept total withdrawal, and Elgin Armstrong was "no slouch." DND liked what DEA was doing for it and felt part of the band of warriors.

Shenstone said that Dave Golden, the deputy minister of defence production, had sent a memo to Trudeau during his leadership campaign, which, unknown to DEA, had great impact in shaping Trudeau's views. The memo called for a phased withdrawal from NATO, maintaining the status quo in North America, and the downgrading of peacekeeping.

The first DND paper on Europe had been submitted in late April 1968 and was not thought even worthy of consideration. In July 1968, a DND/DEA paper was submitted and dismissed. The major review paper that followed was to consider the non-aligned versus the aligned policies. He disagreed that Trudeau just wanted to shake up DEA – he had a profound contempt for DEA.

Referring again to one of his own memos, Shenstone said that the Defence Review was originally scheduled to be completed by September 1968 but was postponed. Cynics suggested that the recent Czech invasion was the cause – ministers might have been too sympathetic to NATO. In January 1969, heads of Canadian missions in Europe met to discuss the review, with Mitchell Sharp present. The views were sterile and cautious. Shenstone heard that Trudeau came in and said that ambassadors should let their staffs travel – "they drink in different pubs than you." In January-February 1969, the final texts of the defence and STAFEUR reviews were hammered out. The STAFEUR line was worked into the Defence Review. Both spent time dealing with non-alignment (though in the end, the cabinet didn't treat this seriously – most ministers favoured alignment).

The main effect of the review process was on DEA. Its officials became even more deeply dedicated to Canadian commitments abroad, and a team spirit among drafters developed that may not have been entirely helpful in the long run.

On Monday, 31 March 1969 (after the cabinet meeting), a PCO draft statement was received at DEA and DND, which contained most of what appeared in the public statement on 3 April. "Phased reduction" was there. The DEA people discussed this into the wee hours, and by 1 April, **Basil Robinson** had redrafted it. Shoemaker of the PCO gave Robinson the Jean-Luc Pepin formula: stay in NATO, phase out the nuclear role, and discuss the conventional role. Rolling with the punches, Robinson put the Pepin formula into the revised draft. At the cabinet on 1 April, Mitchell Sharp was to present the revised version, but there was no indication that he did so. **Paul Martin** said he was glad that he was no longer SSEA. On 2 April, Marcel Cadieux, the USSEA, insisted that the DEA revision had to be accepted. On 3 April, discussion focused on the final text, and Shenstone heard that Léo Cadieux wasn't going to resign. **Ross Campbell,** ambassador to NATO, called repeatedly from Brussels to say that Canada was going to violate its commitments. But when Sharp put this to the cabinet, **Don Macdonald** shot him down by asking which commitments were meant. Sharp couldn't cite any. Marshall Crowe said that diplomats were paid to be embarrassed. Then came the press conference at 3:00 p.m. Nutt briefed Trudeau, and some of his suggestions became policy: fudge the timing and size of the cuts and the air role. Subsequently, this became the basis of a continued DND-DEA effort to get balance. To Shenstone, none of what had happened was motivated by budgetary problems. Instead, Trudeau's view of strategic considerations played the dominant role. Happily, the word "withdrawal" was avoided, and Trudeau even told Sharp that he agreed with the STAFEUR paper. Marcel Cadieux sent a short bitter memo to Sharp after the 3 April statement.

REAR ADMIRAL ROBERT MURDOCH (1918-2004)
INTERVIEW | VICTORIA, BRITISH COLUMBIA, 25 SEPTEMBER 1987

Murdoch joined the Royal Canadian Navy in 1936, served with the navy during the war, and rose through the postwar navy as a communications specialist. He was director of naval intelligence in 1961, director general plans in 1964, and deputy chief (plans) in 1966. In 1967, he was posted to NATO as military representative, where the Trudeau defence cuts of 1969 had to be "explained" to Canada's allies. His last posting was as commander of the Canadian Defence Educational Establishment in 1971.

At NATO and the Defence Review
Murdoch was in NATO as military representative from 1967 to 1971 and spent much time with Ambassador **Ross Campbell,** who, he said, went "to the wailing wall on a daily basis" with his forceful representations about the review. Murdoch himself was asked only for occasional input from Ottawa. He didn't see the DND paper before it went to the cabinet, and his role would not have been deemed important. His task was to explain Canadian policy in Brussels. After the cuts decision, the planning was all done in Ottawa. The role of the supreme Allied commander in Europe was to allocate space to the new Canadian force and to be unhappily diplomatic.

Campbell was bright and sharp, a little, angry man. Murdoch had great regard for him and liked that Ross could be silly if he thought that tack might work. When he was being groomed to go to Japan, Campbell would always refer to "the little yellow bastards" and make DEA nervous. Campbell's post-review explosions were largely ignored in Ottawa, which was the worst thing one could do to Ross.

Ottawa was unable to see the peripheral impact of the NATO cuts. When Cadieux announced the cuts at the May 1970 NATO defence ministers' meeting in Brussels, the Dutch military representative told him that he bet no further contracts would go to Canadair from Holland. (Cadieux was so broken up by the Brussels meeting that he spent his sixtieth birthday in his bath, feeling blue, and wouldn't come to a dinner that Murdoch had laid on.) The Dutch and others felt deserted and believed that Canada was paving the way for the United States to follow its example. The view was that Canada was tearing the fabric of unity, and the allies hoped that crying loudly would force it to reconsider.

Having said that, Murdoch claimed, Canada lost little clout because of the cuts. People still listened to him and talked to him before meetings. Canada held an important place in Europe's heart and mind, as it still did today. His friends were sorry for him, but they wouldn't shoot the messenger. Canada's place in the NATO pecking order was higher than its contribution alone merited, in part because of its past role but also because of the effectiveness of the air, naval, and ground contributions. We did things well and got respect.

Militarily, the Germans filled the gap left by Canada in the Soest area very quickly, and they were not horrified by the Canadian action. Indeed, their attitude changed during his time in Brussels. In 1967, they were still tentative and accepted every request; by 1971, they were aware of their importance, becoming aggressive, and not unwilling to use their ability to replace the Canadians in Soest as leverage to get their way.

Murdoch was not surprised by Trudeau's review. Trudeau was not at ease with the military and could have lived with a demilitarized country. Even so, Joe Clark was more uncomfortable with the military than Trudeau was.

DND had misjudged Trudeau with its review paper; it was bad tactics. The military was always married to the status quo and tended to be gutless – and wedded to its pensions. What was surprising was that so few raised their voices against Trudeau's NATO decision, and it was surprising that the ADMs said nothing either. Trudeau tried no nonsense with NORAD and the Permanent Joint Board on Defence and continental defence. On this, he was sensitive.

Léo Cadieux was too nice. He wanted to stay popular. It was hopeless to pit a man of such softness against Trudeau's steel ...

GORDON SMITH (1941-)
INTERVIEW | BRUSSELS, 8 OCTOBER 1987

He began with the Foreign Policy Review
Smith was working for Peter Dobell in DEA, preparing a Memorandum to Cabinet for the Ministerial Delegation to the December 1967 NATO meetings (where the Harmel Report was being blessed and flexible response okayed).[14] The memo went up through **Basil Robinson** and Marcel Cadieux, but the minister, **Paul Martin,** sent it back with three-quarters of its contents eliminated – all the stuff about political problems in the NATO alliance, compensation to Canada for bases lost in France, and so on. According to Martin, there was no need for this stuff to go to the cabinet. All that remained was boilerplate. This shocked him, Smith said.

After talks with ministers (such as **Donald Macdonald** and Jean-Pierre Goyer), he had become convinced that **Trudeau** and friends were irritated by Martin's refusal to allow discussion of foreign policy. It was clear to him that Trudeau intended a major review of foreign and defence policy. Martin preferred to deal with Mike Pearson, and Trudeau felt alienated from foreign policy as a result. Trudeau was also turned off by Martin's rhetoric about paying dues and contributing to collective security, as there were never any references to Canadian national interests. These, to Smith, were the main reasons for the review, with all options up for consideration. (Trudeau could also use squishy rhetoric, but his head was always strictly calculating national interest.) ...

The DEA and DND papers for the review were only routine regurgitations, especially on the Defence side. They made no effort to respond to the concerns of the new political generation. Very conventional stuff. He saw the papers when he was posted to NATO in May 1968, and he worried about them; he didn't know whether **Ross Campbell,** the ambassador to NATO, worried over them as well.

The NATO force cuts
The original decision after the weekend cabinet meeting was to take all the CF out of NATO. But the government was argued out of this, with Campbell

....
14 Belgian foreign minister Pierre Harmel's 1967 report laid out a dual-track policy for NATO's relations with the USSR: political détente and adequate defence.

helping. The first public announcement was for a two-thirds cut to three thousand men, with the army in a mobile role – no tanks, no heavy equipment. General Michael Dare, the vice CDS, was the key there. The army was appalled by this, fearing that it would be sacrificed in the event of a war. In the process of negotiating with SACEUR, the force was levered up to five thousand.

At the NATO meeting in May 1969, **Michel Dupuy**, the deputy permanent representative, was an expert at negotiating, and he did the subsequent communiqué with the US representative, Tim Stanley, who wanted tough language about Canada. The officials worked on this over lunch, and Dupuy, who had just arrived at NATO and knew nothing of the issues, dragged out the discussion, spoke French, and used the pressure of time. Stanley exploded and left, he was so frustrated. The communiqué presumably was weaker on Canada than might otherwise have been the case.

This was a difficult period in NATO, Smith claimed. The delegation was arguing with Ottawa that the cuts were a mistake (including one telegram that Smith drafted to Trudeau when the die was cast) and simultaneously arguing with the allies; Joseph Luns of the Netherlands was especially harsh. Admiral **Murdoch** and Campbell were fighting over other things. Murdoch was completely opposed to the cuts; Campbell, as a civil servant, had to be more circumspect.

The NATO response was especially negative from the Europeans, who wanted to send a message to the United States (Senator Mike Mansfield et al.). The Americans initially were softer in their response than the Europeans, which made the Europeans redouble their efforts until Washington realized it was sending the wrong signals. The Americans then piled on us. Certainly, the reaction was far greater than the political and military consequences of the cuts.

Smith thought that the cuts did negatively affect Canadian influence at NATO. Our voice was reduced, and we had less influence on European security questions. The allies didn't feel a need to accommodate Canadian views in reaching consensus. But on balance, he could not say that our influence was enormously reduced and could give no examples of harm done, except that **Ivan Head**'s push for the Contractual Link didn't get far. Would it have done any better if the NATO cuts hadn't occurred? They certainly didn't help ...

The Defence White Paper
Don Macdonald spoke to Smith at the Nuclear Planning Group meetings in the fall of 1970. Macdonald had gone to DND with the mandate to produce

a Defence White Paper. During his first months there, he was preoccupied by the FLQ crisis of October 1970. Macdonald had been told that DND had difficulty producing documents that would fly in the cabinet, so Smith was to write the White Paper. He got draft thirteen or fourteen of the papers produced in DND – they read as if the events of 1968-69 had never taken place. He knew this line (produced by **John Anderson** and others) would not fly. To understand where policy was coming from, he read all the cabinet decisions and Trudeau statements. This was also the direction that Macdonald wanted. He looked at some eighteen issues – things such as Strategic Air Command overflights and NORAD Command HQ – that had gone to the cabinet but been held up because Trudeau said there was no conceptual framework to DND policy. **Léo Cadieux** and his department weren't up to producing that. Smith and Macdonald decided to get all of these decisions okayed in the White Paper – and the paper did in fact resolve every single one of those issues.

The process of writing the paper began in Brussels. Macdonald had brought documents over to Smith and talked about the direction over dinner. Smith eventually returned to Canada with a draft. He got all the time he wanted from Macdonald, who spent about fifty hours on the draft, not on how it would sell, but on policy questions. Macdonald also had meetings with academics, including one in Kingston that Professor James Eayrs refused to attend because it was confidential. He listened and talked. Macdonald, who was easy and stimulating, read the draft before it circulated through DND for comment, and he controlled the drafting process. Smith said the civilians and military in DND understood this and were supportive.

There were two areas the paper did not deal with adequately: the shape of the maritime forces and the role of the reserves. That caused problems in DND, but Macdonald decided to treat the two subjects generally because Trudeau was indifferent to them. The White Paper did reach a conclusion on a role for Canada's NATO force, which was important and the most difficult issue to get through the cabinet (it had been left up in the air since 1969). Trudeau disliked going back on the 1969 decision. The decision that Canada would get out of the nuclear roles was clear. The idea was to get out of all nuclear roles as soon as possible, and the cabinet (which Smith attended) agreed. He was astonished to learn that CF-101s in NORAD in Canada retained their nuclear capability into the 1980s. He thought this had simply happened – had the language in the White Paper left a loophole? The United

States strongly pressured Canada to keep nuclear weapons. The Americans were very well informed about the process of decision making on this topic. Were they fed information by DND people, he wondered, or listening in on phone calls?

In drafting the White Paper, Smith took as his framework the principles of 1969. He had no problem with following a national interest line or with concentric circles beginning with Canada, and there was no US or European input at all. That made Macdonald and Trudeau happy. Smith also accepted the idea that there was no direct military threat to Canada and that our only danger lay in a US-Soviet nuclear war. Thus, Canada had to keep anti-submarine capabilities and North American defence to protect the deterrent. And defending Europe was also in Canada's interest, as the Third World War would probably emerge from there.

Once the conceptual framework was in place, Smith had no trouble getting Head, the PCO, and Trudeau onside. To the horror of DND, he spent a lot of time at the PCO and the PMO because he knew that Ivan Head was the critical person. Once he had Head's agreement, he figured that Trudeau was okay. At DEA, he dealt with **Michael Shenstone**, but he felt that if there were differences between the PMO and DEA, PMO views counted most. DND bought the result but with grumbling, and Smith thought that on balance the generals found his work positive. DEA bought in too but complained about how junior Smith was. **Sharp**, he thought, chaired the Cabinet Committee on External Affairs and National Defence. He wasn't in attendance when the White Paper went through Priorities and Planning.

With the framework there, the rest fell into place. Macdonald understood that Smith would push for NATO, but Smith had little trouble persuading him. He didn't cite common values and history but Canadian security interests. Once he was convinced, Smith made the running. The paper easily went through the cabinet, with only Paul Martin, arguing for things that could never happen, showing any pique. Peyton Lyon at Carleton University asked him, "How in the world did you sell this to them? I can agree with everything. It is a reversal." In Smith's view, he had simply worked through a logically based national interest approach, and if the government thought things were different, that could only help.

After the White Paper was through the cabinet and the public, Smith saw his career people at DEA, who told him he was destined for consular work. The White Paper counted for nothing. But he had three or four offers and left in a few days. Later, **Edgar Ritchie** and **John Halstead** asked him why he'd not come to see them.

DND reorganization
Macdonald was disturbed by the way that he as DND minister worked with Elgin Armstrong, the DND deputy minister, who was weak and not in control, with the Defence Research Board, whose head operated in his own world, and with the CDS, Fred Sharp, who was the most solid of the three. Smith attended meetings of the Defence Council, where they fought like cat and dog. It was beyond belief. Macdonald was irritated that the council couldn't produce recommendations. DND was also living with the HMCS *Bonaventure* refit scandal, there was evidence of major financial difficulties, and the new helicopter destroyers (DDHs) were coming along and had to be got right. Smith tried to get Macdonald to do one thing. Coming from NATO, he had been struck by the UK Ministry of Defence, which was an integrated civil-military organization with good career civil servants. (Smith said he had begun in government with the Defence Research Board but had quit because he could see no career there.) Macdonald decided to set up what Smith recommended – the Pennefather Commission to study integrating the civil and military parts of DND. This included Henri de Puyjalon, but the main contact was John Killick, who had the best fix on DND management problems and became executive secretary to the commission. Elgin Armstrong was put out to pasture, and **Sylvain Cloutier** came in, but he decided that the commission report was dynamite, had to be killed, and copies destroyed. He then implemented the report's recommendations on his own, as if the commission hadn't existed ...

HON. DONALD S. MACDONALD (1932-)
INTERVIEW | TORONTO, 5 APRIL 1988

Minister of national defence
Macdonald became defence minister in 1970. He had hated the role of House leader (listening to NDP House leader Stanley Knowles!).[15] But he'd stuck it

---

15   Stanley Knowles had a reputation for being boring and prolix, as well as an expert on parliamentary rules and procedure.

for two years, so **Trudeau** owed him one. When **Léo Cadieux** went to Paris as ambassador, Macdonald asked for the Defence post. He got his mandate from Trudeau: in the aftermath of unification, troop cuts, and the budget freeze, get out and speak to the troops to raise morale, develop a document on policy, accept the NATO decision as final and don't try to push for further cuts, and accept the budget freeze.

He'd been at DND for only a few weeks when the FLQ crisis began in October 1970. He remembered asking Elgin Armstrong, "What the hell do we do now?" The crisis greatly improved military morale – they were doing something useful. Trudeau was gratified too, but Macdonald didn't think this altered his views of the military. That came later, under the influence of German chancellor Helmut Schmidt. Macdonald was convinced that because the two FLQ cells had operated so smoothly, they must have had a bigger organization out there, although there was no RCMP evidence of this. He said Trudeau had little admiration for the RCMP but added that Pearson's decision to keep the police off campuses had hurt their intelligence gathering. Macdonald had no recollection of the military doing intelligence gathering in Quebec, though it did keep watch for separatists in the CF. He couldn't recall any prosecutions for this. In any case, he had not the slightest doubt about the loyalty of the forces.

On DND personnel: Deputy Minister Elgin Armstrong was a fine, diplomatic, and reserved man. Nonetheless, Macdonald was relieved when he left, and **Sylvain Cloutier** replaced him. Syl had the numerate skills that Macdonald lacked and could do financial analysis. When Trudeau had asked him if Cloutier would do, he had said "terrific." General Jean Allard was a tank. General Fred Sharp was very different from Allard, and air officers generally were cut from a different cloth than the brown jobs. Fred Sharp as CDS had good political skills, and Macdonald was impressed with the way Sharp had dealt with him. General Michael Dare as vice chief of the defence staff (VCDS) was an efficient administrator and couldn't be bullshitted by other officers. General M.E. Pollard and Macdonald argued over air defence, but he could roll ideas around.

The Defence White Paper
The White Paper was largely **Gordon Smith**'s. Macdonald had met him in 1967 or so, when Smith was assisting Peter Dobell in running a parliamentary

discussion group on defence questions. Smith, in Defence Liaison of DEA, impressed him, and he had academic training and contacts in the United States and Canada. Macdonald felt that the White Paper couldn't be authored by someone inside DND – he'd get the same kind of stuff that **Mitchell Sharp** got from DEA. Smith was outside but had inside knowledge, and he produced the report, after a lot of consultation (including with him – Smith knew Macdonald's views). Although the paper took a fresh look at Canada and the world, we were locked into certain roles by our equipment. The CF-5 aircraft, for example, was there and something had to be found for it to do. The joke was that the CF-5 had enough range to go from Rockcliffe airfield in Ottawa to Uplands, also in Ottawa, but couldn't get back. The White Paper tried to give Canada a more flexible, mobile force, hence his views against a heavy tank. Also, Macdonald didn't believe that the USSR would use bombers much against North America, and this led to a downgrading of the interceptor role. In his view, we needed a surveillance capability in the Arctic instead, and this led to spirited exchanges with air force officers. Another equipment distortion was the anti-submarine role, which stopped us even getting ships into the Arctic. The White Paper's emphasis on aid to the civil power, of course, was a reflection of the October Crisis. Another task of the paper was to make the public – disillusioned by the Vietnam War – think of the military as useful; hence, it stressed aid to the civil power and disaster relief.

He agreed with the line pursued by the White Paper. In other words, he wasn't against the military. He recognized the need to co-operate with the United States in defending North America, and he saw the importance of the CF in the wake of the FLQ crisis.

During his time at DND, the department and the Treasury Board had essentially declared a truce. They had stopped fighting due to the budget freeze, and their discussions were about defining the freeze, not retarding expenditures. He didn't push to lift the freeze.

On DND organization, Macdonald recognized (after a time) the problems posed by the bicephalous nature of the department, with its separate civil and military organizations. In a budget freeze, DND cost too much money and had too much duplication. The Pennefather Report, which he commissioned, called for a fused structure at DND. Implementing this would mean that the military could fill civilian jobs, but the civilians couldn't do military ones ...

SYLVAIN CLOUTIER (1930-91)
INTERVIEW | OTTAWA, 20 JANUARY 1988

Cloutier served as Public Service commissioner, deputy secretary at the Treasury Board, and deputy minister of taxation in the Department of National Revenue before going to DND as deputy minister in 1971, a post he held until 1975.

Cloutier began with his time at the Treasury Board
His interest in DND started in 1968, when he was at the Treasury Board as deputy secretary.[16] He was trying to change the form of the estimates to give them structure, to present them in a manner that combined legal and financial sides and assisted management in setting and reporting on objectives. Despite its unification, DND was still three services with civilian and military components. He grouped all votes under a single program (except the Defence Research Board) and started cutting fat off the estimates, of which there was a lot. The DND structure wasn't geared to its mission, and the period was one of scandals (such as the HMCS *Bonaventure* refit).

Deputy minister at DND
In 1971, **Gordon Robertson,** the clerk of the privy council, told him he was going to DND as deputy minister. The government wanted a hard manager, and **Donald Macdonald** also wanted him. He didn't know Don well, but they had attended some of the same cabinet committees when he himself was deputy secretary at the Treasury Board. He had no mandate other than to make DND work.

Cloutier arrived at DND in September 1971 and found the Management Review Group (MRG) in operation under John Pennefather, trying to mesh the civil and military portions of the department. Macdonald told him to take an interest in the MRG's operations, and as he thought DND had to be redirected, he was glad to do so. The MRG could provide the way to change direction. But by the time it reported in early 1972, Macdonald was gone,

....

16   This interview and General Dextraze's below were published in a somewhat different form as J.L. Granatstein, "Making the Department of National Defence Work in the 1970s: The Deputy Minister and the CDS Remember," *Canadian Military History* 20, 2 (Spring 2011): 59-64, http://www.canadianmilitaryhistory.ca/wp-content/uploads/2012/03/7-Granatstein-DND-in-the-70s.pdf.

and Edgar Benson was filling in as minister. By then, Cloutier had his own ideas on how to run DND, and the restructure he imposed was not that recommended by the MRG, although in line with its philosophy.

Working with Dextraze

Chief of Defence Staff Fred Sharp was retiring in 1972, and he wasn't a strong manager, something Cloutier had decided by Christmas 1971. Cloutier believed that the CDS had to be strong. General Jacques Dextraze had this quality, and Cloutier got the government to name him CDS-designate early in 1972 so that the two of them could get under way as soon as possible. Sharp was a fine man who went along with the new direction, but he left the hard decisions for Jadex, as Dextraze was known, to handle. In the end, Sharp was sent on tour for the last months of his term.

Within a month, Cloutier had a key meeting with the minister, CDS, and others, and started the restructure rolling. Putting flesh on the bones took two to three months – the submission to the Treasury Board was two or three inches thick. The concepts put forward by Cloutier were novel and predicated on the basis of friendship and co-operation between the CDS and the deputy minister. He and Dextraze worked closely for five years and never once disagreed in public. When they did fight, it was in private; at a meeting, if they disagreed, they'd kick each other under the table and change the subject. Now, there was resistance to having the deputy minister with such power – co-equal to the CDS, same rank, same pay – but the deputy minister was responsible for DND management and the CDS for the operations of the forces. Certainly, Cloutier never gave an order to the CF – if that were necessary, he'd get the CDS to do it.

Restructuring DND

What he did do, Cloutier maintained, was to integrate activities that had been parallel in the three services or in the military and civilian components of the deputy minister's office. The office had about two hundred personnel when he took over; after the change, it had three or four. He created structures that let the CDS and the deputy minister both use them – this eliminated hassles and sped up the process.

The Defence Research Board (DRB) was a Crown corporation with its own budget, and it did what it wanted. In Cloutier's opinion, it needed to do what the military wanted, so it was absorbed in two stages, leaving only an advisory board, which was soon eliminated. The chief DRB scientist became a senior officer under the assistant deputy minister (ADM) materiel. This gave better resource management and made DRB serve military needs.

Cloutier also did a restructure of the CF's commands. He created Air Command, which was negotiated between himself and Dextraze, then done. He brought in General Chester Hull to be VCDS, a big, tough, first-class man and the best manager in the CF – he talked him out of retiring by saying this was the biggest job in the country. He hadn't agreed with the previous VCDS, General Michael Dare, whom he managed to shuffle off to the PCO. In 1972, the government wanted to cut budgets and asked departments to suggest cuts. When Cloutier asked Dare for suggestions, his first offering was to eliminate the reserves to save $30 million. Cloutier, horrified, could see the political fallout and refused.

In his first year at DND, he restructured the department and changed the management. He brought in Lew Crutchlow from the Treasury Board to be ADM materiel and Tom Gregg from business to head the finance side. He created military associate DMs (three-star officers) in materiel and finance, but not in personnel, where the military was on top and a civilian was associate DM.

To Cloutier, as he stated, the military wasn't special. The management of resources and people was the same as elsewhere.

His reorganization created resentment, largely due to its novelty and the fear that civilians were taking charge. This wasn't true, however; the civilians were just making an appropriate contribution. The proof was that when Cloutier left in 1975, the system didn't change. The style was different, but his system survived. There was a strong respect for authority in DND, and that helped. There were also problems with the civilians outside DND. At the Treasury Board, the secretary, Al Johnson, didn't believe in the changes, but Cloutier dealt with him by calling a meeting in which military and civilians talked with Johnson for three hours and swung him round. It wasn't Cloutier, he said – it was "we" at DND.

But he wouldn't have succeeded without Dextraze. They worked out the system together and started on this the first night they met during a mess dinner at Rockcliffe. They then went to Cloutier's house and drank crème de menthe until three in the morning. That persuaded them they could work together.

At one meeting in the summer of 1972, he, Dextraze, and General Ross, the senior personnel officer, plotted postings for the next ten years. All the CDSs for the next decade were on that list, and they determined the kind of experience that generals needed to prepare for the top. To take one example, they decided that Ramsey Withers needed policy experience and leadership of a large front-end command. They gave him both, and he became CDS in 1980.

DND and procurement

The big flaw in DND was in program development, which was tough, as there was no money. In the pre-Cloutier period, a service developed a program and then put it to the deputy minister, who had to re-do it all over again (for how could he okay something without going through it?). In his early days at DND, Cloutier received a huge stack of paper to justify the purchase of forty-eight 707 aircraft. This wasn't on the budget, which was frozen. Why forty-eight? he asked General Sharp. The Orions had to be replaced, and they needed twice as many anti-submarine warfare aircraft. Was this documented? No, Sharp said, but we need twice as many. Cloutier refused to sign.

In 1973, the navy made a case to replace the old destroyers. It started the staff work and made a presentation in two parts: on the ships it then had and on its personnel. Dextraze said what Cloutier wanted to hear. The navy should prepare a new presentation relating its mission to the ships it needed. The navy always thought in terms of where it had been – history, in other words – not of its mission. That was why the frigate program took so long. Dextraze's view was that you might have fewer toys for the boys to play with, but at least you'd have more efficient utilization of resources.

What Cloutier did was to create a programs chief, always two-star military, and integrated him under the civilians who worked in the deputy minister's office. This way, the financial concerns of the civilians could be brought to bear on the process; it worked well and faster, as capital programs had to be gone through once only. Eventually, the 707 became the Aurora and forty-eight became eighteen. He had forced the military to measure the capacity of the aircraft against the need. In his view, the military could choose an aircraft. But he had to insist on testing that choice against the economic priorities of the government and its international commitments. If you bore those in mind, then you could get Supply and Services, DEA, and ITC onside, and the submission to the cabinet would be a complete piece of work that answered all the questions. That way, you got your proposals accepted.

His aim, he said, was to marry resources to purposes; otherwise, you misused resources. When he took over, the capital budget was 12 percent of the DND budget; his goal was to get it up to 22 percent. Indeed, he got the DND budget increased within six months – with a $125 million pay raise, the first since the freeze. That was his first priority. "I'm not dumb," he said. He was also able to get the okay for things that DND couldn't have acquired before. For example, he got a decision for armoured cars reversed. They were good for nothing, and he got the tanks back, though Trudeau disliked tanks. Don Macdonald, by then finance minister, told him, "That's not why we put you there." Cloutier replied, "You should have told me." He had asked the military what tank was best, and it had said British Chieftains or German Leopards. At the same time, the Germans were negotiating to train at Shilo, Manitoba.[17] He learned that the Germans would rent out their tanks, and though the Canadians would have preferred not to use rentals, the choice was that or nothing. As it worked out, they rented tanks initially then bought them, and they could use the German tanks at Shilo when the Jerries weren't.

DND and policy

DND didn't have the people it needed to carry out its commitments. As a result, all units were undermanned. Each day, they'd meet for "morning prayers" and report on readiness. But, Cloutier asked, "Ready for what?" They started examining the shadow establishments, then deciding what they needed as war establishments, then what they could afford. This was a beginning on a White Paper process, a way of using sound analysis to demonstrate the gap between what they had and what they needed. Cloutier claimed there was no evidence of decline in military capability.

He created the ADM (policy) in an attempt to get DND more clout with DEA, which hitherto had made policy and told DND to implement it. The implementer had to have a large role in making policy, and that was why the change. He also started loaning bright young officers to the Treasury Board and bringing Treasury Board people into DND. Later programs were easier to push through as a result.

James Richardson

Cloutier served under twenty-six ministers from 1965 in all his portfolios. Defence Minister James Richardson (1972-76) was a "horse's ass," and Cloutier and Dextraze spent a lot of time trying to prevent him from doing stupid

---

17   A Canadian Forces base near Brandon.

things. At one point, Cloutier was so despairing that when he ran into Trudeau at a party, he asked to be moved from DND and told him why. Trudeau said he had the same reaction to Richardson, but added that Cloutier was in DND because he trusted him. Richardson was a small mind, impressed with his own public relations. He would make speeches only if Cloutier wrote them. Nor was he sympathetic to bilingualism, to which Cloutier had devoted much time. Once, in November 1972, Richardson asked him what he was doing.

"Bilingualism," Cloutier replied.

"It's not a priority."

"It's mine," Cloutier said. Richardson tried to stall the proposed French-language training centre at St. Jean, Quebec, sitting on the memo for three weeks. Cloutier again met Trudeau and told him that Richardson was holding it up, whereas other ministers were asking for it. Trudeau told him to try during the next week to get Richardson to sign, but if he wouldn't, Trudeau himself would. As it turned out, Richardson did sign. He also wanted to close CFB Suffield in Alberta and move the scientists to his own Winnipeg riding. Cloutier got the cabinet to block this. Richardson was the worst minister he ever served.

Trudeau and DND

Cloutier had known **Trudeau** for a long time and knew he wasn't keen on DND. It took two years to get the principle established that the capital share of the budget should be 25 percent, and by the time Cloutier left DND in May 1975, he had the 3 percent above inflation annual budget increase through. The structure that he and Jadex developed was designed to deal with Trudeau – time couldn't be wasted in having the civilians and military in DND fighting each other.

GENERAL JACQUES DEXTRAZE (1919-93)
INTERVIEW | OTTAWA, 12 APRIL 1988

Jadex, as he was known, served with the Fusiliers Mont-Royal overseas in the Second World War, in Korea with the Van Doos, and in the UN mission in the Congo. He was chief of personnel at National Defence Headquarters and became CDS in 1972, a position he held until 1977, when he retired to head the Canadian National Railways until 1982.

As CDS

He was asked to be VCDS to General Fred Sharp, Dextraze began. He said no. Then he was offered the CDS job, instead of Michael Dare, by acting minister Edgar Benson. This surprised him, as he thought he was going to Mobile Command. He said yes, and it was announced the next day (April 1972). Sharp was in the Far East. Dextraze took over in September.

When he became CDS, he applied himself to openly de-unifying where he could – naval ranks, uniforms on ships and abroad, individual ship names on caps. He didn't want new-old uniforms – he could do better things with $50 million.

Air Command was his idea. He told James Richardson, the minister, that all air should be under one command for training, maintenance, and procurement, but naval helicopters, for example, should be under Maritime Command. This was logical, but it did cause fights. It would be easier if each environment had its own air element, but that was costly.

As CDS, he travelled to the troops in the field. The VCDS ran the HQ. He took a sergeant with him to make notes on decisions so there could be follow up.

Relations with Cloutier

He and **Sylvain Cloutier** had met and talked over the necessity of ending the civil-military clash in DND. The forces had been unified, and now the civil-military operations at National Defence Headquarters (NDHQ) had to be unified. It was clear that the minister had to be at the top, with the deputy minister and the CDS together in the box immediately below. The running of the forces was the job of the CDS, and the deputy minister was to support him in getting what he needed. Syl didn't like this, Dextraze said, but was persuaded.

He and Cloutier did the integration of the civilian and military streams at NDHQ. They were both honest; they co-operated and didn't fight in public but went at each other in private. At meetings, Dextraze was in the chair, with Syl on the left and the VCDS on the right. If they disagreed at a meeting, they would delay the decision until they could resolve it in private. During one private argument, Cloutier broke down and cried, and Dextraze took him in his arms and comforted him. He then talked to Syl's wife, found out he was ill, and bugged him into seeing the doctors. It was clear that they really liked each other. He recalled that Syl would agree to divide subjects at cabinet committee presentations but then leap into Dextraze's areas. That was just his style. Once, **Trudeau** smiled at it and asked Dextraze what he had to say. In response, he began with "After hearing Admiral Cloutier –." There was a kind of shyness in Cloutier. Dextraze thought that Cloutier admired his power and strength, and his making him do things. Cloutier was a schemer, which was good, someone who could make things happen.

Dextraze admitted he had made an error in the way they divvied up posts at NDHQ under the integrated system. ADM jobs were to be interchangeable except for finance. Syl wanted policy too, but Dextraze refused. The problem was that the civilians were now taking over at NDHQ because the spots weren't fixed in concrete. Certainly, the old system didn't work. The civilians fought the military, and DND never got anywhere at the Treasury Board, where the deputy ministers always preferred the word of Cloutier's predecessor, Elgin Armstrong – a man who was really difficult to deal with – over that of the military.

As for whether he or Syl ran things, Dextraze was convinced that he did. They worked together, but it was his show. Asked how he reacted to comments that Cloutier had conned him, he was amused (sort of) and said that so long as he got what he wanted, and he did, people could think that.

Getting new tanks

He talked about tanks. Trudeau didn't want any, and Dextraze told him if that were the case, get the troops off the NATO Central Front. **Don Macdonald** also didn't want tanks or fighter aircraft. Eventually, Trudeau agreed to tanks in Europe, but Dextraze persuaded him that there had to be some in Canada, for training. Which tanks did he want? He preferred American ones if they could be secured, as the United States was the closest source of supply, but the US Army was in the midst of developing a new main battle tank. He had to get rid of the old Centurions, and the new UK tank was too heavy. The Germans were re-equipping with the Leopard I (the Leopard II was then on the drawing board), so he saw the German CDS, with whom he was friendly, and persuaded him to arrange a meeting with the German defence minister. He told the minister he needed only a hundred or so, that these could be found by giving the German units a few less. He got him to agree by stressing that Trudeau was usually in disagreement with everything but that he had agreed to a new tank. He was sure that Trudeau thought he couldn't get new tanks. As a result, Dextraze sent his ADM materiel to Germany, and it was all worked out.

Trudeau was not really anti-military. He was honest and hard working, and he had his own ideas of what was best. If you couldn't persuade him otherwise, he would do what he wanted. People were afraid of him, but not Dextraze. He usually saw him once or twice a year – in a crunch.

Dealing with ministers

Dextraze admired DND Minister James Richardson as a well-meaning good fellow. But he also said that Richardson was a dummy and a racist, and was absent when the brains were handed out. The two men fought on French-English questions, and when Dextraze asked, "Do you think you can just bury 6 million French Canadians? They won't lie down," Jim would talk about the costs of having two languages. "So just speak French," Dextraze replied. Richardson was weak in the House of Commons, so weak that he couldn't defend himself, and the Opposition eventually laid off out of pity.

When he disagreed with Richardson, Dextraze would say that he wanted to see the prime minister. Richardson would say no, but Dextraze insisted that as CDS, he had the right to do so. One day, Dextraze wrote to Richardson to tell him that he knew he wanted to be a good minister, which he could achieve if he did various things that Dextraze listed in the letter. He made only one copy and sent the original by hand. Richardson then called him, and Dextraze went over with his copy, which Richardson tore out of his hand and ripped up. "The letter has never been received," he said. But the next day, being a good fellow, Richardson telephoned to say that he couldn't sleep and to apologize. Dextraze and Cloutier had to plot together on how to deal with Richardson. When he resigned, he called Dextraze in Brussels to tell him he was going. Dextraze urged him to wait until he got home, but the next day he read that he'd quit.

Barney Danson, the minister from 1976 to 1979, was much better. He had been a fighting soldier, he understood the troops, and they understood him.

Dextraze liked Don Macdonald for his hard work. As finance minister, however, Macdonald had bitterly opposed the new tanks and was really annoyed when Dextraze kept plugging for them and finally succeeded. But as defence minister, Macdonald hadn't pushed for cuts in NATO.

He knew that the armoured cars in Canada weren't great things, with their lousy 75mm gun. But they were all he could get, they could be used to train tank crews, and they had utility in civil disorders.

IV
Canada and the United States

PROXIMITY AND DISPARITY SHAPED Canadian-American relations under Trudeau, as they have done most of the time since the end of the War of 1812. Geographically adjacent, linguistically similar, ethnically alike, economically linked, Canada and the United States seemed ideally destined for compatibility. And, most of the time, they have been compatible – much more so than the United States' other neighbours, Mexico, Cuba, or the nations of Central America. Compatibility and similarity did raise the question of why the two countries should remain two – why not one? That question exercised Canadian nationalists and alarmed American diplomats. And so, more on the Canadian side than the American, existential questions arose as to the true destiny of the continent. For these questions, American politicians and diplomats had no answer, and hoped to avoid giving one. The status quo must suffice, and would suffice. The political unity of the continent remained a Big Question, with No Answer.

Trudeau was swept into office because most Canadians hoped he could deal with the other ultimate Canadian question – national unity between English- and French-speaking Canadians. Certainly, national unity was tested during his time in office: a terrorist eruption in Quebec in 1969-70; the election of a separatist government in the province in 1976; a referendum on separatism in 1980; and a struggle, ultimately successful, to reform the Canadian Constitution in 1980-82.

Bi-nationalism was not a problem that Americans had had to struggle with, but federalism was, and the resemblances between Canadian and American federalism did not escape notice south of the border. Nor were American governments – those of Richard Nixon, Gerald Ford, and Jimmy Carter – indifferent to or ignorant of the implications for American federalism if the Canadian federal experiment failed. These were international relations of a very special kind, crucial to the Canadians but potentially very important to the Americans, who had enjoyed a stable and unthreatening northern frontier for well over a hundred years. It was one of the foundations of American security, so fundamental, in fact, that it passed as axiomatic. Good vibes and bad weather were what Americans expected from Canada, and fortunately, because of Trudeau's political skill and good fortune, that remained the case from 1968 to 1984. But as our interviews show, particularly with Tom Enders and Robert Hunter, the American government was both concerned and well disposed.

Political stability was paralleled by economic continuity. For Canadians, it was axiomatic that the United States was their biggest trading partner. This was interpreted to mean that Canada was important, unique even. And at times this worked very much to Canada's benefit, securing American attention and consideration during the Second World War and after, when it was strategically important that the two countries work as one against foreign menaces, such as Nazism or communism.

Opposition to the spread of communism was the leitmotif of the Cold War and the mobilization of American and allied resources to deter the Soviet Union and Communist China from any expansion, covert or overt. Canadians were particularly fixated on the Cold War in Europe, whereas the Americans necessarily took a much broader point of view. The whole world was their concern, and American resources and general prosperity sustained an American policy that strewed bases and commitments from Greenland to Okinawa.

For years, the United States had enjoyed a trade surplus with the rest of the world and a positive balance of payments. Economic strength undergirded economic and political self-confidence, making it relatively easy, politically, to give Canada special and favourable treatment – for example, by concluding the Autopact of 1965 that merged automobile production in the two countries, while affording Canada exceptional guarantees for investment and production. American and Canadian trade negotiators took a Canadian balance of payments deficit in automotive trade as self-evident and inevitable; what the Autopact would do was nibble at the edges of the deficit and afford the Canadians some relief.

For the Americans, discovering that Canada had turned deficit into surplus by 1970 was an unpleasant surprise. It was the more unpleasant because no matter where American officials looked, there were deficits. Since 1945, the United States had managed the international financial system, hoping to create a directed, orderly international trade environment, using a system of fixed exchange rates, backed up by a gold-exchange standard, with gold priced at US $35 an ounce. Now the foundations of the system were becoming unstable.

The American government, led by Treasury Secretary John Connally, decided it had to reform international exchanges. Convinced that a high American dollar was contributing to American exchange woes, the Nixon administration – meaning Connally and his advisers – decided to convince America's trading partners to revalue their currencies upward. The policy was one-size-fits-all, and indeed, if it were to work, all of the United States' significant trading partners had to sign on. This was the motivation for a unilateral recalibration by the United States of its international economic relationships, which was announced by Nixon in a televised address to the nation and the world on 15 August 1971. This speech launched what the Japanese accurately termed the Nikuson shokku.

The United States' most significant trading partner – the biggest – was Canada. Some of the interviews that follow tell the story of the shokku as it involved Canada, mainly but not exclusively from the Canadian point of view. The American comments come from officials who dealt specifically with Canada and therefore shared Canadians' preoccupations to some extent. What the interviews do not mention, but what readers should bear in mind, was that Canada had "floated" its dollar in the spring of 1970, abandoning the fixed exchange rates preferred by the International Monetary Fund. The Canadian dollar accordingly rose in US-dollar exchanges by more than 10 percent – a very substantial upward revaluation.

Most Canadian accounts display a fixation on trade and the components of trade, including the Autopact, whose existence was threatened as part of a package of unilateral American trade inducements – in Canada's case, a very negative inducement. Indeed, some threats did emanate from Washington; they were serious, and the people who made them were important, including Connally. Fortunately, American officials who dealt with Canada noticed what Connally proposed to do – cancel the Autopact. With the backing of the US secretary of state, William Rogers, this particular manoeuvre was aborted, as Emerson Brown's interview makes clear, almost at the last minute.

The interviews describe what followed, from August 1971 down to the spring of 1972. The Americans pressed, the Canadians resisted; the Americans argued, and the Canadians refuted. There was no solution until Secretary Connally, for other reasons, resigned, Nixon visited Ottawa – an event amusingly recounted in Ivan Head's interview – and harmony of a kind was restored.

The Canadian-American relationship continued to function but not quite in the same way as before. Trade with the United States no longer seemed to the Trudeau government to be as solid as the Rock of Gibraltar. The shokku therefore gave birth to a Canadian attempt to vary trading relations, using Europe and Japan as alternatives. This policy, called the Third Option, will be examined in the next chapter.

The American government itself recognized that something had changed fundamentally and irrevocably. American economic power was no longer sufficient to keep the world economic system functioning. Instead, the United States sought co-operation with its allies, especially the other significant economic powers. Therein lies the sudden disappearance of confrontation with Canada in 1972, a problem not so much solved as buried.

The new co-operative era was new in another sense as well. The *dirigiste* model of the international economy, in which government(s) imposed and disposed, had received a mortal blow. Slowly, through the 1970s and 1980s, governments gave way to "the market." The market was practical, for it relieved governments of an impossible burden; and it was also mystical and politically inspirational, the invisible hand, or the rising tide that raised all economic boats. Best of all, the eventual consequences did not come home to roost until the first decade of the twenty-first century.

For the time being, the American government, led by Gerald Ford and Henry Kissinger, who was secretary of state from 1973 to 1977, sought co-operation and used a Franco-German idea: annual summits of world leaders – the leaders of the most important countries, economically. The French and Germans saw this as a majority-European affair – France, Germany, Great Britain, and (eventually) Italy, with Japan and the United States, the two largest economies, available to receive instruction. The Americans, meaning Ford and Kissinger, did not see it quite that way. The Europeans needed balance. Canada had a larger economy than Italy, so Canada must join. Though the French resisted, they could not hold out forever, and in 1976 Canada became a member of the G7, the Group of Seven.

The G7 was a more important phenomenon than it seemed at the time. It allowed national leaders the freedom to exchange ideas and to discuss economic policy unshackled by ordinary constraints. Trudeau, judging by his interventions at G7 meetings, was a not undistinguished contributor. In return, he was impressed by what he heard, especially from the German chancellor, Helmut Schmidt, and there were consequences for the shaping of Canada's domestic and international policy, as we shall see in the next chapter. But it should be stressed that Canada's presence at the G7 signalled the country's closeness to the United States, a point that Donald Macdonald's interview makes plain.

Indeed, Canadian relations with the United States in the later 1970s were generally cordial, an important point given the calamitous eruption of oil prices after 1973. Until the 1960s, the United States was the world's largest oil producer, and it used its position to keep oil prices down. Indeed, low oil prices were a major contributor to Western (but mainly American) prosperity. At the end of the 1960s, however, the American position eroded. Domestic production fell, but demand did not. A belief swept the world that oil reserves were nearing exhaustion, that there was a crisis of supply that would only get worse. Oil producers, particularly Arabs, encouraged this belief. The United States fell to third place among oil-producing countries, and the ability of Western oil companies to regulate petroleum markets lapsed. Oil prices rose, and rose steadily. Saudi Arabia, not the United States, became the arbiter of the world's petroleum market, and the Organization of Petroleum Exporting Countries (OPEC), not Esso or Shell, set the world price. This moved in just one direction: up.

Canada was an oil producer. Until 1970, the main objective of Canadian oil policy was to sell as much of the stuff as quickly as possible to the United States. After 1970, that changed, and some of our interviews reflect the contradictory nature of Canadian-American petroleum relations. The oil crisis also promoted the Middle East to be for the first time a major concern in Canadian foreign policy.

Oil and its consequences contributed to President Jimmy Carter's failure to win re-election in 1980. Oil prices, and consequent wage-price inflation, helped precipitate Pierre Trudeau's defeat in the election of May 1979. Trudeau was back by the spring of 1980, but Carter was gone, politically, for good.[1] Instead of the Democrat Carter, there was the Republican Ronald Reagan.

Reagan, as the Canadian ambassador Allan Gotlieb and the American ambassador Paul Robinson agreed, was favourably disposed to Canada. Nobody really knew why (one rumour was that Reagan, a Hollywood actor, knew and liked Canadian actors such as Mary Pickford or Glenn Ford), but it was

---

1 Carter, along with Fidel Castro, would serve as a pallbearer at Trudeau's funeral in 2000.

a sentiment of long standing. In the final interviews in this chapter, Gotlieb and Robinson discuss how Trudeau's aversion to Reagan nevertheless did not lead to negative results, despite nationalistic economic policies in Canada that were aimed squarely at American investment.

IVAN HEAD (1930-2004)
INTERVIEW | OTTAWA, 6 AUGUST 1981

Head spoke on his relations with Henry Kissinger
Kissinger may have got a favourable impression of **Pierre Trudeau** from William Yandell Elliott of Harvard.[2] Trudeau and Elliott had a considerable correspondence that went a long way back and that touched on substantive issues. To his face, Henry Kissinger gave every impression of being impressed by Trudeau.

Kissinger throughout was "principled" in his willingness to hear the Canadian side when it was presented. Head could always get through to Kissinger, who believed in returning his calls, even to or from the California White House in San Clemente. For example, when the Americans were planning to go off the gold-exchange standard in 1971, they held preliminary discussions with the Europeans. The Canadian embassy got wind of it but couldn't break into the discourse. Kissinger took Head's call in Santa Barbara, and they agreed on the viability of Head's argument; it resulted in the December 1971 meeting between Trudeau and Nixon, the one so misreported in the press, where Trudeau was wrongly quoted on things.

It was true that the ability to get one's calls taken implied that one did not use them to pass the time of day. Still, Head claimed that he couldn't remember a single instance when Kissinger had refused a call or was unavailable when Head came to Washington. Theirs was a first-name relationship. Kissinger was a geopolitical power player. He may not have seen the political side of Canada, but he saw the geopolitical. It was useful to the United States to have the Canadians onside and not bitching.

....

2 Elliott was, if anything, as unfavourably disposed to Trudeau as Trudeau was to Elliott. See John English, *Citizen of the World: The Life of Pierre Elliott Trudeau*, vol. 1, *1919-1968* (Toronto: Alfred A. Knopf, 2006), 131-33.

Kissinger could be skeptical, as he was of our "largest trading partners" argument in 1971, but he was helpful in getting US policy on domestic international sales corporations almost all the way back to the starting gate ...

Trudeau and Nixon

In 1968, the United States did not view Trudeau with suspicion. Not much news came Head's way, however, since he wasn't yet much involved; that began with Trudeau's 1969 trip to Washington ...

Trudeau was aware of the importance of his 1969 Washington visit. He instinctively felt more at home in Europe than in the United States. But the Americans "do it to you" – there's the helicopter and the lawn and the Marine Band and the feeling, hey, I've seen this on television. There was the Oval Office meeting with the president, and then it was down the hall to meet the others in the cabinet room.

It's great if you're the guest, but you have to remember that for Nixon you're one of three or four appointments in an afternoon. When Nixon received Trudeau, he still had TV makeup plastered over his face from his previous engagement. Everything in Washington is orchestrated and mechanical.

When Trudeau met other number ones, he was genuinely deferential; he liked to remind Head, when Head was off on one of his jaunts, that receiving Trudeau's emissary was very far down the list for most government leaders and that Head must try to see it from the host's perspective. But on the 1969 visit, Trudeau's modesty at the White House, his "simple graciousness," stole the show.

All told, Head saw Richard Nixon twice more for a couple of hours. The second occasion was in December 1971, when Trudeau came down to Washington some months after the Nikuson shokku. On that occasion, Kissinger and Head were in the Oval Office with their two principals, while the rest of the Americans and Canadians were down the hall in the cabinet room, wrestling unsuccessfully with their problems. Simon Reisman, Head said, described it as "knee deep in blood."

Trudeau was thoroughly briefed, as he insisted on being for such meetings. Some months had elapsed since Nixon had made a gaffe about Japan being America's largest trading partner, and Trudeau had taken a lot of flak for it. He was not deferential to Nixon, giving him a little economics lesson that he had distilled from his briefing materials. He politely left Nixon an out, allowing that the president might have been wrongly briefed. As it happened, Canada that year had a current account surplus with the United States, the only one in ages, if not ever. Trudeau told Nixon that Canada was America's largest trading partner and then led him through the current account balances historically. He said that if Nixon was aware of this, then he, Trudeau, must conclude that the United States had taken the conscious decision that Canada must never, ever, be in surplus with itself, and from that he must draw appropriate conclusions. These were that the only way to get US dollars was from capital account, to sell more and more of Canada to the United States. "He just seized Nixon and forced him into a corner," Head recalled. But at the end, Nixon made demurring noises, and Kissinger took the sense of it to be that the Canadians should be accommodated. It would not work, he said, if Nixon ordered this or that; rather, it would be played just so. And it happened just as Kissinger said it would.

That evening in the White House, Nixon held a small dinner party for the Canadians, with about twelve people in attendance. Nixon had gathered his colleagues, from the chief of protocol through to Treasury Secretary John Connally, to let Trudeau know what they thought of the Canada-US relationship. One by one, he called on them to speak; it was like a seminar. They performed superbly, in Head's recollection. Trudeau showed no deference to Nixon, and Nixon gave no sign that Trudeau was wasting his time. It was "a good evening."

Head remarked again on the two parallel meetings, one in the Oval Office and one in the cabinet room. He had stayed afterward to confer with Kissinger on their understanding of what was said and what was agreed. When he got back to the Madison Hotel, he found long faces on the economists who had been in the cabinet room and a smile on Trudeau's. The conference in the cabinet room had "come to absolute naught," but there was "a sense after the Oval Office that there was movement."

When Nixon came to Ottawa in 1972, it was different. Head realized now that the Americans had decided to bomb Cambodia, and Nixon obviously had things on his mind. The occasion was unpleasant at the start because Nixon's advance team threw its weight around, especially on the question of carrying firearms. Head told his staff to stand firm and refused to see the person in charge; he also told the US ambassador, Adolph Schmidt, that if the fuss persisted he would be willing to call the whole thing off, which caused the advance party to subside.

H.R. Haldeman,[3] an unpleasant creature, came along for the Nixon visit. His contribution was to tell Head and the Canadians that the Americans would not attend the theatre supper that Trudeau had laid on for them at the National Arts Centre. Head and Trudeau found this absurd. So, after the theatre, Trudeau naturally offered Mrs. Nixon his arm and swept the party into the appropriate room, where dinner was soon under way. Haldeman made a scene on the sidelines, and Kissinger appealed to Head, who decided to finesse the situation. He glided up to the head table and explained to Trudeau that Haldeman was insisting the US party must leave. Trudeau very graciously said he could understand that pressing matters called, and of course they could go. Nixon said, no, no, and they stayed.

Could Head account for the "asshole" comment in the Nixon tapes?[4] No, except as a reflection of Nixon's style: profane when he wanted to make a point.

Nixon's secretary of state William Rogers was decent, gentlemanly, and patrician but also down to earth. He came once to Ottawa, where there was a working lunch at Rideau Gate; Head attended and fielded some questions referred his way by SSEA **Mitchell Sharp**. There was no sign of resentment regarding Canada's NATO cuts; indeed, Rogers seemed very well disposed toward Canada. The fuss about the NATO cuts came from the Europeans, from British defence secretary Denis Healey, and not from the Americans. But compared to, say, Cyrus Vance, who knew his way around, Rogers was "just a bit out of it ..."

The Vietnam International Commission for Control and Supervision
On one important occasion, the Americans did "absolutely" take Canada for granted, Head recalled. That was during 1973, in connection with the Vietnam International Commission for Control and Supervision (ICCS).[5] DEA understood that Canada might be called upon for peacekeeping assistance in

---

3 H.R. "Bob" Haldeman was Nixon's chief of staff. See his *The Haldeman Diaries: Inside the Nixon White House* (New York: Putnam, 1994).
4 Douglas Brinkley and Luke Nichter, eds., *The Nixon Tapes, 1971-72* and *1973*, 2 vols. (Boston: Houghton Mifflin Harcourt, 2014, 2015). In 1971, Nixon referred to Trudeau as "an asshole," a remark that was picked up by the White House recording system.
5 The first international commissions for Indochina were formed in 1954 as the International Commissions for Supervision and Control. In 1973, the new International

Vietnam and had studied the matter quite extensively. Canadian thoughts on "supervisory mechanisms" and the fact that they were available were communicated to Washington, where they met with polite interest. (USSEA **Ed Ritchie** even set up a task force to study the subject in 1972. Informed that Canada was ready as a good friend to help out, the State Department showed appreciation.)

Canada was told that the United States wouldn't tout the idea around or use it to embarrass Canada. But once, when Head was en route from South America, he stopped off in Washington for breakfast with Kissinger at the White House. Kissinger indicated that the United States was taking action on the "documentation" of this and that he knew the State Department was not keeping Canada informed. Secretary of State Rogers subsequently phoned Ottawa.

Then, Kissinger suddenly held a press conference and informed the world that the war in Vietnam was over and that Canada was one of the nations to go on the ICCS to supervise the truce. The United States had evolved its own supervisory organization – the ICCS – and had paid no attention to the Canadian ideas.

So, Ed Ritchie, Mitchell Sharp, Trudeau, and Head met. The Canadians worked out "a sophisticated response," saying that Canada would participate in the commission but only for a limited time. They also let it be known they were unhappy about it, unofficially albeit publicly. But, Head said, Kissinger always played the game and always by the rules – very politely, in his experience ...

The Parti Québécois victory, 1976
What then about the Parti Québécois (PQ) election in 1976? Did that lead to a decision to cool it as far as the United States was concerned? No, certainly not, said Head, who returned to the events of the early 1970s. Trudeau was remarkably even-handed where Nixon was concerned, as over Amchitka, the underground nuclear test in Alaska. He was not about to be "eyeballed" by Nixon, but he would work with him and the United States when necessary.

....

Commission for Control and Supervision took shape to monitor the peace in Vietnam. Confusingly, both commissions were usually called the International Control Commission(s), or ICC.

Relations with Ford and Carter
Things generally went smoother under Gerry Ford.[6] Head got along well with Brent Scowcroft, the national security adviser, who was "practically ideal" for the job. Ford was a terribly decent guy too, who saw Trudeau as a player in the North American relationship. He was probably told that Trudeau was a good guy, and that was enough ...

Under Carter, it was different. Human rights turned out to be a problem, and Carter's National Security Council (NSC) adviser, Zbigniew Brzezinski, was playing his own games. Carter tended to work through Brzezinski or through his friends. Even Mrs. Carter had her own foreign policy, and this personalized system was the damnedest thing to work with ...

On Thomas Enders and Brzezinski
As for US ambassadors during this period, they were nice but not outstanding until Thomas Enders. He was the exception, the best of the US ambassadors. "My god, he was good, so very active," Head stated. He was plugged into Kissinger and Scowcroft, and you knew that he could contact them and get results. In Ottawa, he was a "straight shooter." Perhaps Enders had been sent to Ottawa in response to continuous complaints to Kissinger about the quality of US ambassadors. Curiously, Sir Peter Hayman, the high commissioner from the United Kingdom, was effective too.

Head knew that Enders and Brzezinski differed on the Quebec issue. Trading on his upbringing in Quebec, Brzezinski believed that the separation of the province was ordained by history.[7]

Head hadn't known Brzezinski well before November 1976; he had hoped that Richard Gardner of Columbia University would be Carter's NSC adviser instead of Brzezinski. But he professed great admiration for Brzezinski's acuity and eloquence. Initially, Brzezinski was almost deferential in his approaches to Head and company, but this didn't seem to last. On later occasions, Brzezinski would explain to Jimmy Carter, even in Trudeau's presence, that he had his own views on Quebec, which he certainly preferred to Trudeau's. He had once done a paper for the NSC in which he explained

....

6   Ford was Nixon's successor as president, August 1974 to January 1977.
7   The son of the pre-1939 Polish consul in Montreal, Zbigniew Brzezinski (1928-) got his BA and MA at McGill University, followed by a PhD at Harvard. Ironically, he had once aimed at a career in the Canadian foreign service.

his point of view; his views, in Head's opinion, were not in the US interest. The Americans had certainly worked out stand-by positions to protect their interests (such as the use of the St. Lawrence Seaway) in the event of Quebec separating.

Carter, however, didn't seem to reflect this. Where Brzezinski was very hard-nosed with everybody (unlike Kissinger, who was like that with the Soviets only), Carter liked Trudeau and tried to get along with him. He wanted warm relations with Canada and with Trudeau. There were issues: border TV, advertising in *Time* and *Reader's Digest* (the Canadian position was silly), and on our side, the convention tax exemptions for US conventioneers. Carter liked to be a "big picture guy," but he certainly got down into the details of these issues. He was nice: the born-again Christian aspect certainly came through on the three times that Head saw him: Washington, the London G7 summit, and the NATO reunion.

Secretary of State Cyrus Vance, too, was "an awfully nice guy." He was competent and decent – Canadians got along better with Democrats, Head said. The relationship was in good hands with Vance.

Vice President Walter Mondale was also a good friend of Canada; his principal interest was the security of oil and gas supply for exposed border states. While still a senator, under Nixon, he had visited Ottawa in connection with this subject. Head arranged appointments for him, which caused conniptions at DEA, but so what? Head kept Kissinger informed, and Kissinger offered no objections at all.

The United States wanted support for Carter's human rights initiatives. Their fervour took the Canadians by surprise. Now, the Canadians certainly welcomed what Carter had to say about Latin America, and they liked his socio-economic ideas: "good, just like us." But human rights elsewhere "put us on the defensive." Head remembered the press conference after Carter's first meeting with Trudeau, apparently uncomfortably. "It's not what you say about these things, it's what you're able to do," he said, and the United States could do more than Canada ...

RUFUS SMITH (1922-91)

INTERVIEW | WASHINGTON, DC, 14 JANUARY 1988

Smith served in Canada during the early 1960s, was on the Canadian desk in the US State Department from 1966 to 1968, back in Ottawa as deputy chief of mission from November 1968 until 1972(?), and then back in Washington as deputy assistant secretary for Canadian affairs.

Smith began with the Defence Review

He had met **Trudeau** while Trudeau was teaching in Montreal. He knew him as a liberal, no firebrand, an intellectual not directly involved in politics ...

The Foreign Policy Review, or the impression that he received from the PCO, was to be a fresh look, an attempt to define the Canadian national interest. To Trudeau, nothing was out of bounds, and no bias was evident. No one said he was unfair here. Smith received hints of what was happening, what was being questioned, but nothing firm enough to provide a basis for a recommendation to Washington. Perhaps the time might come when the United States had to do something, but he'd learned that lecturing Canadians on their own interests wasn't a good idea, so he was cautious.

When the Defence Review emerged on 3 April 1969, there were sighs of relief that it was less bad than feared. Still, the concern that Canada was getting a free ride remained strong. The US reaction was muted, with no sense that Canada was dissociating itself from NATO. There were hints of disagreement with the policy in DND and DEA. He also remembered hearing of a dismaying NORAD paper written by someone knowledgeable. But because it was by someone who knew the facts, he didn't push hard. This was often the US response, so as not to appear heavy-handed.

Trudeau and Nixon

He had heard nothing to suggest any difficulties between President Nixon and Trudeau. He recalled a governor general's dinner in 1972, when Nixon spoke to an audience that was not predisposed to admire him. He had never heard a speaker hold an audience so well. John Turner, sitting with him, said "gangbusters."

One of Trudeau's concerns was US balance of payments policy. Early in his first term, he spoke to the *New York Times* and referred to the balance of payments deficit with the United States, which could be carried only with a US capital inflow. But the concern was for the long-term implications. What he wanted was a clear statement from the United States that its aim wasn't to get control of Canada. On his first visit to Nixon, he got that statement and was ecstatic at how responsive Nixon was. Nixon, of course, had responded to advice from Rufus and the embassy. Nixon, Trudeau, Kissinger, and **Ivan Head** had met privately and returned to the meeting of the other officials. Trudeau then said, "For one hour, I have been explaining to President Nixon that what we need most is a recognition of our inferiority complex." Nixon laughed.

The Nikuson shokku
The shokku of August 1971 caused immediate concern in Canada. He remembered that a complaining Jean-Luc Pepin, the ITC minister, grabbed him by the lapels. It was unfortunate that there was no prior consultation with Canada, though the secretary of state or the Treasury secretary did try unsuccessfully to reach his Canadian counterpart. Smith thought the shokku measures weren't a significant threat to Canadian interests, but he understood Canada's feeling that it should have been consulted. When Ottawa sent a delegation, Smith told Washington to stay cool and let the Canadians demonstrate that they'd be hurt. If Trudeau had been in the country instead of in Europe, the reaction in Ottawa would have been less, but Finance Minister Edgar Benson and SSEA **Mitchell Sharp** were excited.

During one session with Secretary Connally, Simon Reisman, the deputy minister of finance, stated that the US figures were all wrong. Afterward, Connally said, "Who is that guy? Let's hire him."

Ambassadors and issues
Kissinger and Head hit it off during the Nixon visit. As a career diplomat, Smith resented this channel but admitted that it was positive as long as it was direct communication. And if Kissinger were there, then Trudeau needed Head.

Marcel Cadieux in Washington felt that his ambassadorship was not a success. It was frustrating, difficult to see people on Capitol Hill. Still, he was held in high regard in the State Department. **Ed Ritchie** had readier entrée, as he had served in the United States before and didn't speak English with an accent.

When the Vietnam War was under way, Smith tried to explain it but never to justify it. A Canadian friend told him not to stand with his back to the wall at one of his speeches – otherwise the eggs would splatter and drip on his back. Canadian diplomats who went to Vietnam returned firmly pro-American. More to the point, they'd seen what the other side was like.

Smith was on the Canadian desk when Harold Linder was named as ambassador to Canada, and he went to Ottawa with him, changing places with Joe Scott. An economist and former head of the Export-Import Bank, Linder established an immediate rapport with the Canadian Department of Finance people. He enjoyed the post, wanted to stay, and was shattered when he had to resign after Nixon came in.

Adolph Schmidt replaced him and stayed until 1974. He too was an extraordinary figure. He'd been big in the Mellon Bank and was obsessed by the gold standard, the growth of world population, and the cyclical nature of civilizations. He had sense enough to let Smith run the embassy. He rarely saw Trudeau, made speeches in obscure places (Smith wouldn't distribute them). Schmidt did become convinced that the United States didn't realize how important Canada was to it, and he suggested that the position of assistant secretary of state for Canadian affairs be created. Smith had to tell him that the issue had already been raised by Ambassador Livingston Merchant, required congressional action, and was difficult. So he recommended that the Bureau of European Affairs should become the Bureau of European and Canadian Affairs, with a deputy assistant secretary for Canadian affairs. This worked, and Smith became the incumbent. But when he retired, the deputy assistant secretary was assigned other duties. Now the State Department had gradually returned to the idea of a deputy assistant secretary.

The idea that a special relationship existed between Canada and the United States had superficial plausibility, but it existed just because of all the factors. The Nixon speech in Ottawa in 1972 was said to end the relationship, but nothing changed.

To SSEA Mitchell Sharp, the Third Option meant a shift, and he wanted others to believe this. Smith knew the people who were writing the Third Option paper, and they thought it a crock. Once it appeared, he had to lay a cool hand on the fevered brows in Washington. As a result, there was no significant concern about the option in the United States, although there was always a danger that someone would see it as a betrayal.

A. EDGAR RITCHIE (1916-2002)
INTERVIEW | OTTAWA, 15 MARCH 1988

On Nixon and Trudeau
Personally, Ritchie said, he loathed Nixon, harbouring memories of what Nixon had done to his Democratic opponent Helen Gahagan Douglas, smearing her in a 1950 US Senate race in California as a communist sympathizer. But in early 1969, Ritchie took the line that Nixon would imitate Eisenhower and be statesmanlike. How wrong, in light of Watergate, he thought he was ...

Trudeau and Nixon? Actually, Trudeau spent some considerable time talking to Vice President Spiro Agnew about the problems of the cities, and in fact Agnew was knowledgeable on this topic. But Ritchie had no memory of any particularly impressive discussions. Both Trudeau and Nixon were pretty adaptable politicians, even if antagonistic, as we later learned from the Nixon tapes. On the surface, appearances were maintained.

Ritchie rejected complicated psychological explanations of the Nixon-Trudeau relationship as too subtle. Why not accept that Nixon saw Trudeau as a wild left-winger?

During Trudeau's 1969 visit to Washington, Ritchie held a very successful dinner party for him, to which he invited Senator Mike Mansfield and Justice William Douglas, Scotty Reston of the *New York Times*, *Washington Post* cartoonist Herblock, and the novelist Herman Wouk. In the library after dinner, Reston tackled Trudeau on the question of maintaining troops in Europe. Reston went down the line on the orthodox NATO view. Trudeau was not very favourable to NATO in his comments, and even Scotty was impressed by his dialectic. Mansfield was so impressed that he devoted some of the *Congressional Record* to Trudeau. Douglas, who had been given a copy of Trudeau's book *Federalism and the French-Canadians*, was also impressed. Trudeau was truly one of the best minds we've had ...

The Americans did not try to resist the Canadian NATO cuts, Ritchie claimed, because Nixon didn't take Canada terribly seriously. We were not a factor in his world. This was also true of Kissinger, whom Ritchie occasionally saw during this period. By the bye, the most impressive member of the diplomatic corps in Washington was Israeli ambassador Yitzhak Rabin, who was also the most clear-headed analyst of the Vietnam situation ...

On Ivan Head

"When **Ivan Head** started making his own foreign policy, he was a nuisance," Ritchie stated. "He saw himself as a vest-pocket Kissinger." But note that his contact was really Brent Scowcroft, not Kissinger himself. In a *Financial Post* column of 1971 or so, Bill Wilson commented on how well Ritchie got along with Ivan, compared to Marcel Cadieux. Cadieux used to refer to Ivan scornfully as "the professor." After a while, even the prime minister realized that Ivan had confused his own interests with the national interest. But Ritchie had to admit that things would have been more difficult without Ivan, and Ivan was a better influence than **Michael Pitfield**.

The Nikuson shokku

Ritchie reflected on Treasury Secretary John Connally's bankruptcy. Back when Connally was still governor of Texas, Ritchie had urged strong Canadian participation in the San Antonio Hemisfair on the government. What a waste that was, in terms of influencing Connally's attitudes ...

In August 1971, Ritchie, Jake Warren, and Simon Reisman were the principal officials concerned with the shokku.[8] Ben Benson and **Paul Martin** he remembered from the politicians.[9] Martin dealt with the American ambassador rather vigorously. We wanted an exemption for Canada, and the ambassador said he took Martin's views pretty seriously.

We didn't get what we wanted, but we protected ourselves and didn't suffer as seriously as we had feared. It showed how rough the Americans can be if they want, and that was quite a blow ...

The Autopact

Ritchie had heard rumours that the Autopact was to be cancelled and plainly didn't believe them. Julius Katz and Philip Trezise in the State Department were a little alarmist on the subject.[10] After all, the episode redounded to their credit. Secretary Rogers – he could be helpful as well as unpretentious. The Americans did not give away their own interest, but they saw you had to make an imaginative deal. Phil Trezise had a good mind for negotiation, very good, and Julius Katz was his faithful right hand.

EMERSON BROWN (1919-2009)
INTERVIEW | WASHINGTON, DC, 11 JANUARY 1988

Brown served at General Agreement on Tariffs and Trade and in the Netherlands and was economic counsellor at the US embassy in Ottawa

---

8   Reisman (1919-2008) served in the Departments of Labour, Finance, and Industry, playing a major role in negotiating the Autopact. He retired in 1975 but returned to negotiate the Free Trade Agreement of 1987.
9   Edgar Benson (1923-2011), nicknamed Ben, served in Pearson's cabinet and was Trudeau's finance minister from 1968 to the beginning of 1972.
10 We are using Katz's actual first name. In fact, during the interviews his friends and colleagues invariably called him Jules.

from 1970 to 1973; he was then head of the Canadian desk at the State Department, 1973-75.

Nixon and Canada

Brown heard about Nixon's April 1972 visit to Canada mostly from **Rufus Smith**, who kept muttering about the advance team. Nixon went over rather well in his public appearances and didn't commit a gaffe as Kennedy had done. He actually listened to the ambassador and to Rufus as to what he should say. The embassy staff were assembled to greet the president, only to have Rosemary Woods, the president's secretary, sent in his stead. That was "a little downer." But Nixon did well on his visit, "though I detested the guy." His speech was only to ratify the blunder of August 1971, and that was "a stupidity ..."

In connection with Nixon and Canada, Brown thought it odd that the president's friendship with Bebe Rebozo was overlooked. As an ex-Cuban, Rebozo took an interest in Canadian applications for export licence exemptions. Each transaction had to be individually handled. Every one had to go to Kissinger for approval. Kissinger's special assistant once said that his boss had 125 of them sitting on his desk. It wasn't so much the State Department or even Kissinger, Brown claimed, but Rebozo's mortgage on the Nixon White House ...

Negotiating with Ottawa

When Brown arrived in Ottawa, the Autopact was the great subject of conversation. Canada was running a surplus, and the pact was a hot potato in the United States. The State Department was under very severe pressure from Wilbur Mills, who chaired the House of Representatives Ways and Means Committee, to do something about it. In September or October 1970, Brown attended a meeting "where I first formed a jaundiced view of Canadian officialdom. We only wanted them to state there was a problem on the floor of the House." But Jake Warren, the deputy minister of ITC, just kept saying, can't do it, can't, too political. "That was a lot of crap," Brown recalled.

The Canadians would then turn around and ask, when are you Americans going to exercise some kind of leadership and do something for us? Simon Reisman was the real power and very good. At a certain stage of a negotiation, Simon really would have an understanding of the American point of view. He believed in dealing individual to individual, though he was considered to be tough from way back.

After being "on home leave in August 1971," Brown returned to Ottawa via Washington. "I was told that John Connally had proposed – and nobody had opposed – denouncing the Autopact." Julius Katz had personally stopped it, saying you can't do it that way; so, as Katz said, the press release was put in the shredder.

This news was very closely held in Washington. Back in Ottawa, Brown told Ambassador Schmidt and Rufus Smith, and then went and told Simon Reisman. Letting Reisman in on the precariousness of Canada's position was in our interest, Brown said. Reisman said, "I believe you ..." insofar as somebody might have suggested cancelling the Autopact at some preliminary stage. But Reisman simply refused to believe that it had got as far as Brown claimed. "Here I told him the truth, and he didn't believe me," he recalled.

Around Ottawa, Connally's name became a swear word. Still, if he'd come up to Ottawa, they would have eaten out of his hand. Brown remembered a bibulous Canadian official dinner for touring American reporters, during which Reisman had said, "If Connally were here, I'd tell him to piss up a tent rope." That comment got into the papers, evoking a firm denial from Simon.

Brown believed that if **Trudeau** had not been in Europe during August 1971, when Nixon gave his shokku speech, the Canadians would have handled the ensuing crisis much better. The Canadian attitude was immediately adversarial, uncomprehending: if the Americans are in a bad way, let's not go down with their ship. "There was no appreciation in Ottawa at that time that we were in a pickle," he said.

The initial Canadian reaction to the shokku would have raised all kinds of problems with General Agreement on Tariffs and Trade (GATT); their subsidy legislation was, however, converted to a wage subsidy. The Canadian line was always "we're not the problem." He had lunch with **Marshall Crowe** in the PCO and tried to put across to him what he was thinking, and got in response, oh, we've got to do it.

Brown tried to describe the US attitude up to that point. It was, on the part of agencies and government, that Canada was actually part of the United States, or should be. In the embassy, or in the State Department, we were always very careful to consult Canada on any big multilateral problem, he said. Douglas Dillon, Treasury secretary for Presidents Kennedy and Johnson, used to spend a lot of time on Canada.

But Nixon didn't like Trudeau, and Secretary of State William Rogers was not an important force in his government. That wasn't a bad thing: "In fact, Canada is best ignored." It was ignored in the lead-up to the August 1971 shokku measures, though in fact no US embassy, anywhere, was informed of what was pending.

In August 1971, with the United States in such dire financial straits, we in the embassy weren't very sympathetic to the Canadians, Brown claimed: "But why should we have sympathy for you?" Not that it would have made any difference whether the embassy was sympathetic or not ...

On Canadians and the embassy
Brown's memories of the embassy went back to 1970, and to Joe Greene, the minister of energy, mines and resources, whom he saw perform at the last Canadian-American ministerial committee, the last one that was held "and that ever should be held, from our point of view." That ministerial meeting was a disaster. It was in the Ottawa Conference Centre, and "almost the whole damned Canadian cabinet was there; our side included two lame ducks, and not one of our people had looked at his briefing book before he got on the plane. We realized that this was a losing game. The next one was the Americans' turn to host, and we never set it up." He remembered looking at the banks of Canadian officials sitting there, just like a hockey team ...

USSEA **Ed Ritchie** was a great guy, "though you had to eat his fiddleheads, a much over-rated dish ..."

Brown said he had no particular qualifications for serving in Canada, though he'd known a few Canadians at GATT. He'd read about the heady Trudeau phenomenon in the *Economist,* and it proved to be not that far from the reality. So he had a good time.

On the other hand, the Browns came to Ottawa from The Hague, which was an orderly place, arriving in the autumn of 1970, just at the time of the Quebec bombings and kidnappings. Rockcliffe wasn't quite an armed camp, but it was well supplied with armed guards.[11] The US consul-general in Montreal bore up well under an explicit FLQ threat. Rufus Smith was the shepherd on the situation, though he probably damped down the reporting. There was a science attaché, Miller Hudson, who took a great interest in separatism and probably wrote a lot of crap about it.

Then there was Vladimir Toumanoff, the embassy's senior political officer: "I can remember wonderful talks with him about Trudeau moving Canada

....

11 Rockcliffe was a prestigious Ottawa suburb, home to many foreign diplomats and senior Canadian public servants.

away from the US. He thought there was a Politburo at work somewhere." Brown added, "I guess 'we' never really liked Trudeau; I sort of sympathized with what he was doing ..."

The Canadian civil service, Canadian diplomats, were very good, Brown said, offering more anecdotes about Canadians in negotiation. In connection with energy, negotiations were "absolutely unrewarding. The Canadians were in the cat-bird seat," and at the embassy we knew they couldn't give anything. "I personally sympathized with the Canadian position, which was carefully thought out." Simon Reisman was hard as nails and didn't give an inch. There was "a lot of ignorance in Washington." He remembered a meeting in 1973 or 1974, where somebody said we'd be depending on the Canadians for oil. But the embassy had sent its first dispatch, telling the administration of the depletion, the absolute fall in Canadian oil reserves, in 1971.

"In my experience, I've never been in a bilateral negotiation with Canada where the Canadians didn't tell us their policy was best for us too," Brown recalled with a smile. During a negotiation over strawberries, everything went swimmingly, and for once, none of the Canadians trotted out the line about the benefits of their policy. This persisted throughout lunch, and Brown began to think he'd escaped it, but then some bastard said it. In any negotiation, the topic at hand was ten times more important for Canadians than it was for us; they were always tough and well prepared.

The embassy reported on the Third Option, but then we'd look at the trade figures and say, "Rots of ruck, Canada."[12] Our main reporting was on energy stuff: it was like the last hand of poker, where all the cards were dealt face up, with no surprises. "We used to ask ourselves how such nice people could be so tough in negotiations," he recalled. Americans would moan about not being able to rely on Canada, but that was rather beside the point. "Really," he said, "it was an organic relationship which could use a little trimming here and there." Rufus performed well on the trimmings and could be down on a customs issue like a ton of bricks.

Fisheries? He thought the treaty that applied was the Americans' oldest. He didn't handle the subject, though he once held a staff meeting in his office. How could you tell whether a fish was Canadian or American?

....

12 "Rots of ruck," intended to mimic a Japanese accent and thought to be humorous at the time, translates to "lots of luck." It typically referred to something that had no chance of succeeding.

The Foreign Investment Review Agency (FIRA)? "We were supposed to be very mad at you, and I know Toumanoff read it as an ominous thing," Brown said, but it was a "'rots of ruck' thing. I think you'd have had a hard case demonstrating it kept out any investment." At the same time, Canada had investment incentives all over the place, "and made such asses of yourselves." Take Bricklin, Michelin, and Come-by-Chance.[13]

Adolph Schmidt as ambassador from 1969 to 1974 didn't do anything, listened to Rufus Smith, and was right on some things where Brown was wrong ...

William Porter, who was ambassador later (1974-75), made an ass of himself despite his seniority in the foreign service. He got that job because Kissinger wanted to get rid of him.

Marcel Cadieux was desperate to see Kissinger, and Brown took verbatim notes for their meeting, the first that Kissinger had with a foreign ambassador. Poor old Marcel brought a big, thick briefing book. Kissinger's first line was, "Well, I hope you didn't come here to talk to me about the sex life of the salmon."

Brown also took notes at a meeting between Kissinger and Allan MacEachen at the UN in New York City. They talked more about Cambridge, Massachusetts, than about business. At the end, Kissinger would say, "Oh, here's a few matters my officers say I should bring up with you."

It wasn't easy to be a Canadian diplomat, though they are paid well. He knew it had its hazards. He first heard of Trudeau in 1969, when the Canadian deputy chief of mission at The Hague just disappeared, without making any farewells. "Your officials are better than you deserve," he concluded. "The bunch I knew were men of real stature."

MARSHALL CROWE (1921-2013)

INTERVIEW | OTTAWA, 14 MARCH 1988

On the Nikuson shokku

Crowe went down to Washington with the delegation, which consisted of Simon Reisman, Jake Warren, Jean-Luc Pepin, and Edgar Benson. They had their sessions with Connally and his assistant secretary, Paul Volcker, who

---

13 Bricklin, Michelin, and Come-by-Chance were all troublesome, officially induced investments of the 1970s.

was, by the way, about seven feet tall. Connally had a bunch of papers on his desk; he fumbled in them, selected some, and started reading figures that demonstrated the Canadian iniquity in trade. We'd never heard these figures – they were incredible. So Reisman and Crowe jumped in and said that the figures went beyond the normal Canadian-American discrepancy.

Connally stopped, looked at the heading on his papers, and said, "Son of a bitch, they gave me Japan!" Volcker gently pointed out that the Japanese would be coming in next, and the Canadian papers were over here. They were headed "Canada."

Our argument, Crowe continued, was that they were bound under GATT not to do these things, and that we had this big current account deficit (financed, of course, by US capital imports). Crowe thought that Connally didn't really understand it all. The Americans were trying to make us raise our exchange rate (the Canadian dollar was then at a premium); and Simon Reisman had a big row with Connally over that. It was not true that Simon stubbed out his cigar on Connally's desk, but it was true that he later informed a meeting in Ottawa he'd told the secretary to "go piss up a rope." Really, we just yelped and screamed when we saw the Americans pulling back their fist; what would we do if they ever connected, as they did not in 1971?

PETER TOWE (1922-2015)
INTERVIEW | OTTAWA, 9 DECEMBER 1987

Towe, an economist by training, joined the Department of External Affairs in 1947, serving several tours of duty at the Canadian embassy in Washington. He was ambassador from 1977 to 1981.

Towe spoke at length on the shokku
Between 1967 and 1972, Towe was in Washington with Ambassadors Charles Ritchie and Marcel Cadieux, as senior minister in the embassy. The great event, the watershed in Canadian-American relations, was the shokku of August 1971.

The Americans wanted to negotiate packages of concessions with the Europeans, the Japanese, and the Canadians. This was our first experience of being considered a difficult trading partner by the United States. There had been indications of this for some time, but it was very hard to make people in Ottawa grasp it, or believe it.

Towe remembered a lunch with Philip Trezise, who had negotiated the Autopact, Katz, Trezise's assistant, and Simon Reisman. It was clear that the continuation of safeguards for Canadian auto production was irritating the Americans, and at one point Trezise told Reisman flatly, "Simon, you just don't have any friends down here anymore."

This was a new experience for us. In 1960, the Canadians and the Americans had pooled their resources in the negotiations over transforming the Organisation for European Economic Co-operation into the Organisation for Economic Co-operation and Development, with full membership rather than observer status for Canada and the United States. In those days, our aims, our tactics, were so similar that we had acted as a single team, even sharing our telegrams.

Anyhow, the 1971 shokku measures were not unexpected, but for the Canadians who hadn't believed the signs that the special relationship was no more, they were a real shock.

Finance Minister Benson and Reisman came down and were ushered into Secretary Connally's office. Benson was rumpled and sweating – it was August – and perhaps a little hungover, and he was meeting this patrician from Texas who was dressed coolly and immaculately. Benson put his foot further wrong when he started out by being subservient, telling Connally how fortunate it was that the Americans could choose their Treasury secretaries from wherever there was talent, instead of having to obey the regional choice mechanism that applied in Canada. He was certain that he himself would never have gotten to be Treasury secretary in the United States.

Then Benson started on his brief, rehearsing the historical reasons as to why Canada was not a balance of payments burden on the United States. If you looked at current accounts, even in 1971, Canada was in deficit to the Americans. He told the story of the interest equalization tax and praised Ottawa's record.[14] Surely, American measures that were aimed at other trading partners ought not to apply to Canada, for they bore more heavily on us than they would on others. We were special, we didn't contribute to American problems. The tone throughout was hesitant and apologetic.

Connally replied, "I can tell you, Mr. Minister, that these measures were not aimed at Canada, but I can also assure you that we had Canada very much in mind." Benson was shocked, not least at the possibility that Connally regarded

---

14 In 1963, Canada secured an exemption from a US "interest equalization tax" designed to limit American investment abroad.

him as "an inferior being." During the exchanges that followed, he became increasingly confused, prompting Reisman to say, "What Ben means, Mr. Secretary –." Of course, Reisman had a personality clash with Connally too.

When Reisman was in private, his personality was warm and gentle. He and Towe were close friends and remained so. It was true that Reisman had not gotten over the discrimination that he experienced during his Jewish upbringing in Montreal; it made him combative. "In my judgment, he did more harm than good in negotiations in that period," Towe said. He was so well informed, so arrogant, so determined to make others understand that they knew less than he. This was the total opposite of **Ed Ritchie**, who never said anything but asked pertinent questions, penetrating questions, to which the answer was the one that Ritchie wanted.

The Katz story about the near-cancellation of the Autopact was perfectly true. Julius's attitude was to be helpful and to solve problems: Towe hoped that he himself shared this trait. The two were very good friends. In August 1971, when Towe had had his briefing at the State Department on the Sunday evening and had dutifully sent off a telegram to Trudeau, giving the gist of it – **Trudeau** was in Belgrade and couldn't have done anything about it – he took a tranquillizer and went to bed. Before doing so, he phoned Katz and said he wished he'd had his help in drafting the telegram. Of course, he could have had it, said Katz, and he meant it ...

Anyhow, in August 1971, we were unable to get relief on the surtax, which fortunately turned out not to have too great an impact, and on the domestic international sales corporations, which stayed around for quite a while but never had the effect the Americans had hoped. There were three sets of negotiations: with the Europeans, the Japanese, and the Canadians. Facing Towe were Paul Volcker and John Petty, an assistant secretary of the Treasury. Interestingly, the Canadians were prepared to give way on some points, including the tourist allowance, which the United States wanted raised, but the Americans were keen on getting changes to the Autopact and insisted on treating the negotiations as a package. If one item failed, no others would be concluded. The Canadians had countered the American list with grievances of their own, such as the embargo on uranium; in the event, no agreement was reached, and the Americans rescinded the surcharge, which was a bargaining chip, anyway. Towe added that another Canadian demand was free access to the US market for the oil and gas sector – pre-energy crisis. He had some sympathy for the Americans; they wanted a level playing field, and the Japanese and Europeans were not giving them one.

HON. MITCHELL SHARP (1911-2004)
INTERVIEW | OTTAWA, 8 DECEMBER 1987

On the origins of the Third Option
The shokku of 1971 had made **Trudeau** just as angry as the rest of the cabinet, Sharp began. The special US-Canada relationship had been underpinned by the doctrine, best expressed by Louis Rasminsky, the governor of the Bank of Canada, that the economic and financial affairs of the two countries were so intertwined that the United States could do nothing to correct its balance of payments problems, as Canada was bound to react to its measures. Connally didn't see this, and he blamed Canada for the crisis. That led to the Options paper. Sharp knew that the Americans had almost canned the Autopact. Connally and Reisman were appropriate opponents, but happily, it was Benson who had to deal with Connally, not Sharp. Benson was steady, unimaginative, not charismatic. The Nixon speech in Ottawa also pushed us toward the Options. Certainly, it impressed Sharp. The speech was welcomed here, but it also frightened Canadians. Sharp had realized that the special relationship couldn't last as Canada became a more significant power.

The Options paper, which flatly rejected free trade, had been prepared at his direction and was not discussed with the prime minister. The cabinet had asked Sharp to draft it after Connally and the shokku. He laid out the structure on paper and discussed it with the officials. The paper went to a cabinet committee, but he was not sure if it went to the cabinet. The Departments of Finance and ITC clearly weren't enthusiastic about it, which was why it wasn't issued as a pamphlet. The Second Option had no support at all. In his view, those who opposed the Third Option wanted the First, or pragmatic, option. To him, the Third Option was misunderstood by those who saw only trade in it. There was more. The government accepted the Third Option but did little with it – no internal restructuring, no political will. He admitted that the results – the arts support, culture, and so on – were small beer. He had been at a conference recently with **Michel Dupuy**, who was eloquent on the option and Contractual Link – established to emphasize that Canada was different from the United States, and the link was to show this was so.

The *Foreign Policy for Canadians* series did not include a separate booklet on the United States, because the main one was essentially concerned with that country. If the series had tried to do for the United States what it did for Latin America, the resulting booklet would have been very long. As it was, the Third Option paper was concerned with economic relations with the United States, not all relations.

He talked about accompanying Trudeau to see Nixon. He didn't sit in on the private talks but was in the larger group. On the way back, they decided they couldn't determine how they'd got on with Nixon. He wasn't a person to be trusted. They thought he had was no underlying firmness. As it was, Sharp couldn't imagine two people who were more different than Trudeau and Nixon.

The ICCS in Vietnam

The second ICCS in Vietnam made Sharp "most proud" because it had worked out as he wanted. DEA was unenthusiastic about the commitment, and some officials were strongly opposed. But Sharp believed that Canada couldn't stand in the way of peace, so we agreed to participate but with conditions. The intent was to avoid repeating the farce of the original commission, but officials were still dubious. He talked with Kissinger later about the commission, and he agreed the whole thing had nonetheless turned out to be a farce. At the time, Canada was to announce its withdrawal, and Kissinger called and asked for a delay. Sharp refused to delay the announcement but said he could delay the pullout by a month. Sharp then met Secretary Rogers, who was careful to point out that he (Rogers) had not called. As for the House of Commons resolution protesting the Christmas bombing of Hanoi, Trudeau and the cabinet were strongly opposed to the bombing. The government decided to support the resolution to show its disagreement with US policy. The action caused some problems with Washington.

On US draft dodgers and deserters, Sharp said he instructed his officers to find out what policy the Americans had pursued for Canadian deserters between 1939 and 1941. He discovered that they had done nothing, so Canada did the same, and the United States really did not protest much.

RUSSELL McKINNEY (1922-2001)
INTERVIEW | OTTAWA, 12 APRIL 1988

McKinney joined DEA in 1949, served in a number of posts in Europe, Asia, and the Caribbean, became deputy chief of mission in the United States, and was subsequently assistant USSEA for economic affairs.

On the shokku
McKinney said he was not in Washington on 15 August 1971, when Nixon gave the speech that launched the shokku, but he knew some of the aftermath. There were sore feelings, especially between Connally and Reisman. He could imagine that Julius Katz, with his feeling for the relationship between Canada and the United States, would have done his best to manage it. Therefore, without knowing anything about the status of the Autopact in 1971, he could give some credence to Katz's story that he'd stopped it from being scrapped.[15] In considering the Autopact and economic relations generally, McKinney said, you must bear in mind that Canada was running a heavy surplus with the United States, and that between 1969 and 1974 we were outperforming the Americans on almost any indicator you cared to choose. He remarked, "I can imagine there was discontent and all sorts of complaining and griping ..."

Marcel Cadieux as ambassador in the United States
McKinney was cross-posted to Washington as economic minister, the deputy chief of mission, in succession to **Peter Towe**. He was not aware of any difficulties between the ambassador, Marcel Cadieux, and Towe; he was surprised to hear that there were any, because in his experience Marcel left anything to do with economics to somebody else. Cadieux saw his brief as being legal and political. McKinney's was economics, but he also handled embassy administration. Perhaps that sector was where Towe had the problem.

Cadieux was "an extremely decisive man," who had the ability to hear your evidence and then to render a decision quickly, whether right or wrong. For a subordinate who was trying to get movement, to have things happen, this was superb. Cadieux had habitual insomnia, so he would rise at 4:00 a.m. and would have written a couple of his own speeches by breakfast. He was always ahead of schedule. Not only was he a prolific writer, he had a good style, and in English as well as French. McKinney also fondly remembered Cadieux's sense of humour. He was a tough fellow to handle in an argument,

---

15   Julius Katz (1925-2000), in 1971 deputy assistant secretary of state for international resources and food policy, said exactly that. See interview with Assistant Secretary Julius Katz, 12 May 1995, 60-62, Foreign Affairs Oral History Collection, Association for Diplomatic Studies and Training, Arlington, VA, http://www.adst.org/OH%20 TOCs/Katz,%20Julius%20L.toc.pdf. Katz had much of interest to say on negotiations with Canada from the 1950s onward.

and it was very hard to best him in debate. The Americans probably found him a handful.

Cadieux took fairly radical likes and dislikes where people were concerned. If he took a scunner to you, you were beyond the pale. He was not very discreet in expressing his feelings.

McKinney thought that Cadieux missed the USSEA's power and authority down in Washington, and he got very frustrated with certain people in Ottawa, especially **Ivan Head**. Head was his particular *bête noire*; it wasn't just personal. The very existence of Head's function offended Cadieux's strong sense of hierarchy and form, which may have derived from his Jesuit training. Here was somebody outside the system who was licensed to wheel and deal. It was also true that Cadieux did not seem close to **Ed Ritchie**, but McKinney could not say much about that.

Dealings in Washington

The people we dealt with in Washington included Julius Katz, who was like the Rock of Gibraltar where Canadian interests were concerned. He had a good sense of Canadian policies and concerns, even where he did not agree with them. "I've had many a brisk argument with Julius, who was no patsy," McKinney said. **Rufus Smith** was also there for a while, though he must have left by about 1973. There was Bill Armstrong too, who was assistant secretary for economic and business affairs in 1972.[16] He, of course, had an Ottawa background, as did his wife. Bill was therefore the second-most senior economic man in the State Department, and Julius was his deputy assistant secretary.

Over in the Treasury, there was Paul Volcker as assistant secretary for international affairs. He was the chief US monitor on the famous Michelin tire case, and he called McKinney when they rendered the decision. That was in George Shultz's Treasury, he having succeeded Connally.

Shultz was a friend of John Turner's, which became a factor in how we got along in Washington. Perhaps those two also met later when they worked for Bechtel, the giant engineering and construction company. Rogers as secretary of state was a very decent man, certainly more so than Kissinger ...

16 Willis Armstrong was an economic specialist (and a Canadian specialist too) in the State Department. He was assistant secretary for economics in the early 1970s. As he liked to point out, he was fired by Secretary of State Kissinger.

McKinney didn't think there was any spillover of the low state of political relations to the economic side in 1972-74. "I was never frozen out, though there may have been times" when something was not quite right. It was certainly true that in 1973, Ambassador Cadieux was not *persona grata;* that was because of the Vietnam resolution in Parliament. At the time, however, there was no special rash of economic problems, so for that reason too, the answer was no: he was not frozen out.

Economic and environmental issues
It was, of course, true that particular Canadian actions in the economic field were a problem for the Americans. The Republican administration didn't like FIRA, and Canadian energy policies also got to be a problem in 1973. This was because of Canadian export controls on oil; we were gradually phasing down our shipments during the spring of 1974. That didn't look very friendly, but the Americans did accept that our reserves were declining. To some, it was a nationalistic, excessive assertion of Canadian self-interest. "I remember telling Julius Katz about the export controls," he said. Katz had a way of slowly turning red from the neck up; he displayed it on that day. McKinney couldn't remember what was said, but the visual image stuck in his mind.

As for not keeping one's congressional fences mended, McKinney was mildly scornful. The idea of lobbying the Hill recurred about every ten years, and it was given to each generation to rediscover it. The difficulty lay in whether you were alienating the administration – with whom you had to work – in order to secure the affections of Congress. But having said that, he believed that **Allan Gotlieb**'s cultivation of Congress had been good and skilfully handled.

On energy, the Americans were reactive, not proactive. Not until the free trade negotiations in the 1980s did the idea of a continental energy policy really take hold in Washington. Back in the 1970s, somebody like Katz would have considered the idea a non-starter because of the reaction it would presumably have provoked. The Americans in his day had no over-arching ideas about, or designs on, Canada.

As for FIRA, "I don't think it was as much an issue or irritant as were some other things," McKinney claimed. Granted that under a Republican administration, the State Department was getting feedback from businessmen, but their objections were mostly for theatrical reasons. Most had never experienced it themselves or had had no difficulty. After all, he asked, how many takeovers were refused? "When the rubber hit the road, there was no problem."

But the assistant secretary for economic *and business affairs* (his emphasis) had to take note and repeat what he heard.

Indirect acquisitions were more of a problem than new investment, he went on. "Indirect" meant one US or foreign firm selling its Canadian property to another. Generally, compared to some aspects of energy, to border broadcasting, or to *Time-Life*, FIRA didn't rank as a major concern.

He was once invited to Grand Rapids to speak on Canada's policies at what he took to be the city's version of the Council on Foreign Relations. When he arrived, however, he discovered that the venue was in a suburb of Grand Rapids and that it was owned by Amway.[17] True, the members of the panel he was on were not entirely Amway, but the trend of thought was pretty clear. The Amway prosecution had not yet begun. Mike Blumenthal, then chairman of Bendix and later Jimmy Carter's Treasury secretary, was there; he told McKinney he was pretty brave to have made his speech – outlining differences in economic philosophy between Canada and the United States – in that place. The audience received it without too much abuse, but they were pretty vocal afterward.

Border broadcasting was certainly a headache, McKinney said. This was because of the disproportionate influence that a media-based lobby group can have. A lot of ministers took flak on the issue ...

There were quite a number of environmental situations too. Pittston, "a noisy corporation," was attempting to create an oil depot in Eastport, Maine, which was possibly the most dreadful place in the whole country to try to steer tankers into. There was the West Coast tanker problem too. In North Dakota, there was a strong sector that favoured the Garrison Dam.[18] By this time, Kissinger was secretary of state, and though he was never as knowledgeable or as involved as Rogers or Vance, he took more interest as time went on.

....

17 During the mid-1960s, Amway became involved in a long-running dispute with Canadian Customs that was not settled until the mid-1980s, when the company was found guilty of criminal fraud. See the long, detailed, but fascinating Internet post at "Amway: The Untold Story: The Canadian Fraud Case," http://archive.is/20120729113054/www.amquix.info/aus/canada.htm. Convicted of criminal fraud, Amway was fined $25 million, the largest fine in Canadian history up to that time.
18 It was not so much the dam (a very big dam, finished in 1953) but the diversion of water from the dam and thus from the Missouri River basin north into the Hudson Bay watershed, flowing into Canada and bearing fauna and other non-native elements. The Canadians objected, strenuously, and over many years. A water treatment plant was eventually installed to treat the overflow water.

McKinney did not see much of Head's role in Washington; his connection was with Scowcroft. That was genuinely handled at another level, in a different manner. His recollection was that Head's interventions were usually about trips and similar subjects. "I don't recall that it undercut us in any significant way," he said, "but there was a natural bureaucratic resistance to losing control of something."

However, Ivan may well have played a part at summits. The Puerto Rico summit was the one where Ford insisted on inviting us; but McKinney just couldn't remember much. Summits were really Head's line of country.

On the difference between Canada's relations with Ford and with Carter, McKinney said, "We expected and found that the Carter administration would be more congenial." Carter was a lot more popular in Canada than he was in the United States. Cy Vance, Mike Blumenthal, Bert Lance, director of the office of management and budget – what a group. "I think we were pretty excited about Jimmy Carter," McKinney recalled. He was a new guy, but he had old pros like Vance and Blumenthal, "whom we knew pretty well." There was Mondale, with his special brief for relations with Canada; everything seemed open and optimistic. Still, McKinney stated, "We had a lot of respect for Ford, who was a very decent caretaker president."

During his almost twenty years of dealing with the United States, only two things that Canada did actually made an impact on most Americans. One was the exclusion of Taiwan from the Montreal Olympics in 1976. That rated us three unfriendly editorials in the *New York Times* in two weeks, and the feeling went right across the country. He was then chargé and had the experience of being grilled on the subject on the McNeil-Lehrer news show on PBS; a storm had knocked out the air conditioning, so the place was steaming. Unfortunately, they got the power on just in time to run the program, so he had to sit there and answer hostile questions, with sweat dripping from the end of his nose. Even Gerald Ford was making statements over Taiwan.

The second occasion was with Ambassador Ken Taylor's rescue of American diplomats from Iran in 1979.

RICHARD POST (1929-)
INTERVIEW | WASHINGTON, DC, 13 JANUARY 1988

Post spent much of his State Department career in Africa and Portugal. He was deputy chief of mission at the US embassy in Ottawa, 1975-76.

Mid-1970s issues

Post began by noting that he served under Ambassador William Porter, who was on R&R after his previous heavy tour handling the peace negotiations with North Vietnam. Porter was a low-key man who probably kept a low profile because of the anti-Americanism in Canada and because the Third Option was then the rule. That low profile lasted until late 1975, when he let loose during a speech and caused a storm. He had not exploded under instructions, Post said, but had bottled up things. Porter thought that his comments were beneficial to the US-Canada relationship, as it was important for Canadians to know what the United States thought about potash, *Time*, TV advertising, and what Canadians were doing to the United States. Canadians, Post said, think the United States pays no attention to them and that therefore they can get away with things. That's true for the general population, but not for US special interests. The general reaction to Porter's speech was that the media said they agreed, and Kissinger offered a near apology. Anti-Americanism was always out there, though it didn't hamper business. What annoyed Americans was the holier-than-thou attitude of Canadians.

As it was, Post claimed that the Third Option helped the United States by enhancing Canadian credibility in the world. It was clear that Canada sided with America on the important things, and Canada was obviously independent ... The economy side was harder. He disliked complaints about investment since, after all, the United States had been invited to invest in Canada. Saskatchewan's nationalization of phosphate hurt a great deal, though it was not seen as a national security problem. Canada got into trouble whenever its actions hurt large numbers of American citizens (as with pipelines or oil pricing). He thought Canadian policies were formulated with US effects in mind, but sometimes this was not considered until too late.

On the environment, the key issues were not acid rain, but the Garrison Dam in North Dakota and the Maine refinery, with its tanker traffic. He seemed to support Canadian positions here and talked of having sent telegrams to Washington, putting his own arguments into the mouths of the Canadians he was quoting.

THOMAS ENDERS (1932-96)
INTERVIEW | NEW YORK, 13 MAY 1988

A professional FSO, Enders had served, controversially, in Cambodia during the US bombing campaign there, which made him politically toxic in Washington. Secretary of State Kissinger sent him to Ottawa to remove him from the line of fire. After Ottawa, he held a number of senior posts in the State Department and ended up as an investment banker in New York.

The PQ, Quebec's status, and the United States

Enders began with his assessment on the subject of Quebec, when the Parti Québécois won the provincial election in November 1976. It didn't take the US government long to adopt an attitude on that question, and private initiative played a role in it. As soon as the election was over, everybody began to think about what was going to happen. It became clear that an assertive Quebec government wanted to establish privileged or beneficial relations with the United States in order to use such relations as a balancing factor with Ottawa. And its efforts to detach Quebec from Confederation were very real.

There were two questions for the United States, Enders recalled. First, was this a process that we viewed with indifference, or did we have major stakes in the outcome? Second, how were we to handle Quebec's efforts to establish a relationship? "I think this occurred with Carter's election in the background," said Enders. "The outgoing Ford administration had looked at the question" but declined to deal with it. So within the US government, the initiative on Quebec rested with the embassy as the only body with sufficient information to come to grips with it.

We thought it through, roughly as follows: First, if Canada did begin to split up, we could see no benefit for the United States. It had once been a major force in the security area and was still a significant foreign policy influence and a successful democracy in a world that had few of them, so its disappearance would be a loss to us. Second, whatever economic benefits that might accrue to individual American interests (such as better access to energy supplies in Quebec or elsewhere) would be swamped by the fact that the separate pieces of Canada would be less dynamic than a single country could be. Finally, "I even raised the question of whether the American union might not be adversely affected." The United States had just had its own confrontations between producers and users of oil; he did not want to see an example of balkanization on America's border.

"These lines of reasoning encountered no dissent within the US government," Enders remarked. Nobody could see anything but loss in the breakup of Canada. But the last thing that Ottawa or anybody else wanted was to see Washington taking sides or becoming actively involved. On the other hand,

Ottawa wanted to keep the US attitude just short of cordial. And Ottawa wanted the Americans to be sensitive to the perils of Quebec's desire for any kind of contact. It wanted there to be no question that Washington might accept such relations with the Province. "I made a recommendation that we comport ourselves in such a way as to leave no doubt of any possible support" to Quebec, said Enders.

"I communicated this, but not in person, to Carter at his transition camp," Enders remembered. It was probably done through Zbigniew Brzezinski, the national security adviser. Enders received an approval; in any case, Vance instinctively knew it was the right thing to do. Enders then communicated this to Trudeau and to the SSEA, "and handled our Quebec contacts accordingly."

The private initiative now made itself felt, Enders said. Ian Sinclair, the president of the CPR, and Paul Desmarais, the president of Power Corporation, went to see Trudeau. With "his acquiescence, they came to see me on his behalf to urge the United States not to appear indifferent or supportive of Quebec."

Trudeau, who did not know or understand the United States or Americans particularly well, or some of his entourage, feared that Washington would adopt a different attitude – that the continentalist urge was predominant in its policy. The idea was that redrawing the map would be in the US interest. Enders observed that nobody he ever met was either aware of such an urge or proposed gratifying it.

The effect of the "enormous preoccupation" with Quebec "inevitably" was to limit Ottawa's preoccupation with cutting transborder flows of various kinds: it didn't stop Canada's efforts but did mean that they weren't added to.

Enders did speak with Carter very early in his administration – probably in January 1977 – and Carter explicitly approved his approach to the Quebec problem. Enders had wanted to make sure that Carter did so approve.

As he recalled, "I did other things" in connection with Quebec. In New York City, he encouraged "a questioning reaction to René Lévesque's pitch" to the Economic Club in December 1976.[19] He wanted to ensure that other governments and opinion-makers would not lend themselves to Quebec's ploy. Scotty Reston of the *Times* was especially helpful in this.

....

19 Properly, "The Economic Club of New York."

Enders also spoke to Trudeau about the Quebec issue. Trudeau's attitude toward dealing explicitly with the Americans was one of caution and uncertainty. He did not want to be the *demandeur*. But from Ian Sinclair and Paul Desmarais, and through **Michael Pitfield**, Enders received many signals as to Canada's attitude. He and Pitfield went over it very thoroughly. So he had a number of occasions to express it to Trudeau, who made clear that it was important to him.

It would have been astonishing if the United States had taken any other position, Enders stated. But Trudeau hadn't hung out with many Americans and had virtually no close friendship with any American. He was certainly not an easy or frequent visitor to American society.

Enders did not think that PQ strategist Claude Morin had any grounds for asserting that some foreign envoys had promised to recognize a sovereign Quebec on the day after a separatist referendum succeeded. Nor did Morin's claims that the Quebec government was not trying to involve other countries ring true. If that were so, what was Lévesque's Economic Club speech all about?

In general, Trudeau was intellectually well equipped for the direction of foreign policy. He was brilliant in argument ... His economic policies ran the gamut from Hayek to Galbraith. Prior to 1976, Enders had observed Canadian attitudes toward cross-border exchanges, as on investment or trade, "but I was unable to detect a general philosophy towards the US." There was no systematic Canadian nationalist policy that he could see. There was no overall plan, no long-term objective. All these objectives were considered subsidiary to the protection and defence of the Canadian union.

And though it was true that Trudeau tended to be uncomfortable with Americans, he was uncomfortable with many people; admittedly, he was somewhat better with Europeans. As to Trudeau's relations with Carter, perhaps it was true that Carter was disappointed in him; but Carter wanted more of everybody than he could possibly get. He was "a meliorist" in the fullest sense of the word. Enders remembered the meetings between Trudeau and Carter as awkward, both men being terribly anxious to get down to the agenda laid before them – but there was usually not enough on the agenda really to carry it off.

In sum, during this period Washington did not behave in ways that caused Trudeau great problems, and by 1977 it was vice versa too. In that sense, the period was a happy one; but when Trudeau got back into power in 1980, things would be different.

Enders reasserted that as far as he knew, Brzezinski did not favour Quebec separation, and he hewed to the same line on the subject as the rest of the administration.

ROBERT DUEMLING (1929-2012)
INTERVIEW | WASHINGTON, DC, 12 JANUARY 1988

Duemling spent thirty years in the US foreign service. He worked in the Far East and after his four years in Ottawa (1976-80) was an ambassador and a senior officer at the State Department.

On Enders and the embassy
Duemling went to Ottawa as deputy chief of mission (DCM) because Tom Enders, his friend since college, had asked him to go. Enders, like other ambassadors, had the privilege of choosing his own DCM. We should not think that he was just being pally in picking Duemling; it didn't work that way. Duemling was then an assistant to the deputy secretary of state, on the management side. This meant he customarily dealt with the top people in the State Department – an asset for any ambassador who later employed him. "I had a reputation as a manager," he said, "and I knew he [Enders] could get along with me – and so could his wife. Enders knew that with me, he could get fast to the top people – though he knew his own way around." But if Enders could call them directly, so could Duemling, which allowed Enders to concentrate on other things.

Enders had been assistant secretary for economic and business affairs. Kissinger admired him; he wanted to give Enders a mission, and a good one. Enders had already been chargé in Cambodia, and his time had come.

In coming to Canada, whether it was Enders's perception or somebody else's, there were important issues to be resolved. These were energy, George's Bank and fish generally, and the environment, especially the Garrison diversion and acid rain. "I knew that Enders himself considered them all to be important issues, worthy of his time and efforts," Duemling said. "Enders was very issue-oriented and liked engaging himself on important issues." Later, in Spain, he had the EC and NATO as important subjects to engage him.

Enders and Duemling felt that the Ottawa embassy needed a considerable upgrade. Duemling was assigned to clean out the political section. This meant upgrading the staff and making the embassy and its constituent posts much more productive. In this, "I was Mr. Inside, Tom was Mr. Outside." He kept a sharp eye on personnel to energize and activate them. Enders also chose Don Bouchard as administrative counsellor. He was a junior, but he'd worked closely with Lawrence Eagleburger, who had been executive secretary to the secretary of state. "I was suspicious, but Bouchard was very able in fact," Duemling recalled.

"I turned my hand first to the political section," Duemling said, "and replaced the political counsellor, **Richard Post**, first." Then he shopped around for better juniors. He replaced the chief consular officer, and Enders took responsibility for housecleaning the economics section ...

Dealing with the Ottawa bureaucracy
Embassy contacts were with the Bank of Canada, the Treasury Board, ITC, and DEA, passing data back and forth, much of them highly technical. The fact of life is that Ottawa and Washington officials have their own channels, and he had to decide how to handle this. On the whole, it was an asset. "We encouraged constant contacts," he remarked, "which in any case we could not have prevented." He and Enders wanted to be kept informed, however; they realized that many issues were time-sensitive and could not wait for regular channels to clear. He tried to persuade embassy personnel to follow up such contacts and to keep some kind of permanent record.

Long-standing relationships existed between the Department of Agriculture and the Wheat Board, the FBI and the RCMP, the CIA and whatever there was, and the State Department and DEA. This was constructive and productive.

One day, he sat in on a meeting of agricultural specialists. They had dealt with each other for years, and "I was the outsider" at the meeting, just sitting there listening.

In the embassy, you dealt with people who had authority, people in power; he was in a position early on to size up changes. There were overlapping sectors of authority. He might get a call from the PMO or the PCO before he heard from DEA about some issue. "I made a point of cultivating mid-level people," Duemling said, and ensured that they could get a quick response when they needed it. Sometimes the PMO would tell him that DEA would call soon. He himself had contacts with **Michael Pitfield**, though Enders saw him more, with **Ivan Head** and with Bob Fowler. The embassy found that DEA was not always in the know, so it made a point of keeping DEA informed of what other agencies were doing: "This is in the nature of the relationship."

They kept tabs on Alan MacEachen's movements. In regard to MacEachen, "the Canadian press were very generous." "I don't recall ever having an experience" where USSEA **Basil Robinson** couldn't reach his minister, as had happened to other embassies. In Duemling's opinion, Robinson and Bob Johnstone, the deputy minister of ITC, "did okay." Nor could he remember people at DEA being paralyzed; had that happened, the embassy would have gone to the PMO for action. Yes, Head was very powerful, and Pitfield also spoke with authority.

In comparative terms, Duemling estimated, the Canadian diplomatic service was very good, among the top six of the world: in across-the-board ability, the Japanese, the Brazilians, and the Canadians were superior to the Americans. "We've abandoned quality for quantity," he said, referring to the American service, whereas its Canadian counterpart remained more selective. "My impression was that External Affairs, in my generation, was clearly the pre-eminent service in Ottawa." The proof, he said, was the number of DEA types who had become deputy ministers in other departments. The route to the top was through DEA. The Canadian service was relatively small for the size of the country, and its training was very good.

In terms of the Canada-US relationship, it's fair to say that the United States loomed larger in Canada than vice versa. In Canada, the better people gravitated to the American relationship. On the US side, the State Department did not give adequate attention to it. But you couldn't make a full career out of Canada, though John Hickerson and to a degree **Rufus Smith** did. It had no pizzazz, it wasn't sexy. So the people who worked on Canadian issues had no Canadian background. This probably wouldn't change, though some peculiarly Canadian issues, such as the environment, have now become universal, and you could make a career out of them.

His improvements in Ottawa stuck, Duemling claimed. Enders was able to give prominence to the relationship when he was there, and, as mentioned, the environment has come much more to the fore ...

The United States and Quebec separatism
The story about Enders and Carter on Quebec separatism was true, as far as he knew. From the US standpoint, a strong federal government, an able and

responsive partner, was highly desirable. That such a government had been undermined or wounded was not in American interests. But for the Americans, dealing with the issue was very, very delicate. They could not intervene in an internal matter in such a way as to provoke a backlash. They had to find a delicate way to make their position clear but without offending either Quebec or Canadian nationalists. Oblique statements from Carter were the solution.

They were always, Duemling stated, but always, correct with Lévesque and the separatists, and they knew that Lévesque was trying to influence the American position. Lévesque's visits to the United States were discussed at the highest level between the Canadian and American governments.

Washington was anxious that its behaviour be seen as friendly and supportive; fortunately, the shared political assumptions of both countries included a desire not to be seen as bottling up free speech. But Lévesque was never received in the White House or, officially, by Kissinger or Vance. He or his officials may have been received below that level.

Duemling said there was little interference on the Quebec question from the National Security Council (NSC). In the mid- to late seventies, the NSC did not take a great interest in Canadian affairs. The subject was left primarily to the State Department, and in any case the NSC deferred to Enders and to State. Enders devised a remarkable way of influencing American policy. He would write speeches on important topics and send them down to Washington to be cleared. Given about four days' notice before delivery, the Canadian desk would have to take the speeches around and sell them. "He made policy by corralling the town," Duemling said. "If people are tough and resourceful, they can do it."

US business was very interested in the Quebec subject. He doubted that Enders ever thought Quebec would separate or even achieve a great deal of autonomy. Energy issues did not greatly interest business, whereas Enders felt that energy was very important. Duemling thought that Enders believed the pipeline issue worked as well as it could have under the circumstances.[20]

---

20 There were two pipeline issues: one, transporting Alaskan oil to the lower forty-eight states via Canada; two, transporting Canadian oil from the Arctic southward and onward (it was hoped) to the United States. Canadian hopes were disappointed on both.

Trudeau and Carter

FIRA regulations were thought to be detrimental to US interests, and economic nationalism was in the same category. What became apparent was that **Trudeau** was not prepared to take the forward positions that Carter wanted, either in Latin America or on human rights.

The relationship between Trudeau and Carter was civil but not particularly warm. There was no meeting of temperaments. That Carter never visited Canada was indicative. When he did plan a visit, it was three-quarters through his term – and it never happened. Perhaps he felt that his priorities lay elsewhere. As Duemling recalled, no major issues figured in the proposed Carter visit – it was just a neighbourly call ...

Final impressions

Duemling summed up his impressions of Canada by recalling a conversation with the newly arrived Dutch ambassador. The keenest insights come during the first month. The Dutchman told him that the two most important men in Canada were Trudeau and Enders. They were very bright, tough, proud men.

Trudeau's office was always very much on edge about Enders. They watched him constantly, very carefully, very suspiciously. "I don't blame them," Duemling said. They didn't know what he'd say or do next. A successful prime minister controls the evolution of political thinking in his own country. Enders threatened that because he had success, because he moved constantly, spending as much as six weeks on the road. Trudeau's office was unnerved and considered it destabilizing.

Kenneth Curtis, who replaced Enders as ambassador, was exactly his opposite. He was a puppy-dog. He didn't travel, and he never figured out the power structure in Canada. His greatest buddy was Ed Schreyer, the governor general. He was a populist, straightforward, very nice, and he never got angry. And that was all one could say about him.

HON. DONALD MACDONALD (1932-)
INTERVIEW | TORONTO, 5 APRIL 1988

G7 summits

Macdonald attended the Puerto Rico and London G7 summits with **Trudeau** in 1976 and 1977. They were a waste of time. Nothing emerged. The communiqués were boiled up weeks beforehand. Why did we want in? – *amour-propre*. He thought that Canadian and US interests were generally the same and that Ford and Carter, who lacked international experience, seemed in awe of Trudeau. Carter was so respectful, and he had such naive trust in Trudeau as the other North American, that Trudeau was touched. Washington felt that it could rely on him more than on the Europeans and the Japanese. At the London G7 summit in June 1977, Macdonald was speaking about the need for agreements on grain. Helmut Schmidt interrupted to say that grain didn't interest him. Carter then jumped in to say that grain interested the United States, so maybe the United States and Canada should go and arrange things between them. The other German delegates pulled at Schmidt, and he backed off. Macdonald wondered whether this was the beginning of the Schmidt-Carter antipathy. Trudeau and Schmidt had a real rapport, and the British prime minister Jim Callaghan was so smooth that everyone felt they had rapport with him.

ALLAN GOTLIEB (1928-)
INTERVIEW | WASHINGTON, DC, 14 NOVEMBER 1988

On Trudeau at the G7 summit
Trudeau was not marginal at the G7, but summits could be so goddamned high powered. The Bonn summit in July 1978 saw France's Valéry Giscard d'Estaing and Germany's Schmidt, both economists, launched into a discussion of the Kondratieff cycle before ten minutes had elapsed. Trudeau had spontaneously proposed the anti-hijacking resolution, so his role wasn't negligible.

Jimmy Carter was very weak at the summits, "flabby" compared to the Europeans, who behaved with "tremendous arrogance." Carter was not impressive in a group; he was "not a very aggressive person," and Gotlieb was "surprised he didn't fight back."

Yet Trudeau genuinely liked Carter, especially in 1977-79: "He liked the way Carter was on top of the files." He didn't need "cue cards." Trudeau had a good regard for Carter "and never thought he was weak." Carter's policy on Canada, at a time when we had an active secessionist movement, was "very high-minded," very Boy Scout. He never interfered but let it be known that he supported a united Canada ...

INTERVIEW | WASHINGTON, DC, 30 JUNE 1986

Canada and Carter
Gotlieb thought the depiction of the Carter period as "paradise" was at odds with the swift descent into hell that followed.[21] Granted, the periodization was right, with 1980 as a watershed, but there were some special factors that made the period 1977-80 unusually tranquil.

The first was Don Jamieson, "the most pro-American foreign minister we ever had," "genuinely pro-American ... almost a lapdog of Cyrus Vance." Gotlieb recalled Jamieson's support for union with the United States in Newfoundland from 1948.

The second was that "Trudeau was immensely in harmony with Carter's general world outlook." This was best expressed in Carter's Notre Dame speech, which proclaimed that containment of the Soviet Union was over and that the Soviets no longer posed a threat. This was crucial; Carter later moved, witness Afghanistan, but Trudeau remained where he was. He recalled Trudeau "raging over Afghanistan"; his statements in opposition on that subject were "adamant." Though very sympathetic to Carter over the Iranian hostage incident, he was totally unsympathetic over Afghanistan.

Third, there was "the total state of shock over Quebec." "We just couldn't dream of criticizing the United States; they held our future in their hands. We didn't know how long the Quebec problem would last. If they [the Americans] had decided to play footsie with Quebec rather than with the federal government, or to pursue a divide and conquer policy," things would have been very different in North America.

Fourth, Trudeau picked up resonances from European leaders, particularly Helmut Schmidt, who was outrageous on the subject of Carter. Undoubtedly, Carter was weak vis-à-vis the Europeans, and Trudeau saw that. It wasn't that he went along with Schmidt entirely, for he believed that the interests of nations transcended personalities, but he couldn't avoid it either. He saw Carter as diminishing, and Carter was very weak at summits.

The fifth factor was the very grave opinion in Ottawa regarding the ineffectiveness of Carter. All countries found him unreliable and discovered that he couldn't deliver on his promises. The failure to ratify the fisheries

---

21 This interview was conducted by Robert Bothwell and Professor John Kirton.

treaty was a real shock; after all, it was his treaty. The convention tax in Congress and the problems over border broadcasting did not help. He wasn't delivering very well, and though he was intelligent and a liberal, his standing sank.

In looking at Trudeau's period in office, one can discern two kinds of policies, those sponsored by the ministers and those emanating from the prime minister himself, when he was moved to intervene due to his disappointment in a minister. When that happened, the minister was dead in the water. Witness Allan MacEachen over the Peace Initiative: "So it's a complex picture."

Gotlieb mentioned a 1979 speech that Trudeau gave to the Advertising Club of Toronto, when he promised three specific extensions to FIRA. "That rattled the hell out of them down here" in Washington.

Gotlieb had heard it said that Zbigniew Brzezinski was "convinced that Canada would fall apart." He had his own contacts in Quebec in both communities, and that appears to have been their message.

The Toronto speech, then, was a bit abnormal during a period when Trudeau had to deal with Lévesque. He took a while to recover his self-confidence, and there was a freeze on Trudeau's policies as a result.

Gotlieb in Washington under Reagan

Gotlieb spoke of the "key players" in Washington. "When I got [to Washington], there were a number of contradictory impressions that I had," he recalled. There was a "tremendous discontinuity between the two administrations." The new Trudeau policies of 1980 meant that we were the "odd man out in the industrial club; we were an industrial country with Third World policies." That view dated back to Carter, but it was not strongly expressed. **Peter Towe,** who was in Washington until November 1981 as ambassador, "was convinced that the Carter people would not make a big issue over the NEP." Given his personal relationships (for example, his wife was friends with Mondale's wife), the election, Iran, and the sense he got from living in Washington, he did not expect much. "I don't think the Carter people had shown the full extent of their antagonism."

When Reagan came to Ottawa in March 1981, there was a debate as to whether he would mention the NEP and FIRA. He started mildly, and he held back at first; it was believed that the Americans were restrained by considerations of the approaching G7 summit at Montebello, Quebec. Only in July 1981 did Treasury Secretary Don Regan come, and "it started for real and NEP turned into a crisis." His arrival led Trudeau to back off and say no more NEPs and FIRA. "There was a tremendous sense of a crisis brewing," Gotlieb said. In the White House, there was a feeling that the Canadians were going off half-cocked. Reagan was affected by a lot of his California kitchen cabinet friends, some of whom had oil interests in Canada. They were very anti-Trudeau, very antagonistic to us. This was working on Reagan. It showed up in staff studies in the White House and in the State Department. Malcolm Baldrige and Bill Brock were really mad,[22] and "Haig shared their views." Al Haig thought he was a moderate. Reagan got the "Canada the bad boy" message from California, Bush from Texas: All the interests, including broadcasting, came together to put the finger on Canada as the bad boy. The State Department was probably the most conservative in that area; the push came from the domestic side, the White House, and the US trade representative.

"When I came here [to Washington], **Enders** was still in Ottawa," Gotlieb said. "December 1, 1981, Enders was back here. Enders, who was doing the Central American job," said at that time that "we were pretty stupid because we didn't know how to play it." In Reagan's book, Canada was a very good thing – trilateral, North American. Canada had a unique advantage – it could do no wrong.

Reagan had a very short list of absolute beliefs: "One of them was that North America was special and should get along." Enders said that we should exploit this more. This, despite the tremendous campaign against us and against Trudeau as a socialist/communist. The real sentiment about Canada came from the White House – this is the central area of foreign policy. It thought that Canada was a good thing. Hence, Reagan's first trip outside the United States was to Canada. Just after Gotlieb arrived in Washington, Richard Darman in the White House said that "the great mistake Canada made was not to be part of a special bureau, Canada-Mexico-US. You would have gotten a much better deal."

Canada-US relations really went sour in 1982, Gotlieb went on. This was due to the White House, which felt that Trudeau had behaved very badly at the Bonn NATO summit and the G-7 Economic Summit at Versailles. At Bonn, a group of us were standing outside, and the assembled journalists were asking Reagan about the recent Israeli invasion of Lebanon. Trudeau

---

22 US commerce secretary and US trade representative, respectively.

told them to "ask Al,"²³ implying pretty clearly that the president didn't know anything. That generated a very bad feeling. Gotlieb had enjoyed great relations with Lawrence Eagleburger. This feeling came from William Clark, then at the NSC, the wives, and particularly from Michael Deaver in the White House. Did Reagan himself feel insulted and betrayed? All the people around him, all the California group, did. Their view was to protect the old man – Trudeau had been unkind. That was reinforced by steady insertions from his right-wing friends – that Trudeau was a communist. "I had it on high authority that Reagan read Lubor Zink's article in the *National Review*. Of course he did," Gotlieb said. Bill Buckley, the editor of the *National Review*, and his wife, who was a Canadian, were very close to Reagan and "very anti-Trudeau." So Reagan got it from California, Texas, New York, and the right. The dominant attitude toward Canada was injected through the White House.

MacEachen's influence

But there was a slow change at work late in the Trudeau years, Gotlieb recalled, which occurred because Allan MacEachen was appointed SSEA. George Shultz loved MacEachen. They went to school together. When MacEachen became SSEA, Gotlieb said, "I was worried. MacEachen had a reputation – Third World, immigration, Paris. MacEachen could be seen as anti-American. But he was almost as pro-American as Jamieson. He was very constructive and deliberate. He was very anxious to rebuild in the Jamieson mode." Shultz saw MacEachen as a very strong player. He liked and knew him. They shared personal traits, such as long silences at breakfast. MacEachen began the road back. Shultz's quarterly meeting became important, and Shultz became a positive factor. MacEachen steadily improved. So there were two foreign policy periods: 1980-82 and then the MacEachen one, when he was SSEA until the summer of 1984. In 1982-83, MacEachen was trying to hold back from disputes with the US policy such as the NEP and to slowly rebuild. He and Shultz were problem solvers ...

....

23 Trudeau was referring to Al Haig, the secretary of state. In Robert Service, *The End of the Cold War, 1985-1991* (New York: Public Affairs, 2015), Chapters 1 and 3, there is a good account of Reagan's strengths and Haig's weaknesses, as well as appraisals of the other major American figures.

The US governmental system
What was overwhelming in his experience, Gotlieb said, was that the United States really had no foreign policy toward Canada. It may have come close to one during the Carter period due to Quebec, but the relations with Canada were an aggregation of domestic policy thrusts. The issues on the agenda came out of the legislative or regulatory environment. Therefore, the responsibility centre was somewhere in the domestic system. For example, the Clean Air Act caused acid rain to be important, there was the Garrison dam issue, nuclear waste sites, and on the economic side, energy disputes, trucking, civil aviation, broadcasting, and communication. An enormous number of the problems arose because the Americans changed their regulations, so they wanted us to change ours. So we now had an unfair advantage.

The State Department had no weight on those issues, and the real actors were elsewhere. Shultz made a great show. He was very conscientious, he liked Canada, he really tried. He played much more heavily on these things than the State Department did. It had little to do with trade. The US trade representative belonged to the White House and the National Security Council. The White House and the NSC were the only ones who mattered on such issues ... We kept the State Department informed, Gotlieb went on. On pharmaceuticals, it was James Baker and the Treasury. Often the State Department said it couldn't help us. We now played on the domestic agenda of the United States. Fortunately, Shultz was a heavy. When he or John Whitehead, the deputy secretary of state, got to the Economic Policy Council or the NSC, they had weight. People listened to Shultz, but it was personal. His department played little role. The State Department was not a central agency.

In 1984, the NSC had a particularly negative view of Canada, right down the line to the desk officer level. This was true for the State Department too. They were unwilling to help Canada. We would get support at a high level at the State Department but nowhere else. This was due to the Peace Initiative. But then Mulroney was elected. Before, when Shultz was there, we could use the Shultz-MacEachen link, but there was a sea change in the White House when Mulroney came in ...

Vice President Bush had not had a role. When Trudeau was prime minister, he came to Ottawa for a day, the day on which Reagan made his Star Wars speech. Bush had not had a role thus far, but it was he who asked for this last trip to Canada. Gotlieb did not think that Shultz would welcome a Bush role.

So Bush was not a major player, but the trip to Canada was largely initiated by him ... When Trudeau visited Washington in July 1981, it was Bush who led the attack on Canada. Reagan was still new, but Bush was familiar with the issues, so he served as the key interrogator ...

The central thing was that the United States was a "virtually ungovernable society." It consisted of division of powers within division of powers. If the centre of the system worked in your direction, as it did on acid rain, that was a help, but even then most of the time it just couldn't control the whole galaxy ...

One thing to emphasize in any discussion of the Carter period, Gotlieb concluded, was how badly it sapped America's national will. That's why Peter Towe felt the way he did about the United States not making an issue of FIRA and the NEP. And Carter's aborted trip to Canada was not exactly "prevented by Iran," Gotlieb argued. "It was a public decision not to go. He was heavily criticized for it later. That's when the Russians began to hold him hostage in the White House, and he was the only president never to make a visit to Canada during his term of office."

INTERVIEW | WASHINGTON, DC, 14 NOVEMBER 1988

Canada and the United States
The Reagan period around 1982 was horrible, with periodicals like *Business Week* firing at us, and congressmen getting into the act. There was the 1982 recession as well. The Liberals knew they could take bad relations only so far, and they started to improve through smoke and mirrors.

As SSEA, **Mark MacGuigan** had been publicly damaged by two contradictory impressions – that he was Al Haig's pal and the idea that things were awful.[24] Gotlieb had no great expectations of Allan MacEachen as SSEA, whom he regarded as a "tiers-mondiste," concerned with North-South and the like. But he turned out to be a second Don Jamieson, a real Maritimer rather than a Toronto Liberal. MacEachen accepted the legitimacy of some of the US complaints. Trudeau's increasing tilt to Third World issues stimulated his desire to mediate. In fact, by mid-1983, MacEachen's reputation was very high ...

....

24   Haig was secretary of state from 1981 to 1982.

As for Reagan's 1983 invasion of Grenada, Trudeau behaved strictly according to his notion of spheres of influence. True, he loved Cuba and kept a line of communication open there, but he "did not choose to tweak the giant's nose." Soviet intervention in Poland came before Grenada, and Trudeau may have seen Grenada as a legitimization of his stand on Poland. There were no real anxieties; we made more of the fact that we hadn't been consulted about the invasion.

Back in Washington, Gotlieb was busy defending the NEP. The Americans were complaining bitterly, and George Shultz called it "outrageous" in conversation with MacEachen. They could see that the NEP was unravelling, and some took pleasure in watching the Canadians shoot themselves in the foot.

There was another bone of contention too. The Duncan-Lalonde (US) formula had ratcheted up the price that Canada charged the Americans for its natural gas, along with the international oil price.[25] This, despite the fact that Canada had no other market for its gas than the United States, so it was a highly artificial link. But then the oil price went down, and the shoe was on the other foot.

Malcolm Baldrige, the commerce secretary, continued to give us both barrels on energy. **Lalonde** had a hard time down in Washington, and Herb Gray was actually persona non grata – nobody wanted to see him.

The back-off from FIRA, however, improved matters considerably. We grasped that it was an administrative mess, so we tried very hard to improve its administration. The fact that we were allowing 95 percent of investment applications helped.

So did the Cruise missile. The American request to test it in Canada made sense to Trudeau, and despite his inert cabinet, he decided the matter. Then people criticized him, and he'd not rest until he demolished his critics – very gutsy statements. Gotlieb circulated them widely, and people were impressed ...

As for sectoral free trade,[26] Gotlieb had had no special connection with the subject, but he did have two general inputs. One was to tell Ottawa that US protectionism was a serious long-term problem from 1982 on. The status

....

25 Named after Charles Duncan, US secretary of energy, 1979-81.
26 Modelled on the Autopact, sectoral free trade would have established Canada-US free trade by industry, or economic sector, rather than all at once.

quo was not viable: "I was shocked by what I saw here." There was a deep sense that Canada was not playing fair on economic matters. There was the Dingell Report on Canadian investment.[27] Wherever you went, there were soreheads. By 1982, he was advising getting out of the multilateral option. One of his colleagues accused him of advocating the "prostitution option," going to bed with whoever paid most. That was essentially true, Gotlieb said.

He was not against the sectoral approach. It was functional, but it was stillborn. The United States was glad to try it, and we agreed on four sectors – steel, computers and software (hard to define), etc. The US steel industry was opposed to the approach, and Bill Brock said it was too narrow to succeed. The sectoral idea was probably associated with Ed Lumley, but really it must have come from the trade policy division of ITC.

EDWARD NEF

INTERVIEW | WASHINGTON, DC, 12 JANUARY 1988

The son of a Swiss diplomat, Nef joined the US foreign service and was posted to Africa, Latin America, and the Peace Corps. He was legislative director for Senator Max Baucus of Montana.

On the congressional view of Canada after 1980
The post-1980 oil crisis and the cuts in Canadian petroleum exports to the United States brought a major recession to Montana. As a staffer to Senator Baucus,[28] Nef was much involved. Montana depended on Alberta crude, and there was substantial refinery work there. Baucus, who thought he knew Canada and Canadians, was hit hard by the cuts, and this was the start on the Hill of a tougher view of Canada among senators and representatives from Washington, Michigan, Minnesota, and Montana. Canada, it turned out, could inflict substantial harm in key areas – potash, oil and gas – and the bureaucrats in Washington had kept the policy to themselves. The feistiness on the Hill reflected a resentment versus Canada *and* the Executive Branch.

....

27   John Dingell (Democrat-Michigan) was the longest-serving member of the US House of Representatives (1955-2015). He took a consistently skeptical view of Canadian policies as they affected his auto-industry constituents.
28   Max Baucus, Democratic senator from Montana, was also skeptical of Canada and Canadians, and fairly consistently hostile to Canadian interests.

On the failure of the fisheries treaty, Nef faulted the Canadians and the Executive Branch. He told the Canadians that they had failed to assess the changed relationship of the Executive with Congress. The Canadian embassy had the views of the State Department and the White House, but on the Hill the politicians knew that their constituents were being hurt. It was hard to go into a town where 70 percent of the population was affected by Canadian policies on lumber. A politician had no choice but to make an issue of fish or stumpage. On lumber, Congress itself had little power and was reluctant to pass legislation for individual industries.

ROBERT HUNTER (1940-)
INTERVIEW | WASHINGTON, DC, 15 NOVEMBER 1988

Hunter was on the National Security Council handling Western Europe and Canada between 1977 and 1981.

Trudeau in Washington on Quebec
Hunter got involved at the beginning with the preparations for Trudeau's February 1977 visit to Washington. Ivan Head came down and talked with Zbigniew Brzezinski. Ivan had a very good relationship with Zbig and an "excellent entrée" everywhere. They discussed what was on Carter's mind, and on Trudeau's, a very workmanlike and proper procedure.

During the conversations between Trudeau and Carter, Hunter took notes, as did **Vernon Turner** for the Canadians. Afterward, they went over what they'd written.

"Oh," Turner would say, "the prime minister couldn't have said that. He did? Well, what he meant was this." And he'd write down the opposite. It was an education for Hunter.

Afterward, Hunter and Brzezinski had excellent relations with USSEA Gotlieb: you always knew where you stood with him.

The overall US position was clear. America was not neutral on the question of Quebec. Even to be perceived as neutral was wrong, Hunter said. It implied that Canada's survival was a matter of indifference, when in fact it was very much in the interest of the United States.

The NSC would have done a study on Canada, as it did on a lot of countries, but Hunter couldn't remember it. He *did* recall "bemused" and highly speculative conversations about how many states Canada would comprise if

Quebec separated, and what the effect on the electoral college would be if Canada split up. More practically, barely, there were discussions of how to handle relations with the two parts of a divided Canada. But the consensus was that a divided Canada would be bad for North America.

One of Canada's strengths, he argued, was "that you don't get taken too seriously." This meant that Canadians could get away with more than others did.

As to Carter's relations with Trudeau, they were excellent. Both men were autodidacts and very smart. They both felt that policy was superior to politics; indeed, the good impression Trudeau made was misleading because it may have led Carter to expect too much of Canada. Yes, Carter did have use for Trudeau's ideas; he believed that ideas transcended personalities and position. Trudeau was much more sophisticated than Chancellor Helmut Schmidt, who was an arrogant, talkative bore, partly because President Ford had indulged him, some said by parking the phone and working while Schmidt raved away. The chancellor believed that he had had a master-pupil relationship with Ford and should have one with Carter as well. As early as March 1977, he had passed the word to American diplomats that Carter must shape up. Hunter had seen the dispatch and Carter's comments on it. The president was not amused. Carter simply did not intend to be dealt with as Ford had been.

HON. MARK MacGUIGAN (1931-98)
INTERVIEW | OTTAWA, 19 JANUARY 1988

Trudeau and Carter and Reagan
MacGuigan said he saw the two together at the Venice summit and felt that their relations were good but not close ...

As it was, we had the NEP to contend with, thereby complicating matters; why bring out hostility "through our own stupidity?" The NEP was the first thing Haig and Shultz would bring up at meetings. Businessmen were contacting the US administration. In retrospect, however, MacGuigan believed that we got "a bad rap" on the NEP, with only one important exception. That was the back-in provision, made retroactive.[29] He could never justify it to

---

29 In the Trudeau government's National Energy Programme (1981), Ottawa appropriated a 25 percent interest in (particularly) petroleum leases on federal lands,

himself and tried to get it modified. But he was very supportive of getting US companies here to give equal contracts, equal treatment, to Canadians.

He remembered a 1981 meeting in Ottawa that brought up Treasury Secretary Donald Regan, "a peculiarly nasty man in philosophy and in person." Finance Minister Allan MacEachen, braced by **Michael Pitfield**, refused to modify the back-in; the Canadian government, he said, had a need for confidential energy information that only equity could give.

MacGuigan said that he had learned about the impending NEP as a member of the cabinet and assumed **Gotlieb** had heard about it through the Pitfield network. They were *told* in the cabinet, but because it was part of the budget, there was no normal consultation, and DEA's view was not sought. MacGuigan said he liked it in general, was indeed one of NEP's strongest supporters in Cabinet, so why jib at consultation? He did try to get MacEachen to vary the back-in, but **Marc Lalonde,** the minister of energy, mines and resources, said he could live with it; and MacEachen, or more likely Pitfield, was intransigent. In any case he didn't focus on the back-in as an issue at first ...

MacGuigan had a number of objectives when he became a minister in 1980. One of these was relations with the United States. There, he and Trudeau differed, but at least he was aware of the need to get on with the Americans. In MacGuigan's opinion, Canada had to be clearly on the US side on everything to do with the USSR; that allowed for leeway for differences over NATO and the Third World. To Trudeau, this was paying an unwelcome price; to MacGuigan, it was just reality, our policy, and in our interest too.

Despite the attitudinal differences, he and Trudeau never quibbled over anything fundamental. Yet, MacGuigan added, "I felt Trudeau was irrationally aggressive, suspicious, towards the Americans ..."

PAUL H. ROBINSON, JR. (1930-)
INTERVIEW | CHICAGO, 1986

A Chicago insurance executive and Republican fundraiser, Paul Robinson was US ambassador in Ottawa from 1981 to 1985. He managed to be both staunchly conservative and pro-Canadian, reflecting his own Loyalist

including on previously granted leases. It was this latter point to which the US government vehemently objected.

ancestry. He had particularly strong views on Quebec separatism and its leader, René Lévesque. As he told a later interviewer, "Although not a Canadian, I have strong pro-Canadian views. To me, [separatism] is treason. I mean, if the governor of Illinois was saying the things that Lévesque said, we would hang him."[30]

Reagan on Canada

Reagan's own opinion of Canada was unformed but positive.[31] In posing his candidacy for 1980, he mentioned what had been announced on 13 November 1979, "the North American Accord," but he left it purposely undefined, so as not to upset either the Canadians or the Mexicans. Robinson had "any number of" contacts with Jack Gavin, the US ambassador to Mexico, to further the idea, and he knew that it was close to the president's heart. It helped that Reagan thought a great deal of Brian Mulroney, and he added that Trudeau and Reagan also got on "just fine."

Becoming ambassador and dealing in Ottawa

Robinson started preparations for his ambassadorship with two months of off-and-on briefings in Washington; they took that long only because of delays in getting Senate confirmation of his appointment. The briefings, as might be expected, reflected departmental or agency positions. They did not appear to have made a tremendous impact on Robinson, whose impression or preferences toward Canada were already formed. Among other things, he had taken his wife and daughter from Toronto to Calgary by train in July 1980. He was a strong believer in the idea that cultural similarity makes for the closest and best relations; on reflection, he included French Canadians. He did not like to do business outside the English-language countries, though perforce he did because some of his clients were involved in, say, France ...

Within half an hour of presenting his credentials in Ottawa, he saw Trudeau. He asked whether he could have easy access to the prime minister and his ministers, and found Trudeau agreeable. This was important, given the attitudes of some of the ministers. Once, when Robinson was explaining an idea of selling all Canada's surplus hydro, gas, and oil to the United

---

30 Interview with Paul H. Robinson, 1989, 16, Foreign Affairs Oral History Collection, Association for Diplomatic Studies and Training, Arlington, VA, http://www.adst.org/OH%20TOCs/Robinson,%20Paul.toc.pdf.
31 This interview was conducted by Robert Bothwell and Professor John Kirton.

States under some kind of guarantee at market price, the relevant minister responded, "What's in it for America?" Some thought that the wily Yankee always had a trick up his sleeve.

Robinson found that in some departments, "I was being very politely stonewalled." Herb Gray, the minister of ITC, apparently had nothing on his mind but the Detroit Tigers, and Robinson quickly figured out that he would get nowhere with Gray. So, he tried to sideline Gray and made a point of calling back on Trudeau. He found himself on Trudeau's plane flying to Grand Rapids, Michigan, for the inauguration of the Gerry Ford Presidential Library and chatted about this, to make the point that Canada was changing the trade rules in the middle of the game. "We discussed this" – Trudeau, Reagan, Haig, and himself – but got nowhere.

The impact of FIRA and the NEP
Robinson naturally attended all the meetings between Trudeau and Reagan. At the first one, held in Washington during July 1981, Trudeau and Reagan were getting on well, but "the atmosphere was heavy," and there was a lot of sniping going on at the ministerial level. Even though Trudeau and Reagan were not "soulmates," they had enough respect for one another's positions and countries to keep things civil between themselves. In this, as in other things, the Canadian press had it all wrong ...

Perhaps the greatest crisis of Robinson's ambassadorship came in October-November 1981. Through Judge Bill Clark, the Reagan crony who was deputy secretary of state and "a very special friend," he got to appear before the entire US cabinet in formal session to argue the case against retaliation against Canada for FIRA and the NEP. There were "very powerful men" who wanted retaliation, and they were in the room (presumably these were Bill Brock, the US trade representative, and Malcolm Baldrige, secretary of commerce). It did not, apparently, include Donald Regan of Reagan's staff, who showed up in Ottawa to meet with Allan MacEachen at Robinson's house. Regan, Robinson said, "later became a good friend" and a key to keeping the lid on the relationship between the two countries.

One of the ideas then circulating was to drop Canada from the newly established quadrilateral group on trade relationships set up by the G7 summit; it hadn't yet met but was scheduled for Key Biscayne. Robinson had had the temerity to predict failure for the group and to insist that Canada be invited, though of course he had no power whatever to control who was invited. He met Ed Lumley, who became ITC minister in September 1982, and Lumley saw Brock, and Canada got the coveted invitation. At some point, Trudeau gave Lumley a mandate to clean up FIRA's activities, and he did.

RICHARD SMITH (1932-)
INTERVIEW | WASHINGTON, DC, 12 JANUARY 1988

Smith served as director of Canadian affairs in the State Department (1978-80) before moving to Ottawa as deputy chief of mission from 1980 to 1983.

The impact of the NEP
The dividing line in US-Canada relations, as Smith recalled it, was the NEP. Prior to October 1980, 1978-80, relations were pretty good ...
The NEP struck with no warning at all. Even **Gotlieb** seemed to have been left out. It was hatched between Mickey Cohen, the deputy minister of finance, and Ed Clark,[32] one of its key drafters. Was it anti-American? Perhaps, perhaps not, Smith said. He never thought that **Trudeau** himself was anti-American, and not even Clark really qualified as such. But Clark and the others were edgy, and on balance there was an anti-American tone. It was reasonable to conclude that the ascendancy of people such as Clark, who was socialistically inclined, made you less enamoured of the American way of doing things. There had been a period of confusion and weakness under Prime Minister Joe Clark, which allowed people like Ed Clark to do their homework.
Although Smith had his difficulties with Ed Clark, he never had any problem getting to see Energy Minister **Marc Lalonde** for office time or for dinner. Indeed, he had no access problems at any time, right up to the prime minister. Some of the Trudeau children were attracted to Ambassador **Robinson**'s pitching machine at the residence, so there was contact that way. There might have been tensions, but they were never personal.
Smith thought that Clark had based the NEP on a rapidly and continuously rising price of oil, and if you bought his assumptions, then the NEP made "a bit of sense." In fact, however, it encouraged a shift from equity to debt just as interest rates were hitting 18 percent. Clark's idea had been to get

---

32 Clark later became the CEO of the Toronto-Dominion (TD) Bank.

back equity from the United States and exploit the opportunity of higher prices, but eventually even Trudeau recognized the folly of Clark's program.

The tension resulting from the NEP was manifested in the run-up to the Reagan visit in 1981. Notes were sent but then pulled back as too extreme. There was a sense that the relationship between the two countries had been betrayed. Our meetings with the Canadians were tense; the exchanges between Ed Clark and Meyer Rashish, the under secretary of state for economic affairs, were acerbic.

There was talk of punishing Canada for the NEP ... But what happened was that realism won out. Canadian investment began to stream down to the United States. Some people actually wanted to stop it, but why on earth should they? It seemed that every action that could be taken against Canada was also in some way against the American interest. "I did a little public diplomacy in the expectation that the reality would sink in," Smith recalled. As for the ambassador, he was onside: there were no inappropriate countersteps. The conclusion was that "we should pursue our own interests and see what was happening."

V
Canada and Europe

NEXT TO THE UNITED STATES and Great Britain, Western Europe was a major focus for Canadian diplomacy. Canada maintained embassies in every European country west of the Soviet bloc,[1] partly for symbolic reasons but usually because cultural affinity and sometimes immigration (from the Netherlands, Germany, Portugal, and Italy, for example) kept links alive even when there was very little political or trade business to transact. The embassies served another useful purpose, by relieving the pressure of senior officer overpopulation in the Department of External Affairs. Thanks to Europe, and to a wise policy of purchasing sizeable embassy buildings in the 1940s and 1950s when European real estate was cheap, diplomats who merited reward always had something to hope for.

There was a point, however, to maintaining a noticeable diplomatic establishment abroad: the cultivation of goodwill and the determination that if anything arose where interests were entangled, Canada, and Canada's opinions, would not be forgotten or ignored. In countries with similar problems and similar interests, it was possible to cultivate diplomatic co-operation, as at the United Nations or within the NATO alliance.

France played a special role in defining Canadian relations with Europe. The reasons were not economic, or political, or military – though at various points in the past, they were all three. Canadian troops had defended France in the First and Second World Wars, Canada gave France substantial loans after 1945, and until 1968 the Royal Canadian Air Force kept bases in France as part of NATO. During the Second World War, Canada both maintained relations with the Vichy government of France and supported the Free French movement of General Charles de Gaulle. France and Canada were not close during the 1950s, especially because France was preoccupied with colonial wars in Indochina and Algeria.

....
1 Luxembourg, San Marino, Monaco, and Andorra excepted.

Once those wars had been lost, President Charles de Gaulle, as he had become (1959-69), turned his attention to shoring up what remained of French influence and prestige elsewhere in the world. His eye lighted upon Canada, and as early as 1964 he determined on a policy that would encourage the autonomy, and possibly the independence, of Quebec. After all, Quebec was home to the largest group of French-speakers outside France itself. There followed de Gaulle's famous visit to Quebec in 1967,[2] and his subsequent promotion of Quebec independence and the demise of Canadian federalism.

Many of the interviewees represented in this book (and some others, such as Marcel Cadieux, who is a frequent presence in these pages) had a role in promoting, frustrating, or negating Gaullist interference in Canada. The Lalonde interview in Chapter I and the Max Yalden interview below are important here. It was clear from our interviews that almost all members of the French professional foreign service were unenthusiastic about de Gaulle's Quebec policy. (The exception was Jean-Daniel Jurgensen, who is referenced in some of the interviews that follow.) Some, such as François Leduc, were discreet, whereas others, such as Jean Béliard, were outspoken. In this, the diplomats mirrored the population of France, who were certainly not inspired by de Gaulle's romantic adventure in North America. De Gaulle was soon sent packing in January 1969, though his successors as president, Georges Pompidou and Valéry Giscard d'Estaing, maintained a passive hostility to Canada or Canadian projects, such as membership in the G7 group of leading economies.

Under de Gaulle, France had formally wound up most of its overseas possessions – as colonies. But in some cases, such as Niger (mentioned below), France retained substantial interests, and French troops were available to friendly governments to cope with coups or other forms of disorder. Accordingly, some French-speaking African republics, nominally independent, were in fact French satellites. At the same time, the Canadian government, largely for domestic political reasons, was trying to establish itself as a friend of "La Francophonie" – the cluster of French-speaking states (or moderately French-speaking states). Thus, Canadian engagement in La Francophonie did not please important segments of the French government,

....
2 In July 1967, during a state visit to Canada, de Gaulle addressed a large crowd from the balcony of the Montreal City Hall, concluding his speech with "Vive le Québec libre," the separatist slogan.

because it created an alternative to dependence on France for the new countries of Africa.

Finally, under Giscard, France stopped blocking Canada's admission to the G7 and permitted a Contractual Link to be negotiated between the European Common Market (which was a kind of Franco-German condominium) and Canada, in pursuit of Trudeau's Third Option policy. Perhaps the French expected that little would come of it in the immediate future, and they may have been right.

The other European country represented here is the Federal Republic of Germany. West Germany, as it still was, had Europe's largest economy and most prosperous citizenry, having eclipsed both Great Britain and France. West German foreign policy was carefully designed not to make its Western European neighbours, or the United States, nervous. The Germans also pursued an active policy of engagement with the Soviet bloc, to which, by 1987 when we did our interviews, they had become essential sources of funds – paymasters, in effect, to the communist states of Eastern Europe.

Because of its size and economic importance, and its political centrality, Germany was a natural focus for Canada. Canada maintained a large embassy in Bonn, the West German capital, and sent some of its most seasoned diplomats there. The Germans reciprocated Canadian interest, though the links between the two countries probably did not fully mature until the prime ministership of Brian Mulroney, who followed Trudeau.

The G7 provided Canada with an entrée to Europe but especially Germany. Relations between Trudeau and Helmut Schmidt, the German chancellor, were notably friendly, and Trudeau certainly admired Schmidt, who through Trudeau considerably influenced some of Canada's domestic policies. The interviews with the German diplomats Heinz Schneppen and Rüdiger von Lukowitz accurately portray this relationship. At the same time, readers should bear in mind some of the American comments on Schmidt, notably those of Robert Hunter in Chapter IV.

HON. GÉRARD PELLETIER (1919-97)
INTERVIEW | OTTAWA, 14 AUGUST 1987

La Francophonie
When Pelletier became a minister in 1968, he originally wanted to be a junior minister (minister without portfolio) in DEA; but the department's view,

reported by Jules Léger, was that two ministers, the prime minister and the SSEA, were enough.

Nevertheless, **Trudeau** asked him to become minister responsible for La Francophonie, a subject on which Pelletier had spoken at a riding meeting in his Mount Royal constituency in 1966. By then, DEA policy had changed under Pearson and some of the aid was very generous (for example, to the association of francophone universities). Generally, things went well for Pelletier and for La Francophonie at this time; in fact, they went so smoothly that Trudeau forgot he had assigned Pelletier to the task. Only after Pelletier became ambassador to France did Trudeau phone him and ask why things were no longer going well; when Pelletier reminded him of the ministerial arrangements, Trudeau said he had quite forgotten; and he appointed Jean-Pierre Goyer to the job. Goyer, Pelletier said, was less modest about the task than he himself had been.

Canada and France
He discussed the "Vive le Québec libre" incident, which occurred during de Gaulle's July 1967 visit to Canada. Did de Gaulle intend to scandalize, or did he not? On the one hand, he prepared his remarks carefully; on the other, he must have had a second speech that would be given later, in Ottawa. What was in it? A few months afterward, in the fall of 1967, de Gaulle asked the ambassador, **François Leduc**, whether the Canadians had recovered from the shock he had given them. Leduc thought they had and that things could be patched up. Well, said de Gaulle, "The Canadians had gotten along for a hundred years before him, and presumably they could get along for a hundred more."

Asked about support for Quebec separatism in France, Pelletier said that it amounted to twenty-seven people, no more, no less. They included some ex-ministers, some Quai d'Orsay types, and so forth. There was Philippe Rossillon, a multi-millionaire who could travel everywhere at his own expense. Rossillon may have had a nominal government job and salary, but he took his vacations whenever he wanted. He also peculiarly was not in good health, once fainting on Pelletier's bed in Liège. If you spotted only twenty-six of them out for a Quebec festivity, it was a matter for comment and grave speculation. Pelletier was certain that the French secret service had not intervened in Canada; it did so only very cautiously and for important reasons, though in Africa admittedly things might be a bit looser. The 1986 escapade in Auckland, New Zealand, blowing up the *Rainbow Warrior*, an environmentalist vessel, showed that the firm, guiding hand they once had was absent.[3]

The Rossillon affair in Canada was just a flash in the pan.[4] The Manitoba incident in September 1968 was the result of an unchecked, panicky phone call that Derek Bedson, the senior civil servant in Manitoba, made to Trudeau. Unfortunately, he called just before the House sat, or before a press conference, and Trudeau went overboard in his comments. Later, Pelletier told him he'd gone rather far; and when Bedson was asked, he agreed that the information he gave Trudeau was very much on the run, unconsidered, and unverified. And Rossillon's tiny donation to the Acadians did no harm, probably the contrary.

The key to understanding French policy toward La Francophonie was to realize that the French were not very interested if they had to share power with another nation. The British were better with their Commonwealth, according to its secretary-general Arnold Smith, though even there Smith said it became an enjoyable or challenging place to work only after it moved out of London, away from the shadow of the United Kingdom.

The difficulties of the French attitude may be discerned from an incident at the second Niamey conference. With his minister in attendance, Jean-Daniel Jurgensen told Pelletier that he and Canada had better give satisfaction "to Quebec's legitimate demands" or the conference would fail.[5] And, Jurgensen added, "We're well organized to blame you." Pelletier retorted that he could no longer talk to Jurgensen after receiving such a blackmail threat. Jurgensen protested that he hadn't meant that, but Pelletier replied that they spoke the same language and he understood Jurgensen very well. He thought that Jurgensen got a little spanking from his minister afterward because the French and the Quebeckers became more reasonable.

....

3   A Greenpeace ship, the *Rainbow Warrior* was in the South Pacific to protest French nuclear testing. Divers working for the French intelligence service covertly attached two mines to its hull, and the resulting explosions sank the vessel.

4   Philippe Rossillon, who had been a supporter of France's attempt to retain its colony in Algeria, switched his attention to Quebec and "Acadie" in the later 1960s and the 1970s. He played a role in the French bureaucracy, supporting the French language and culture abroad, which brought him to Canada with subsidies in his hand. Ottawa reacted severely to what it saw as foreign interference.

5   Jurgensen (1917-87) was a senior French diplomat with a particular interest in the defence of French culture, which led him to promote the cause of Quebec independence.

His valedictory dispatch from Paris in 1981 (picked up by a *Le Devoir* reporter off the desk of a federal minister in Ottawa, or so the minister later told the RCMP) argued that there was no French policy toward Canada and no Canadian policy toward France. The two countries reacted to each other by improvising ...

FRANÇOIS LEDUC
INTERVIEW | PARIS, 12 OCTOBER 1987

Leduc was French ambassador to Canada from August 1965 until August 1968.

De Gaulle in Canada
Leduc talked of the high point of his embassy in Canada – de Gaulle and "Vive le Québec libre." He linked the incident to de Gaulle's emotion, his exhaustion at age seventy-one after a day on the road. He himself had no advance knowledge of what de Gaulle would say. He heard it over the loudspeaker, like everybody else. But given de Gaulle's sympathies for Quebec, they would have erupted sooner or later.

He rehearsed all the difficulties that preceded de Gaulle's arrival. Quebec was seen as primary, Ottawa secondary. The Canadian authorities worried about security, as they had to; de Gaulle insisted on an open car, on touring Expo '67 on foot, on going to the American pavilion.

For de Gaulle, the visit was a historic occasion in a true sense; the present did not count. He was there to compensate for what France had not done two hundred years before.

Really, the "scandal" was not what de Gaulle said, but his failure to go on to Ottawa, that's what caused the impact. "Ils ne m'acceptent pas, puis je m'en vais," de Gaulle said. Obviously, it wasn't good for Franco-Canadian relations. But it did accelerate "la crise de conscience" on the place of Quebec in Canada.

French interference?
The Rossillon affair was much exaggerated, the subject of an RCMP phobia. Even Leduc's own phone was tapped. The French never gave subsidies to the separatists. Rossillon's own subsidies came from the office of the French prime minister and certainly not from the Elysée. If Marcel Cadieux believed that the embassy was involved, he was indulging in an act of psychological

transference. Anyway, why give subsidies? Canadians were richer than Frenchmen. Of course, Leduc met separatists, like Masse or Morin,[6] but it was in the course of his reporting duties.

Overall, he concluded, his mission was difficult, because he had finally to put events, in Quebec and in Canada, in context.

MAX YALDEN (1930-2015)
INTERVIEWS | OTTAWA, 21 APRIL 1988 AND 5 AUGUST 1988

Yalden joined DEA in 1956 and served in Moscow, Ottawa, and Paris. He then became ADM to the secretary of state, under secretary of state, deputy minister of communications, and official languages commissioner.

INTERVIEW | 21 APRIL 1988

The French and Canada
In 1967, Yalden was Marcel Cadieux's adviser on federal-provincial relations, on France, and on the Constitution. He wrote a paper on federalism and international relations, and one on federalism and international education conferences. Why did he get that job? **Gotlieb** was one of Cadieux's closest advisers, and Gotlieb was a friend. Cadieux wanted someone to chair a task force and to develop a coherent strategy.

On the night that de Gaulle gave his Montreal speech, Yalden and his wife were watching it on TV. Just watch, he said to her, there'll be no surprises. But there certainly were. The next day, when he came in to the office, he found everybody running around like chickens with their heads cut off.[7]

....

6 Marcel Masse (1936-2014) was a nationalist Quebec politician, who early in his career flirted with separatism. He later served as a minister in the Progressive Conservative government of Brian Mulroney. Claude Morin (1929-) was a Quebec civil servant whom Ottawa saw as very sympathetic to separatism. He later became an overt separatist and served in the PQ government from 1976 to 1981.
7 The Central Intelligence Agency assessed de Gaulle's remarks and believed he had "overreached himself." But it concluded somewhat bizarrely that the "immediate result of De Gaulle's visit ... may be to bring French and English Canada closer together." "France-Canada," *Central Intelligence Bulletin*, 26 July 1967, 4, CIA Records, CIA-RDP79T00975A010100210001-5, https://www.cia.gov/library/readingroom/docs/CIA-RDP79T00975A010100210001-5.pdf.

They were in no doubt as to what Claude Morin and company wanted. "We took it for granted, rightly or wrongly, that what Morin wanted was what Canada had done in the 1920s and 1930s, meaning the slow but steady acquisition of the foreign affairs power," he said. Morin and his men were trying to make contact with virtually any organization, and some of them found themselves enmeshed in exchanges of letters that they were completely unprepared for. This went on until we made it very plain that signing accords of the type proposed by Quebec would be regarded as an unfriendly act. Only the French and their African clients did it. We believed that what we were doing was necessary.

Marcel Cadieux was a passionate, *very* passionate man. He believed profoundly and with a great deal of emotion that the French were trying to screw us – as they were. Marcel didn't accept any of the excuses. "In the time that I worked for him, he was interesting," said Yalden. "I liked him." It was true that Cadieux was not supported by most of the French Canadian officers; in the terms of the day, they were more doves than hawks. They were troubled by what they considered Cadieux's extreme views. But they didn't speak out, knowing that you crossed him at your peril. Some, two or three, shared his attitude and his tough line.

Lester Pearson's attitude in 1967-68 fluctuated in his waning days. **Trudeau** was becoming stronger and stronger. **Martin** was not very influential on this; for Martin was a dove too, and in thrall to Couve de Murville. So, in the department, there was a certain tendency to take Quebec issues straight to the prime minister, not the minister. That meant Pearson himself, not **Marc Lalonde**. All this time, there was a state of great flux.

We had the Gabon fiasco, and then came Trudeau. For Cadieux, this was a very different ball game. Now we had another French Canadian, and Cadieux was no longer the top French Canadian. The friction between the two men was much more complicated than a simple dislike or a failure to get along. Cadieux *disapproved* of Trudeau, of the swinging, of the cavalier attitudes. Now that Trudeau, Marchand, and **Pelletier** were on the scene, he had become less relevant. Pelletier was "pretty dovey" during that period.

INTERVIEW | 5 AUGUST 1988

Dealing with La Francophonie and Quebec
Yalden stressed several times that there was a break in his career in early 1969: he transferred to secretary of state, as ADM. Thereafter, his connection with La Francophonie was as Pelletier's personal in-house adviser.

Where did the people in the Quai d'Orsay get their mandate? In Yalden's view, people such as Bernard Dorin, or Jacques Foccart,[8] or Rossillon, and especially Jurgensen, could not have acted without authority. He remembered Rossillon in a swimming pool in Niger, wearing a big cowboy hat, and incidentally sharing the pool with Julien Chouinard from Quebec.[9]

Indeed, he remembered the Niger president Hamani Diori's special counsellor, who was French but of indeterminate nationality, probably Lebanese.[10] This man was fairly friendly to Canada. And Yalden thought he recalled being present when the counsellor came to see Lalonde. Of course, Lalonde took a strong line, as "we all did."

During this period, Yalden himself was involved in discussions with Quebec, both in Ottawa and in Quebec City. Julien Chouinard sat in on them, at Premier Bertrand's instruction, and it was not unusual for him, as the cabinet secretary, to be used for that purpose. Morin was always around, though it was Chouinard who headed their delegation at Niamey II.

"Julien was a gent, a man who would never play a devious hand," Yalden said. He represented his authorities in an honest and forceful way; in his conduct at Niamey, he was very different from Marcel Masse, then a Union Nationale minister, the year before. It is plausible that Chouinard, as a federalist, changed the tone of negotiations between 1968 and 1969 – but that's as far as Yalden could go.

He remembered a discussion with Julien in Niamey about the idea of "government participant." He and Julien knew we were under the gun from the French, thereby limiting very severely our freedom of manoeuvre. The federal diplomats were engaged in "damage control." This was because "the French controlled the whole game ... They could cook our whole goose." But Julien played a quiet, reserved role, waiting for the French and the Canadians to come to some arrangement. Although it was true that Chouinard in 1970 was doing nothing wrong, the people on his delegation were doing a great deal of hanky-panky.

....

8 Bernard Dorin (1929-) was a French diplomat with an interest in La Francophonie. He was later French ambassador to the United Kingdom. Jacques Foccart (1913-97) was a French politician with a somewhat louche background, who in the 1960s and 1970s dealt with post-colonial French interests in Africa; he was known as Monsieur Afrique.
9 Julien Chouinard (1929-87) was secretary to the Quebec cabinet. A lawyer, he was later appointed to the Supreme Court of Canada.
10 Hamani Diori (1916-89) was president of Niger, 1960-74. Niger was of great interest to France, and to Foccart, because of its uranium deposits.

Yalden never had the impression that the Africans had any profoundly rooted views about these questions. President Hamani Diori wanted to play more of a mediating role, but we had no intention of allowing any foreigner to mediate between Canada and one of its provinces.

The year 1968-69 was taken up with pamphlets and White Papers, one virtually every five minutes, or so it seemed. But the boat on the federal foreign affairs scene was leaking very badly. Nevertheless, "I concluded we won the game with Quebec, but it took a while."

The Quebec tactic was to traipse around from body to body, such as the World Health Organization or UNESCO, and arrange meetings to deal with its "provincial" responsibilities. Then it would speak as if it were a sovereign state. UNESCO did not approach Quebec: it was the other way around. By and large, the international organizations responded very well; the exceptions were those countries or bodies that were heavily influenced by France.

"UNESCO continued to cause us problems," Yalden recalled, because, though it was an international organization, its mandate dealt very largely with provincial issues. But UNESCO was co-operative with us. Where the involvement was innocent, we were able to put a stop to it, and we more or less neutralized the French thrust. He remembered seeing, with Pelletier, "a whole raft of these people," but it was hard to remember who or when.

As secretary-general of La Francophonie, Jean-Marc Léger played fair, by his lights.[11] Though he may have manoeuvred, he was not a cheat. Pelletier's judgment was that we should let his appointment go ahead. Léger certainly saw himself as a "grand commis de l'état international," and some of his pomposities were the least pleasant aspect of him.

In summation: "It was all, in a way, so damned foolish." But he recalled once again the hot July day of 1967, when he tuned into de Gaulle's speech with the assurance that he would say nothing new: "And he sure did surprise me." ...

PIERRE-MARC SIRAUD (1907-93)
INTERVIEW | PARIS, 12 OCTOBER 1987

Siraud was a French diplomat and ambassador in Canada from 1968 to 1972. Like some other French diplomats who dealt with Canada, he had an African connection in the French foreign service.

---

11   Jean-Marc Léger (1927-2011), journalist, separatist, and international civil servant.

In Ottawa

Siraud represented France in Canada from August 1968 to June 1972. Before leaving for Canada, he saw de Gaulle, who sketched for him an America with vast English-speaking, Portuguese, and Spanish populations, and with Quebec the French language's only toehold. He must encourage *le fait français*, its culture, its language. French Canadians had a choice between resistance and contraction. That was "le fond de sa pensée." De Gaulle said that the Canadians had misconstrued his intentions. He also stressed, however, that "l'avenir du Québec appartient aux Québécois."

Some had thought that de Gaulle should have gone farther; he had to resist these tendencies. There were certainly "les ultras" in the French bureaucracy ("dans les bureaux") and in journalism. Siraud described Rossillon as a minor figure, though one who brought a certain amount of publicity in his train.

He depicted **Trudeau** as "brillant," a man with guts à la Truman but with "plus d'éclat." He had "grande volonté, grande fermeté, et des idées précises."

He and Trudeau met amiably over dinner, and Trudeau used to say, "Mais je ne comprends pas la France," arguing that his bilingualism policy was the right one for Canada, Siraud responding that France's policy surely helped bilingualism and its objectives.

When Pompidou succeeded de Gaulle in 1969, he continued the same policy. Siraud saw Pompidou, unusually for an ambassador in mid-term, who confirmed it. What was that policy? "Coopération culturelle," founded on the 1965 *accord cadre*, or perhaps even before that, to the origins of Franco-Quebec co-operation in 1961.[12]

As ambassador, he met the Ottawa press; he saw Premier Daniel Johnson about a month before his death; and he saw his successor, Jean-Jacques Bertrand. The consulates definitely came under him. There were no formal contacts with the separatists through the consulates; instructions were firm on that. (He meant this in the sense of formal approaches; he did not mean that contact was excluded in the day-to-day operation of the consulates' reporting functions.) "Nos services sécrets" followed what was happening "de près" but did not interfere.

....

12   The accord cadre was a device that extended a federal umbrella over Franco-Quebec agreements, thereby preserving Canadian sovereignty over Quebec's international initiatives.

Johnson told him that "il fallait frapper assez fortement pour obtenir quelque chose" in Canadian politics. Premier Robert Bourassa after 1970 stressed the economy more, rather than politics.

Siraud admitted that French investment in Quebec and Canada was rather minor: there was Lafarge, there was Renault. He used to say to Bourassa, you can get money and capital anywhere, but you can get culture only from France.

There were disagreements, "malentendus," on the application of the accord cadre. France did not wish to interfere on the Canadian Constitution: he used to say, it was a Canadian affair. As for Niamey, all France wanted was for Quebec to be recognized; in sum, Niamey was "un peu comique." Perhaps Ottawa took it too seriously. Yet on the French side, too, he implied, culture was given too much importance ...

HON. LÉO CADIEUX (1908-2005)

INTERVIEW | OTTAWA, 9 DECEMBER 1987

Ambassador to France
Cadieux was named ambassador to France in 1970. The position had its problems. Jules Léger had had a difficult time, and his successor, Paul Beaulieu, was frightened of the job. **Trudeau** was looking for someone to take over and asked Cadieux in the Commons lobby ... Cadieux asked **Sharp** about the offer and was reassured to be told that Sharp was happy if he went to Paris, as we needed a "tough guy" there. Cadieux thought about the offer for five or six months before accepting. He told Trudeau that he wanted the post for not less than five years, and this was agreed.

In 1944, when Cadieux was a war correspondent for *La Presse* in Paris, he had got to know Maurice Schumann, who was now foreign minister under President Pompidou, which was very useful. The problems he encountered in Paris were largely caused by the Quebec Délégation Générale, which was very active. It made no difference whether the délégation was Liberal or PQ, but his whole life was conditioned by the necessity of finding out what it was doing. The French didn't want to offend Cadieux and wanted to co-operate, but their ideology was so flexible that they always found excuses – a provincial matter, cultural questions, and so on. He had to keep constant watch on the activists in the Quai. There were a few stooges of the délégation there.

For example, when Pompidou died, Trudeau came for the funeral on his advice. As Cadieux and **Si Taylor** waited at the airport for Trudeau to arrive, they began to wonder what would happen if Premier Bourassa met with acting French president Messmer but Trudeau didn't. So he browbeat a French official at the airport into giving Trudeau an appointment, and explained this to Trudeau when he arrived. After the funeral, Cadieux had a reception at his residence, with Bourassa in attendance, and left with Trudeau to see Messmer, Bourassa having said nothing about his plans. After the interview, he and Trudeau met Bourassa on the way in for his own interview ...

Cadieux was very courteous to the délégation staff and always invited them to receptions. Jean Chapdelaine was in charge of the délégation. He was okay but slippery, though not hostile. He had a job to do and did it well. When Bourassa was coming to visit Paris, Cadieux and Chapdelaine agreed that the embassy would have a lunch and the délégation a reception. But Chapdelaine sent out invitations to a reception, and when Cadieux called to ask what was up, he was told that Quebec City preferred a reception. There were occasional victories – once he unveiled a délégation plaque in the absence of a Quebec representative.

Pompidou was an Auvergnois and thus really tough. He was pleasant to Cadieux, but when Cadieux tried to promote a spontaneous invitation for Trudeau to visit France, he found that his efforts went nowhere. He succeeded only when Pompidou was dead. Cadieux blamed Trudeau for the impasse. Early in his administration, he was skiing in France and told the press that there were too many places in France where one could eat well to take time to visit Pompidou. Pompidou didn't forget.

The Contractual Link
At first, France was not in favour of the Contractual Link with Canada, along with other EC countries. Canada as a North American country would set a bad precedent for the United States to get into the EC. Cadieux informed Ottawa that the attitude was negative, but DEA got impatient with him and France. He found it difficult to understand the Third Option (we seemed to want to be in Europe, out of NATO, and in league with the United States). Explaining it to the confused French was difficult. Finally, he was sent some help and went off to the Quai to see the key official, who was opposed. This was the day before the vote at Brussels. The minister was in Poland and due back that evening, so Cadieux insisted on waiting in the office until he returned. The minister arrived at 9:00 p.m., dead tired, and Cadieux told

him this was vital for Canada on political grounds. The minister said he had no instructions and went to see President Giscard. The Quai officials said it was hopeless; we are against. But the next day, the minister voted in favour at Brussels. Why? He told Giscard he'd seen Léo and that his officials were opposed to Canada. But Giscard interrupted and said this was a political question and that France could not vote against Canada: "You will vote for." As it was, the link died a natural death.

JOHN HALSTEAD (1922-98)
INTERVIEW | OTTAWA, 9 DECEMBER 1987

The Third Option
After the Nixon shokku of August 1971, Halstead recalled a conversation with **Ivan Head** that made clear that **Trudeau** now wanted to give Europe more attention. The prime minister had been criticized for neglecting Europe, but now he was ready to move. At the time of the shokku, Halstead was assistant USSEA for Europe and defence relations, and he also acting USSEA, as **Edgar Ritchie** was on holiday ... It was clear that the response to Nixon's 15 August shokku speech was to be in the cabinet, which wouldn't wait for DEA to advise. But to him, this was a prime example of Canadian vulnerability, reinforcing his conviction that it had to be reduced.

Out of this and subsequent discussions came the Options paper, which was largely drafted by Goldschlag. The idea went to **Sharp** early on, who liked it, contributed to it, and took real interest. Halstead wasn't directly involved in the paper, but he pointed out that the Third Option was first and foremost a domestic policy. The recommendations on Europe were never called the Third Option – they were for diversification. To Halstead, this was two sides of the same coin. The Third Option was designed to strengthen Canadian institutions and the economy in order to reduce vulnerability to external forces, especially the United States. But the foreign policy dimension that predated the Third Option was diversification – Europe and Japan.

After STAFEUR and *Foreign Policy for Canadians (FPC)*, there was a systematic and detailed implementation of recommendations by DEA. Instructions went to embassies to implement, to promote cultural and scientific exchanges (which caused difficulties with the Department of Finance). Initiatives were taken to strengthen trade representation and promote economic co-operation. These steps were well received in Europe, but it took time for results in these areas to become apparent. The early implementation of these measures was through bilateral missions.

To succeed, Canada had to integrate diversification and the Third Option. The problem was that the option had to be implemented by domestic departments, and even though it was adopted by the government, it was not implemented. There was no cabinet directive to departments, no follow-up machinery, no examination on a government-wide basis. Why did DEA not push for it? Halstead said that Jim Hyndman in Policy Planning of DEA drafted stuff but got nowhere. If a fuss were to be made, it had to be by the USSEA and the SSEA, and both had other fish to fry. To Halstead, although the Third Option was adopted, the government really followed the First Option – adhocery – unconsciously. What went wrong? Option Three split the bureaucracy, with DEA in favour of the option and Finance and ITC opposed to it. By and large, economic specialists opposed and political specialists favoured.

The Contractual Link
The Contractual Link idea came after the PMO indicated an interest in Europe. In implementing FPC, DEA had been trying to get ministers to go on visits to Europe and vice versa, and now it wanted to get Trudeau involved. This was unsuccessful until Ivan Head indicated that Trudeau was ready for a visit to Europe. But what was he to do there? It had to be important, so Halstead had to find something. "What about Trudeau giving a push to the idea of a more institutionalized relationship with Europe?" he asked Head. "Yeah," Head replied, "but what will he do?" Halstead then produced the Contractual Link and had to work out the idea of a framework agreement with Finance and ITC.

It was difficult to get the EC to agree. It thought this was for the birds. Europeans (and Canadians) thought that Canada's only real business was with the United States. Moreover, the EC was seen as protectionist when the United Kingdom joined (which cut Canadian aluminum, wheat, and other exports). There was no question of a preferential agreement with the EC, critics said, as the United States would never allow it. Gradually, the idea developed that a link might do no harm and could offer some scope for economic co-operation. It could reaffirm the GATT principles. It could be a way of watching out for trade disputes. Eventually, the link developed into the idea of a framework.

But how could this be sold to the EC, as there was frankly little in it? Halstead hoped it might be the first step toward something, but the EC had never negotiated anything like this with an industrialized country and had to be persuaded that it was worth the trouble. Halstead handled the political argument, **Michel Dupuy** the economic.

The crucial meeting on the political side was on 24 September 1974, in New York City, where the EC political directors of foreign ministries met each fall to co-ordinate their UN policies. This meeting was essential to clear up problems, and he got them onside politically, the Germans being especially helpful. Even the French said they were prepared to examine the idea. Halstead got the *nihil obstat* he wanted. Then the serious groundwork on the economic side was prepared by Dupuy.

Trudeau's trips to Europe occurred against this background. In fall 1974, he visited Paris and Brussels, and went to most of the other capitals in spring 1975. His Mansion House address in London, as originally drafted by Head, said nothing about Europe. Halstead redrafted it and added some mention of Europe; his draft was rejected, but some of the Europe references stuck.

To Halstead, Trudeau was a dilettante. If he said something, he assumed that it would happen; people who knew nothing of diplomacy made that kind of mistake.

JACQUES VIOT (1921-2012)
INTERVIEW | PARIS, 13 OCTOBER 1987

Viot was extremely senior in the French foreign service. He was ambassador to Canada from 1972 to 1976, then ambassador to London and inspector-general in the foreign service.

Canada-France relations
Prior to Viot's 1972 appointment as ambassador to Ottawa, Canada-France relations were virtually non-existent. His mission was to restore them.

Official visits between the two countries were difficult. When **Mitchell Sharp** had condemned French nuclear testing, he'd made some people in Paris rather angry, which blocked a visit by Michel Jobert, the foreign minister. So the Giscard invitation to **Trudeau** in 1974 was the first fruit of Viot's efforts.

The general French policy toward Canada in the mid-1970s was shaped by the perception of many who recognized that a divided Canada would lead only to absorption of English Canada by the United States. This was not in the French interest, although the French could do little to prevent it if it were in the cards. So the existence of a bilingual Canada with an independent foreign policy became a French desideratum.

Some people in the Quai d'Orsay and elsewhere did believe in Quebec independence, but their views were individual ones, not government policy. He himself did not share their opinions. Whenever he was asked in Canada what French policy was, he would say that it was to maintain cultural links with Quebec no matter what. He cited the Jean Lacouture–derived arguments about the French abandonment of Canada and the need to redress it.[13]

On Trudeau
Trudeau gave Canada an international persona that was beyond its real power. He had an outstanding personality. He had sympathetic views on the Third World, which were by and large correct. His desire for independence of the United States was admired. His views on Quebec were consistent and structured. Although he did not get on with Giscard, that was on personal grounds; nevertheless, it was Giscard who had invited Trudeau to visit.

How did Viot meet the prime minister? The French embassy was next door to 24 Sussex Drive, and the Trudeau children's balls sometimes came over the fence into the embassy garden. Madame Viot, who was sitting in on our interview, said that when Trudeau came to retrieve them, she asked him whether his visits were private or official ...

On Quebec
Separatists? Part of Viot's job was to report what was happening in Canada, so making contact with diverse groups was necessary. But it was also part of the job not to interfere, and French officers were so instructed. Certainly, there were contacts through the consulates-general in Quebec and Montreal.

....

13 In 1986, Jean Lacouture, a French journalist and biographer, had just published the last volume of a massive three-volume biography of de Gaulle, and our interviewees showed that they had read it and perhaps had adjusted their memories accordingly.

With Premier Robert Bourassa, there was a private agenda one could not know. He held his cards very close to the vest; his political resurrection was a sign of his political skill. Canadian security? Viot did not know whether he was followed or his phone tapped.

The French were very cool to the Contractual Link, but because it was a political necessity for the Canadian government, they acquiesced. The Canadians understood this response. For Canada and Europe to have some kind of special relationship was a good idea.

Canadian affairs handled at the Quai were under a sous-direction for North America, and possibly one or two of the officers there dealt with Canada. But there was also a cultural division and a La Francophonie office in the prime minister's own department.

Viot personally had no objection to Canada sharing some of the burden of La Francophonie, though some people were disturbed by it.

Rossillon? Madame Viot said to her husband, "You were very disturbed by him at the time, my dear." Rossillon's activities were "nonsense," Viot said, disclaiming any responsibility for him. As for General de Gaulle's famous "vive" speech, Viot implied that he disapproved of it. It did the general no particular political good at home. Remember that it led to Giscard's comment about de Gaulle's "solitary exercise of power," which he made just after the incident ...

MICHEL DUPUY (1930-)
INTERVIEW | OTTAWA, 18 JANUARY 1988

A long-time DEA official, Dupuy served at Brussels and at NATO, negotiated the Contractual Link with the EC, headed the Canadian International Development Agency, and was ambassador to the UN and to France.

Beginnings of the Contractual Link
The Contractual Link story began on the economic side, the political organization of the EC still being weak then. When Canada started to look at the possibility of negotiating with the EC, the goal was modest. What were the priorities of the EC?

1. Completing the internal market and developing internal priorities
2. Enlarging itself
3. Association with developing countries
4. Relations with the United States
5. Relations with Western Europe
6. Relations with Australia and New Zealand
7. Relations with Canada.

At that time, the EC was more important than Japan as a Canadian trading partner, so Canada's position on the EC priorities list worried Ottawa.

Dupuy had been deputy head of the Canadian mission to the EC for five years from 1963 to 1968 (under the same roof as the embassy to Belgium). Canada would file notes and never get satisfactory replies on significant issues.

The key in the move to seek a link was the Nixon shock of August 1971. After Canada failed to get the United States to recognize the special relationship between them, even its Canadian proponents had to recognize the new era. Even Simon Reisman accepted it (though when Dupuy returned from Europe in the late 1960s, Reisman had told him not to waste time on Europe – the United States was where the action was). This was the point at which **Sharp** directed a review of the US link. The cabinet chose the status quo option, not the Third Option, in real terms, so qualified was the Third Option with caveats. The Third became well known because of DEA's squabbles with ITC and Finance, and because it let DEA boost its policy thrusts.

The Third Option paper dealt only marginally with foreign policy, and most of it was domestic. In fact, the link was to include the EC and Japan. The North-South push came out of discussions with **Trudeau,** who began by saying that, so far, his foreign policy was just doing the obvious. Canada had adjusted to some major events (China, NATO) but little else. What to do now? The Senate had produced its report on EC relations. Trudeau said that apart from the United States, Europe was the most troubling aspect of our policy. Instead of going straight to northern European countries, Trudeau asked, couldn't Canada develop its relations with Scandinavia and Africa, and, by operating in the backyard of Europe, begin to be perceived by the Europeans as important? **Head** and Dupuy disagreed with this approach. Strike at the heart, not the periphery, they urged. The Europeans had interest in Canada, as they sought a voice in North America that was independent of the United States (Dupuy confirmed this later, when he was ambassador to France). This conversation was the origin of the link, not the Options paper.

The Interdepartmental Committee on External Relations after August 1971 concluded that the best way to engage the EC was to negotiate with it. Dupuy had re-created this committee in the early 1970s. This was a considerable challenge because Canada already had bilateral relations with most EC countries. And the balance of the trade relationship was covered by GATT. Thus, when the EC looked at Canada, it saw no need for a link. The only type of agreement that it had negotiated was for preferences, and their machinery had no room in which to include Canada. How then could a link be negotiated?

Desiderata
The Canadian link was designed to solve the problem by reaffirming GATT, reaffirming bilateral relations, and creating machinery under the general roof of vague principles. The EC saw in negotiations a chance to get access to Canadian resources, guaranteed, secure, and immune from Canadian domestic policies. This had to be resisted, and the cabinet gave no authority in this direction.

Trudeau's European visits had real impact. There was a certain sympathy for Canada in the United Kingdom, Germany, and Belgium, but things were tricky in France and Italy. The issue at the EC was difficult, as the EC had never negotiated a treaty like this with anyone and feared setting a precedent. The EC was also concerned with energy and saw that Canada wanted to keep control of its resources. There were also fears that Canada – the agricultural Japan of the world, as Dupuy called it – would push its products on Europe. The French were the most difficult, and negotiations there had to be carried on at the highest level as a political move. Canada-Quebec-France didn't enter into this at all. Dupuy had no recollection of **Léo Cadieux** lobbying. Trudeau certainly discussed it with Giscard and Chirac, who showed a certain sympathy for us. But Chirac said, "Don't be more European than the Europeans – you want more than we [the EC] have reached."

Was there empathy between Trudeau and Giscard? Dupuy could offer only hearsay. The first time they met, Trudeau had been told that Giscard liked to talk on a high plane, something that Trudeau had no difficulty with. But after the meeting, the feedback from Paris was that Trudeau didn't know his dossiers and spoke only in generalities. The next time they met, Trudeau talked details, and the feedback was that he had no vision. At a dinner during Trudeau's 1975 visit to Paris, Giscard replied to his friendly, witty remarks by saying that "in the old days when kings ruled the world, they used to call their fellows 'cousin.' I am pleased to welcome a cousin."

On the framework negotiations, the EC was more imaginative than Canada. The only hard negotiations concerned energy. Certainly, there was great skepticism in Ottawa. Dupuy met Jim Grandy, who told him the "link was as dead as a dodo," a typical ITC response. The technical departments thought that DEA was trying to achieve something out of nothing. DEA always had its own ongoing debate on the worth of the link idea, which didn't make great waves there. You could lose little here and could achieve only little gains. The negotiation wasn't protracted – three years. The negotiations were on the agenda of the EC Council of Ministers all that time – and this alone, by drawing attention to Canada, achieved the main aim of the link idea. Indeed, for three years the ministers got a basic course on Canada from the commission (the EC's executive arm) and the negotiators. And as a result, relations changed for the better, with a degree of seriousness and open lines of communication.

Failure of the Contractual Link
Still, Dupuy said, they had hoped for more. Meetings between EC and Canadian officials could identify problems and so on but couldn't create an environment that would generate more investment and trade. They lacked the leverage for this. Dupuy was involved here as director general for economic affairs and as assistant USSEA for economic policy. After the link was signed, there was agreement on sectoral missions, and there were two or three of these encounters, though they produced few results. Trade did not rise dramatically after the link, as the stagflation of the late 1970s and the recession of the early 1980s hurt. Then there were money problems. He once had a chat with the French finance minister, who told him that France had planned to open its economy after the early 1970s to help expansion, but this had been abandoned after the energy crisis. This also hurt Canadian efforts in the EC.

Trudeau lost interest in the link after it was signed. Dupuy also thought that the job was done, and it wasn't something for which you'd go to the wall. Given the world situation, it was clear that the link was unlikely to produce much in the short term. You couldn't invest much ministerial time in something that was going to cruise for a while.

The link had two deficiencies in operation. The first was inadequate effort: there was no attempt to pave its way. Second, Trudeau put the link into too high visibility, with his two European trips. Originally, a more modest prime ministerial role was looked for. It was Trudeau who decided on the second trip for reasons unknown to Dupuy.

The link sank "quickly into relative oblivion," but it shouldn't have appeared so dramatic a gesture. Still, it was worth the effort, and it was a creditable achievement, a neat and tidy operation, especially given the difficulties of negotiating with the EC ...

Ambassador to France, 1981-85
The fundamental issue was a lack of substance in the relationship between France and Canada, plus the complexity of managing Canada-France-Quebec issues. The economic relationship was weak, and Canada had been unable to expand it. The blame was shared. Trudeau had told Dupuy that he wanted to get to the root of the matter – were Canadian officials biased against French proposals (such as Airbus)? Dupuy concluded that they weren't.

There were two silver linings in his time as ambassador. Investment rose in unprecedented amounts, and not solely to Quebec, thanks to François Mitterrand's nationalizations, and the composition of exports changed to include more manufactured goods. Still, committee consultations were disappointing; Canada wasn't a priority to France or vice versa – Dupuy was the first "economic" ambassador to France.

On Canada-Quebec-France issues, Ottawa had realized during the 1970s that it had little leverage to stop French meddling. The relationship between the two countries wasn't substantive, so Canada had little clout. But people such as Giscard and former French premier Raymond Barre realized that something had to be done. When Dupuy arrived, Mitterrand made it clear from the first that Canada was special to France, that his government would respect Canadian sovereignty, and that if there were difficulties, to let him know. This was genuine. It allowed Dupuy to work on a strategy to anticipate friction and forestall crises. He relied on men of goodwill and escaped the vicious circle. There were no problems in his time, and he even got Louise Beaudoin, the Quebec delegate, to co-operate.

Trudeau had recognized the privileged nature of Quebec-Paris links before Mulroney did. On a visit to Paris in 1982 or 1984, in Dupuy's presence, Trudeau had accepted this. But he spoke in confidence, and Mulroney did it in public.

DE MONTIGNY MARCHAND (1936-)
INTERVIEW | GENEVA, 11 JULY 1988

Failure of the Third Option
Although Marchand hadn't finished his study of the Third Option in Europe in 1979-80, he had formed tentative conclusions, more than tentative, really. He thought he could defend them if he had to. His method was to do in-depth interviews, half a day, with senior officers of various European companies (bankers, manufacturers, and others) that had to do with Canada. They gave him excellent co-operation and understood that his brief was not to advocate but rather to investigate. So some of them were remarkably candid. He wanted to find out about their trading and investment experiences. For this, he had prepared a whole series of questions that were designed to elicit both a recital of experiences and an appraisal of why things went the way they did.

So why did the Third Option fail? Reason number one was that on the ministerial level, it really had only two defenders: **Sharp** and **Trudeau**. Sharp believed in the thing in his gut, and Trudeau found it convincing intellectually. The rest of the cabinet did not but conceded what it thought the prime minister wanted. Trudeau defended the idea brilliantly in the cabinet, and it was adopted. But people such as John Turner, Simon Reisman, James Grandy, Al Johnson, and Jake Warren – they didn't believe in it.

Because of this, the Canadian banks got the message that the Third Option policy was not on. Their multiplying effects in terms of influence and general impact could have helped it succeed.

That determined what happened next. The Third Option was just an elegant piece of argumentation buttressed by a clever accord with the EC. And the EC was puzzled by the whole thing, especially its vice president, Lord Soames, who was inclined to oppose it. Repeated visits and arguments from **Michel Dupuy** finally brought him around to the understanding that the accord couldn't hurt, whatever else happened. So the EC gave us the benefit of the doubt, signed, and waited to see what would happen next. The answer to that was – nothing.

It must be conceded that the times were out of joint. When the Third Option got going, trade with the United States was lagging. There was capacity to spare. But by the mid-1970s, things were looking up in American trade, our order books were full, our production lines occupied. So the progress that had been made with the Europeans was simply jettisoned by

Canadian businessmen who could look no farther than the US market as the be-all and end-all.

The designers of the Third Option had made "a strategic mistake" in relying on our businessmen's "appetite" for markets, because there was something skewed about that appetite. Again, the banks were mostly at fault. They had no sense of business banking à la British, no tradition of it; they were really just big savings institutions functioning in a protected home market. They had no real competitive instinct.

Some Canadian businessmen operating in Europe told Marchand that they had got nowhere with their own banks; if they succeeded, it was despite what the banks had done, not because of it. In one case, the business had dumped the Canadian institutions in favour of Barclay's. And that was just one example.

In addition, Canadian business entrepreneurs were unprepared and intimidated at the idea of doing business in Europe. In Germany, Marchand had interviewed many industrialists and bankers who told him that the Canadians just didn't know how to do it. For example, for the Canadians, business seemed to be a nine-to-five phenomenon; for the Europeans if you were doing business, they wanted to see the complete picture and get to know you, family, weekends, and all. "This scares the hell out of us, we're uncomfortable with it," Marchand claimed.

Canadians might be competent, interesting, and even charming, but that extra edge – staying power – that the Europeans liked was not there. In the mid-1970s, few of the more dynamic Canadian businessmen in Ontario spoke French or German. The absence of language was part of it, but the fact that the Canadians did little to support their initial effort, made so little follow-up, was also part of it. The Europeans just could not establish rapport with their Canadian interlocutors – as they understood it.

Now that we have free trade with the United States, can we say that things have really improved? The bedside manner of doing business is probably still lacking, and it's a serious handicap.

In addition, because our product runs were short, Europeans who had established a successful contact with a Canadian supplier found that they could not be accommodated when the magic American orders reappeared. We just couldn't supply them, even when we had established a record of doing so, when the US market beckoned. That was true in lumber, for example, and it was true in some manufactured goods.

The second category of reasons for the Third Option's failure, beyond business attitudes, was our lack of sophistication in disseminating knowledge of ourselves in Europe. For instance, Marchand once visited a construction firm in the Ruhr that specialized in turnkey projects. Its executive vice president was boasting to him about his company's international vocation. It had just completed a hospital in Saudi Arabia, down to the sheets and scalpels. Now, as Marchand knew, there was a very fine Canadian company that made operating tables, very specialized and very sophisticated. Why had the Ruhr firm not sought supply there? The vice president called in his supply manager. The latter said, well, the Saudi Arabia project was generally known and written about; the Ruhr company had let it be known that it was interested in bids; it was mentioned in the trade press; and no bids were received from this or any other Canadian firm. Canadians make good products, Marchand said, but we don't let people know about them. More than excellence is required. Even if we were embraced by the European market, we wouldn't know what to do.

The FIRA effect and other negatives
Investment was the other side of the picture, Marchand said, and there he was convinced that FIRA's negative impact had been much exaggerated. Frankly, the question in investment, especially from European bankers, was where was monetary policy made? This was a natural question from bankers, who listened very attentively when Gerald Bouey, the governor of the Bank of Canada, explained to them that when the United States caught cold, Canada also sneezed. They admired Bouey but were left "speechless" by his candour. So they had no trouble figuring out which was the tail and which the dog. If you were investing, you would wish to do it where you were closer to the real source of decisions, the Federal Reserve, and thus be closer to where you might hope to exert some influence. This was the attitude of the Frankfurt banks. Yes, they mentioned FIRA, but more as a pretext.

Some investors also worried about Canadian immigration laws and whether they would be able to bring in the skilled personnel they might need to operate a plant. Now, under free trade, we were officially giving preference to US firms in that regard; the concessions made to the Americans have not been made to the Europeans, who thereby feel disadvantaged.

There was also the question of how Canadians viewed Europe, Marchand continued. There were Britain and France, to be sure, but in the mid-1970s Britain was thought to be on the skids, and France was effectively the enemy:

a decadent United Kingdom and a mischievous France. Germany was therefore the real target. It was our only interesting putative partner. This, he said, was something the Europeans didn't mention and was his own conclusion. The government for this purpose should have had a more serious study and rationale behind it all. But it was people such as **John Halstead** and Klaus Goldschlag, on one side as pro-Europeans, and Jake Warren on the other.

After his European stint in 1979-80, Marchand thought that the Trade Commissioner Service should be privatized as a way of giving it credibility abroad. He raised this idea on the Canadian Manufacturers Association, the Chamber of Commerce, and the Canadian Exporters Association, where he got a good response, but not in government ...

Dealing with France
The salvation on the issue of dealing with France, which he dealt with as associate USSEA from 1980 to 1985, was the advent of President François Mitterrand in 1981. That changed everything, especially on the foreign minister level: the previous presidents had been hostile and dangerous, "had pissed in the soup." Anyway, Mitterrand's arrival meant that we could create a new type of relationship. This was true at the top and was also true on the ministerial and on the political director level.

Marchand's own French counterpart was Jacques Attali, who was Mitterrand's summit sherpa. The advent of Attali, **Jean Béliard**'s arrival as ambassador in Ottawa, and Claude Cheysson's 1981 appointment as France's foreign minister – this was a very happy conjunction; this created a new dynamic that made it possible to revisit de Gaulle's policy of buttressing Quebec's aspirations. "I think Mitterrand himself felt he had to regain some respect for France in the rest of Canada," Marchand suggested. That was the point about Mitterrand: he saw Canada as continental in scope and not simply confined to the region of Quebec. He was basically an admirer of North America and took an interest in northern sovereignty.

Attali's response to Marchand on a number of occasions made it clear that he spoke for his boss. Cheysson was interested in bridge building, in North-South, and in France-Canada. When he got papers shoved under his nose by his pro-Quebec subordinates, Marchand saw him dismiss them with a wave.

As to Ambassador Béliard, he didn't have that notorious inferiority complex of the French, which they express by being so very snotty or Pavlovian in their responses. He had been consul-general in Chicago and knew Americans; his command of English was excellent.

JEAN BÉLIARD (1919-2010)
INTERVIEW | PARIS, 30 SEPTEMBER 1988

A long-time member of the French foreign service, Béliard had served in the US and NATO, and was a spokesman for the French government in Paris from 1969 to 1973. He became ambassador to Canada in 1981 and remained until 1984.

On de Gaulle and the pro-Quebec group in the Quai d'Orsay
Béliard knew General de Gaulle well but never spoke of Canada with him. They always dealt with immediate concerns ... The only point on which Béliard and J.D. Jurgensen disagreed was on Quebec. Jurgensen wrote about Quebec and was of the opinion that the French could survive in North America only in a solid structure, not a province but a state. But Béliard realized that the Québécois were North American, not French. Still, it was very hard to say what Jurgensen's influence was on French policy ... but he was left more or less alone to develop his thesis. Certainly, he could write memos to be read by the minister and the president ... The result of the 1980 Quebec referendum, he said, should have been a turning point for those in the Quai who favoured independence.

The consul-general in Quebec City from 1967 to 1972, Pierre de Menthon, was an ardent *indépendantiste*, Béliard recalled. As ambassador from 1981, he himself was responsible for the consulate and saw the correspondence.

Béliard's views
To Béliard, it was always bad for a friendly country to get involved in another's politics. This was banal but true. He believed that Quebec should be helped out in every possible way, but there was a clear distinction between help and support for independence ...

He had met René Lévesque, who said to him, "So, you're not in favour of independence." Béliard replied, "I'm not here to get mixed up in Canadian affairs; that was the last thing I should do. Canadians as an independent, adult democracy could handle their own affairs." That was always his answer. And "in all modesty," Béliard maintained, "I was right."

On Trudeau and SSEA MacEachen
Béliard's relations with **Trudeau** were excellent. They were neighbours on Sussex Drive, and Trudeau, who loved the embassy's architecture, visited

frequently ... In his valedictory dispatch, Béliard said that Trudeau was a great man who did more for La Francophonie than those who had preceded him.

He thought that MacEachen was very nice, blunt, open, intelligent. You didn't waste time with him.

On Giscard and Mitterrand
One should be careful of characterizing Giscard, Béliard maintained. He threw out "épater les bourgeois" opinions, or he might be talking of a trend in history. As for Mitterrand, he and Trudeau were both highly intelligent, politically oriented men, well read with a scope that allowed them to approach problems or topics at a high level ... Béliard attended two of their meetings.

DRS. HEINZ SCHNEPPEN (1931-) and RÜDIGER VON LUKOWITZ
INTERVIEW | GERMAN FOREIGN MINISTRY, BONN, 19 OCTOBER 1987

Schneppen and von Lukowitz were Canadian desk officers at the German Foreign Ministry who reviewed the departmental files for the authors.

The Third Option
The Third Option was very positively received in Germany, which welcomed this reorientation of Canadian foreign policy. The United States had found its identity in opposing Europe, but this was not a natural situation for Canada. But at the same time, Canada's seeking a Contractual Link was something of an intellectual exercise. The facts could not be ignored – Canada lived near a dominant, impressive neighbour, which created a gravitational pull that was difficult to escape. Moreover, it was difficult to alter the existing pattern of relations in and between European nations. There were limits to the possibilities of change. For example, even if Canadian trade with Germany were doubled (from 1 to 2 percent of German trade), this would not change the basic situation. That was probably the reason the Contractual Link policy failed.

If Germany had perceived the Canadian position as anti-American, its stance might have been different. Probably, Germany didn't care very much. There was no indication on file that Canada's NATO military cuts had affected the German position.

Schmidt and Trudeau

Schneppen and von Lukowitz translated a page of Helmut Schmidt's autobiography, *Menschen und Macht*, for us. Schmidt wrote that **Trudeau** was "wise, pensive, thoughtful, always very serene" and a good host at Montebello, where he chaired the G7 summit in "an efficient and detached way."[14] Generally, in Germany, he was seen as highly intelligent, probably brilliant, a man of good character, a high flier.

Trudeau's relations with Schmidt seemed warm, or so the files suggested. They showed that Schmidt had arranged "a very personal meeting" with Trudeau and had written warm thank-you notes after Montebello. Trudeau's meetings with Schmidt during the late 1970s and early 1980s were the first intensive exchange of views between Germany and Canada, and relations have never been as close since. From 1978 to 1982, the two men met at least once a year in Bonn and in Ottawa. This had some policy spinoffs, as when the link was used to resolve the uranium question. They had protested Canada's "rigidity" on uranium sales to Germany and the EC. Surely, they said, this was an area where Germans "had a good record."

Another result was the appointment of special representatives, who met to enhance trade. Schneppen and von Lukowitz had the impression that this led nowhere and ultimately lapsed.

FIRA, they noted, had a negative reception in Germany. Business people looked in a negative way at the Canadian investment climate. This may have been a factor working against the Third Option.

The German assessment of Trudeau

Schneppen and von Lukowitz concluded by reading an assessment that the Foreign Ministry had prepared on 30 June 1984, summing up Trudeau's career:

> When he came to power Canada was searching for its position as a nation. In domestic politics, his greatest task was to sustain the federal entity, threatened by long quarrels between French and English and by demands for Quebec autonomy. In terms of foreign policy, the need was to find an identity versus the US, to establish independence, and to find a profile of one's own. In his 16 years, Trudeau tried to solve these problems.

---

14 Helmut Schmidt, *Menschen und Macht* (Frankfurt: C. Bertelsmann Verlag, 1987), 294.

"As for national identity," the assessment went on,

it was of considerable satisfaction to Trudeau that an independent constitution was formulated and put into place. Both languages have the same status. In foreign policy, his policy to the US at times led to considerable irritation, but Trudeau tried successfully from the beginning to work towards détente and East-West dialogue. His understanding of Third World problems was important and brought Canada much respect there. Nonetheless, the end of the Trudeau period was characterized by a number of problems. The East-West situation had hardened, there was a deep recession in Canada, and economic contingencies had forced more and more concessions to the US that hurt economic independence. Still, the close relations between Canada and Europe, between Canada and Germany, will scarcely be affected by the change in government.

VI
Canada and the Soviet Union

DURING THE TRUDEAU PERIOD, the Soviet Union was not a major bilateral diplomatic or economic player for Canada. But the Soviets were the Cold War enemy, the empire that invaded Czechoslovakia in 1968, held down the Eastern Europeans, staged adventures in Africa, and invaded Afghanistan in 1979. As a member of NATO, as a neighbour and ally of the United States, Canada was, and had to be, interested in what Moscow thought, believed, and wanted. The Soviets were, in effect, ever-present.

Pierre Trudeau challenged some of Ottawa's orthodox policies toward the USSR. He had travelled to Moscow in 1952 for an International Economic Conference organized by the World Peace Council and the World Federation of Trade Unions, both communist front organizations, and on his return, he had written sympathetic but critical articles about the Soviet Union in Montreal's *Le Devoir*.[1] Sixteen years later, Trudeau was prime minister. He was not pro-Soviet so much as, unhappy with the Cold War and its dangers, willing to try a different tack toward the USSR. The 1968 crushing of the Czech spring by the USSR and its Eastern European satellites delayed any initiatives, and so too did the FLQ crisis of October 1970. But in mid-May 1971, Trudeau paid a visit to Moscow, one of the very first by a Western leader since the events of 1968 had chilled relations.[2] What resulted were meetings with General Secretary Leonid Brezhnev, in which Trudeau gave away none of the NATO positions but did say that Canada's halving of its NATO force was a gesture to reduce tensions. Premier Alexei Kosygin told Trudeau that

---

1 The fullest account of Trudeau's rationale for going to Moscow and his observations in the USSR may be found in Max Nemni and Monique Nemni, *Trudeau Transformed: The Shaping of a Statesman, 1944-1965* (Toronto: McClelland and Stewart, 2011), Chapter 9.
2 French president Pompidou had preceded him in visiting the Soviet Union.

the USSR saw the troop cut as exactly that, "an act contributing to the reduction of tension in Europe."[3]

The highlight of the visit, however, was the signing of a Protocol on Consultations, the origins of which remain somewhat vague. The protocol called for issues of importance, not only crises, to be discussed between Ottawa and Moscow; the Soviets welcomed it because they probably saw it as evidence that Trudeau's Canada might be sliding out of the American orbit. For the same reason, Washington, not consulted in advance, fretted about Trudeau. So too did some in the cabinet in Ottawa who had not been informed of the protocol.

What upset many Canadians – and Americans – were Trudeau's words at a press conference in Moscow on 20 May. He pointed out that Canada was a friend and ally of the United States but added, "Canada has increasingly found it important to diversify its channels of communication because of the overpowering presence of the United States of America and that is reflected in the growing consciousness amongst Canadians of the danger to our national identity from a cultural, economic and perhaps even military point of view."[4] A week later, Trudeau raised another storm when he compared Ukrainian nationalists to FLQ separatists. If Trudeau "were an agent of Moscow," right-wing columnist Lubor Zink wrote in a 31 May 1971 article for the *Toronto Telegram*, "he could hardly do better." That Kosygin promptly paid a visit to Ottawa (where he was attacked in front of the Parliament Buildings by a protester shouting "Free Hungary") increased the concern. But in fact, the protocol and an exchange agreement reached a few months later would have little real impact on bilateral Canadian-Soviet relations.

What did influence the relationship were the roles played by two longtime ambassadors: Robert Ford, who served Canada in Moscow for sixteen years, and Alexander Yakovlev, who was posted in Ottawa from 1973 to 1983.

Ford's influence was very strong, and not only in Ottawa. A respected poet himself and an able translator of Russian poets, he had unique entrée into cultural circles and wide contacts in Moscow that made him well respected by ministers and in the Soviet bureaucracy. He took a realistic view of the USSR and Soviet policy, seeing the country's domestic weaknesses and its

---

3   J.L. Granatstein and Robert Bothwell, *Pirouette: Pierre Trudeau and Canadian Foreign Policy* (Toronto: University of Toronto Press, 1990), 193.
4   Ibid., 195.

foreign aggressiveness plainly. He generally favoured a tough line, believing that you gave away nothing unless you received something in return. To Ford, Trudeau was sometimes a bit naive, even credulous, about the USSR.

On the other hand, there was Yakovlev, exiled to comfortable Ottawa as light punishment for his views on Soviet policy and ideology. Highly intelligent and much less dogmatic than many Soviet figures, he and Trudeau hit it off, meeting regularly and talking at length. Yakovlev understood the Canadian leader's ideas, and he formed a clear sense of Canada's weight in the world, limited but not insignificant. It was Yakovlev who encouraged Moscow to dispatch Mikhail Gorbachev on a visit to Canada in 1983, where he met Trudeau and spent three weeks touring Canada with Eugene Whelan, the Liberal agriculture minister, and seeing its farms and agricultural production.[5] And it was Yakovlev who rose to be a full Politburo member and a key adviser when Gorbachev became general secretary in 1985. His time in Ottawa and on the road with Gorbachev and Whelan may have played a substantial role in the USSR's change in policy toward *glasnost* and perestroika under General Secretary Gorbachev; certainly, Yakovlev later said as much.[6]

This chapter contains interviews with several of the key Canadian players in this period – Paul Martin, Ambassadors Robert Ford, Peter Roberts, and Geoffrey Pearson, and William Hooper from the intelligence and security

....

5 The US embassy in Ottawa wrote a full report on Gorbachev's visit, and this was passed to the CIA. US Embassy to Secretary of State, "Politburo Member Gorbachev's Visit to Canada," 2 June 1983, CIA Records, CIA-RDP85T00153R000300060040-9, https://www.cia.gov/library/readingroom/docs/CIA-RDP85T00153R0003000 60040-9.pdf. The telegram, based on conversations with Canadian officials and US analysts, clearly pointed to Gorbachev as a rising star. His visit to a supermarket was especially noted by Herbert Meyer, vice chairman of the CIA's National Intelligence Council, in an 8 June 1983 note to the deputy director of intelligence: "I would give anything to know what flashes through the mind of a Politburo member ... who, on his first visit to the West, wanders through a supermarket." Ibid.

6 "Shaping Russia's Transformation: A Leader of Perestroika Looks Back – Interview with Aleksandr Yakovlev," *Conversations with History* (Berkeley: Institute of International Studies at the University of California, 21 November 1996), http://www. uctv.tv/shows/Shaping-Russias-Transformation-A-Leader-of-Perestroika-Looks -Back-with-Alexander-Yakovlev-Conversations-with-History-7137. A recent account of Yakovlev's influence on Gorbachev and the USSR is Richard Pipes, *Alexander Yakovlev: The Man Whose Ideas Delivered Russia from Communism* (DeKalb: Northern Illinois University Press, 2016). On Soviet political and economic problems in the 1980s, see Stephen Kotkin, *Armageddon Averted: The Soviet Collapse, 1970-2000* (Oxford: Oxford University Press, 2008), Chapters 1 and 2.

side of DEA. The view that emerged from these interviews was generally realistic in its assessment of Soviet policy and conditions in the USSR, but Pearson, ambassador to Moscow in the chilly early 1980s, appeared less willing to condemn the Soviet Union's position on the issues of the era. So too, in the judgment of most interviewees, was Pierre Trudeau.

Most Canadian observers, and especially Ford, concentrated on the political-military side of the Soviet Union. Peter Roberts, on the other hand, noticed and reported on signs of dilapidation and decay in the civilian economy. The implications this had for Soviet foreign and military policy were unclear, and most Soviet specialists in the West, including Canadians such as Robert Ford, placed more emphasis on Soviet military strength than on the signs of economic weakness. As events after 1984 showed, however, Roberts's perception was prophetic.

RT. HON. PAUL MARTIN (1903-92)
INTERVIEW | WINDSOR, ONTARIO, 10-11 FEBRUARY 1987

Kosygin in Canada, 1971
Martin escorted Soviet premier Alexei Kosygin around Canada when he visited in 1971, but he had met him before, in 1967, at the UN and in Moscow in 1965, when Martin was trying to get some life back into the ICC in Vietnam. "I said to Andrei Gromyko, the long-time foreign minister, that Kosygin should see President Johnson," he recalled. In 1967, Gromyko resisted; they needed an invitation. "So I saw Secretary of State Dean Rusk and said Johnson should see Kosygin," said Martin.

When Rusk replied, "It takes two," Martin countered with "They don't say no." And eventually, they did meet at Glassboro, New Jersey, in June 1967. When it was over, Kosygin came to thank Martin at the Canadian hotel. Mike Pearson was jealous that he hadn't been involved, Martin recalled.

When Kosygin came to Ottawa in October 1971, on an official visit, Trudeau asked Martin to take him across the country. During his visit, Kosygin was assaulted in front of Parliament, and there were demonstrations wherever he stayed, including one very large one outside the Inn on the Park in Toronto. Kosygin, who was unnerved by it all, told Martin, "Your country's in a bad way, no discipline, drugs, etc., etc." Martin replied that if Kosygin lived in Canada, he'd be a Tory, at which Kosygin's daughter chimed in: "That's true, Dad."

The Kosygin tour had its incidents. They travelled to Montreal from Ottawa, Ambassador **Robert Ford**, Martin, the interpreter, Kosygin, and a Russian diplomat. When they reached Montreal, Kosygin attempted to get out of a dinner that Premier Robert Bourassa was hosting. Martin tried the direct approach and strode into Kosygin's bedroom. He still remembered him lying there, looking pale and exhausted. But he prevailed, and Kosygin attended the dinner. Meeting Bourassa wasn't of any consequence.

In Vancouver, they were scheduled to take in a hockey game, and again Kosygin was reluctant. But he went and he enjoyed it. There was also his meeting with the Canadian cabinet, attending one of its sessions ...

On Robert Ford
Robert Ford was "easily our best ambassador, anywhere," but "I always thought he was a little too hard on the Russians." He was the same type of man as George Kennan. His illness (some kind of muscular degeneracy) had something to do with keeping him in Moscow. The Moscow embassy building was practically at grade, so there were no steps for Ford to climb, which was helpful, given his illness. He was so well respected, even by the Russians. He had an entrée because of his extra-curricular activity, his poetry.

Martin's connection with Ford went back to the day when Ford's father, Arthur, of the *London Free Press*, a crusted Tory, was damning the Mackenzie King government and saying that his son couldn't get a government job: "That bastard Mackenzie King, he goes too far." Martin told him there was no substance to his complaint; he saw the USSEA, Dr. Oscar Skelton, who arranged for Robert to write his exams. He passed and his first assignment was Windsor, where he was a passport officer. Martin saw something of him and urged him to study a language. So Ford took up Russian with Father Znamensky of Holy Trinity Russian Orthodox Church. He did so well that by the end of the year, the Russian community gave him a banquet at which he orated in Russian.

Martin remembered a meeting in Moscow at which he was to have dinner with Gromyko. He walked down the corridor, where Gromyko met him, and poor Ford hobbled along so slowly, but Gromyko had no problem waiting. And he told Martin (as he may have done to other foreign ministers) that Ford was the best ambassador in Moscow.

Negotiating with the Soviets, the Americans, and the British
What was Martin doing in Moscow? It was a time when Canada was having

problems with the Americans on a number of subjects: China, the Dominican Republic, and Haiti, where they wanted us to take action. They wanted Canada to raise the matter of a Quebec Catholic convent in Haiti, which had been taken over by President Papa Doc François Duvalier. Dean Rusk phoned to say that if Canada asked, the United States would send in the Marines on the issue. But Martin refused.

Anyway, Martin suspected that the Russians knew of these disagreements. Yet, then and later, though we had disagreements with the Russians, "we didn't have much to talk to them about." Lyndon Johnson suggested that in all fairness, the Canadians should give the Russians the same treatment they gave the Americans.

Negotiating with the Russians was not easy. They were not as frank with us as the British sometimes were. With the Americans, "I always found you could talk frankly to Rusk; he never pulled a Dean Acheson on me" – that is, he never high-hatted him. In spite of our differences with the Americans, our rapport with Washington was better than with Moscow. With British prime minister Jim Callaghan, there was also good rapport. It was a little more difficult with Prime Minister Harold Wilson, but when Martin was high commissioner in London he could always find somebody in the Foreign Office who would talk indiscreetly, depending on the issue and the position that person was taking.

ROBERT FORD (1915-98)
INTERVIEW | VICHY, FRANCE, 15-16 OCTOBER 1987

After joining DEA in 1940, Ford served in Latin America, Egypt, Yugoslavia, and the USSR, where he was ambassador from 1964 to 1980. He was also a distinguished poet and translator.[7]

Ford began this extraordinary two-day interview with his time in Moscow The staff in Moscow was much expanded over what it had been during his first posting just after the war. Now staff lived out, there were enough guards

---

7 Ford's memoir is *Our Man in Moscow: A Diplomat's Reflections on the Soviet Union* (Toronto: University of Toronto Press, 1992). See also Charles A. Ruud, *The Constant Diplomat: Robert Ford in Moscow* (Montreal and Kingston: McGill-Queen's University Press, 2009).

(subject to Russian entrapment, but all married, at least – their failing was the temptation of the black market). The Canadian embassy grew in ratio to the Soviet embassy in Ottawa – though the latter, because the USSR was a superpower, was perforce larger ...

In the Soviet Foreign Ministry, Canada, Britain, Australia, and New Zealand were the province of the Second European Department. "We were quite happy to be lumped together," Ford said. All the Russians in the department spoke good English, and almost all had experience in one of the four countries. The First European Department dealt with Western Europe; together the departments were headed by an assistant under secretary of considerable standing. In the Second Department, there were ten or twelve officers, four for Britain, three for Canada, and three for the Antipodes. Besides this, there was the Institute of the USA and Canada, previously the Institute of the USA. Its head, Georgy Arbatov, had delicately consulted Ford as to the change in title and mandate.

The Foreign Ministry took a good and essentially non-ideological view of Canadian politics. Ford felt that it understood Canadian politics better than American. It was totally opposed to Quebec independence, seeing it as a means of delivering English Canada to the United States, which would then become a super-superpower. There was no comparison to the Soviet nationality problem. There was, however, some fear or concern for Canadian encouragement of Ukrainian nationalists. The ministry could be quite strange on the United States. Watergate was interpreted as a plot against US-Soviet rapprochement.

The Russian understanding of Canada was superior to that of France. When Giscard came to dinner at Ford's home at Vichy in September 1987, he said that he could not understand why Canada was not part of the United States. Ford explained, but he drew a blank with the frigid economist.

There were lacunae. The Canadian Communist Party was not taken seriously except as a convenient echo of the Soviet line for quotation against the Eurocommunists. Once, when in Yalta, he was told that a rest house (formerly a palace) had just been vacated by "your great leader," meaning William Kashtan.[8]

The foreign policy branch of the Central Committee was kept at arm's length – or kept itself there. But if one knew someone, such as Valentin

---

8   Kashtan was general secretary of the Communist Party of Canada from 1965 to 1988.

Falin, who became ambassador to Germany, contact could continue up to a point.

There could be rivalry between the Foreign Ministry and the Institute of the USA and Canada. The head of the Second Department, Vladimir Suslov (no relation to Mikhail), was rather jealous of the institute and Arbatov. And though Arbatov had been to Canada, he was primarily interested in the United States. It was true that the talent deployed in the institute's Canadian section was less than that in its American section – for the Russians, there was only one other power.

After the Cuban missile crisis, he heard Gromyko and others repeatedly say that they would never again allow the USSR to be "blackmailed" by the United States. They had got there largely because of Khrushchev's peasant failure to understand a wider world and his habit of risk taking. They never suggested that Cuba had been wrong; certainly, the buildup in Soviet forces dated from that time.

The Russians would not mention the Sino-Soviet split but would happily discuss it if you brought it up. Ford recalled a 1974 trip to Ulan Bator to present his credentials, after which he went to Beijing. It was not a happy visit, as the Chinese were in the middle of an anti-Confucian campaign. Afterward, he told Kapitsa, the head of the Foreign Ministry's Far Eastern Department, that Ulan Bator made him feel back in Europe. It was horrible, but it was recognizably European. He did not add the qualification, and Kapitsa beamed with pleasure. There were no suggestions at any time of an actual alliance against China, merely the affirmation that the Russians knew where the Chinese nuclear facilities were and could take them out in short order.

The Russians saw the Chinese as their natural enemies, much more so than we were. There was also the historical legacy of the Mongol invasion. Their ideal was a superpower condominium that would put the Chinese, the Germans, and everyone else in their place. Their nightmare was a billion Chinese pouring over the Soviet border, Ford said, and recalled a conversation with the mayor of Khabarovsk. The great fear was the Chinese plus Western technology from Taiwan and Hong Kong.

After 1965, Vietnam dominated US-USSR relations. Of course, Vietnam allowed the USSR to expand its forces, and the Russians were delighted to let the Americans be bogged down in the war. But the expansion would have occurred anyway, and the economy allowed it.

Ford had little contact with the Chinese until Canada officially recognized the People's Republic; after that, the invitations were frequent. The first one encompassed every member of the embassy, including the guards: they were most impressed. There was the inevitable toast to Norman Bethune, of whom 90 percent of the Canadians present had never heard.

The Moscow diplomatic corps had changed and expanded. The Africans suffered because of the cold weather. One actually came to him as dean of the diplomatic corps to ask whether a January invitation to Moscow was an attempt to kill his president. But the Africans were all treated like dirt and had a miserable time.

On Soviet culture

Culturally, Ford was lucky. Just before he left his first posting in 1954, Pasternak's *Zhivago* poems were published. During his years away, he translated them, though he never met or corresponded with Pasternak. In early 1964, when he returned, Khrushchev was still in power, and access to Russians – intellectuals, poets – was still relatively unfettered. After Khrushchev's ouster in October 1964, others found contact difficult, but Ford's literary contacts were not stopped, either because the authorities were embarrassed to do so or because they knew Ford was translating them. The contacts were not selfish or frivolous, because through them one got a sense of intellectuals' thinking, Yevtushenko being an example. One must examine words, phrases, implications. One must also take into account Russians' great love for poetry – a Yevtushenko reading attracted an audience of sixteen thousand. Even members of the Politburo were familiar with the Russian classics, certainly more cultivated than the average Canadian politician. The military may well not be, Ford said.

The intellectuals were looking for a bit more freedom; they did not want to overthrow communism, but they didn't want to be its tools either. Brezhnev couldn't understand this and considered it subversive. He thought them proWestern, and indeed they were interested in the West and did not wish to go on repeating nineteenth-century formulas. The whole clampdown was absurd. The intellectuals wanted a little liberty, but the bureaucrats wanted conformity.

Soviet leaders

Gromyko was extremely intelligent, extremely able, a devoted communist who served his masters well in sheer weight of knowledge and argument. When there was a Canadian issue at the UN, fish or whatever, he was perfectly briefed. A busy and distracted Canadian minister would not be.[9]

General Secretary Leonid Brezhnev's period was divided in two by his health collapse in 1974. The first phase also had a turning point, 1968 and Czechoslovakia. The period 1964-68 was a time of reform under Brezhnev and Kosygin, but Czechoslovakia froze it. Then 1968-74 witnessed a gradual thaw in East-West relations. After 1974, there was total immobilism.

The improvement in USSR-Canada relations started with Ford soliciting a visit to Canada from Vice Premier Dmitry Polyansky, who was responsible for agriculture. Since the USSR "owed" Canada a visit of parliamentarians, Polyansky came as its head in 1966. He stayed behind for a week and visited Manitoba, Saskatchewan, and southern Alberta.

The STAFEUR report

The STAFEUR report originated in Trudeau's 1968 desire for a reappraisal of policy. (He was coy as to just how he knew, but he reiterated that he knew.) Paul Tremblay was made co-chair, perhaps because he was French Canadian. Ford would fly out to Brussels, where Tremblay was ambassador, and together they worked up the outlines of the report. They recommended that Canada not withdraw troops from NATO; the Russians would misinterpret this as a prelude to the weakening of the American commitment. The report was fleshed out by detailed fact checking in Ottawa, where Ford spent a lot of time. It argued that Canada's major foreign policy interest was in the prosperity of and trade with the United States and Europe. (Japan was not yet a large factor.) Canada had to consider how withdrawing troops from NATO would affect relations with its most important partners. "I knew perfectly well what Trudeau wanted," he said, "but I was determined to oppose it."

He met Trudeau on 8 April 1968, when he was back in Canada because of his father's death and was staying with the Roland Micheners. Governor General Michener gave a small dinner party for Trudeau, who took Ford aside to tell him of the importance he accorded Canadian-Soviet relations.

STAFEUR was formed after the Czech invasion of August 1968, which "had a good deal to do with how we shaped the report." They consulted a good deal with **Ivan Head**, with DND, Transport, and Communications, but not with academics. None of Trudeau's people were "blatant enough" to be explicit about the line they wanted, but there were "lots of hints and innuendos, from Ivan at any rate."

....

9 In his memoirs, Gromyko was quite complimentary about Trudeau. See Andrei Gromyko, *Memoirs* (New York: Doubleday, 1989), 228.

At the time, Head was "very pro-Soviet, reflecting what he thought Trudeau wanted to hear." That meant "tending to downplay the Soviet threat, to downplay anything negative about the Soviets." Canada-US relations were where the danger lay. And Head was "pretty woolly" on disarmament. Now, there were lots of people – not foolish – who thought that way, and it was in the context of the 1960s.

Trudeau's impact
Two days after he won the leadership of the Liberal Party, Trudeau dined with Ford and explained that he wanted to make improved relations with Russia a priority. The Czech invasion provoked a soft Canadian response, however, Ford said, softer than he himself wished.

Sharp and DEA agreed with Ford, wishing to keep in step with the rest of NATO about the "Brezhnev doctrine,"[10] which justified the crushing of the Prague spring. But Trudeau and Head disagreed: Ford was certain about Head, less so about Trudeau. In the end it was power politics: we couldn't, wouldn't, do anything about it.

About three months later, Trudeau sent clear signals that he wanted to break the ice. Though Vietnam was still an issue, plans proceeded for his visit to Moscow. He had to cancel at the last minute because of the October Crisis in 1970. The Russians really couldn't understand why it was a crisis – kill them all and put the rest in jail!

During the pre-visit period, Ford was back and forth to Canada to brief Trudeau. We had an agenda; how best to handle it? The Protocol on Consultations was to be signed. The Russians wanted it: it provided for consultation on a crisis. We did not consult with the Americans in advance, a shock to them and a mistake by us. In any case, it was a dead letter for everyone. Ford tried to use it, but it didn't signify; the Russians didn't take it seriously.

The first American reaction was quite strong. The Americans thought it a first step out of their orbit. And if Trudeau meant what he said during the visit, he saw it as a step toward new directions. But Trudeau was very intelligent: "He knew it didn't represent anything." The Russians hoped nevertheless, and the quick invitation to Kosygin was taken as another good sign.

---

10 The Brezhnev doctrine proclaimed, in effect, that once a country was communist, it would always be communist, even if the Soviet Union had to help it along. It was not enunciated until November 1968.

Really, Head had merely looked at the calendar for a free date that was sufficiently before the next election. "I told the Russians" not to count too much on it and told Ottawa it was too quick. And yet ...

The USSR and the United States

On the Foreign Policy Review, Moscow was naturally pleased at anything that seemed to distance Canada from the United States. As to the Third Option, it was nonsense, but the Russians were fascinated. Of course, they could hardly offer to be a balance – they could barely offer us goods, let alone capital.

In 1972, while chatting with Kissinger and a Soviet official in the Kremlin, Ford suggested that the 1971 Canadian opening had an effect on Washington's relations with Moscow. "What total nonsense," said Kissinger.[11] But the Soviet said, "Sorry, the ambassador is right." Kissinger repeated his denial. He was one of the most brilliant tacticians, and one of the most arrogant men, whom Ford had ever met.

Ford reiterated that the USSR was really interested in only one country, the United States. During Gromyko's visit, all he wanted to talk about – apart from his formal and official conversations – was whether Nixon had extended a genuine olive branch in his state of the union address. When relations with the Americans were going badly, the Russians become more interested in Canada, and the reverse was also true. The fact that Canada was closely allied to the United States gave it more influence; he argued this constantly to Trudeau. As long as Canada had the strength of the alliance behind it, it had significance; otherwise, its meaning for the Russians was to be used as a pawn. This did not convince Trudeau.

The US-USSR rapprochement was followed in 1972 by SALT, the Strategic Arms Limitation Treaty, which Ford strongly approved, both the arms limitation and the emergency consultation facilities, which showed their worth during the Arab-Israeli Yom Kippur War in 1973. "We had no input in this that I could see from Moscow," he said.

....

11 Kissinger received a Canadian report on Trudeau's conversation with Brezhnev, which he forwarded to President Nixon. See "Document 261: Memorandum from the President's Assistant for National Security Affairs (Kissinger) to President Nixon," 18 June 1971, in *Foreign Relations of the United States, 1969-76*, vol. 13, Office of the Historian, https://history.state.gov/historicaldocuments/frus1969-76v13/d261.

On Angola and Mozambique, the Russians got the signal that the Americans did not care and assumed that the two countries were not a vital security interest of the United States. When the Portuguese left Mozambique, they handed it to the Soviets on a platter. But the Soviets underestimated the magnitude of the task, and they did not take into account how the use of Cuban troops in Angola would affect the United States emotionally. Moreover, Ford's understanding of détente was that it allowed either side to extend its influence peacefully.

Africa was a sore point among Russians. They resented the amount of money and effort that they expended on Africa and the Arabs. One reason for Khrushchev's overthrow was his visit to Egyptian president Nasser in September 1964, in which he spouted promises of aid. Sure, it was partly racist on the part of the Russians, but who does like the Arabs? When weighing aid, the Russians had to contemplate the dilapidated state of their own economy.

Incoming embassy staff were usually surprised to see Moscow looking as good as it did. So Ford used to send new officers to Voronezh or some similar town on a Sunday to look at the unpaved streets, the empty shops, and the street pumps ...

Academic exchanges were most useful at the student level – where they did some good. Some students went on to join DEA. But on the whole, the exchanges were not very important. There was little of significance on more senior academic levels. As for exchanges in connection with the Arctic, it was the same story. Once, we stupidly gave the Russians some muskoxen, which they badly wanted for experiments. It was costly, but we foolishly got no reciprocity guarantees. There was no follow-up: no Soviet publicity, no thanks, and nothing in return. Ford recalled, "I got absolutely furious, and told a minister that you don't give anything to the Russians unless you get something in return."

It was true that Farley Mowat received special treatment in Russia, going to places that no other westerner had been to (the best we could do was a few ministerial visits to Yakutsk).[12] But he was already strongly prejudiced in the Russians' favour when he arrived.

....

12 Mowat (1921-2014) was a prominent Canadian author and controversialist, best known for his books on the Arctic and his strongly negative views of the United States.

Gromyko, Brezhnev, and Kosygin

The hard-line change in Russian policy coincided with two things: Nixon's fall and Brezhnev's illness. Moscow tried to carry on under Gerald Ford, but Jimmy Carter was fatal to a détente that was already crumbling. The Russians had been developing the SS-20 nuclear missile since at least the late 1960s, and when the project matured, it seemed natural to deploy them. So they sited twenty, and nobody noticed or complained. They then set up another twenty, and people began to get nervous. Brezhnev couldn't perceive this. It needed an intelligent man like Mikhail Gorbachev to see it. Brezhnev could not see how unfavourable to the Russians the situation really was – but in 1980, Ronald Reagan was elected president on a violently anti-Soviet platform. At the same time, the Soviet economy began to stagnate, leading to comment by intelligent Russians that the burden of military spending must be reduced. Gromyko would not say this: he was part of the pack, had survived Stalin, and had a survivor's instincts. He was not the person to oppose a Brezhnev policy.[13]

Ford saw a fair amount of Brezhnev during this period. As dean of the diplomatic corps, he was the first ambassador to be received by Brezhnev as president; he was there to convey congratulations. According to the American ambassador, who was present at a Carter-Brezhnev meeting, Brezhnev's poor physical state allowed him to concentrate for only fifteen minutes maximum on one subject.

Ford liked Kosygin very much for his personality and intellect. Although he must have been tough, in manner he was very gentle. In 1965-67, he did try for economic reform, but Brezhnev was obviously not very enthusiastic, and the Czechoslovakia invasion put an end to it. Still, he had the right ideas.

At any rate, down to 1978-79, Russians saw their standard of living rise by the only measure 90 percent could apply – their own past experience. Then the rise stopped ...

Afghanistan, 1979-80 and after

The Russians failed to understand the Western stand on Afghanistan. A coup had toppled the monarchy, another had overthrown the republic and installed a communist regime, and there had been no reaction in the West. But the

---

13 There is a well-researched account of the Soviet leadership in Robert Service, *The End of the Cold War, 1985-1991* (New York: Public Affairs, 2015), Chapter 5.

Soviet invasion of 1979 marked a real breakout from an agreed or understood situation. Still, Ford was told by one Russian official, "You're stupid; you're going to have to swallow it, like Czechoslovakia."

After Trudeau won the 1980 election, Ford was back home again for consultations. Trudeau showed signs of wanting to re-examine the US-led boycott of the Moscow Summer Olympics, which was intended as a protest against the invasion. Ford argued that if Canada were the only NATO country to attend the Olympics, this would show that it legitimated the seizure of Afghanistan. Trudeau shrugged and admitted that Ford was right. In September 1980, Ford left the position of ambassador.

His succession was a problem, because several qualified Russian-speakers turned it down, and it fell to **Geoffrey Pearson**. "Pearson was a disaster in Moscow," Ford said flatly. "That's why he was brought home." **Peter Roberts**, his successor, got the job he'd always wanted. And **Vern Turner** held the position for a decent time. None spoke Russian, but that's true of 90 percent of ambassadors. The Russians accept it, partly because it gives them an advantage in communication.

The arms race under Reagan increased the burden on Russia but not to the point where its economy might collapse. Ford had argued the point with hardline American academic Richard Pipes and found him completely unrealistic. His line was "absolute nonsense." A vast economy like that of Russia does not collapse, Ford told Pipes, and though the Russians didn't want to spend the money on armaments, they would if they had to. Besides, if the Soviet regime did collapse, it would mean 1917 all over again, with the country coming apart and an enormous nuclear arsenal as the prize. Pipes hadn't seen it in that light.

As Ford explained, "It's not in the interest of anybody that the arms race should continue. If the Soviet economy can improve, it will give the Soviets exposure to the outside, a real standard of comparison. A lot of westerners in Moscow hope the Russians never get it together" (and without some kind of free market, they wouldn't), "because if all that talent were unleashed they'd rule the world. They'd be a real menace then." The Russians' great fear was of the 1 billion Chinese on their doorstep advancing faster than they themselves could.

Ford after Moscow

Ford departed Moscow to attend a human rights conference that SSEA **Mark MacGuigan** had convened in Montebello. When Ford retired, Trudeau, probably on **Allan Gotlieb**'s recommendation, asked him to participate in Swedish politician Olaf Palme's commission on disarmament and security issues. It produced its report, a sensible one that nobody read, in 1982.

Ford, Marcel Cadieux, **John Halstead,** Klaus Goldschlag, Bruce Rankin, and **Si Taylor** were also appointed to a Foreign Policy Advisory Group,[14] which met at least twice a year to ponder large issues. It was a think-tank, not dependent on the latest dispatches or in-depth study, and it looked at issues such as East-West relations. It was Gotlieb's creation, and SSEA MacEachen liked to sit in, but it languished after Gotlieb went to Washington.

Ford also became a special adviser on East-West relations. He received assignments from the USSEA, who wanted his reactions, or "sometimes I would take the initiative." (This might have included vetting Geoffrey Pearson's dispatches from Moscow, which reportedly reduced Geoffrey to a froth, or writing a report on the USSR and Latin America.) He wrote a long, quite detailed report, "A Study of East-West Relations," an examination of all current issues and an attempt to project the future. It was finished during Yuri Andropov's year as general secretary, but that made little difference. Only after Konstantin Chernenko's death did things move, and then the speed surprised him. Indeed, Gorbachev had some of Khrushchev's rashness – witness his invitation for a Reagan meeting in 1987. Reform in Russia must come from above, Ford said. Gorbachev was like Alexander II.

During this period, Ford travelled to Ottawa for two- or three-week stints. When his wife died, he resigned all but the Palme commission and a geopolitical institute in Paris.

On journalists: Peter Worthington was able and bright. David Levy was also good, but the *Globe and Mail* man, Lawrence Martin, was not.

Last thoughts on Trudeau
What should one make of a prime minister who in 1952 had visited Moscow to attend the conference of a front organization? He'd enjoyed the Hotel

....

14 These men were all distinguished senior officials from DEA. Ford's recollection of the membership is faulty: for example, Cadieux was dead by the time the group first met. Its formal title was the Group of Foreign Policy Advisers, and it met twice, in 1981 and 1982. Trudeau attended at least the first meeting. John Hilliker, Mary Halloran, and Greg Donaghy *Canada's Department of External Affairs*, vol. 3, *Innovation and Adaptation, 1968-1984* (Toronto: University of Toronto Press, 2017), 338-39, 473.

Rossiya food for a week before he came to the embassy for relief dinners, after which he ate well enough and clung to the embassy. But he gave no explanation of why he was in Moscow. Then there was his dinner with Ford in April 1968. Then Trudeau's 1971 visit to Moscow, with the press conference that "irritated the Americans beyond belief." And how could he take his three boys to the USSR for a Soviet-government-paid vacation in 1984? This was quite inappropriate for an ex–prime minister. Ford drew no drastic conclusions but wondered if this behaviour weren't Trudeau's anti-establishment trait coming through. Yet why did Trudeau personally not raise human rights, as his government did? ...

The World Economic Congress that Trudeau attended in 1952 was sponsored by front organizations. No respectable economist went, and Trudeau was not even an economist. But he came to the embassy, "and he liked us and we liked him." The embassy treated him well, as one of three Canadian visitors between 1951 and 1954. He discovered that he liked caviar, a foretaste of his imperial attitudes. And "he always contrasted the treatment he got from me with the treatment he got in other embassies. He never forgot it." He had "a long memory," positive and negative.

Really, Trudeau was one of the brightest and most attractive people whom Ford ever met. They were on first-name terms – Pierre and Robert. Trudeau wanted to be sure that Ford was in Moscow for his prime ministerial visit.

Overall, Trudeau's Russian policy had a good effect – improved relations were good, and keeping the Russians interested in rapprochement with the United States was good. He gave the Russians an idea of our real importance. Ford never agreed with his consistently anti-American line. Amusingly, Trudeau, like many French Canadians, was very anti-French. At a reception in Moscow, he spent a long time talking to the Chinese chargé, even speaking some Chinese to him. Next was the French ambassador. There was the barest "Bonjour," and Trudeau turned his back to talk to the next in line.

Certainly, Trudeau and Giscard couldn't stand each other – Giscard said so at dinner. His hauteur would make any French Canadian angry; it rolled off arrogant Anglo-Saxons' sense of superiority. When French Canadians were posted to Paris, they took about six months to shed their starry-eyed enthusiasm.

Trudeau's "Third Option nonsense" indicated that he would go out of his way to irritate the Americans. And "the peace mission was a foolish and useless move," in which the Russians took no interest once they saw that

Trudeau carried no American concurrence. No doubt, Geoffrey Pearson had something to do with it: "Anything half-baked is likely to come from Geoffrey."

Yes, Trudeau was something of a dilettante. Look how he dropped East-West after 1971. It was his turn to visit after Kosygin, and he never came.

On DEA, Ford repeated that the quality of young officers was better in the 1970s than in the 1950s. Perhaps overall, things were worse because of demoralization at the transfer of power to the PMO and the disastrous integration of Trade and (especially) Immigration people in the foreign service, with some senior posts reserved to them.

Personalities
Ivan Head "played a sinister role," undercutting DEA, arrogantly asserting his standing, displacing Ford from the customary seat next to Trudeau at the Kosygin talks in 1971. He was "his master's voice."

Marcel Cadieux hated Trudeau, hated his ideas, and hated the French.

Allan Gotlieb was a good USSEA, with a brain like a trap, a bit arrogant and not wildly popular; but he was respected by Trudeau. "His views on East-West tended towards mine," Ford said. And he was a good administrator.

Ed Ritchie was a close friend, but neither he nor **Basil Robinson** was as effective as Gotlieb. They were too nice, and both had health problems. Neither was a good administrator.

The worst minister was Don Jamieson, "really pretty awful," with no background, no preparation, and no languages.

Mitchell Sharp was the best. He played a moderating role with Trudeau and succeeded after 1970. Perhaps that was because Trudeau was losing or had lost interest.

JOHN HALSTEAD (1922-98)
INTERVIEW | GRAINAU AND AUGSBERG, GERMANY, 20-23 FEBRUARY 1988

Trudeau and the USSR, 1971
During Trudeau's 1971 trip to the USSR, the Soviets produced the Protocol on Consultations, and Trudeau decided to sign it. They played him right – knowing he'd be receptive to more dialogue and to a Canadian contribution to it. Halstead didn't remember the form of the first Soviet draft, but changes

were made to ensure that nothing therein prejudiced Canada's alliance links or altered its basic orientation. This was an acknowledgment of the usefulness of talking to each other. The appearances here worried DEA but not Trudeau. He was prime minister and believed he could sign the protocol on his own. It didn't require legislation, and he decided there was no need to consult the cabinet. **Ed Ritchie** was there as chief adviser, and Halstead especially was concerned about how this would look. The officials were nervous. In the end, however, the protocol did no harm and made no difference. Canada invoked it after Afghanistan and got the same story the USSR gave the rest of the world. What did more harm in the USSR was Trudeau's off-the-cuff remark on a Soviet icebreaker at Leningrad about US military pressure on Canada ...

PETER ROBERTS (1927-2003)
INTERVIEW | OTTAWA, 5 FEBRUARY 1988

Roberts was in Moscow from 1957 to 1960, on the USSR desk at DEA from 1960 to 1962, in Hong Kong and Vietnam from 1962 to 1965, in Washington (watching China and the USSR) from 1965 to 1969, and in NATO from 1969 to 1970. Then he served in the PMO as press secretary from 1970 to 1973, as assistant USSEA for culture from 1973 to 1979, in Romania from 1979 to 1983, and in Moscow as ambassador from 1983 to 1985.

Trudeau and the USSR
Trudeau's 1971 USSR visit was a lot of fun – though not for Roberts, who had to mind more than seventy Canadian journalists. He did the briefings and sat in on meetings. Trudeau was well received, uniquely so in that the USSR opened Norilsk to him, the first time that foreigners got there. The journalists were also given free rein, which was unique, and the Canadians had more freedom than resident correspondents.

The Russians saw Trudeau as amenable to their influence, sympathetic to them, and coming from a different quarter than the United States. Trudeau was an eclectic personality who didn't believe in labels. He believed in people, not slogans or movements. The United States and some people in DEA saw him as naive, but he wanted to see for himself. That was why he cultivated Alexander Yakovlev, the Soviet ambassador from 1973 to 1983. He saw brains there. His meetings in Ottawa with Yakovlev made DEA angry. When Trudeau went to Moscow for Andropov's funeral, Yakovlev invited him to his home for a family dinner, a great and unprecedented gesture. This swept Trudeau off his feet. Roberts thought that the link with Yakovlev had some policy spinoff, in that the USSR got an accurate read on Trudeau. Trudeau had a clear view of Yakovlev too, though Roberts wasn't sure if he passed this on to DEA (though he probably did to ministers).

Ambassador to the USSR
In Moscow from 1983 to 1985, Roberts found less change than expected. Between his first posting in 1959 and the Trudeau visit of 1971, the change was enormous. But between 1971 and 1983, it was less so, and the problems were still the same in leadership, economy, and mentality. Only when Gorbachev came in was there change.

Roberts had good access to people in Moscow, especially in the economic ministries. He could see Foreign Ministers Gromyko and Eduard Shevardnadze when he wanted and could see deputy ministers. He could even see Yakovlev one-on-one when he was the Communist Party propaganda chief. Access to the cultural world was good, and literati would come to his residence. Once, Maya Plisetskaya showed up uninvited.[15] But he still couldn't invite ordinary citizens for dinner, though junior officials in the embassy had more ordinary contacts. It was possible to get a better read on things than twenty-five years before. Statistics were more reliable, and you could have a good conversation with officials on what was wrong with the oil industry. Travelling was easier too.

Embassy business was 40 percent trade (a staff of three), 40 percent political (a staff of three or four), and 20 percent ambassadorial administration. The consular section was busy. During his first tour in the USSR, there were three hundred visitors in two years; now there are thousands. The cultural link was almost completely dead after Afghanistan. Canada shot itself in the foot by cancelling the General Exchanges Agreement. All he could do was watch for visitors to Western Europe and bring them to Moscow for an evening performance in the embassy, with room for forty or so guests. As he was leaving the USSR, culture was opening up again.

....

15   Maya Plisetskaya (1925-2015), Russian prima ballerina at the Bolshoi and later ballet director.

WILLIAM HOOPER (1924-2010)
INTERVIEW | OTTAWA, 21 APRIL 1988

Hooper joined DEA in 1950 and served in Latin America, India, Africa, Britain, and Ottawa. He worked mainly on the intelligence side of the department and was director general for security from 1978 to 1982.

DEA and intelligence
Hooper worked on the intelligence side of External Affairs. From there he moved on to the Soviet desk as a kind of natural extension. For example, between 1961 and 1964 he was working on such things as Russian intentions. He had also been posted to Tanzania and to London, where he was our liaison with British intelligence, one of the few areas in which the British actually listened to what we had to say ...

Hooper emphasized that he was on the DEA side of the intelligence community; Deputy Commissioner Bill Kelly was his "RCMP nemesis." He himself dealt, *inter alia*, with large parts of the file on Mikhail Klochko, the Soviet chemist who defected in 1961 while attending a conference in Montreal; he worked on China, where we were among the first Western analysts properly to appraise its break with Moscow. Kelly, of course, refused to believe it; it was just another commie ploy, fiendishly clever. In that period, DEA's people were already working on the problem of Eurocommunism; it was obvious in the early 1960s that even the Khrushchev variant was not working with the satellites. "We on the intelligence side had to explain to people that the monolith was deteriorating," Hooper recalled. Unfortunately, the belief in the superhuman, if not supernatural, qualities of the KGB was so ingrained that the Canadian analysts had an uphill battle. The skepticism derived in part from domestic perceptions. Any observer could see that the Canadian Communist Party was utterly subservient to Moscow, assumed this was the natural state for any Communist Party, and could not understand that other Communist Parties were in fact rather different. Hooper recalled, "I used to say, let the communists take power in Chile: what will it avail the USSR?"

The gut feeling in Canada, therefore, was that the Americans and the British had it wrong. Hooper found, for example at NATO, that we tended to be more sophisticated about communism than the US or UK spokesmen – spokesmen, by the way, and not the experts underneath them; their experts by and large had it right. In the Kennedy years, it was easier to deal with this, even though JFK himself seriously misjudged what Khrushchev was all about.

So Canada in world affairs tended to play a moderating part, at least until about 1976. The key period for this trend was under Trudeau.

The Czech invasion

Hooper was on vacation in August 1968, when the Soviets invaded Czechoslovakia. "Everybody went berserk," he remembered. But why? The invasion was no surprise. Months earlier, we had concluded that they would go in, that they would have to go in. The Brezhnev regime in the USSR was so insecure that it could not tolerate the fragmentation of the Soviet satellites.

Marcel Cadieux was not surprised by the invasion. He understood something that few other Canadian negotiators did: the Russian mentality. He was "a Cartesian of the best school," and he applied philosophy to dealing with the Russians, which entailed being "confident, logical, and unwavering." Don't back down from your position unless you get a concession first. The same lesson should be applied to the French but not to the Americans. Dealing with the Americans is different, because unlike the French or the Russians, they want to be loved.

In 1968, we did all the standard things in expressing our dissatisfaction to the Russians: protest this, suspend that. "We're to a large extent in the hands of NATO, but it's quite clear in my mind that **Trudeau** and **Sharp** knew we weren't going to change anything in Eastern Europe. It was better in any case to have a stable Russian satellite than a destabilized government, because that's exactly what the Czechs did have before the invasion – the Czechs went nuts," prior to August 1968.

We knew the Russians would have to do something; what we really didn't like was the rigid Stalinist government that they imposed – Husak and company.[16] Thereafter, the Czech government moved in lockstep with the USSR, which almost meant that there was no point in having relations with it. Our relations in Prague were indeed very poor and stayed that way at least until 1976. We even recommended to DEA's cost-cutters that our Czech embassy be closed on the grounds that we didn't need it. We would tell the Czechs this whenever they got especially difficult (such as refusing to talk about family reunification or trade), and it would drive them round the bend. Stalinists or not, it hurt the Czechs because they considered themselves so

---

16 Gustav Husak (1913-91) was secretary general of the Czechoslovak Communist Party (1969-87) and president of Czechoslovakia (1975-89).

European. Hooper did not mean that individually the Czechs were a problem, but as a group they were impossible. So we refused any ministerial visits and declined to schedule anything. We even tried to get NATO to adopt a similar policy.

Sharp "bought our line" about how to treat the Czechs. He too was unhappy about their government. (Both Sharp and Hooper knew that actually closing the Canadian embassy in Prague was politically impossible.) What could you do with a government that had only four or five competent people? The only thing to be said for it was that it could deal with the problems of a very divided country. He added that Czechs and Slovaks had no sense of co-operation, of belonging; they had no sense of individual nationalism without actual separateness. And Canadians thought *we* had a separatist problem!

Finally, after a lot of pressure, the Czechs turned around. In the late 1970s, for example, we got a large contract for building a paper mill.

Dealing with the Russians
The Russians liked negotiating with us because we were so clear in what we stated and what we did; as they said, with the Canadians "we know where we are." Otherwise, they'd have you for breakfast. Yakovlev would tell Hooper that "we always get an answer from Canada, and it's always clear."

Take the example of Jewish emigration from the USSR. The Soviets took the view, very strongly, that this was an internal matter. We would not debate that. What we did was to say that whatever the definition of the problem, it was causing difficulties in Canadian-Soviet relations. We wanted certain people out in that context. It was concern for our relations that caused us to raise this matter again and again, or so we said.

Hooper recalled that "Yakovlev would over and over say 'thank you, I can convey this to Moscow, and I won't get in trouble.'" Formulating the problem in this manner wouldn't get him into trouble and provoke Moscow into demoting him further. When Yakovlev was sent to Canada, he was clearly being demoted. In Moscow, he belonged to a very interesting group, which took the line that the USSR had no business being in places such as Africa. As he would say, there's no proletariat in Africa. He would add, "I'm not a Marxist; I'm an Engels man." Socialism must be based on developed industry.

Hooper saw a good deal of Yakovlev when he was in Ottawa; he used to be invited round to his house and they would sit and talk. Of course, he briefed the RCMP on his discussions, and there was no problem there.

One mistake that Canadians and other westerners made in dealing with the Russians was assuming too great a cultural similarity. In fact, "they are as different from us mentally and socially as are the Chinese." They had a different concept of government, authority, and morality: not less, but different. Fundamentally, their view was "tribal." So few Canadians understood this, though **Paul Martin** was not bad in this area.

Martin also grasped the kernel of the problem with Vietnam. He kept telling the Americans that there was no military solution and that we would not support one.

Sharp was the best minister Hooper ever had for taking a briefing, though Allan MacEachen was also pretty good. He was much more a political animal, though. Sharp could take his briefing and then lay it right on the line in whatever negotiation or situation he might find himself.

We knew that the Russians had to have certain things in their negotiations with us; the question was, what? The answer to that used to drive the Russians mad because of the rigidities of their system. On one occasion, Gromyko told Sharp that he would have to return to Moscow for a Politburo meeting (very important, though; for before becoming a member Gromyko was a mere executor, not an originator, of policy). At any rate, Gromyko said that the forthcoming meeting would be a total waste of time: "We will decide on a model of shoes," or something like that. "You wouldn't believe it."

Trudeau and Europe
One day in London, Hooper got a frantic phone call asking him to come home to Ottawa and take over the Soviet desk. This was in June 1970; Trudeau wanted to visit Russia, which would mean that Canada was the first Western nation to have any serious post-1968 high-level contact with the Soviets.

We took the attitude that Canada was a European country; of course, so was the United States. Was this a function of Trudeau? It may have been more general. We felt that we'd made our point in 1968; now we should look to our own interests. Could we not broaden our relations, such as trade? This subject "was always at the top of Sharp's mind." Some also believed that we should extricate ourselves from the economic grip of the United States, "though I never bought this facile idea." Hooper agreed with economist Harry Johnson that economics and ownership did not govern our relations with the United States; it was a question of political will for Canada to remain separate. Anyway, our view was that we must stay in Europe. The Brits were busy saying goodbye to us, so that they could go into Europe and enjoy being preoccupied with the "British disease." So we had to be involved with the other Europeans, not because of Pearsonianism, and we had to be seen as not totally aligned. We also had to be seen as distinct from the Americans.

This was Sharp's vision. We were not getting away from the United States; it was not a choice of either Europe or the United States, but a case of both Europe and the United States. This implied NATO, the Conference on Security and Cooperation in Europe (CSCE), and East-West relations. We remained in constant contact with the Europeans through NATO. During the mid-1970s, Hooper found himself operating in and through the European capitals and in Helsinki and Geneva and so forth.

Trudeau's projected visit to the USSR was interrupted by the FLQ crisis of October 1970. Hooper was diverted to the DEA Operations Centre. That operation would have gone better if the deputy solicitor general had been kept out. At that time, DEA was the only source of a large number of people who could manage a crisis. But when the crisis was over, the centre went back to its standby and part-time status. Hooper himself turned out the office lights on its last day. When he became director general of security and intelligence in the 1980s, he revived it as an emergency centre; until recently, however, it was not manned on a round-the-clock basis. Nevertheless, we had space, people, and infrastructure.

In this as in other intelligence questions, you don't see the whole picture until you see the raw material. We're in trouble all the time unless we do our own work. We have our reciprocal relation with the United States; the major Canadian input there is into assessments of what Hooper called "the threat to North America."

Dealing with communists
Hooper talked about his relationship as Soviet desk officer to Ambassador **Bob Ford**. He recalled one occasion in 1974, when the department was scrambling to find a new number two for Ford, because Ford used to be rather hard on his deputies. Ford wanted someone who could understand him and run his office; he asked for Hooper. Hooper was not enthusiastic. He had no Russian, and he was not anxious to go to Moscow; he was just becoming a director. But Ford had seen Hooper operate at the CSCE, and he knew that the Russians trusted him as someone they could deal with; Ford had some problems along that line. "I got on with Ford's nemesis, the head of the second European division, Vladimir Suslov," said Hooper. He was "an

awful old drunk," but he had extremely good contacts in the KGB and in the party. Ford couldn't stand him, possibly because he was an extremely tough character; but perhaps Suslov was afraid of Ford, who could come down on him as an uncultured boor.

Ford was finally asked, do you want Hooper in Moscow or do you want him handling your things in Ottawa? Ford gave in, and Hooper remained his Ottawa agent.

Though Ford's Russian was very good, Hooper said that it was a very difficult language to negotiate in. There can be four Russian equivalents for one English word. You must be extremely careful because of the philological difficulties and semantic problems posed by Russian. So you may find yourself inadvertently changing the meaning of agreed positions. Take the phrase in the CSCE negotiations, "freedom of movement of people": for "people," the Russians wanted to use the word *narod*, though the correct translation, as we had intended, was *lyudi*.[17]

Hooper then talked of the role of the KGB in diplomacy. "I've a lot of time for them," Hooper said. They were not afraid, and you could deal with them. They were the sole possessors of information: thus, they took the place of both a free press and a free Parliament. They were essential. Look at Juan Perón, the Argentine dictator: when his secret police ceased to report accurately, his regime cracked.

In the USSR, there was also the party press summary. It was the job of the Novosti and Tass correspondents, every day, to collect data from the capitalist press; this information was then sent to Moscow and published in a restricted circular. (Yes, he had read an example.)

As a diplomat, you knew that if you talked to a KGB or Tass person, what you said to him might very well get straight to the top. Yakovlev told Hooper that whenever he wanted a message to go through, he always sent it via the party network, through the Politburo secretariat and not the Foreign Ministry. When Hooper served in Tanzania, he used to chat with the KGB resident there, who was in a position to tell him how the Russians saw things there.

....

17 Alison Smith, a Russian historian at the University of Toronto, commented, "Lyudi really wouldn't be right, because it's not abstract enough. Litso/litsa/lits (singular, plural, genitive plural, which is how it would show up in the formulation) would have been a better word to suggest." We are most grateful to Professor Smith for her help.

Thus, if you used the other fellow's intelligence system properly, you could have a major input. In London, "I was constantly feeding impressions and analysis into British assessments of situations." That probably had more impact on the way the British thought or acted than the official ministerial communications. He commended the British edition of *Puzzle Palace*;[18] it was a really good account of what went on.

Trudeau's Russian visit, 1971

In contrast to Sharp, Trudeau did not brief well: you just could not say to him, "you can't say that." In addition, USSEA **Ed Ritchie**, who went along to Russia, "didn't have a clue. He thought the sun shone out of the Russians' backside. We had a terrible time getting him not to sell the shop. He knew less about Russia or East-West relations than any other under secretary."

Ivan Head was "a good type." The only problem was getting to him, because he had so many irons in the fire.

What was Trudeau up to in Kiev? He probably saw something in the Ukraine that he was familiar with in Canada: the problem of a huge linguistic minority. The thing was that Trudeau was in the business of upsetting people, "and what he said [in Kiev] had occurred to me."

Again, when you looked at Russia, there were the similarities to Canada: language problems, space, nationalities. The only thing was, the Russians themselves were not like us. We'll never become the same in this millennium or the next, if we survive that long. Contacts between top-level individuals could be distorting or distorted. You saw only the top men and their sycophants. Understanding and communicating with Poles, Hungarians, and even Indians was easier, though, of course, on a human basis you could get close to a Russian. You couldn't even do that with a leader.

One evening in Warsaw, Hooper and MacEachen took a stroll, and of course some obviously "official Poles" tagged along with them. They saw a group of youths at a bus stop; the kids scattered and fled. When they reached the bus stop, the reason for their flight was obvious to Hooper: he could smell marijuana. The official Poles had no idea; and of course neither did MacEachen, who had no children to learn from.

---

18   James Bamford, *The Puzzle Palace: A Report on America's Most Secret Agency* (London: Penguin, 1982). *The Puzzle Palace* deals with the National Security Agency, a US intelligence organization.

PETER HANCOCK (1938-)
INTERVIEW | BONN, GERMANY, 21 OCTOBER 1987

Hancock worked on Trudeau's 1971 trip to the USSR, in Policy Planning, and as director general for the USSR and Eastern Europe. He was a major player in the 1983-84 Peace Initiative.

Trudeau in Moscow and Canada-USSR relations
The Moscow trip had been postponed from October 1970 to the spring of 1971. Hancock was the advance man in March 1971. There was a lot getting ready to happen, such as German-USSR arrangements and a four-power meeting on Berlin. Despite the Czech invasion of 1968, it was remarkable the way the West was picking up momentum on East-West relations. France's Pompidou had gone to the USSR, the Italians were there, and a US-Soviet deal was cooking. Hancock thought that Canada was ideally positioned to approach the USSR: it was behind France, Italy, and Germany, and ahead of the United States. He thought positioning was part of the genius of Trudeau's foreign policy, and he attributed it to **Ivan Head**. He had done the same with the official recognition of China.

The key result of the Moscow visit was the Protocol on Consultations. This wasn't a friendship treaty, and it proved useful over the years. It gave Canada a claim on the time of the Russians.

The talks in Moscow were good. Kosygin was still strong, and the USSR surprised us by quickly accepting our invitation for him to visit Canada. The visit helped wheat sales and let us try to crack the USSR market for industrial sales. (The year before, Jean-Luc Pepin had signed an Industrial Exchange Agreement with the USSR.) Trudeau signed a General Exchanges Agreement, which allowed academic exchanges. The visit was timed right – if it had come after the United States, Canada would have got nothing ...

Trudeau's visit to Norilsk was not a statement on the Gulag. As Canadians, we had to be interested in large northern cities, so we had to see it, even if it was built by slave labour.

We got Arctic exchanges. During an Arctic visit, Jean Chrétien began this process, which takes time and is now beginning to produce. There was the hockey series, which was fun, important – and we won. But Hancock admitted that the rot had set in by 1979. After a decade, little had resulted except disillusionment. The USSR couldn't deal sensibly with the West, and even before the Afghan War, regular meetings with the Soviets got tougher. Dealing with the Russians required sweet-and-sour sauce, with the mix having to be varied.

After Afghanistan, Trudeau suspended the exchange agreement in 1980, and this drew the academics out of the woodwork. The idea of sanctions against the Russians had been kicked around in January 1980, and Trudeau was back in power in February. He adopted the broadest and toughest range of sanctions. The head of the National Research Council had cut off exchanges on his own hook.

Ambassador **Ford** had real standing in Moscow. His ability and stature were formidable. The Soviets didn't always like him for his contacts with intellectuals to whom his poetry and translations gave entrée. To work for Ford was no easy task.

Trudeau and Yakovlev had a special rapport. Hancock and others used to grumble about the dinners at Sussex Drive. Still, look where Yakovlev was in 1987 and how firm the picture he must have had of Canada. The important thing about the 1983 Gorbachev visit was that it happened, that Canada was an okay place for the USSR to send its high flyer. This was a tribute to the work done during the 1970s on the relationship between the two countries. There are pieces of Canada in Gorbachev's head, with possibly a later payoff.

VERNON TURNER (1930-)
INTERVIEW | MOSCOW, 27 FEBRUARY 1988

Turner joined DEA in 1954. He served on the ICC, in London, Warsaw, Dar es Salaam, New York, Ottawa, and Washington. He was ambassador to Israel from 1982 to 1986 and to the USSR from 1986 to 1990. He retired in 1991.

On the Russian desk at DEA
Turner came back to Ottawa in 1969 to the USSR desk. After the August 1968 invasion of Czechoslovakia, there was a deep freeze with Moscow, but in 1969 Canada decided to relieve the tension by inviting Gromyko to Ottawa – on three weeks' notice. That Gromyko accepted so readily was undoubtedly due to the possibility of a meeting with Trudeau. Trudeau was a different kind of Western leader, who was bound to intrigue the Soviets. Turner had to provide the briefings for **Sharp** and **Trudeau**. One day, Gromyko was

scheduled to have tea with Trudeau, and Turner accompanied the prime minister to 24 Sussex Drive to brief him en route. Trudeau asked wistfully, "Will he ask us about our Indians?" Turner demurred, suggesting that Gromyko simply wanted to meet him. Over tea, Gromyko asked Trudeau for his perspective on global developments. Trudeau's reply took the form of lengthy and masterful monologue. Gromyko's response: "You know, prime minister, you don't look at all like your pictures."

Trudeau seemed naive about the Soviets, and not just the Soviets, but he wasn't soft on communism. He knew the kind of system it was. Certainly, he wouldn't accept conventional wisdom on the USSR. He questioned everything and everybody, which was his way of learning and developing his views. Perhaps that made him seem naive. But he listened to people and wanted their opinions.

Turner became head of DEA's Eastern European section in 1970. Trudeau's visit to the USSR was postponed from October 1970 to May 1971. A Protocol on Consultations had been discussed before the visit, and Turner remembered telegrams being exchanged with our embassy in Moscow. The response of officials in Ottawa to this Soviet proposal was reserved because of concern that such an agreement could raise questions about Canada's political orientation in the East-West context. Trudeau, however, thought the protocol a good idea. He favoured increased contacts and would have seen them as a contribution to détente.

High-level visits to the USSR also let Canada push it to improve on human rights. Trudeau did this, and Joe Clark did too. The Soviets eventually accepted it as normal that Canada would raise bilateral family reunification questions – even questions about dissidents could be raised too if carefully done. Those were political questions best posed by politicians in the first instance, but then officials could follow up. The Helsinki agreements and the CSCE obliged the Soviets to accept the situation.

JAMES (SI) TAYLOR (1930-)
INTERVIEW | OTTAWA, 30 AUGUST 1988

Taylor joined DEA in 1953 and had an extraordinary forty-year career. He served in Vietnam, India, France, the USSR, Belgium, NATO, and Japan, and was USSEA.

Service in Moscow, 1967-70

His time in Moscow was, Taylor said, mid-Brezhnev. There was still a kind of triumvirate at the top, but Nikolai Podgorny, the chair of the Presidium of the Supreme Soviet, was clearly on the way out, and Kosygin was dipping perceptibly below Brezhnev in importance. Kosygin was trying his economic reforms, which were running into the sand; Brezhnev meanwhile had made himself the patron of the military establishment, which meant that some of the salient characteristics of the later period had emerged.

What that meant was that the press were forever cooking up stories of the war and Brezhnev's service at the front; all this was associated with Great Russian nationalism; and all was linked to the problem of maintaining revolutionary enthusiasm in a post-revolutionary generation. The cult of monuments, the tours for schoolchildren of battlefields, these were part of it.

By 1967, almost all traces of the war had disappeared from the physical fabric of Russia, even in Leningrad, where there were some scars on the faces of buildings. Even the tsarist palaces around the city were well on the way to restoration of their facades.

The regime sensed that it was unappealing, Taylor stated, and it was using the past to bolster itself, as an excuse, really. The emphasis on the suffering of the Russian people masked the fact that other countries (though not, obviously, Canada) had suffered as much. Consider Finland, which lost a major part of its territory to the USSR, not to mention its main timber port (the Finnish economy turns on timber). Despite its territorial and economic losses, Finland remained a much more dynamic country than Russia. You could argue the Finnish example pretty plausibly. You had the feeling that the Russians deluded themselves about the gravity of their own failures by constant reference to their suffering during the war.

Soviet invasion of Czechoslovakia

The most important event of his time in Moscow, Taylor said, was the Czech invasion in August 1968. There was plenty of speculation backward and forward about whether the Russians would actually invade – only "a hard-nosed minority" predicted they would; and then after the fact, there were the analyses. In fact, the Russians issued no immediate plausible justification or rationalization beyond the bogus allegations of imminent German expansion or NATO intervention. It was analysts in the West who invented the term "Brezhnev doctrine," which was first issued as a newspaper article, therefore semi-officially: really a kind of try-on. Brezhnev only later endorsed it in a speech in Poland. At the time, people tended to consider it a programmatic doctrine; some in the West believed that it furnished a blueprint for taking on Yugoslavia. "That's nuts," Taylor said. The Russians invaded Czechoslovakia because they believed it was in their national interest. They knew damn well that the "Brezhnev doctrine" was "a tendentious rationalization."

The Russians didn't worry much about the Canadian reaction. The one Canadian opinion that mattered to them was Bill Kashtan's, the Communist Party leader. The approval of anybody was important and was played up.

Every time something like this happened, Western governments had to do something and had to be seen by an expectant public opinion to be doing something. The basic attitude of the West through this period, 1967-84, was expressed by NATO's Harmel doctrine, but you must remember that it consisted of two tracks. One of these was negotiation, and the Czech invasion "pulled up that track."

All we could do was express outrage, Taylor continued. Going to war over an issue like this was no longer an option. And the fact of the matter was that we saw the USSR as a relatively remote country in terms of our bilateral relations, and considered in bilateral terms, the same was even true for the United States. Our reactions were political symbolism. If we tried economic retaliation – we won't accept your money for our grain – we lost as much as we gained. In wheat, for a whole generation, the Soviets have been our most important market. It's "you have our wheat and we have your cash – bilaterally balanced trade."

The Soviet economy was disorganized and chaotic. There was so much to be reformed in the system. How do you get people to work properly? How can you take up the slack in the system? "While I was there," Taylor said, "the Soviets had just had one of their economic experiments among farmers." It was to give them individual responsibility and advantage. As you might expect, it proved that productivity rose right away. The more you did it, the better.

During this period, the Russians were altering the strategic balance. You could see the new weapons systems trundling through Red Square every November. But this was also the period of their ill-fated supersonic airliner that blew up. And at the time, the Russians were genuinely admiring of such American achievements as putting a man on the moon. They certainly weren't grudging in their comments.

Agreements with Moscow
Initially, the Soviets weren't sure what to think of **Trudeau**. After Czechoslovakia, they did come to appreciate that he was "trying to civilize the relationship." There was the *annus mirabilis*, 1971, when he visited Moscow and Kosygin came to Canada. In 1971, in Ottawa, we signed agreements of some substance, not bogus ones. This set the framework through which we conducted our relations until 1979. After the Soviets invaded Afghanistan during that year, it was emptied of content.

The results of the exchanges were spotty; it worked well in some disciplines and not well in others. And, of course, there was the question of whether official sponsorship got you as far as private, friendly initiatives. Even some of our government scientists found that they could get farther with the Russians in visits on their own than they could through government mechanisms and Canadian sponsorship. For example, they could be granted access to forbidden regions. One of our permafrost experts got as far as Yakutsk, where officials could not have gone. You couldn't get anywhere if the permafrost expert didn't think he gained by the exchange. After-dinner orations talked about our "northern neighbour" and so forth, but the reality was more limited.

There was also the question of balance in exchanges. You try to exchange where you can derive some profit. But the Canadian economy (technology) was generally ahead of the Russian. Some of their technology was first class, but that was rare. Why spend limited exchange funds on the USSR when you could derive more marginal advantage in exchanging with the Netherlands?

GEOFFREY PEARSON (1927-2008)
INTERVIEW | OTTAWA, 30 AUGUST 1988

> *The son of Lester B. Pearson, he joined DEA in 1952 and served in Paris, Mexico, Ottawa, and India before becoming ambassador to the USSR from 1980 to 1983. He then worked on Trudeau's Peace Initiative and headed the Canadian Institute for International Peace and Security.*

On Robert Ford and the USSR
Robert Ford's time in Moscow was coming to an end by 1980, and the people who might have succeeded him (such as Blair Seaborn) had gone on to other things. What Pearson meant was that Ford had been there for so long that

the logical successors all gave up hope of getting Moscow, and the USSR desk became a dead end. Why was Ford left in place so long? Every few years, the prospect of posting him was raised. But it was convenient that he stay, and he wanted to. Ford was senior, so there were only a few places he could go. His physical handicap also became an excuse for not moving him. After a decade there, his reputation was such that he became an asset to Canada as the voice on what was happening. His reports were read in the United States, the United Kingdom, and NATO. And, Pearson said, his reputation was justified. He coincided with the Brezhnev years, and he made it safe to say that nothing in the USSR would change, and nothing did, though this stance did make it harder to anticipate change under Andropov, for example.

In effect, governments had come to expect that the USSR would never change. They took for granted a hostile regime that would always threaten them except for brief periods of détente. Pearson wasn't suggesting that Ford was responsible for this. Other ambassadors shared this perspective as well, but he reinforced the entrenched view.

Pearson wouldn't characterize Ford as hard line, but he was definitely skeptical of the prospects of change, of the idea that the West could have an influence on the USSR, of any left-wing ideas that the West could work with the USSR. Still, Ford was no professional anti-Soviet. He had contacts with the intellectuals, understood Russia's culture and soul. He didn't write them off – he just didn't believe their system would change.

Ambassador to Moscow

Pearson had had no experience of a communist country when he arrived in the USSR six months after the Afghanistan invasion. He didn't know what to expect and brought an open mind that let him notice things others might not have seen. For example, some Soviet academics would say to him that nuclear war was unwinnable and out of the question, which others might have dismissed as currying favour. But he took it seriously and soon discovered that this was now USSR policy. Pearson's views were seen as naive "by those who had been in the USSR for sixteen years," meaning Ford, but there were undercurrents there.

Pearson knew that Ford saw his views as those of a naïf. That didn't surprise him – it was normal for a sixteen-year ambassador to be critical. Ford as a special adviser was a cross that Pearson had to bear; certainly, it wasn't for Pearson to criticize Ford's continuing usefulness to the department. But he did object that he never saw Ford's reports.

Still, the criticism didn't bother him, he said unconvincingly, as he was reporting on his own impressions and interests. With the help of his wife (who learned kitchen Russian), they talked to everyone, KGB or otherwise. He compared views with other ambassadors (especially Arthur Hartman, the American, who was also new, even if a Reagan appointee), and he didn't feel that his impressions were out of place. He recognized that expertise could be a trap.

To him, the USSR was a Third World country – poor, defensive, insecure (like India or Mexico). He didn't see it as a great power but as a relative newcomer in the world and one extraordinarily sensitive to criticism. He didn't seek monocausal explanations for things. For example, he thought he'd never called the USSR totalitarian in his reports; it wasn't. There were all kinds of underground ideas, *sotto voce* asides, etc., just as in Mexico. All these cross-currents impressed Pearson, and he found that the Russians opened up if you showed you weren't hostile. It was hard to get invited to homes, but that was because they were ashamed of how they had to live and because they were encouraged not to invite foreigners. Still, one of his staff went everywhere. Pearson admitted that the DEA view of his reports was the Ford view. The department, like NATO, took a conservative view of the future.

Trudeau, however, felt that Canada had to take the USSR seriously but didn't pursue this. In 1971, he had influenced events, and the protocol was useful. By the end of the 1970s, it was falling apart, however, and the international situation was worsening. The Afghanistan invasion stopped everything dead, including consultations under the protocol. Pearson's advice from Moscow was to soften Canadian policy and to resume exchanges as soon as possible. Canada lost more than the USSR did due to the cessation, especially on the academic exchanges. But no one listened, and Canada was very slow in resuming the exchanges. Pearson didn't know why we were at the end of the line behind even the United States, though he thought that the atmosphere created by Reagan or the substantial influence of ethnics in Canada might have been responsible. He was at pains to point out that he thought Afghanistan was an example of Soviet aggression and that he wanted pressure kept up. But sanctions didn't work. He agreed that high-level consultations should stop, but he thought the low-level (i.e., academic) ones ought to go on. In the end, Ottawa agreed and changed policy.

VII
Canada and the Far East

PIERRE TRUDEAU CAME TO power in 1968 with few fixed positions in foreign policy, but one was that it was long past time for Canada to recognize the communist regime in China. Trudeau had gone to China briefly in the late 1940s and again in 1960 with his friend Jacques Hébert, the latter trip recounted by Hébert and Trudeau in a book, *Two Innocents in Red China*, first published in 1961.[1] As a new MP and parliamentary secretary to Prime Minister Lester Pearson, Trudeau was part of the Canadian delegation to the United Nations in 1966, and he had raised the question of recognition with SSEA Paul Martin. The Cultural Revolution was then in full swing in China, the United States remained adamantly opposed to Beijing, and he made no headway, but he and his roommate in New York, Toronto MP Donald Macdonald, agreed that change was necessary. In power, they would act. During the election campaign of 1968, Trudeau clearly stated that "our aim will be to recognize the People's Republic of China Government as soon as possible and to enable that Government to occupy the seat of China in the United Nations, taking into account that there is a separate Government in Taiwan."[2] That was a "one China, one Taiwan" policy. But by October 1970, after long and difficult negotiations in Stockholm that revolved around the wording of the status of Taiwan, Beijing and Ottawa had worked out a formula that let Canada recognize China without throwing Taiwan completely under the bus: "The Chinese Government reaffirms that Taiwan is an inalienable part of the territory of the People's Republic of China. The Canadian

---

1 The best account of Trudeau's late 1940s travels is in Max Nemni and Monique Nemni, *Trudeau Transformed: The Shaping of a Statesman, 1944-1965* (Toronto: McClelland and Stewart, 2011), Chapter 5. Jacques Hébert and Pierre Elliott Trudeau, *Deux innocents en Chine rouge* (Montreal: Les Éditions de l'Homme, 1961); Jacques Hébert and Pierre Elliott Trudeau, *Two Innocents in Red China* (Toronto: Oxford University Press, 1968).
2 Office of the Prime Minister, press release, 29 May 1968.

government takes note of this position of the Chinese Government."[3] In other words, Canada neither challenged nor endorsed Beijing's claim to Taiwan, but it agreed to "take note of" its position. Trudeau accepted this formulation; in Beijing, Chairman Mao and Premier Zhou Enlai did as well. This formula would soon be used by Belgium and Italy.

The genesis of the Canadian position on China is covered here by Paul Martin, who was Lester Pearson's SSEA and leader of the government in the Senate under Trudeau. The course of the negotiations from the Chinese side is explicated by Yao Guang, a senior Foreign Ministry official who became ambassador to Canada soon after recognition. And Ottawa's view of the negotiation is given by John Fraser, who had earlier been based in Hong Kong and then served in Stockholm during the recognition meetings. By 1972, Canada's embassy in Beijing had opened, and Maurice Copithorne was the number two. He had a bird's eye view of Trudeau's visit to China in 1973 and a hand in negotiating the agreements on consular services, family reunification, and sport and public health exchanges that marked the visit. So too did Yu Zhan, later ambassador to Canada.

China was, of course, the key player in Asia, but Canadians had dealings with Japan as well, and trade was substantial, though not as voluminous as Canadian business hoped. The interview with Yasuhiko Nara, a 1970s ambassador to Canada who became friendly with the Trudeaus, puts such issues into the Japanese context and adds much of interest on Trudeau's personality and marriage.

The other subject covered in this chapter is Vietnam. Canada had been involved in Indochina since the Geneva Conference created the International Commissions of Supervision and Control (ICSC, though usually called the ICC) in 1954. Diplomats and military officers served there for two decades, a very substantial percentage of the officers in External Affairs holding posts on the commission. Most returned home with very strong impressions: the North Vietnamese could not be trusted; the Hungarians and Poles who sat on the commission unwaveringly followed the Communist Party line;[4] and the Indians, supposedly the neutrals on the four-nation commission, were devious and often untrustworthy. One other impression was gained: the United States was more right than wrong in its Vietnam policy. This view shows very clearly in Thomas Delworth's interview.

....

3   Canada, *House of Commons Debates* (13 October 1970), 49.
4   The Poles alone were on the ICSC, and the Poles and Hungarians were on the ICCS.

When Henry Kissinger succeeded in negotiating a peace accord with North Vietnam on 27 January 1973, the United States strong-armed Canada into taking a position on a new International Commission for Control and Supervision (the ICCS, though usually still called the ICC), along with Polish, Hungarian, and Indonesian officials and officers, to monitor the agreement. Unhappy, Ottawa agreed to provide 290 Canadian diplomats and military personnel to serve for a sixty-day trial period and to extend that commitment if the new commission worked as hoped. The commission managed to get almost all US prisoners of war out of North Vietnam, but that was its only success, and there would be only one extension for the Canadian commitment. In any case, Ottawa extraordinarily adopted what it labelled an "open mouth" policy, going public with the commission's work and pointing out North Vietnam's regular violations of the agreement and the obstructionist tactics of the Poles and Hungarians. Richard Gorham elaborated this policy in Ottawa, and Michel Gauvin, heading the mission in Vietnam, implemented it. Gauvin had served on the earlier commission, and he was tough-minded enough to use the open mouth policy effectively, holding press conferences after every commission meeting. Canada withdrew on 31 July 1973. Gorham and Gauvin's accounts tell the story.

RT. HON. PAUL MARTIN (1903-92)
INTERVIEW | WINDSOR, ONTARIO, 10-11 FEBRUARY 1987

Canadian relations with China
First of all, Martin said, Prime Minister Louis St. Laurent and Lester Pearson wanted to recognize China (St. Laurent after his India trip in 1954 and Pearson earlier). At the time, Martin was against it, as were other cabinet members. "I was influenced by some of the missionaries," he said. In any case, Pearson gave up on the idea. As for St. Laurent, Prime Minister Jawaharlal Nehru and Escott Reid, the high commissioner in New Delhi, had convinced him, especially Reid, in whom St. Laurent reposed great confidence. But for Martin, the US position and missionary influence predominated. There was never a good discussion in the cabinet, and even after Taiwan obstructed his 1955 efforts to get new members into the UN, Martin did not really change his view.

In 1955, the question arose of representing divided states in the UN, such as Korea and Vietnam. When he went to Vietnam in 1956, he found that our non-recognition of China prevented him from seeing Zhou Enlai; the two men were doing practically the same tour, but they could never meet because of the recognition question. Martin was advised against it.

By 1963, this had relevance as his position had changed. As the Vietnam War developed, Martin came to view China as more moderate than the Russians on the subject. But the Cultural Revolution was under way, which was hardly a popular attraction in Canada, and that helped to discourage efforts at recognition. Pearson was especially sensitive to that point. The US reaction continued to matter. The Chinese refused to let in retired diplomat Chester Ronning as a peace emissary, even though he was well known there, though they did admit a bunch of Alberta businessmen with an Alberta senator; he never could find out why.

The most Martin could get out of Pearson was to let Canada abstain on the Albanian resolution to admit Beijing to the UN. When Martin informed President Lyndon Johnson of this over breakfast at the president's ranch, Johnson did not seem especially disturbed. It was Secretary of State Dean Rusk who was upset. That abstention, however, didn't impress Beijing because it was linked to a two-China policy. In the event, what **Trudeau** was later able to do, Pearson would have liked to have done.

Trudeau moves

When Trudeau came in, he set up an External Affairs Committee on which Martin sat. Other members were Jean-Luc Pepin, **Mitchell Sharp,** and one or two more (but not apparently **Léo Cadieux**). Under the rules of the cabinet at that time, the decision of a cabinet committee in the absence of opposition from anyone was to be considered a decision of the whole cabinet unless, of course, the prime minister decided to refer it to the whole body.

The committee gave the okay to exploratory talks in Scandinavia, Oslo, or Copenhagen: the Chinese wanted "a neutral place." We didn't know a hell of a lot about the People's Republic of China (PRC), Martin said, neither the cabinet nor DEA. And, of course, the missionaries' views were very one-sided. In the department, we didn't have many very well-informed people; there was little able help, practically no one. Arthur Menzies was elsewhere, and **Basil Robinson** was no expert.

On China, Trudeau never indicated what he wanted, but everybody knew that he favoured recognition. He and **Donald Macdonald** were members of our delegation at the UN in 1966, and Martin had talked to him about it then. The committee went into the whole matter, and with little discussion we agreed.

YAO GUANG (1921-2003)
INTERVIEW | BEIJING, 25 MAY 1987

In the PRC Foreign Ministry from 1964 to 1970, Yao was ambassador to Canada from March 1972 to September 1973 and vice foreign minister from 1982 to 1986, among other postings.

Yao began with China-Canada relations
Yao said he would cover the negotiations for recognition and the early period after recognition.[5] He began with a long disquisition on the three phases in Canada's relations with the PRC:

- 1949-52: This period encompassed the new China, the Korean War, and the Canadian withdrawal of officials from the PRC.
- 1952-68: This period entailed two Chinas and the status of Taiwan. Due to US pressure, Canada did not recognize the PRC ...
- 1968 to October 1970: **Trudeau** had indicated in his election campaign that he would try to establish relations, and after he took office, he ordered officials to contact the PRC to select a suitable location for talks. During this period, it was clear that Canada saw the PRC as the only China and that once it had recognized China, it would give up its recognition of Taiwan. But there was still a problem: Taiwan was an inalienable part of China's territory, and the Canadian view was unclear here – and Ottawa hoped to avoid the issue. This became most important in the negotiations and was the main reason for their lengthiness.

Canada starts recognition negotiations
As director of the Department of Europe and the Americas, Yao was involved in Beijing, making policy on the recognition negotiations. He was also in charge of the negotiations themselves. His view, and the general PRC view,

---

5 This interview was done by Granatstein with York University professor Bernie Frolic.

was that Canada wanted to establish relations because the demands for recognition in Canada were greater than the opposition, as shown in the 1968 election campaign. Trudeau was smart to seize on this because his views suited those of the people. But there was still pressure from the United States. The PRC had understood this even before the Cultural Revolution. China understood that Canada's big neighbour was a problem and that Canada had difficulty in acting; we understood and were prepared to wait patiently. Thus, once Trudeau proposed negotiations, the PRC was ready at once. Yao was unsure why Trudeau was able to act when Pearson couldn't; perhaps if Pearson had been in power after 1968, he might have acted. In any case, Trudeau needed courage to have moved.

On 6 February 1969, Canadian diplomats in Sweden called the PRC embassy and said they wanted to talk. First contact came on 11 February, and progress was made, the Cultural Revolution notwithstanding.

The US pressure was mostly in connection with the Taiwan issue. Before 1968, the Canadian view that recognition of the PRC was tied to Taiwan was US-inspired. This two-China policy was a US policy. The resolution of this problem developed step by step during negotiations. The PRC couldn't give up its principles just to establish relations, and the first stage in negotiations was the exploration of these principles. Beijing could wait one or two hundred years if necessary.

The US influence

Yao explained why he believed that the United States had let Canada act. In the 1968 election in the United States, it was clear that America's attitude to the PRC was changing, not enough for Washington to support Canada, but enough not to oppose the Canadian move for recognition. If Canada had not acted, the United States wouldn't push Ottawa. Check Richard Nixon's article in *Foreign Affairs*, which discusses the PRC and the Vietnam War, Yao said.[6] PRC-US negotiations resumed in Warsaw after the end of 1969 – after the Canada-PRC negotiations were under way.

There were no direct connections between Canada and the US-PRC negotiations. The talks with Canada were for diplomatic recognition, whereas those with the United States dealt with the status of Taiwan. Canada didn't occupy Taiwan, but the United States had interests there. Thus, the negotiations were different.

....

6 Richard M. Nixon, "Asia after Viet Nam," *Foreign Affairs* 46 (October 1967): 111-25.

The fundamental point, he said, was that there was no real conflict between the PRC and Canada. They differed on certain areas, but Canada did not occupy Taiwan, as the United States did. There were no obstacles between us, no tough issues left by history. For example, the Ming Sung Company issue was not a major obstacle and was easily solved after recognition.[7] Even Taiwan as an inalienable part of China, once clearly explained, was easy to understand. With the United States, the PRC could not have accepted "take note of" as a solution, given the US treaty with the Kuomintang and its troops in Taiwan. But when "take note of" was proposed by Canada, after it had shown its understanding of the PRC position, this was okay. Canada was the first to get this formula, which was soon used by others, including Italy. The formula was not appropriate for the United States, but it was for countries that were close to the United States, such as Canada. The PRC understood Canada's difficulties with the United States.

Understanding Canadian policy
During the Cultural Revolution, there was domestic chaos in China, but foreign policy was not basically affected, as it was decided by Mao and Zhou. Even when the Gang of Four was riding high, their fingers didn't touch foreign policy. At that time, he was director of a division in the Ministry of Foreign Affairs, and he always had direct contact with Zhou, and when Zhou read reports they went to Mao. Although there were some ambiguous views of Canadian policy about Taiwan, the PRC had a basic understanding of Canadian policy. The PRC understood the problems, so when Canada took the initiative, there was no way to reject it, and the PRC didn't set preconditions. This was different from negotiations with Vietnam or the USSR, for example. The PRC simply set out its principles to Canada. Yes, Yao said, the decision to negotiate was made by Zhou and Mao, and the final formula – "take note of" – was okayed by them.

There were no special envoys in the PRC-Canada negotiations, and Canada, so far as he knew, had no involvement in the Kissinger initiative to start talks on US recognition of China. The PRC embassy in Ottawa helped promote relations with the United States, as American friends wanting to visit could go there.

....
7   The Ming Sung Company operated Canadian-owned ships that had been seized by the PRC as it came to power. The dispute was resolved soon after recognition.

Yao said the Sino-Canadian relationship was not affected by US-PRC relations. The PRC did not look down on Canada. He arrived in Ottawa in March 1972, when his predecessor Huang Hua went to the UN. While he was ambassador, Trudeau decided to visit the PRC, and he and **Ivan Head** discussed arrangements. He met Trudeau several times and found him easy to approach, not like many political leaders. In 1972, the PRC had an exhibition in Toronto and invited Trudeau, who attended and was presented with rugs. It was a pity, Yao said, that he himself couldn't accompany Trudeau on his PRC visit.

Yao indicated that at least on relations with the PRC, Canada acted on its own and did not seem subject to US pressures.[8] Of course, there were also changes in the United States, which lessened pressure on Canada. What the PRC appreciated most was that Canada decided to act before the United States did. If Trudeau had been in power in 1964, the PRC would have agreed to talk. Trudeau was special. Yao didn't want to dump on Pearson or Howard Green, who was SSEA under Diefenbaker, but Trudeau was special. Of course, relations with both the Liberals and Conservatives in power were good.

JOHN FRASER (1935-2010)
INTERVIEW | OTTAWA, 15 JUNE 1989

Fraser joined DEA in 1958 and served in Hong Kong, Beijing, Washington, Warsaw, and Belgrade.

The two-China proposal
On 23 November 1966, when **Paul Martin** made his two-China proposal at the UN, the Beijing Chinese, and not just the Americans, were furious. This was reflected in the abrupt cancellation of the regular Canadian six-month visit to Beijing from Canada's office in Hong Kong, in which Fraser would have participated. It was cancelled directly because of Canada's unfriendly act. When the next visit was due in June 1967, the first item of business in Beijing was a lecture on the iniquity of the two-China proposal.

---

8 The United States was not happy with Canadian recognition of the PRC. President Nixon said that it was "strictly political," and Kissinger thought the "wheat deal" played a significant role in the decision. See "Document 93: Memorandum of Conversation," 25 October 1970, in *Foreign Relations of the United States, 1969-76*, vol. 17, Office of the Historian, https://history.state.gov/historicaldocuments/frus1969-76v17/d93.

Negotiating recognition

Very little of our approach to China was due to the lure of commerce, Fraser said. The conventional wisdom among the Trade and Commerce people was that our practical relations with China were just fine and that there was no realistic hope of expanding our exports there. Indeed, they saw the approach to establishing diplomatic relations as fraught with peril, for if the process broke down, our commercial relations might be harmed as a consequence.

In his reports from Hong Kong, he said, with the end of the Cultural Revolution the Chinese were perhaps more receptive to the outside. Trudeau's speech of 29 May 1968 pointing to recognition gave rise to the first draft of a revised paper in DEA;[9] indeed, it was more of a book. But it was really a huge collection of every kind of information: "Everything you wanted to know about Beijing but were afraid to ask." It had all the options and every possible international reaction. Our mental picture regarding recognition was that it would all go quite quickly. We originally expected the fruits of the approach by October 1968. Of course, it took much longer.

We were able to say to the Chinese that it was not our intention to recognize Taiwan. Plainly, the issue was that both governments claimed to rule all of China, and one could simply not recognize both simultaneously. Our starting point had been that this Canadian position was none of the PRC's business. On the other hand, the PRC's reaction was far less severe than it would have been five or ten years earlier.

As for the negotiations, our number two in the Stockholm embassy spoke Chinese and had established contact with the Chinese consulate there. In some ways, holding the negotiations in Cairo would have made better sense, since that was where the sole remaining Chinese ambassador was stationed (the others had been recalled during the Cultural Revolution). But we told the Chinese originally that Stockholm was fine.

The derivation of the phrase that we would "neither challenge nor endorse" Beijing's claim to Taiwan came from what **Mitchell Sharp** had said in the House of Commons. At first, he said something that was overemphatic on one side, and he then hastily recovered and said, "and not challenge either."

We had to satisfy the Chinese of our serious intentions and good faith. At the beginning, we came up with a draft communiqué that was modelled on the French one. We wanted to include a reference to establish an exchange

---

9 See J.L. Granatstein and Robert Bothwell, *Pirouette: Pierre Trudeau and Canadian Foreign Policy* (Toronto: University of Toronto Press, 1990), 180-81.

of ambassadors, so as to avoid the fate of the British and the Dutch (who had chargés ad infinitum). The Chinese wanted much more extreme language. This negotiation eventually produced another funny scene in the House of Commons, where Sharp was upbraided for inconsistency. Sharp finally said, well, if the policy announced varies from that previously announced, then it varies.

Canada was as good as its word in 1971. In 1970 at the UN, we had voted for both the admission of Beijing and the "important question" resolution.[10] As a result, Fraser got a wigging from the Chinese Foreign Ministry.

The recognition deal specified that there would be "no government-to-government relations with Taiwan." This meant that we expected people-to-people trade to continue, though Canada in fact has been rather purist about interpreting it, with none of the subterfuges the Americans have used. Remember that the minister's statement and the communiqué on recognition were a package. Ambassador Margaret Meagher and Fraser read out the minister's statement to the Chinese in Stockholm. In fact, right up to the end we were uncertain of the outcome. Fraser went to Stockholm with two pieces of paper, one announcing failure and one success.

Had the United States been on the other side of the table, the "take note of" phrase would not have been used. The Shanghai declaration (when Nixon and Kissinger were in China) really amounted to much the same kind of thing. In terms of significance, the Canadian recognition was a post–Cultural Revolution watershed. The French recognition in 1966 had not been followed by anything, but Canada's was. The Belgians and the Italians were proceeding at almost the same time. We kept in touch with them throughout. Because Canada had started first, the Chinese gave us a two-week lag on announcements. He remembered the final discussion as to what kind of paper the communiqué would be on: it was decided to use neither Canadian nor Chinese, but Swedish. And whether it should be signed: the Chinese wanted it, but we didn't see the necessity. Then there was the question of what Chinese sign to use for Margaret Meagher's last name (pronounced "Mar"). The Chinese had two words that were pronounced as "ma": one meant horse, the other precious stone. The precious stone character sign was used.

....

10 United Nations General Assembly Resolution 1668 (XVI) deemed the issue of China's representation an important question under the UN Charter; any proposal to change the representation required a two-thirds majority vote.

Throughout, Canada was aware of the Cultural Revolution, which we had followed from Hong Kong. By 1971, one could see the cult of Mao Zedong winding down almost week by week. Even the statue of Mao in the hotel lobby disappeared overnight. When Fraser inquired about it, staff asked back, "What statue? Oh, that one. It's being cleaned." So the frenzy of the revolution was being abated. People who'd previously given no sign that they spoke English revealed that they had PhDs from Stanford or wherever.

Immediate results?
There were still problems. In 1971, we could travel only to Tientsin, so we slapped corresponding restrictions on the Chinese. They were annoyed because regulations in China applied to all foreigners, and ours applied only to them. We used to joke that if they'd allow us to go to the Ming tombs, we'd let them go to Smiths Falls.

The Chinese made a conscious effort to direct some trade our way, as if to show that our efforts were appreciated. Zhou Enlai even mentioned the Ming Sun ships. Chinese negotiators had treated the issue as peanuts, but in 1972, Zhou said something like, well, we've had the use of them for so long, perhaps we'd better pay for them. This, Fraser said, was quite a surprise.

MAURICE COPITHORNE (1931-)
INTERVIEW | VANCOUVER, 23 SEPTEMBER 1987

After joining DEA in 1956, Copithorne worked in Ottawa and abroad. He was legal adviser and director general of legal affairs, and he served in China during the early 1970s, as ambassador to Austria and UN agencies in Vienna, and as Canadian commissioner to Hong Kong. He retired in 1986.

On China-Canada relations
"I had done my time in Ottawa," Copithorne said, and though he had no Chinese background, he was not notably worse off in that respect than other officers. Those few who knew China had given up or done other things. The Canadian arrival in 1972 after recognition was the first of a wave (there had been a wavelet earlier) that included the Austrians, Italians, and Belgians. Everybody who undertook recognition anticipated some kind of payoff, but

by 1972 the *Globe and Mail,* wheat, and some Canadian businessmen had all established their own meaningful connections. In fact, as soon as you touched down in Beijing, you lost your leverage: "They had you, and you had to compete with other missions."

You couldn't quantify the warmth of the reception for Canadians, and though Copithorne had thought that, for example, the Bethune name would help, this applied only so long as all other things were equal. They seldom were.

There was also political turmoil in China, where Zhou Enlai's cosmopolitan policies were an element in internal conflict. It was pretty difficult to get a handle on it, and several dozen people were constantly preparing notes inside and outside the embassy.

It was a pretty unworldly atmosphere, but it was relieved by an unusual service: two publications were delivered to one's apartment every night, one in blue being the digest of world news and the other, in red, a précis of Hsinhua, the official press agency. Neither was then available to the Chinese people.

There was also a rather incestuous atmosphere among the small group of foreigners, diplomats, and journalists in Beijing. They were divided into the "in-thing-to-be-in-China" crowd, who were often swiftly disillusioned. Though frequently of high quality, they soon became frustrated, especially the Africans. Others had been following China and had a good idea of what they were getting into.

"My expectations were not couched in those terms," Copithorne said. The Canadian response to China reflected the professional interest of our officers; though frustrated on a day-to-day basis, they were not otherwise.

The Trudeau visit to China, 1973

"I was very much involved in **Trudeau**'s visit in 1973," Copithorne stated. As second-in-command of the mission, "I ran the communications link between the guest house and the embassy." He sat in on some meetings and was present for Trudeau's interview with Zhou. The two men could communicate very well, and Zhou's comments were relevant and meaningful to Trudeau.

Zhou was clearly the dominant figure on the other side, and Trudeau's role was similar to his. Trudeau had a wonderful native curiosity and sensitivity. He had identified the right briefs to read and was never at a loss on any part of any agenda item. Copithorne suspected that Trudeau was one of the best interlocutors the Chinese had.

Ivan Head was a very important figure in the process. It was clear that he had a significant influence on the prime minister's thinking. He had a sense of the outside world. Copithorne didn't think there was resentment of Head in DEA, though there may have been some on specific issues.

Copithorne was involved in three agreements while Trudeau was in China. The first was consular, including the right of access to our nationals – "very meaningful stuff." He got a proper definition of Canadian citizens, as opposed to racial Chinese. The second involved the reunification of families, and there was another on sport and public health exchanges. The negotiations took place late at night, after the banquets were over. Clearly, Zhou wanted agreements at least as much or more than we did, but the visit was what made them happen.

When Trudeau gave a speech, we insisted on having a Canadian read the Chinese translation, which was an innovation. It was an attempt to level the playing field.

To the Chinese, we were a window on North America, until the Americans came along. The Chinese always talked of the export trade, but clearly politics was at the top of their agenda.

YU ZHAN (1921-92)
INTERVIEW | BEIJING, 27 MAY 1987

Yu was vice minister of foreign affairs from 1972 to 1982 and ambassador to Ottawa from 1983 to 1986.

He began with a long statement on Ottawa-Beijing relations
The relationship between Ottawa and Beijing was excellent, not just good, Yu claimed.[11] It had steadily developed, and all parties in Canada had the same policy. He expected future relations to be beautiful. The political relations were good, the leaders exchanged visits, and there was a system of consultation between the Foreign Ministries. There were consular relations, ten twinned cities/provinces, and, of course, Norman Bethune. The trade and economic relations had developed fast – from 1970 to 1986, trade increased by 8.5 times ...

....

11 This interview was done by Granatstein with Professor Bernie Frolic.

Trudeau's relationship with the PRC

The foundation of the Canada-PRC relationship, Yu said, despite the different social systems of the two countries, was common ideas on peace and development. The leaders wanted to develop the relationship. **Trudeau** came to China several times – not by chance but because he was interested in China.

As a youth, Trudeau came to China and he revisited in the early 1960s. This prepared him to recognize the PRC when he became prime minister. "I learned in Canada that he made the decision to seek recognition despite US pressure and some domestic opposition. This is action with foresight and courage," Yu stated. "I never forgot that Trudeau was an old friend of China, and I had many contacts with him. During meetings we discussed many things. I feel he was a far-sighted politician and statesman who had vast knowledge of Canada and international affairs. He was always very interested in world developments. Each time we met, he took the initiative to discuss domestic and international developments." He was "very friendly to Chinese ambassadors." He was very approachable. "When I visited his house," Yu recalled, "he showed me every room, including some under renovation. He invited me to dinner and rode in my car to his house. He was very flexible. I invited him to a Chinese acrobats show, but he had an engagement and suggested the next day. He said that he always took his children. But the next day I had an appointment to see a provincial premier, so he changed his schedule and attended. He could only stay for the first half of the show, but his kids stayed. Before he left, he went on stage and shook hands with the cast." Another example: "At a Chinese exhibition in Montreal, I invited Trudeau to attend, though he was not in office any more. It was the ceremonial opening, and the mayor and federal and provincial ministers were to attend. If he attended, he might draw press attention. But he wanted to go, so I asked him how to do it. 'I can find a way,' he said. Sixty minutes before the ceremony, he attended while I was eating with the mayor. Trudeau didn't eat, just toured, and when the ceremony started, he left. I also walked on the street with him and saw the way people nodded or shook his hand."

Trudeau's visits to the PRC

In 1973, Trudeau talked with Zhou and met Mao. The purpose, shortly after recognition, was to discuss how to develop the relationship. He stayed a week and had two formal rounds of talks with Zhou Enlai and many informal talks. Both raised domestic problems. They had broad and deep exchanges on international issues and bilateral relations, and signed several agreements and laid foundations. It was a very successful visit, beyond the expectations of the Canadians. "I was involved in officials' talks," Yu recalled. A trade agreement was signed for which no preparations had been made on the PRC side. They reached agreement during the visit, which was possible only when both had the desire. There were also other agreements – an exhibition of Chinese relics in Canada, "which I signed," and a consular understanding that decided on cultural programs, on sports exchanges, teachers, science programs, and public health exchanges.

On international questions, Trudeau and Zhou talked about how to maintain peace and secure disarmament, on USSR-PRC relations, PRC-US relations, the Middle East, Vietnam, and the law of the sea. Trudeau appreciated the PRC's support for Canadian sovereignty in the Arctic. Zhou appreciated Trudeau's contribution to the establishment of diplomatic relations, as he had done this despite US pressure. Canada was not only the first North American nation to recognize China, but it also gave a push to Western Europe.

During this visit, Trudeau invited Zhou to Canada, but Zhou said he was already in his old age and indebted to too many countries, so he couldn't accept. He already had cancer, in fact. Later, the PRC sent the vice president of the people's congress, a vice premier, and the minister of foreign affairs to Canada. Zhou also accompanied Trudeau on his trips around China, and Deng Xiaoping accompanied him on another trip, the first time Deng had emerged since the Cultural Revolution. Trudeau and Deng become friends.

In 1979, when he was in Opposition, Trudeau made a private visit to China. He went to Beijing, Lhasa, and Chengdu, and Deng and others met him and invited him to dinner. Zhao Ziyang, then the leader in Szechwan province and soon to become premier of the PRC, invited him for dinner. Deng said the PRC would not forget Trudeau's contribution to the establishment of diplomatic relations. Although he was no longer prime minister, his visit nonetheless contributed to the development of relations. They discussed PRC-USSR and PRC-Vietnam relations, as Trudeau was very interested in those.

During this trip, he went to Lhasa. When he returned, he talked to Deng about his "deep impressions." He said he thought the PRC policy in Tibet was respecting Tibetan traditions and religion, developing the economy and improving people's lives. He said in twenty years China could respect the character of Tibet and maintain unification of the country, though this was not easy. Trudeau explained his goodwill and said he hoped future Tibetan intellectuals would continue to support the unification of China so as to avoid being left in the hands of other countries. He thought this generation would support the policy, but coming generations might have other ideas – according to his own experience. Trudeau believed that it was good for a minority to stay with the majority, but there was a precondition: the majority had to respect the minority's traditions ...

In 1983, Trudeau visited for one day on his Peace Initiative. He explained his fears about the tense world situation and his proposals, which he hoped could reduce tensions and lead to disarmament. Deng met him to exchange views. He expressed an understanding of the dangers of the situation and appreciated his efforts for peace. And they gave the PRC's views. The PRC had some similar ideas – it too thought the international situation was very strained and felt that statesmen of every country should make efforts to reduce tension. But at the same time, Beijing felt that the main danger was from the USSR and the United States, as both were competing to gain hegemony. They had the most weapons, and only they could start a war. For the three other nuclear powers, their weapons strength was much less. All these powers should press the Americans and Soviets to reduce their weapons stockpiles. Before the superpowers did so, calling a meeting of the five nuclear powers was not realistic and might create confusion while diverting attention from the USSR and the United States. So when Trudeau asked for Zhao Ziyang's ideas, the reply was that if he wanted a five-country conference, it would be better to have more countries present ...

YASUHIKO NARA (1917-2013)
INTERVIEW | TOKYO, 20 MAY 1987

A long-serving Japanese diplomat, Nara was ambassador in Ottawa from February 1975 to September 1978.

On the Trudeau marriage
Nara's relations with **Trudeau** were personal and private. They were good friends, not ambassador and prime minister. He did not know Trudeau before he arrived in Ottawa, but **Ivan Head** arranged the first meeting, and then they began to see each other. He was closer to Trudeau than any ambassador and to Margaret too (she visited Nara twice in Tokyo after she and Trudeau separated). Nara used to preach to Margaret, and he would tell Trudeau that

though he was unhappy, she had given him three sons, so why complain? Sometimes, Trudeau and Margaret would fight in front of Nara and his wife, and once, to their embarrassment, Margaret breastfed Michel in front of them, ten days after his birth. Trudeau had married Margaret because she was an Anglo – this enticed him. The split between them was all her fault, as she wanted her own way. Trudeau went out of his way to accommodate her, but she was a child. Not crazy, but erratic.

Personal diplomacy
Only on two occasions did Nara use his close relationship with Trudeau for political purposes. He never reported to Tokyo on their talks, except for these two instances. One concerned the uranium embargo on Japan. Canada was insisting on a strict bilateral agreement, and Japan rejected this. Nara then approached Trudeau at one of their dinners and made a direct appeal. Japan had been sending its uranium to the United States for enrichment, and Canada insisted that this must cease unless strictly regulated. This annoyed Japan because uranium was already subject to US regulation. Trudeau agreed that ore sent to the United States for enrichment would be allowed as a direct export from Canada, and Canada would accept the US controls as satisfactory.

The second occasion came when Trudeau, unhappy because Canada was not in the G5, asked Nara to help. Foreign Minister Miyazawa was a close friend of Nara's, and he was asked to help counter France's opposition to Canada and Italy. Miyazawa then contacted Kissinger, who was in favour. The United States and Japan pressured France, but Giscard still said no, primarily to keep Italy out. The next summit with President Ford as host in the United States saw Canada get in. In return for Japan's help, Trudeau did some favours for Tokyo.

On Trudeau
Trudeau had the same kind of mind as Lee of Singapore (where Nara also served). He had real likes and dislikes, and only a few people really knew his mind. Nara used to talk about Trudeau with Chrétien and Jean-Luc Pepin. Trudeau had a shield up all the time, and Margaret couldn't get through it.

He was very interested in foreign policy and used to talk about his trips before he went into politics. He knew the leaders well. His major contribution was to delineate Canada from the United States – by recognizing China.

Japan perceived the differences, especially because of the China issue, where Trudeau had acted to show that Canada was different. Why did this not produce much for Canada? "You have nothing to offer them," said Nara.

Trudeau felt no animosity for the United States, but he didn't like all US policies. He understood the USSR better than Washington did, but he didn't like the Russians. Trudeau wanted to tame them, not confront them. Incidentally, Trudeau's relations with US ambassador **Tom Enders** were the same as with all other ambassadors (except with Nara).

Nara accompanied Trudeau to Japan. The Framework for Economic Cooperation agreement between Canada and Japan was "not too important," as the two countries were good friends without it. The problem in their relations was that Canada inevitably played second fiddle to the United States in Japan, as Japan did to the United States in Canada. Japan's trade with Canada was only one-tenth of its trade with the United States.

Nara said that Canadians didn't like being preached at and got angry if they were. When the Hisao Makita trade mission came in October 1976, and business conferences were reactivated, Vice Chair Eiichi Hashimoto was attacked by the press for his complaints about Canada's mail, labour unions, strikes, and so on.[12]

THOMAS DELWORTH (1929-2012)
INTERVIEW | UPPSALA, SWEDEN, 26 OCTOBER 1987

With the ICC in Vietnam
Service in Vietnam created a special breed of diplomat in DEA. Every FSO who was posted there believed that the United States was fundamentally right, and a third of all FSOs served there over the 1954-68 period. This helped create a kind of hardline attitude in DEA and may have delayed recognition of China. It helped create a massive turnoff toward India, after dealing with the Indians and their concept of truth on the ICCs.[13] That love affair was over. There was no divergence between Ottawa and the field on Vietnam, but there were anti-US attitudes in DEA. Still, this wasn't the basis of policy in

---

12 Frank Langdon, *The Politics of Canadian-Japanese Economic Relations, 1952-1983* (Vancouver: UBC Press, 1983), 89-91.
13 The plural refers to the three commissions: Vietnam, Cambodia, and Laos.

the department. Delworth added that **Paul Martin** as SSEA had worked hard to get the Nobel Peace Prize, but the people who had served on the ICCs wouldn't give him the words he wanted to say, and the policy tended to skew. Of Martin, he said, "the ship of state is the only one that leaks from the top." In his view, Canadian policy on Vietnam looked ludicrous to Washington, with Martin trying to use our ICC connection as a chastity belt. Martin tried to create a special relationship to the Vietnam problem, but the DEA professionals saw him as transparent.

Trudeau was uninterested in foreign policy when he came to power in 1968, but the Trudeau of 1980 was very different from ten years before. His view of the world and of Canada's potential had changed. For example, after 1968, the Vietnam job disappeared, and Delworth on the desk was put to recruiting and personnel. Trudeau had no interest in Vietnam. To Delworth, he had distorted priorities by being too uninterested in Vietnam. Martin had made it overblown ...

Canada and the Pacific
The Japanese were in diplomacy to sell and weren't delicate or subtle. He remembered an Ottawa cocktail party in which, during a sudden hush, Ambassador **Yasuhiko Nara** was heard to say to Trudeau, "What are you doing with your Margaret problem?"

Indonesia, where Delworth went as the youngest ambassador in DEA, was the biggest Association of South East Asian Nations state. As such, it was one of the underpinnings of our Asia policy, a fairly important aid and trade partner. Trudeau had come to visit in 1971 as part of a process of registering Canadian interest in non-Commonwealth Asia. Delworth had to arrange the visit three months after his arrival in Jakarta. He saw the secretary of state of Indonesia and talked about the program, pointed to one empty slot, and asked if Trudeau should do option A or B. The answer, in true Indonesian style, was yes. Trudeau went over very well there. He played things by ear and travelled with one security man and no bodyguard, which impressed the Indonesians all to hell. A ride in a rickshaw was arranged, and Trudeau put the driver in the seat and pedalled. The Indonesians loved this spontaneous gesture to de-pompous-ize the prime minister.

The Pacific is important to Canada, but Delworth said he got angry at those who saw it as an alternative to Europe. He once argued with Marcel Massé, who said that Canada had to choose between the two. To Delworth, both Europe and the Pacific were necessary. Canada for too long had assigned too little weight to Asia, and he himself had created the Asia Pacific Foundation with private-sector help. But, he said, it was Europe that gave us our sense of identity, and Canada couldn't exist without links to Europe ...

RICHARD GORHAM (1927-2011)
INTERVIEW | BEIJING, 24, 26, AND 28 MAY 1987

After joining DEA in 1952, Gorham was ambassador in China from 1984 to 1991. Over the course of several days, he talked about his time in Ottawa, Japan, and China.

Canada's "open mouth" policy on the ICC
Gorham had instituted the open mouth policy as head of the Press Section of DEA when the ICC for Vietnam was being set up in 1973. Deciding that there should be detailed press briefings about Canadian policy, he informed his boss and got a discreet okay. SSEA **Mitchell Sharp** was not told. Gorham saw the press at his home and gave them coffee and brandy while he read the files to them. The reporters were puzzled but pleased. The next day, Sharp appeared on TV and said many of the same things, so Gorham told him of the briefings and got his okay. Sharp was an excellent SSEA.

The head of the Canadian ICC, **Michel Gauvin,** was told to be open. He held press conferences after every commission meeting, and when his colleagues protested, he told them that he had a stenographer at the meeting to ensure that everything he said was correct, and he asked other delegations if they wanted to hold press conferences with him ...

Trudeau in China
On **Trudeau**'s last visit to China in 1986, Gorham wanted him to ask Chairman Deng about the economic reform process. Trudeau willingly made the attempt, but Deng put him off by saying that he could ask Zhou those questions when he saw him ...

Regarding the 1973 trade agreement with Beijing, Gorham left no doubt that the Canadian side had made extensive preparations because Canada wanted an agreement. Zhou said China didn't but would do so if Canada wanted one. So there was a flap on the PRC side to get it done.

A prime ministerial visit is useful primarily because it serves as a spur to get things done in readiness, if only so that the big fish have something to sign. But visits don't accomplish as much as the public think. A visit tells the bureaucrats that Canada is a friend, which helps down the road. If the prime minister can say in discussions with the other leader that this or that concerns him, this helps get a resolution. The PRC, for example, didn't like communiqués, but it helped later to be able to point to a clause in which some action was promised.

The Norman Bethune syndrome, he added, was a real help in the PRC.

MICHEL GAUVIN (1919-2003)
INTERVIEW | OTTAWA, 12 APRIL 1988

Gauvin served in the infantry and won the Distinguished Service Order in the Second World War. He joined DEA in 1946, had postings in Ottawa, Europe, South America, and Africa, and served in Vietnam twice in 1955-56 and 1973. He retired from DEA in 1984.

The ICCs and Canadian diplomacy
Gauvin talked about Indochina and its effect on those who served there; he wanted to put it into the context of the overall attitude of DEA. It was true that those who served in Vietnam were strongly affected, though he denied that all emerged as fervent anti-communists. The point was that most Canadians did not look at foreign affairs and foreign policy as an essential defence of Canada's interests abroad. In DEA, this was amplified by the policy of giving the benefit of the doubt to your left-wing opponents ("to those who spoke the doctrine") because, whatever their deficiencies, they were moving in the correct direction. So you started by conceding them 50 percent and then moving along. We were inclined to take a moralistic approach, for example, to the role of the United States as a big power. We were inclined to suspect Britain as a power with a colonial past, rather like Roosevelt preferring Stalin to Churchill in Second World War conferences ...

A second tour in Vietnam
The second time round in Vietnam in 1973 for the ICC, he was seconded from Greece where he was our ambassador. He had all kinds of promises from DEA, the open mouth policy (somebody in Ottawa coined that), and so on. At home, the hierarchy was Ralph Collins on top, someone called Archer, and Daniel Molgat below; Molgat, at least for the first couple of

months, saved Gauvin from clashes with the head office. He called Molgat "Mr. Vietnam in Ottawa," a "very bright and very wise" man who took all possible points in Gauvin's favour and neutralized those that might be questioned.

You do not go out of your way to disobey orders, even when they are couched as "suggestions" or "advice," Gauvin said. If you do, they wait for you to make the least slip and then chop you up. You might be thought to be lacking in breadth, and you would not gain the support of either the professionals or the politicians. In any case, you do not, as an ambassador, make policy; you apply it.

"When I went," he said, "I was determined not to be the Canadian you could roll over ..." He chose his second-in-command, **Vern Turner**, who was tremendously supportive and very useful. He was lucky in his other subordinates, people such as Manfred von Nostitz, "my pet," but he did not choose them.

Canada was on the ICC with the Hungarians, the Poles, and the Indonesians. For four of the six months, the Indonesians leaned our way, but after that (knowing that we were getting out of the commission), they must have concluded that whether South Vietnam survived or not, there would always be a Vietnam, and Vietnam was their neighbour, and thus an important factor to consider. As to Ambassador **Tom Delworth** in Jakarta, he did what he was supposed to and represented the Indonesian point of view. Gauvin saw copies of his telegrams and found nothing exceptionable in them. Like the Indonesians at the end of Canada's role on the ICC, Delworth was very cautious.

Gauvin did not believe at the outset that South Vietnam was doomed. He understood that the Americans had promised to return in the event of renewed North Vietnamese aggression. "I don't think the South Vietnamese believed that, but the Americans compelled them to believe it," he claimed. When you are forced to grasp at something, you frequently do believe it.

Negotiation in the ICC

In the ICC, the Hungarians and the Poles were up to their old abusive tactics; they played "the broken record," so Gauvin did it too. The chief Hungarian was a professional bastard, but that did not prevent Gauvin from getting together with him at the end of the day and having a drink. Indeed, they had lunch relatively recently in Ottawa; Gauvin seemed to be warmly remembered.

When **Mitchell Sharp** came to Vietnam on tour, he and Gauvin took a walk in the garden. Gauvin had concluded that the mission was futile, but he was determined not to advise Sharp, merely to let him draw his own conclusions from inescapable evidence. The South Vietnamese had on display a North Vietnamese army type, who was not supposed to be in the South. Sharp, who had recently visited Hanoi, actually questioned him on landmarks there, and he replied satisfactorily. So Sharp authorized the writing of a report saying that the North's army was still in the South.

But would this report be a commission report? This issue caused a crisis because naturally the Hungarians and Poles would not agree, and unanimity was the rule. But Gauvin was chairman that month. So they barracked back and forth as the end of the month approached. Ottawa finally told him to give way, not insist, and actually sent him a form of words that he was to read. He had it in his pocket and would have read it at one minute to midnight. But not before.

He held a marathon session. The lunch break was cut back, and the usual siesta was cancelled. There was no dinner break. And he kept at the broken record tactic. Finally, late at night, they cracked; Gauvin could sign the report as chairman, which implied that it was a commission document. Ottawa was apparently incredulous that he had got by without reading aloud its instructed piece. At one point, Gauvin had told Sharp that he could send him back to Greece at any time; he would willingly go. So Ottawa informed Gauvin that his wish would be granted. (The Canadian Forces commander on the ICC, Major-General Duncan McAlpine, was not displeased at this, saying that they could get along without him.) But then Ottawa had cold feet and cancelled the order on the day before he was to leave.

The other incident he remembered was that of the two missing Canadians captured by the North Vietnamese. He knew that the North Vietnamese commander of their mission at Tan Son Nhut would know of it, so Gauvin went directly to him. Of course, he was told that they knew nothing, which Gauvin found impossible to believe. The Canadians might have been detained by over-zealous subordinates, but Gauvin added that he would hold a press conference at which he would say that the obvious reason the North was denying it was because it had killed the two men. His conference would be at 4:00 p.m. the next day.

At 3:30, he got a phone call. The men had been found! Fine. They then negotiated the rather complicated conditions for retrieving them. Gauvin insisted that their two Vietnamese employees would be released with them. The North said no: they would be released or dealt with separately. Gauvin then went to the Hungarian or the Pole on the ICC and said that, of course, we wanted the Vietnamese back. Why? asked the communist. Surely, the return of the Canadians was enough. No, said Gauvin, Canada would not take the racist position that the two Asians were of no concern. So the Canadians who were sent to pick up our men were to collect them too. Moreover, they were to sign nothing other than a receipt. Naturally, once they arrived, they were confronted with a long document admitting that we had been spying (Gauvin had made very sure with his Canadian general that this was not the case). Ottawa had instructed the delegation to sign the document, saying that it was under duress. Gauvin told his men to take a tent with them and to be prepared to stay the night.

Sure enough, a certain time after the delegation had rejected the first document, another modified one was brought forward, obviously prepared in advance. Finally, the Canadians were asked to sign a mere receipt for the jeep and radio equipment (which the North Vietnamese were keeping). The answer was still no. Dusk was approaching, and they had no radio equipment and could not fly at night. Finally, at 4:30, ninety minutes before sunset, the North gave in, and off they flew.

VIII
Canada, the United Kingdom, and Patriation

THE CANADIAN CONNECTION WITH Great Britain goes back centuries. When Trudeau became prime minister, the British Empire was well within living memory, and Canada's colonial connection had not completely vanished. Because of the inability of the Provinces and the federal government to agree on a method of amending the Canadian Constitution – the British North America Act – the power to amend it remained with the British Parliament. Although in all other respects Canada was sovereign, this vestige of the British Empire remained. As a junior civil servant, Trudeau had worked on constitutional amendments in 1949-50 and had seen them shipped overseas to be duly passed by the Parliament in London.

In the 1940s and 1950s, Canada and Great Britain were political and military allies, through NATO, and linked through membership in the Commonwealth. The prime ministers of the Commonwealth met from time to time, formally, in London.[1] The British government set great store by these meetings because they helped maintain the perception that Britain was still a world power, with connections and influence in all parts of the globe, through the Commonwealth. The truth was, however, that the Asian and then the African members of the Commonwealth increasingly went their own way. They were united only in blaming the British for the colonial or post-colonial remnants of the empire – white-supremacist Rhodesia and South Africa – which by the end of the 1960s gave a neuralgic quality to Commonwealth meetings as far as the British were concerned.

From 1932, the Commonwealth countries were linked through a series of bilateral trade agreements, establishing what was known as Imperial (later Commonwealth) Preference. As the name indicates, Commonwealth countries gave each other specially low tariffs. Other trade arrangements, particularly

---

1   These were called Commonwealth Conferences until 1971, when the name became Commonwealth Heads of Government Meetings, pronounced "chog-um."

the multilateral General Agreement on Tariffs and Trade of 1947, overtook and then superseded Commonwealth Preference. British trade with much of the Commonwealth, and especially Canada, shrank as a proportion of the total, until in 1961 the British government decided to abandon the Commonwealth as an economic unit and applied for membership in the newly founded European Common Market. The British were unsuccessful, as was also the case for their second try in 1966 – both times blocked by France. The third time, however, they were lucky, and reached an agreement with the Common Market that took effect on 1 January 1973.

Not surprisingly, the economic uncoupling with the Commonwealth mitigated British enthusiasm for what many British politicians saw as a meaningless remnant. British Conservative prime minister Edward Heath (1970-74) was a notable exponent of this point of view; it was therefore quite conceivable that the Commonwealth would be wound up during his watch.

In a remarkable turn of fate, Pierre Trudeau, anti-imperialist, irreverent, skeptical, became an enthusiast for the Commonwealth. He was instrumental in containing Heath and keeping the Commonwealth going at the Singapore meeting of prime ministers in 1971. At the time, it seemed that only Trudeau and Queen Elizabeth could prevent its dissolution, and they did.

Indeed, the Commonwealth overshadowed strictly Anglo-Canadian relations in the 1970s, though those improved once the chilly Heath and his oleaginous successor, the Labourite Harold Wilson (1974-76), were out of office. Wilson was succeeded by James ("Sunny Jim") Callaghan, his chancellor of the exchequer (finance minister). Callaghan was that rare bird among British politicians, someone who actually liked Canada – so much so that he undertook a cross-country tour of the place. Callaghan's visit had real significance because, when asked by at least two provincial premiers, he made it clear that if Ottawa sought change or changes in the Constitution – presumably in the matter of amending it – any British Parliament under his control would simply comply, regardless of the objections of the Provinces.[2]

....

2 The two premiers were Robert Bourassa of Quebec and Allan Blakeney of Saskatchewan. The information regarding Callaghan is from Terry Empson (1931-2012), late of the Foreign and Commonwealth Office and formerly attached to the British High Commission in Ottawa. Bothwell and Granatstein interview, 8 October 1987, London (not included in this volume).

In the late 1970s, with a separatist Parti Québécois government in Quebec, constitutional reform was very much on Trudeau's agenda. René Lévesque's PQ government used every means at its disposal to advance its cause, including Quebec's mission in London, as Paul Martin's interview shows.

Lévesque scheduled a referendum for May 1980 that would have been the first stage of a process leading to Quebec independence. When Trudeau unexpectedly returned as prime minister in March 1980, he took Lévesque on and contributed to the decisive defeat of the referendum. The following September, having failed to reach agreement with most of the Provinces, Trudeau proceeded with a constitutional package that included amending the Constitution,[3] in the future, entirely within Canada, but also a Charter of Rights and Freedoms that would enshrine the fundamental rights of Canadians. Once passed, Trudeau's altered Constitution would proceed to London for passage, with the support of only two of the ten Canadian Provinces.[4]

Had Jim Callaghan still been prime minister, Trudeau's Constitution would have had clear sailing. But Callaghan had been defeated in a 1979 election, and the Conservative Margaret Thatcher was now prime minister. She and Trudeau first met in London in the summer of 1980 and subsequently at a Commonwealth conference in Melbourne in October 1981, as Trudeau's amended Constitution was proceeding through the Canadian Parliament. As the interviews describe, these meetings were merely incidents in a complicated and unhappy episode.

RT. HON. PAUL MARTIN (1903-92)
INTERVIEW | WINDSOR, ONTARIO, 10-11 FEBRUARY 1987

Going to London
His London posting happened thusly, Martin said. **Trudeau** summoned him and pointed out that three of his cabinet ministers represented the Windsor area (Martin himself, Eugene Whelan, and Herb Gray). This was too many, so someone would have to go. But there was no way to exclude Whelan and

---

3 "Prime Minister's Meeting with Mr. Pierre Trudeau ... 11.30 AM, 25 June 1980," PREM 19/189, Thatcher Papers, Churchill Archives Centre, Churchill College, Cambridge.
4 The two were Ontario and New Brunswick.

Gray. Plus, the 1974 election was coming on; they'd have a better chance of retaining their ridings if they were still cabinet ministers.

So, what would Martin like? Speaker of the Senate? That made no sense, he'd be seventy-five soon, so Martin declined. What about ambassador-at-large? No, Martin said, he'd had two of those posts in his time, and they ended up doing nothing. Then what about Washington? No, he wouldn't have a minute's peace. So Trudeau offered London, and Martin agreed.

"I'd never thought of taking over a mission," he said. "I'd thought it beneath me." But he reflected on Talleyrand and his mission to London. "Of course, England isn't as important as it once was, but the Foreign Office is still a great institution. It's a great laboratory for foreign policy discussion and formulation. Every foreign policy issue that came up, I got interested in. First, I'd query Ottawa for our material, which sometimes turned out to be nothing. I'd master it and then go to the Foreign Office as if I'd been instructed to go and discuss it. That gave me access to their materials."

The social side of London was necessary, but he didn't like it much. The best part of it was having Jim Callaghan ask him where he got his information; he replied that he got it in Callaghan's own shop. He remembered "the magnificent library" at the Foreign Office (FO).

The Commonwealth

The Commonwealth Secretariat was the next subject. Arnold Smith saw Martin and Mike Pearson about his great idea of a Commonwealth Secretariat.[5] He'd already discussed it in London, "unknown to me." Martin responded as Mackenzie King would have: he resisted because of the overtones of a common foreign policy. But eventually he came round, understanding that the Commonwealth was not what it once was, but an association of equals. Smith was a combination of dynamism and nuisance. After Pearson nominated him, and he was appointed as secretary-general of the Commonwealth, he turned out fine. He was a tremendous secretary-general, though he had his trials with the British. In any case, without the Commonwealth, Britain would be a much reduced state in terms of world influence. So they put up with the embarrassments.

As high commissioner, Martin was active at Marlborough House, the home of the Commonwealth Secretariat. He tried to establish regular meetings of

---

5 Arnold Smith (1915-94) joined DEA and served in Moscow and Cairo among other postings. He became the first Commonwealth secretary-general (1965-75).

high commissioners and tried to persuade the foreign secretary to preside. But the British couldn't disclose enough information to them to make the meetings meaningful. This was shades of old Krishna Menon, who, when he attended such meetings forty years ago, used to act as a leak. He was caught, and Eden had to discontinue the meetings.

Sonny Ramphal was okay as secretary-general,[6] though he and Trudeau had their differences about demands for Canadian aid, as with scholarships. Trudeau wouldn't see Ramphal for a period. On a visit to Ottawa, Ramphal phoned Martin in frustration and complained about Trudeau's attitude. So Martin called **Ivan Head** and Trudeau himself. In the event, Ramphal was useful to Trudeau during the Peace Initiative of 1983-84.

Peter Carrington and Martin were very good friends. Martin saw him regularly in Opposition, and the day he became foreign secretary, Martin phoned him. All the high commissioners had been meeting, and they had become exercised over Rhodesia. They were indignant at Thatcher's opposition to majority rule. Martin had never seen anything like the anger of the high commissioners, but he felt strongly on the subject, and so did Trudeau.

Carrington invited Martin round to his apartment that night, to have Martin warn him about Britain's impending isolation over Rhodesia. With Trudeau's consent, Martin gave a stern warning, and the British did change their Rhodesia policy. When this occurred, the Queen was very helpful about it.

Trudeau and the United Kingdom

In 1978-79, Trudeau visited Britain on Martin's suggestion that he spend a few days. The idea was somehow to seek renewal in friendly contacts, politician-to-politician. Trudeau liked Jim Callaghan, and Callaghan liked Trudeau, so it seemed to make sense. Anyway, Martin wanted to use the visit to get satisfaction from the Brits for the great Anglo-Canadian issue of the day – namely, whether Air Canada could stay at Heathrow or was to be booted out to Gatwick.

Martin suggested to Callaghan that he assemble the relevant ministers for dinner with Trudeau. Martin briefed Trudeau beforehand, but Trudeau said nothing about Heathrow during dinner, and the party gradually ebbed to its end. As Trudeau still said nothing, Martin finally raised the subject, looking

---

6   Sir Shridath Surendranath "Sonny" Ramphal (1928-) succeeded the Canadian Arnold Smith as secretary-general of the Commonwealth in 1975 and served until 1990.

straight at Trudeau, who said nothing. So, since it was up to Martin, he spoke, gave them an earful for half an hour. Later, going home, Trudeau said, "Paul, you certainly handled that Heathrow stuff beautifully." Martin was furious, but he reflected that Trudeau may well have thought it was not important enough to bring up ...

The monarchy

Trudeau and the monarchy was touchy. He recognized that there would be a problem for national unity if he actually tried to change it. He sometimes said things that were a little naughty, such as his verbal indifference before the students at Oxford. When Martin remonstrated, Trudeau replied, "Well, it would get reported back in Quebec and have a favourable impact there."

There was one very odd incident. On the first day of the Trudeau government, **Sharp** brought up the question of the monarchy and suggested "to my amazement" that we could do without it. Martin spoke up and said that attempting to dissolve Canada's connection with the Crown would cause infinite trouble for the Liberal Party. He recalled a lunchtime conversation between Mike Pearson and the Queen on the future of the monarchy and how he had warned Pearson at the time that it would get out and do harm. Some did, though not as much as he had feared ...

Dealing with the provinces in London

During his time as high commissioner, seven provinces had agents in London. They all worked hard on trade; he remembered especially good men from Saskatchewan, Alberta, and British Columbia. They were trade men primarily, "but as human nature dictates, they try to find their way."

You treat provincial representatives as important persons, Martin said, have them to dinner, show them consideration. But after Lévesque came to power in 1976, you had to be careful. If a provincial minister wanted to see a British minister, the High Commission would arrange it, and a Canadian diplomat would be at the meeting. For Ontario and Quebec, that usually meant someone senior, such as Martin. The agent-general for Quebec, Gilles Loiselle, was a wise and prudent man but a strong nationalist.

One day Robert Burns, a Lévesque minister, came to see Martin and told him that he'd seen the home secretary the day before. Now he wanted to see the foreign secretary. Martin explained the practice, which cut no ice with Burns. He understood, but he would do as he wished anyway. Martin later complained to the home secretary because he'd departed from protocol in seeing Burns; the minister pleaded ignorance of the nuances.

Ontario also caused problems. Darcy McKeough was coming to Britain and wanted to see the chancellor of the exchequer.[7] The Ontario agent-general complained of the established practice. He came over and ranted on about it, but when Martin emphasized why it was necessary, especially because of Quebec, he calmed down a bit. This was when Lévesque himself was threatening to come; if he'd seen the foreign secretary, all hell would have broken loose. On this occasion, Martin thought it useful to phone Darcy McKeough and explain the situation. In confidence, he told him about the attitude of his agent-general.

Loiselle was doing propaganda work against Trudeau's constitutional plans and spending a lot of money. The Canadians had a source inside Quebec House, a spy who was one of the maids. She was a friend of the stenographer of our trade commissioner at Canada House.

There was some meddling, especially from British MP Anthony Kershaw, who established an informal committee to examine what would happen in the event of a unilateral reference on the Constitution from Canada. "There was never any doubt in my time or before what the British response would be," Martin said. Clement Attlee had settled the matter and stated the precedents back in the 1940s.[8] However, it was inevitable that there would be a lot of discussion. "I thought I'd better formalize this," Martin said, "and Justice Minister Ron Basford and Donald Thorson, the deputy minister of justice, came over." Basford had come to London to speak with the Queen regarding some important changes being proposed for her role and that of the governor general – a new bit of phraseology. (The Queen was pleased by the consultation.)

Martin arranged a dinner with the prime minister, the attorney general, the home secretary, and the lord chancellor. "We had a wonderful discussion about what would happen," he said. It was very interesting, though Basford had some slight disagreement with Martin about the actual relationship of the Provinces. Martin said he was pleased that Trudeau and the British agreed with his position, not Basford's.

....

7 Darcy McKeough was the Ontario treasurer (finance minister).
8 British prime minister, 1945-51.

HON. MARK MacGUIGAN (1931-98)
INTERVIEW | OTTAWA, 19 JANUARY 1988

Patriation
On the Constitution, DEA was essential for dealing with the United Kingdom, though secondary on events within Canada. MacGuigan was a very strong supporter of the government's constitutional policy.

He had first mentioned patriation in caucus in 1973, urging a unilateral approach by the federal government, with a charter of rights created by federal power alone. MP Herb Breau spoke against it, and the other MPs were indifferent. But then, the Parti Québécois election win of 1976 and the aftermath of the 1980 Quebec referendum precipitated action. In response to the PQ's opening of the issue, we did what we wanted and not what the PQ wanted. In the cabinet, MacGuigan and John Roberts were the strongest supporters of the constitutional policy.[9]

First dealings with the British
The first contact with the British came at Singapore in the summer of 1980, MacGuigan recalled.[10] We didn't bring the whole package then, but he and John Roberts did bring it over to England in October. It was not entirely pleasing to Prime Minister Margaret Thatcher. For one thing, her government's control over backbenchers had slipped in recent years, and Thatcher was not keen to go to the wall with the Canadian Constitution and lay her own prestige on the line. For another, she was not willing to have a charter like ours in her own country. But she felt obligated to put the matter to Parliament and to try to get it through. She stated her unhappiness because she opposed such a package at home.

There are lots of lines of communication to the United Kingdom. There are family ties, business ties, personal ties. There are British Tories with links

---

9 A former FSO turned Liberal politician, Roberts (1933-2007) occupied a series of ministerial posts in Trudeau's various governments.

10 MacGuigan's Singapore reference could not be confirmed; apparently, the first time Trudeau raised the issue with Prime Minister Thatcher was on 25 June 1980 in London. Both agreed that the United Kingdom had no choice but to act. "Prime Minister's Meeting with Mr. Pierre Trudeau ... 11.30 AM, 25 June 1980," Thatcher Papers.

to the Tories in Canada too. MP Jonathan Aitken played a role in this, a large role. And some on the Kershaw committee in the British House of Commons had connections.

Patriation in the cabinet
Also in 1980, Chief Justice Bora Laskin was quietly lobbying for the constitutional matter to be referred to the Supreme Court, in the belief that it would turn out favourably for the federal government. He probably meant well and thought that his court would approve because people such as his fellow justice Brian Dickson usually did vote with Laskin. Another factor was that **Marc Lalonde** changed his mind to favour a reference to the court. There was very significant tension in the cabinet that led Allan MacEachen to threaten his resignation unless such a reference were made. This would have been in the late fall of 1980.

What happened was that "a group of us" was determined to force the issue, and **Trudeau** was inclined to go along. So the cabinet decided to push it through at all costs. After the decision was made, MacEachen told his colleagues that he would have to consider his position in the government – his exact words. He was not opposed to the legislation, but as a person with great affection for the House of Commons, he thought it an improper way to proceed (presumably using closure at that stage). Trudeau rescinded the cabinet decision after an adjournment, so he could discuss the matter with MacEachen. He knew that if MacEachen resigned, we couldn't get the Constitution through Parliament. We therefore withdrew pressing forward as a tactic and temporized.

Our difficulty was to tolerate months and months of debate. That is what led Lalonde and others to the idea of a Supreme Court reference. In a sense, this was a victory for the Opposition.

The struggle in London
Reeves Haggan came to London and lobbied the British. He arranged for MacGuigan to give a major address in London in March 1981. Several weeks before it was to occur, Trudeau told MacGuigan not to proceed. He wouldn't say why, but MacGuigan divined that it was due to Jean Chrétien's jealousy of him. The prime minister had taken the easy way out in cancelling the speech. Once he understood what was up, MacGuigan suggested that Chrétien speak in his place, and this was arranged in a few days. Unfortunately, it

turned out to be a big mistake, because when Chrétien did speak, his approach did not make a very good impression.

In Britain, we were dealing with a kind of emotional claim, that of the British to be the protectors of the downtrodden, in this case the provinces and the Indians. This was a peculiarly British Conservative notion. It was the foundation for the last-gasp emotional opposition to our efforts. But on balance, MacGuigan thought that the Provinces' lobbying was less effective than the federal government's.

As time passed, the situation for the Constitution became steadily worse in the United Kingdom. Eventually at Cancun in October 1981, Peter Carrington told MacGuigan that the repatriation bill would not pass the House of Commons, and even if it did, it would not pass the House of Lords.

His own inclination would have been to proceed with the issue despite Carrington's warning. Had the bill failed, the Canadian reaction would have depended on our domestic political situation; personally, he would have favoured a unilateral declaration of independence.

He remembered "the very nefarious influence of **Sir John Ford**," the British high commissioner in Ottawa, who was an old-style colonialist with happy memories of the East Indies. He was very strongly opposed to our interests and played a role in organizing opposition here in Ottawa, probably due to a misplaced sense of imperialism. When Roberts and MacGuigan were in England during the fall of 1980, **de Montigny Marchand** told them he had heard rumours of Ford's activities and asked whether he should make representations. Ford's superiors in England must have known what he was up to, but they were prepared to disown him when he was caught. We sent **Gotlieb** over to London. We didn't want a fuss because the Opposition would have claimed that Ford represented the real UK attitude.

What happened was that Ford chose to lobby New Brunswick premier Richard Hatfield, who promptly called MacGuigan. And he lobbied NDP leader Ed Broadbent, who told MacGuigan that he would ask a question in the House about it. Gotlieb left for London the next day. MacGuigan was certain that Ford really did represent at least some people in England. A NATO ambassador told MacGuigan that he had reported Ford's activities to his own government and wondered how long it would be before he was caught.

Then came the Supreme Court decision, which waffled and made things so much worse. Trudeau must have been tempted to retaliate by refusing to promote Brian Dickson to chief justice, but in the end he did not.

Jean Wadds was a very effective high commissioner in London, super, totally loyal.[11] She was the best person we could have had. She was so good that MacGuigan kept Don Jamieson from succeeding her. The effect of Jamieson in London would have been much worse than Jean Chrétien's speech; Wadds could at least move around the Conservative establishment there. Even before MacGuigan left his swearing-in ceremony, he was asked whether Wadds would be kept, and he said yes. Prince Charles, passing through Ottawa a few weeks later, convened MacGuigan at Government House to urge him to keep Wadds, saying how highly the royal family valued her; MacGuigan used this comment as an argument with Trudeau.

John Roberts and MacGuigan had been very careful to brief the Queen in October 1980 at Balmoral. She was very well informed, very sharp in the sense of asking pointed but good questions, and she "appeared" to be in support. MacGuigan recalled, "We hoped this might help at the margins, hoped that it would be advantageous."

SIR JOHN FORD (1921-)
INTERVIEW | PALM BEACH, FLORIDA, 23 FEBRUARY 1989

Ford joined the British foreign service in 1947 and served in London, Europe, the Middle East, and Indonesia. He became high commissioner in Canada in 1978, remaining in that post until his recall in 1981.

....

11 A Progressive Conservative MP and national secretary of her party, Jean Wadds (1920-2011) was appointed in 1979 by the Joe Clark government to succeed Paul Martin as high commissioner in London. The Trudeau government kept her on, and she served until 1983. She was present at Trudeau's interview with Thatcher on 25 June 1980 and met Thatcher again on 26 June. The office of the agent-general for Alberta learned the next day that "Mrs. Wadds indicated that Mrs. Thatcher found Mr. Trudeau to be neurotic and paranoid regarding patriation." Trudeau had predicted that he would have to proceed unilaterally with the patriation of the Constitution. Wayne Clifford to Oryssia J. Lennie, 27 June 1980, Government of Alberta, Department of Federal and Intergovernmental Affairs, Thatcher Papers, http://7f11a30961219bd1a71e-b9527bc5dceodf4456f4c5548db2e5c2.r10.cf1.rackcdn.com/800627%20Alberta%20mnt%20(MT%20on%20Trudeau).pdf.

The beginnings of the patriation issue with Britain

When **Trudeau** met with Prime Minister Thatcher in England during the summer of 1980, Ford sat in on their meeting.[12] During their discussion of the patriation issue, there was no mention of the Charter of Rights. Ford's implication, of course, was that Thatcher's assurances about passing the repatriation bill were, even at this late date, made without knowledge of the added complications that Trudeau would throw in.

When Ford returned to Canada, he met separately with **Gotlieb** and with **Pitfield** in August and gave them his personal views on the possibility of getting the patriation package passed in the British Parliament. He told them that the prospect of passage would be much brighter if Ottawa did not complicate the package it sent to the British government. Politics being the art of the possible, Ford advised, they should make things as easy as possible. It was his personal view that without a majority of provinces backing the deal, passage would not be easy, perhaps not possible.

In September, the Michael Kirby memo was leaked, with its paragraph about the possibility of unilateral action without provincial consent. Early that month, Ford met Allan MacEachen at a cocktail party and told him that it would be best not to send a package to Britain that was disputed in the courts, as this would only complicate things. MacEachen replied that the British Parliament had no authority over the matter and would be obligated to pass whatever it received from the Canadian government.

When **MacGuigan** went to see Thatcher in early October, he misrepresented her qualms about the inclusion of the Charter, emphasizing her pledge to "do her best" to the exclusion of any qualifications and reservations she may have had. Soon after this meeting, a *Globe and Mail* article corrected the record and showed the real problems that the Canadian position presented to Westminster. Based on British government and civil service leaks, it nicely revealed what Ford referred to as the "duplicity" of Canadian ministers in this case. St. John Stevas, the leader of the House of Commons, was the only British minister to comment publicly on the anticipated difficulties of passing the package, however. The legal advice from the Foreign Office concluded that, although there was no precedent for patriation, the government really had no option but to pass the bill – this advice itself was hotly disputed from other quarters.

---

12 This interview was done on our behalf by Professor Paul Litt.

The difficulties caused by Trudeau

By December, however, the extent of opposition to the patriation of the package was obvious in London. As Ford contemplated the scene, speculating on all the possibilities, he was struck by how difficult Trudeau was making things for the British government. He expected it to stick to a pledge that it had originally made without any knowledge of the Charter, and he'd infamously said that the MPs should simply "hold their noses" and pass his bill. Ford wondered whether Trudeau was deliberately trying to provoke a confrontation between the British and Canadian Parliaments, perhaps hoping that Britain would ultimately not pass the patriation package. Using this failure to fan nationalist outrage in Canada, he could then sever all ties with Britain, including the monarchy, and establish a completely independent Canadian republic, with himself as its first president.

Ford qualified these remarks later in the interview by saying that he was not maintaining that this was definitely Trudeau's hidden agenda; he had no proof. It was his job to try to imagine all the possibilities, and this was just one of the possibilities he contemplated. But Trudeau's belligerent conduct "made one wonder if this was not in fact his intention." At the very least, Trudeau's actions were not consistent with wanting to help the British government pass the bill. Nor could his behaviour be the result of simple ignorance. The visit of the British minister of defence, **Francis Pym**, to Ottawa on 19 December 1980 had left him with a clear picture of the increasingly complicated and treacherous scene in London.

Thatcher's problems

Thatcher's government was new, and its hold on power nowhere near as certain as it would be after the Falklands War. Moreover, at this particular time, the Conservatives' popularity was low, whereas Labour was riding high in the polls. All in all, Ford said, Trudeau's handling of the constitutional issue was remarkably unfriendly toward the British government. He put Thatcher in an impossible position, stuck between a pledge falsely extracted despite her eagerness to patriate and have done with the Canadian connection once and for all, and the real prospect of defeat in Parliament over the Canada bill, which would mean the defeat of her government. Throughout this entire episode, there was little sign of any Canadian attempt to show some understanding of Westminster's predicament.

The Foreign Office had general policies by which, of course, all of its personnel were guided. But its agents abroad, such as Ford as high commissioner, did not simply follow specific instructions from home. Instead, they operated autonomously toward fulfilling the best interests of their government according to their assessment of how best to do so. Ford felt that part of his responsibility as high commissioner was to keep Ottawa informed of what was going on in London and vice versa.

The Rideau Hall conversation
Ford frankly recounted the salient features of the Rideau Hall skating party episode. What he said to the NDP MP there differed from his remarks the previous summer, in that before he had been projecting what might happen; this time he was describing what had happened. Ford's remarks gave his opinion on the existing state of affairs in London at the time, but they were interpreted as a dictum of British government policy. He believed that NDP leader Ed Broadbent deliberately twisted the meaning of his comments to exploit "colony phobia" and inflame nationalist sentiments to his own partisan advantage.

Broadbent's ploy was ineffectual, however, perhaps because it was premature. In fact, it backfired on supporters of the patriation package because it gave Ford nationwide publicity through press conferences and so on, which allowed him to disabuse the Canadian public of the delusion promoted by its government that the British Parliament could not or would not do anything but pass the bill. He believed that there was considerable relief in London as a result of his actions because the government no longer felt quite the same pressure of being put in a false position by Trudeau.

In regard to his Queen's Park visit, Ford did not recall making a special trip to see Ontario premier Bill Davis at any time. He visited all the premiers annually, and any visit to Ontario was just one of these routine calls, albeit one at which the constitutional question naturally arose. However, Davis was well informed on the issue and did not particularly need Ford to update him.

REEVES HAGGAN (DIED C. 1997)
INTERVIEW | OTTAWA, 4 FEBRUARY 1988

The patriation issue
Haggan stayed at Solicitor-General for seven years, and the way he got out was when they realized they'd bitten off more than they could chew with the Constitution. So Michael Kirby called him at eleven in the morning and told

him to be at the PCO at two. No, his deputy didn't know yet, but he would by then. Haggan insisted that they tell the deputy with a bit more consideration, but in short order he was back. "I guess having decided to make a smash-and-grab raid on the Constitution, they decided they needed operatives," Haggan said. He became "director of institutions," which meant he was responsible for the Senate and the Supreme Court. But Roger Tassé was handling the Supreme Court, and Ron Watt was doing the Senate. David Cameron and Haggan were principally concerned with drawing together activities and writing memos every few days to Trudeau: "Barry Strayer, David Cameron, Gérard Veilleux, and I were the principal writers of the 'Kirby memorandum.'" Haggan did the part that is always quoted, with Machiavelli, "the strategic bit that caused so much trouble." The memo was constructed in forty-eight hours.

Why was Michael Kirby involved with the Constitution issue? **Gordon Robertson** and the others would never have been able to pull the Constitution through. **Trudeau** knew Kirby, who was amazingly quick, so quick that it "used to terrify me." If Kirby liked a stray idea, he'd set a task force on it; but he'd drop it immediately if it didn't work out. He saw himself as an important adviser to the prime minister, "but in my view he was not," Haggan said. "He was driving this bloody great train, but he was not laying the tracks." And you couldn't argue with Kirby.

Going to London
Haggan got to London as part of a "reactive process." If Quebec hadn't been so active, he wouldn't have gone. **Pitfield** and **Gordon Smith** sent him, not Kirby.

Haggan was suitable because he "knew London, Whitehall, Westminster, from an earlier life." As a British barrister of the Middle Temple, he had standing. It helped to have somebody who could speak the British language. For example, Canadian English can be very imprecise, and it sometimes mystified the British as to what a Canadian visitor might have meant. The Canadians would fail to understand that the British were baffled: mutual incomprehension.

So Haggan had to translate. He would brief the visiting ministers not to call their British counterparts "sir." "The ability to talk to the English is not given to all Canadians," he commented. One thing that bothered the English was the Canadian tendency to take everything so seriously. So it helped to have somebody who could do the job. This was in no way a criticism of Jean

Wadds. The office of high commissioner was not set up to deal with the Constitution of Canada. The high commissioner dealt with government, not with legislators.

Wadds told Haggan that "my house, my table, are at your disposal." She was very good, "because if I had to see **Pym** or St. John Stevas, she had to go in her official capacity and I went as a member of her staff." After the necessary pleasantries, they would then turn to Haggan for business.

As a high commissioner should be, she was "very good at the abbey, the palace, and the airport." That was not true of her number two, Christian Hardy, who was "a bloody nuisance to me" because he would fight for his turf – over offices, for instance – even if he was bound to lose, as he was. He was "a bit barbary," perhaps because the Constitution was against all his instincts. Haggan observed to one of Hardy's officers that what really mattered was the Constitution, not Hardy's agenda.

Haggan always behaved as a member of the high commissioner's staff. He "never attacked the Provinces," but he would explain their position when necessary. Where the position was so very different, as with Quebec, he simply refused comment. He never had any difficulty in explaining the BC stance, for example. In fact, he had good relations on a personal basis, even with Gilles Loiselle, the Quebec representative.

"I had enough power to keep Canadian ministers out of London," he said, and in one case he used it. No, it was not New Brunswick premier Richard Hatfield, though his speech was very embarrassing; the worst Canadian speech was by *Globe and Mail* publisher Roy Megarry, a childish performance, even calling the prime minister a communist.[13] That was one time when Haggan got angry.

It was true that the English were not crazy about Trudeau. As one of them said, "He's too damn smart, and he's not afraid to show it."

Haggan went to the meetings of Anthony Kershaw's committee the week he arrived in London.[14] The committee had as adviser Sir William Wade, the master of Gonville and Caius College, Cambridge, a man who had announced at the very first session that he had been retained by the Province of Quebec. Apparently, that little confession excused anything he might say thereafter.

---

13 *Globe and Mail* publisher Roy Megarry was a fierce opponent of Trudeau's Constitution.
14 Conservative British MP Anthony Kershaw chaired a parliamentary committee that examined the Canadian request for constitutional amendments.

In London, Haggan had to deal with three groups: the government, the senior civil service, and the Lords and Commons. The latter two were enormously superior to anything one might find in Ottawa. Of the two hundred active lords, most were life peers; only Douglas Home came from the very old aristocracy.

"Was I a lobbyist? I would say I was explaining our side of the issue. I never said the thing was perfect, but I was very broadly in sympathy," Haggan recalled.

The British situation on patriation

Trudeau made a mistake when he said there should be a three-line whip to get the Constitution through the British Parliament. He didn't understand the UK system. If it was a party platform, on which MPs ran, then yes, the government could impose the whip. But if something came from left field, and you added a whip, it maddened the members. They saw themselves as separate from and senior to the cabinet. The House of Commons existed long before the government did. Moreover, they did not see constitutions as the business of government. From the Thatcher government's perspective, 1980-81 was not a high point in its popularity. It couldn't afford to have the Constitution defeated, and it didn't have a lot of political capital to spend.

They saw Canada House as allies helping them with a difficult task, Haggan said. "My opposite numbers" in the Foreign and Commonwealth Office (FCO) could not themselves leak what was going on in the British cabinet, so they did it via a junior to **Daniel Gagnier** at the High Commission. And yes, the Constitution was discussed a number of times in the British cabinet, though on a technical basis. Haggan's job was to reduce the noise around the government.

The MPs and lords listened more to us than to the Provinces because they liked us better, and we knew how they'd operate. The Quebec agent would wine and dine them, and when they made polite noises, he would take out his pencil and tick off a list. But he didn't understand how things worked with the Brits. They proceeded by indirection, so you had to interpret their signs rather than their words.

The Labour Party was more fun than the Tories, constantly going off in all directions. Though it was an Opposition tactic always to waste government time, Labour Party leader Michael Foot read the Riot Act on the Constitution issue, telling the Labourites to stay in line. Jim Callaghan, though favourable to Canada, was pessimistic, and his pessimism infected Trudeau, who at times believed that the bill would not get through. But if it had been beaten, a key ingredient would have been that Foot had decided to use it as a tactic. (Haggan added that Robin Sears, the NDP's national director, not Ed Broadbent, was his source for information about the Labour Party.)

"I was much more fearful of the Indians than I was of the Provinces," Haggan claimed. The noble red Indian is a part of every British childhood. Cowboys are villains. Just look at Grey Owl, whom Haggan remembered from his Belfast childhood. Fortunately, the Indians took the wrong tack, and "in the end they cocked it up ... We were very vulnerable and I advised the government so ... Had the government listened to reason on the Indians, they could have been settled. But there is a fear in Ottawa government circles" that concessions to the Indians are "a slippery slope."

What was wrong with the Indian tactics? They were awful liars. Even Labour MP Bruce George, their champion, had almost had enough of them, and he told Haggan that he pitied those who had to spend their lives dealing with them, negotiating with them.

Haggan was confident that the Constitution would have passed, though the burden of carrying it measurably increased when the Supreme Court decision came down.

PETER MEEKISON (1937-)
INTERVIEW | EDMONTON, 21 SEPTEMBER 1987

Holder of a PhD in political science, Meekison served the Alberta government from 1974 to 1984. From 1977 to 1984, he was deputy minister of intergovernmental affairs. When he started as head of research and plans at Intergovernmental Affairs, the unit had a staff of twenty or twenty-five and a budget of $1 million. When he left, it had a staff of a hundred and a budget of $5 million.

The patriation fight in Canada and Britain
Meekison spoke of the Constitution, the Meech Lake Accord, and patriation. Patriation was left over from the Statute of Westminster, of which nobody could find a copy. **Trudeau** had warned in 1976 that the present situation could not endure indefinitely, but nobody took him seriously. As for the 1979 first ministers' meeting, that lasted only two days and was too vague for any

real agreement. The summer, as described in Roy Romanow's book,[15] was pleasantly and constructively spent. Then came the Kirby memorandum of 30 August 1980 and the meeting of September 1980. That soured federal-provincial relations in a hurry, though Meekison also admitted that the Kirby document could be seen as a normal bureaucratic memo listing options and alternatives. The meeting was a very low point, in which all kinds of tensions came to the fore. Yet though he could not swear that Alberta premier Peter Lougheed liked Trudeau, he averred that the premier had great respect for him. Personal animosity was not a factor in Edmonton-Ottawa relations; the discord was institutional, not personal.

September brought a crisis unlike any previous one. There was no six-month hoist to await a better time and calmer tempers. Trudeau just went ahead with his two-punch package: the Charter of Rights and the Victoria amending formula. That October, the ten Provinces met in Toronto and discovered that they were divided on Trudeau's package 6-2-2. The six then began to plot their "defensive alliance." This had three lines: court appeals, publicity to win opinion in Canada, and action in Britain.

Appealing to the United Kingdom was not illegitimate, Meekison argued. The case of the Constitution was unique. Patriation had been left to Britain in 1931, and in that sense the Provinces were not foreign parties to the dispute. It is true that Garde Gardom, the BC attorney general, really had his doubts about the propriety or dignity of going, but Meekison did not think that BC premier Bennett shared his hesitations.

Had Prime Minister Thatcher scheduled a debate right away, the Provinces would have been dead in the water. But she didn't, and the court action, once commenced, gave hope for delay, for mustering forces. The British parliamentary schedule was very tight, much tighter than ours, which was apparently a revelation. Perhaps it helped that Thatcher's relations with Trudeau were not supposed to be cordial; it did not help that Canada House kept British ministers very strictly away from their provincial counterparts. Only Romanow got through and then only to the junior minister in the Foreign Office. The British placed some value on the continuation of cordial relations with Canada. Still, when and if it came to a vote in the House, the

---

15 Roy Romanow, *Canada – Notwithstanding: The Making of the Constitution, 1976-1982* (Toronto: Methuen, 1984).

Provinces hoped that Thatcher would put on only a one-line whip. After all, all she could absolutely rely on was the "payroll vote" of about a hundred MPs. British support was of several kinds, some perhaps interested in the provinces, some interested in Indians and Aboriginal rights. Meekison listened politely and with interest to this latter variety.

Up to a point, he had qualms about the role of Quebec in all of this. But that apparently meant not very far. Once, in Winnipeg in May 1981, the Quebec delegation sailed in, and Claude Morin let slip that in any conceivable circumstance (court rulings of either kind or British parliamentary action pro or con), "we win." Perhaps if Morin had repeated himself or expanded his point, there would have been a problem, but fortunately they broke for lunch, and Morin returned to his normal circumspection. Meekison agreed that the Québécois had their own agenda, but in this defensive circumstance, they were on the same side.

The Provinces certainly spent money in London but not a lot. Meekison's agent in London, James McKibben, enjoyed the work and threw himself into it. There was not perfect trust between the Provinces. For example, Quebec would not give Alberta House its list of winees and dinees. They had a letterhead chosen (Meekison handled the competition) and printed, and they had a letter drafted. But it never went out.

Was this "bush league?" (The phrase plainly bothered Meekison.) Finally, he said that the effort to block the Constitution was legitimate because 1931 left no option, and in any case "bush league" meant amateur – this effort was anything but.

DANIEL GAGNIER (1946-)

INTERVIEW | OTTAWA, 5 FEBRUARY 1988

Joining DEA in 1970, Gagnier served in Mexico, Yugoslavia, and Ottawa, and in the United Kingdom from 1980 to 1982. He was in the PCO from 1984 to 1987, was loaned to Saskatchewan as a deputy minister, and returned to the PCO in 1990.

The patriation situation in Britain
Gagnier went to London in June 1980. When he got there, and for months thereafter, nobody in the High Commission, apart from Jean Wadds and

Christian Hardy, knew anything at all about the Constitution or what it might imply. Only when John Roberts and **Mark MacGuigan** arrived in October did the net widen: "they needed a bag-carrier," and Gagnier was it. When the authors mentioned **Haggan**'s negative characterization of Hardy, Gagnier replied that Hardy was cautious, preferring to do things with a minimum of fuss.

When Haggan arrived, Gagnier recalled, he took the role of senior counsel, the man who understood the nuances, who knew the system, who knew how to convey Canadian arguments. Gagnier said that he himself was the one who had to knock on 650 doors around Whitehall. He understood that the best federal tactic was to be reasonable; as the Provinces became increasingly agitated, it was well for the High Commission to grow more calm.

Where patriation was concerned, a number of British attitudes were at play, Gagnier maintained. Some Brits regretted the loss of the white dominions and were nostalgic for the empire. Mrs. Thatcher was definitely not one of those; she had remarkably few illusions on that score. Some Brits went beyond dominion status and thought Canada in some way subordinate. And some, such as Enoch Powell (who was very bright), objected to the Charter on principle.

Canada House's relations with the British government were always very good. The doors to **Francis Pym**, Lord Carrington, and Home Secretary Willie Whitelaw were always open. Relations were so close that the Canadians were usually privy to what was happening, or about to happen, in the cabinet on the Constitution. Only once, in December 1981, did the British tell them to back off: they needed a couple of weeks to recover from having the Canadians "inside their heads." They wanted to work on their legislative strategy without having the Canadians muttering in the foreground.

Nicholas Ridley, minister of state at the FCO, was active too. Gagnier remembered a session with Ridley and his officials in which they gave their reading of where they thought British MPs stood on the patriation issue; actually, the Canadian estimate was closer than theirs.

Relations with the FCO, with the prime minister's office, were reasonably close, correct, and proper. In the FCO, they were really worried about what bad management of the issue might do; the monarchy was always in the front of their subconscious. John Day was one of the officials, and Vivian Hughes, desk officer for Canada at the FCO, was another; she was lucky to have that job when for the first time in twenty years there was an important

Anglo-Canadian issue. She was very bright and "quite tough." Leonard Harris, Pym's legislative assistant, was an outstanding civil servant. He took the whole situation with considerable and refreshing humour. With all the above, Gagnier went on, matters were very easy because there was no fundamental disagreement on how the thing should end up.

You could enlist Anthony Kershaw, but you couldn't control him. He was very bright and open enough to realize that if he gave the Canadian bill a whitewash, he wouldn't be taken seriously. But no, he was not strategically minded enough to have deliberately planned his impact on Canada.

Sir John Ford had a certain latitude in Ottawa, and he had become convinced that the Western Canadian provincial position was the right one. He had the misfortune of hawking his personal views around without the protection of "background" or anonymity. **Gotlieb** came straight over to London and handled the matter well. Ford was recalled. The reports of the Haggan entourage went right to **Pitfield**, Kirby, and the PMO. The UK government's attitude was that it wished it could do patriation without any fuss; it worried that the controversy would make it burn up valuable parliamentary time. So it hoped for unanimity at home in Canada.

The agents-general were ecstatic at the issue. Finally, they had a role and could entertain important people. Quebec was doing it out of conviction, as were Alberta and British Columbia. Saskatchewan was active when Premier Blakeney came to town. When the High Commission staff attended the Tory Party annual shindig at Blackpool, they found that the agents-general were there as well. Gilles Loiselle was the most prominent and the most consistently active, but Alberta's was pretty active too.

Gagnier's job in particular was to know more about what everybody else was doing and bring that added value to Haggan. He had to be sufficiently informed through his "networks" so as to block something the Provinces tried before (or if) it happened. If he had exceptionally good sources, Gagnier didn't confirm this.

He had to be very active with Labour MPs because Michael Foot was in no position to control his members. They were not about to submit to Foot, and Quebec canvassed them very heavily. Callaghan and Denis Healey were certainly on the Canadian side; their relations with Chrétien, who appealed to the British, were especially good. Really, Healey functioned as friend and adviser to Canada, explaining how things were done. The same was true of Callaghan.

Ministerial visits

There were many ministerial visits to London. There was always a constant stream of VIPs from Canada, raising the question of whether the High Commission was in fact a travel bureau. Gagnier said they were very careful not to buy opinions from travelling experts; if they wanted to render favourable opinions "clean," that was fine. MP Doug Frith was very good, as were MP John Evans and John Roberts, with his Oxford connections. There was one minister whom they didn't want back, but it wasn't Serge Joyal, who learned more than he influenced, or Yvon Pinard, Trudeau's House leader, who was extremely successful, both proper and charming, with his British counterpart. Still, "We tried to maximize the strengths of every minister, official, and professor who came over."

As far as the British were concerned, the patriation issue went through three stages. In the first, before the Supreme Court reference was initiated, the British sat back cautiously, in a kind of "hooo-boy" reaction. In the second, during the reference, the mood was relief – we've gained some time – and there was hope that a clear verdict would lift the burden. In the third, post-decision, the reaction was "oh my god – what does it mean?" This was a new dimension, and all the chickens were in the race again.

The British became very strategic, adopting a trust-us-and-we'll-manage attitude. They assured us that their objective remained the same as ours, but they would run the show and tell us what they were doing. Their timetable said that the bill would probably be debated in the spring. "I don't think anybody doubted it would get through," Gagnier stated, "but they didn't want a tight vote."

Reeves Haggan gave the Indians "wise counsel" – that they should not go the course. Gagnier sat through the hearings with Reeves: "We thought they'd just blown it." He remembered Jean Chrétien telling Labour MP Bruce George that there was no such thing as a generic Native; he thought that George understood what Chrétien was getting at, and he heard in the end that George was disappointed in his Aboriginal clients. Perhaps it was their inability to negotiate consensus among themselves that did it. And after eighteen months, you have to get more concrete in your demands or your reasoning.

What about the media? There was an unholy fear that the Canadians would wash their dirty linen over in England. The *Telegraph* supported what the government did and said; the *Guardian* went the other way; and the *Times* stressed the facts. There was an air of unreality to all of this. Gagnier recalled one British MP who was invited to 12 Upper Brook Street for supper when they got round to the Constitution.[16] Not realizing that Gagnier was a French Canadian name, he confided that "the only thing wrong with your country is that the Frogs are in charge." Some MPs thought that **Trudeau** was a Marxist, which was a problem; and there were the common-law fanatics, and the pro-Natives, and all kinds of other factions. "We met with every kind," Gagnier said.

Jean Wadds took her role as high commissioner very much to heart, whatever her own views. She understood the government's objective and threw herself into it with more zest than most ambassadors would have. She felt that this was all part of Canada maturing and that the nation could not be "rebuked" at this stage. She was never obstreperous.

What about Roy Megarry's visit to London? Perhaps his speech had more impact than Manitoba premier Sterling Lyon's did. Once you got the idea that the whole battle was about rights and prerogatives abroad, you had to accept the exercise of these rights and prerogatives. Megarry did it, and the High Commission reacted pragmatically: it adjusted.

As for the Queen, "My understanding was that our constitutional monarch accepted the decision of the government." She was not at all petty about it, and she was very, very well informed about Canada ...

The British cabinet discussed the subject of the Constitution many times during each of the three chronological phases. The discussion tended to focus on how to handle the issue. The position that Thatcher took initially defined the stance of the government throughout.

The Lords, he thought, were more interesting than the Commons. The High Commission met with an awful lot of them, but Gagnier didn't think they were as persistent as the provinces were. When Chrétien came to London, we organized a supper with about fourteen or fifteen peers. Most of them, including Lord Shinwell, who at the age of ninety-something came to the House of Lords to speak, addressed the real issues in their debate. We had not lobbied Shinwell, but he made an outstanding speech, one to look at. Not all of them were like that, and you had to be careful about some of them, including the one who asked after Mackenzie King.

---

16 The residence of the Canadian high commissioner, which had exceptional facilities for stylish entertainment.

A number of different networks were at play. For example, Pitfield had one with Sir Robert Armstrong, his opposite number in the British system. The relationship between Pitfield and Kirby was important. There was also the Kirby-Haggan-Pym network of importance.

There were no threats. "We never had any illusions about how big a stick we should carry," Gagnier stated. Haggan, who had emigrated to Canada from Northern Ireland, had the right touch: "My dear Lord Chancellor, I trust that the country of my adoption won't be as much of a burden [to you] as the country of my origin."

MacGuigan's dark estimate of the Constitution's chances of passage was wrong. It would have caused the British loss of sleep and heartburn, but they would have passed it. It was unthinkable that the duly elected Government of Canada should have been rejected. The British just did not want to see Britain saying no.

Still, leaving the field would have been a major blunder. The British government might then have asked, "Why should we do your work for you?"

Not all the contacts were pleasant. Chrétien came over for the final debate and had the experience of hearing MPs compare Canada to El Salvador. Gagnier walked him round the London Sheraton, getting him to cool down.

"We all gave our liver in the cause of our country but none more so than journalist Jonathan Manthorpe, a special adviser at the High Commission," Gagnier concluded. They were a tight group, with real esprit de corps and a sense of mission: "It was an exceptional time."

THOMAS WELLS (1930-2000)
INTERVIEW | TORONTO, 23 NOVEMBER 1987

Ontario's minister of intergovernmental affairs at the time of the patriation crisis, Wells was the Province's agent-general in London from 1985 to 1992.

Patriation
Wells was heavily involved in the events of the summer of 1980, the Chrétien mission and so forth. Ontario premier Bill Davis told his caucus to "trust me," and it did. There were no problems with the provincial party, but there was trouble in the ridings. Obviously, there was a division between those who followed the Joe Clark line and those who followed Davis, though in

fact Ontario was not opposed to the Supreme Court reference that Clark forced. In the event, because there was a happy ending, there was no permanent damage.

The agent-general in London was not instructed to be active in defence of the Ontario position, Wells insisted. For the agents-general to fight it out abroad was thought to be improper; Davis and the Ontario government generally thought that Canadians should fight their battles at home. Of course, they knew that the other five agents-general were very active, and it is true that Ross de Geer, the Ontario agent-general since 1978, did send around letters with speeches and convened MPs for receptions when Wells or Roy McMurtry, the attorney general, were in town. Ontario also hired a British lawyer to advise on the constitutional aspect and to keep a watching brief regarding what was going on. And he and McMurtry spoke when they were in London.

It was easy to accept Ottawa's leadership in London. The federal government had people on the ground, such as **Reeves Haggan,** and Jonathan Manthorpe was writing some of the speeches. Above all, as leader of the federal team, there was Jean Wadds, who was well known and trusted in Toronto.

Wells had his own source of information in the British government, Nicholas Ridley. Ridley had visited him at Queen's Park when he was government House leader and had sat around his office for chats between the multiple divisions that day. So, knowing Ridley, he could drop in on him. Ridley, close to Thatcher and "an optimist" by nature, always assured him that there was no trouble, no problem, that he had just added up the numbers.

On the other hand, there was **Sir John Ford**'s story of **Francis Pym**'s visit in December 1980 for some NATO ministerial meeting. Pym was said to have had a meeting with Trudeau, during which he informed him that the UK government was very reluctant to proceed without greater consensus among the Provinces. Ford told this story around Ottawa, and he telephoned Wells to set up lunch at the Park Plaza. This was the story he gave Wells. Wells believed that there was some substance to it but wasn't sure how much.

He passed Ford's story on to Davis, but it had no particular impact. Davis and Trudeau were close on the Constitution; Davis was "a key player" and far closer to Trudeau than was Richard Hatfield. Wells supported Davis's position "completely." Ontario favoured "one last try" in 1981, though he declined to say anything much about the cabinet meetings on the subject. On the night that the deal was struck, he, Davis, and their entourage were having Chinese food at the Four Seasons in Ottawa, and Davis was called away to the phone. Davis talked to the prime minister for half an hour and reported that everything was fine, that matters might now precipitate themselves.

The nature of Quebec's position was to be isolated, Wells concluded. How could the rest of the Provinces agree on something that was satisfactory to Quebec or vice versa? Everybody understood that Lévesque couldn't walk away as one of the parties to an agreement. Wells believed that **Trudeau** did his best to keep Quebec at the conference, to find a way, and persuaded Lévesque not to walk out, as he had intended, a day and a half earlier.

RT. HON. LORD PYM (1922-2008)
INTERVIEW | LONDON, 9 FEBRUARY 1989

Francis Pym, a Conservative, served in the Thatcher government as defence secretary, foreign minister, and leader of the House of Commons.

Patriation of the Constitution
Pym said his first involvement in the Canadian Constitution issue came in November or December 1980, when he was defence minister. Thatcher and Carrington asked him, as a specialist in House of Commons procedure, to check the Constitution file for any problems that might arise. He read the file and was horrified – he could see problems in the House if it went forward because of the troubles between Ottawa and the Provinces.

At the invitation of the minister of national defence,[17] he went to Canada in December 1980, where he secretly met **Trudeau** for a long talk. Pym told him that Westminster would unquestionably pass the patriation bill but only with an awful fuss that could damage Canada-UK relations for a long time and make both countries look like fools. He had made this clear to

---

17 Although this is technically correct, Thatcher had proposed the visit. Thatcher to Trudeau, 5 December 1980, Thatcher Papers, http://www.margaretthatcher.org/document/119754.

Trudeau three times, he insisted.[18] The problems had to be sorted out in Canada first. He also feared the time necessary to get the bill through in London. The talk with Trudeau was supposed to be secret, but word soon leaked, probably from DEA.

To Pym, it was only natural that the UK House would take an interest in patriation. The purpose of Parliament is to express disagreement, and the MPs, having the bill before them, were obliged to take it seriously. His estimate was that fifty MPs were interested in the measure, "more than enough to cause problems." When the bill passed almost unnoticed, that was, he said modestly, a triumph for the way he had handled it. He seemed extraordinarily proud of his skills in managing the House.

In this connection, he went on, the select committee under Anthony Kershaw was useful. Kershaw was a permanent backbencher, a man of limited IQ but nonetheless sound. His select committee, an innovation at the time, raised the issues and, Pym suggested, more or less dealt with them. Had the committee not existed and the issues come up in the House, there would have been delay.

If **Sir John Ford** said anything improper regarding the Constitution issue, he was acting on his own. Certainly, Pym stated flatly, there was no linkup between UK Conservatives and Ottawa Conservatives.

Margaret Thatcher and Trudeau did not like each other. She thought that he proposed measures for which others had to pay. He, Pym, liked Chrétien greatly.

EDDIE GOLDENBERG (1948-)
INTERVIEW | OTTAWA, 29 AUGUST 1988

Goldenberg was Jean Chrétien's closest adviser.

....

18 Pym (and Thatcher) much preferred that Trudeau ask for patriation only and abandon any attempt to include his Charter of Rights in the legislative package to be sent to London. He said this in a discussion with Trudeau on 19 December. In response, Trudeau indicated that he would make a public issue of British obstruction, with serious consequences for Anglo-Canadian relations. Back in London, Pym repeated his hard line to the Canadian high commissioner, causing Thatcher to comment that she was "a little bothered by the line Mr. Pym is taking." Minute by Thatcher on copy of Carrington to High Commission, Ottawa, 23 January 1981, PREM19/397 f147, Thatcher Papers, http://www.margaretthatcher.org/document/125544.

Patriation in London

Goldenberg was only peripherally involved with the London end of the Constitution.[19] He always believed that Thatcher's hesitations were pure bluff and that in the end the British would, as **Trudeau** advised, hold their noses and pass the patriation bill. Be that as it may, he was over to London twice. The first was on a swan. He'd been working hard, wanted a vacation, wanted to go to the theatre, and thought that London would be a good rest. He applied to Michael Kirby, who had him on a plane to London for a week. His duty was to have lunch every day, and in the evenings he could go to the theatre. He recalled one Labour MP who liked to proclaim that he was 90 percent convinced of the Canadian case; that way, both sides would keep inviting him to lunches and dinners.

There was one moment on the Ottawa end. He had a couple of friends at the British High Commission – the economic counsellor and his wife. She was the most junior person in the place, fourth secretary or something, and she was put in charge of Nicholas Ridley when he visited Canada. Goldenberg believed that Ridley had relatives in Canada and simply wanted Westminster to pay for his visit, so he decided to "carry a message" to the Canadian government from his own. Goldenberg's friend phoned one day and begged him to put Ridley into Chrétien's office for a few minutes so that he could justify his trip; no other minister would see him. So he got Ridley in, and he also got a thank-you dinner that Friday.

In England, he met **Francis Pym**, one of those Englishmen who like to tell you within five minutes of meeting you that his family have been in the House of Commons for three hundred years: putting the colonials in their place. Goldenberg didn't like Pym. Perhaps he was better than St. John Stevas, but that didn't make him attractive. He lunched with Harold Wilson, whom he found very intelligent, not especially tippling, and strongly committed to the Canadian side.

During his second trip to London, Goldenberg had come over with Chrétien for the passage of the bill. All these snobbish Brits claiming the sanctity and inscrutability of the great British parliamentary process. After all, they'd say, we've been doing it for three hundred, or five hundred, or eight hundred years. It used to drive Chrétien wild. He would ask when the bill

---

19   Goldenberg's memoir is *The Way It Works: Inside Ottawa* (Toronto: Douglas Gibson Books, 2007).

was to come down for whatever reading. Oh, that will be decided by the House. Gee, said Chrétien, don't you decide it in the government? Oh no, we've been at this for centuries, don't you know. So on it would go.

But, Goldenberg said, he remained convinced that it was all bluff.

Afterword

Canada's constitutional package finally made its way through the British Parliament and received royal assent on 29 March 1982, the 115th anniversary of the passage of the original British North America Act in 1867. Trudeau lost no time: on 17 April, Queen Elizabeth signed the new Constitution in a ceremony on Parliament Hill. Margaret Thatcher was invited and accepted the invitation, but the Argentine invasion of the Falkland Islands intervened. The image of Thatcher attending as Canada's constitutional midwife, Charter of Rights included, would have signalled a graceful, if ironic, conclusion to the constitutional affair.

IX
The Peace Initiative

THE COLD WAR WAS IN grave danger of spiralling into a major military conflict in 1983. The Soviet Union had placed new SS-20 missiles in central Europe, and the United States and NATO responded with Pershing and Cruise missile deployments. The Soviet occupation of Afghanistan continued, and the leadership in the Kremlin was geriatric and hostile. In the United States, President Ronald Reagan boosted American defence spending while talking darkly of Star Wars and the USSR as an "evil empire." Neither side seemed willing to talk seriously to the other. Then, on 1 September 1983, Soviet fighter jets shot down a Korean Air Lines passenger aircraft that had strayed over the Far Eastern territory of the USSR, killing all aboard. The United States – and Canada too – called this murder and imposed sanctions.[1]

Pierre Trudeau had few illusions about Canada's power and its ability to ameliorate global tension, but he had the urgent sense that he must try to do something. He had already begun talking to his closest officials about the need to ease Cold War tensions. He may have wanted to remain in power,[2] but he was three years into his fourth term in office, and he had persuaded himself that if he were to do anything for peace, it had to be done while he held power and had an entrée abroad as the senior Western statesman in terms of service. Other leaders had crusaded for peace after leaving office, to no avail. After the KAL007 shooting and the resulting global tension, he vigorously pushed his officials forward. At the initial meeting of ministers and senior bureaucrats from DEA, DND, the PCO, and the PMO

---

1 For Trudeau's response to the KAL007 downing and the genesis of the Peace Initiative, see John English, *Just Watch Me: The Life of Pierre Elliott Trudeau, 1968-2000* (Toronto: Knopf, 2009), 593-602. Our account is in J.L. Granatstein and Robert Bothwell, *Pirouette: Pierre Trudeau and Canadian Foreign Policy* (Toronto: University of Toronto Press, 1990), Chapter 14. A later version by Bothwell is in his *Alliance and Illusion* (Vancouver: UBC Press, 2007).
2 English, *Just Watch Me*, 602.

on 21 September, Trudeau put his hands on his head, rocked back and forth in his chair, and said that Canada had to do something. But what? No one had more than a hint of the general direction that he wanted to pursue, no one believed there was much chance of success, and some officials thought that the Canadian public would see a Trudeau initiative as politically motivated. Leave politics to the politicians, rejoined Trudeau.

Over the course of the next few weeks, a plan took shape for a bold Peace Initiative, one held closely in Ottawa and not shared with allies in the drafting. On 23 September, a steering committee and a working group began the task of producing ideas; the one fixed point on their calendar was a speech that Trudeau was scheduled to deliver at the University of Guelph on 27 October – there, the Peace Initiative would be launched.

Trudeau had the opportunity to rehearse his preoccupations with Margaret Thatcher in private and in public, using her entirely coincidental but fortuitous official visit to Canada from 25 to 28 September as a platform. At a gathering in Toronto, he approvingly quoted Carrington during an exchange of speeches "and also took up, in public, a theme that he had pursued in the Cabinet Room that morning, on the need for politicians to take a hand in strategic issues and not leave [them] to the 'nuclear accountants.'" As Trudeau spoke, the British high commissioner observed that Thatcher "ominously began to make notes." She then delivered a Churchillian response, stressing alliance solidarity and resolve "in the face of Russian pressure."[3] The Trudeau-Thatcher debates were a dress rehearsal for what was to follow, for as she flew back to London, the prime minister's Peace Initiative took a more definite shape.

The bureaucrats came up with twenty-six proposals, each one following the same format – background, evaluation, upside and downside, and negotiability – and each running to four or five pages; in the end, six proposals were recommended. On 7 October, the senior group, with Trudeau having the final say, picked five: a five-power conference; a beefed-up nuclear non-proliferation treaty; a foreign ministers' meeting in Stockholm; the speeding

---

3 Lord Moran, high commissioner, to Sir Geoffrey Howe, foreign secretary, "The Prime Minister's Visit to Canada, 25 to 28 September 1983," 5 October 1983, Thatcher digital archive, Thatcher MSS (Churchill Archive Centre), THCR 1/10/55 f178, http://fc95d419f4478b3b6e5f-3f71d0fe2b653c4f00f32175760e96e7.r87.cf1.rackcdn.com/831005%20UKHC%20Ottawa%20despatch%20MT%20VISIT%20TO%20CANADA%20THCR%201-10-55%20f178.pdf.

up of Mutual and Balanced Force Reductions (MBFR) negotiations;[4] and a ban on high-altitude anti-satellite weapons. Trudeau had liked the process that produced the ideas, and he agreed with the officials' urgings that his efforts should be aimed at leaders, not at the general public; that entailed a heavy travel schedule to Western Europe, Asia, Moscow, and Washington. An election was likely in 1984, Trudeau said, but "we have to act as if we are eternal, taking action now if we believe we are right."[5]

The Guelph speech on 27 October went well, getting a very positive response in the Canadian media – and briefly in the opinion polls. It contained whispers of "equidistance," a lumping of the United States and the USSR as equivalents, which had put Trudeau into difficulty in the USSR in 1971 and in a Notre Dame University speech of 1982, but there was no doubt that he had struck a chord with Canadians.

Events abroad might have caused an eruption before the initiative got off the ground. A NATO command post exercise called Able Archer had started on 2 November. The exercise simulated a period of conflict escalation that culminated in a nuclear attack and involved the participation of some heads of government. In the tense international situation, some Politburo members apparently believed that Able Archer was a cover for a NATO attack on the USSR and readied their own nuclear and air forces. Happily, NATO forces did not respond with an alert of their own, and the crisis ended when the exercise concluded on Remembrance Day, 11 November.

How much of this Trudeau or his interlocutors knew remains unclear,[6] but his visits to Paris, The Hague, Brussels, Rome, the Vatican, Bonn, and London were brief, the conversations tepid, the press coverage minimal.

....

4   A series of NATO–Warsaw Pact negotiations on military matters held between 1973 and 1989 in Vienna.
5   Granatstein and Bothwell, *Pirouette*, 368.
6   Individuals who were senior Canadian diplomats at the time do not now recall anything about Able Archer or a possible war scare. Searches in Canadian archives have not turned up any documents or files that would clarify its impact on Canada, if any. Beth Fischer of the University of Toronto sees Able Archer as a crucial episode. See Beth Fischer, *The Reagan Reversal: Foreign Policy and the End of the Cold War* (Columbia: University of Missouri Press, 2000). The best and most useful analysis of the Able Archer crisis is Nate Jones, ed., *Able Archer 83: The Secret History of the NATO Exercise That Almost Triggered Nuclear War* (New York: New Press, 2016). It is clear that Trudeau's instincts about nuclear peril in the fall of 1983 were correct, even if he knew few if any details of the very real danger.

Returning to Canada on 13 November, Trudeau gave a second speech, unfortunately to a Liberal Party gathering, a fact that called his motivations into question, and he then left to attend a Commonwealth Heads of Government meeting in New Delhi. Support from the Commonwealth was useful though not vital, but the Chinese indicated that they were willing to receive Trudeau, and a visit to Beijing immediately followed. However, the Chinese leadership did not like the idea of a five-power meeting, seeing it as unrealistic and a diversion of attention from the two superpowers, and Trudeau had to sit through an hour-long oration from Chairman Deng. Among other things, Deng told Trudeau that with its vast population China had the best chance of surviving a nuclear war. There was no progress there.[7]

Nor was there much in the United States.[8] On 15 December, Trudeau flew to Washington to meet President Reagan. The Canadian leader was not much admired in high Republican circles, as we have seen in earlier chapters, but, advised by Ambassador Allan Gotlieb, he pitched his line cleverly. Telling the president that he knew he was a man of peace, Trudeau said that Reagan's message was not getting through. The reaction to this approach was not wholly positive, some of Reagan's key advisers believing that Trudeau had treated Reagan as a simpleton, but the presidential rhetoric seemed to soften over the coming months.

The Peace Initiative had gained little traction as yet, and Trudeau returned to Europe early in the new year. The Soviet satellites were showing signs of restlessness as Moscow's leadership crisis continued, with General Secretary Leonid Brezhnev dead, his successor Yuri Andropov dying, and no able, healthy successor yet in sight. Trudeau visited Prague, Berlin, and Bucharest, the East Germans and Czechs being obliged to station the USSR's SS-20 missiles on their territory and clearly realizing that any general war would see

---

7 John Hilliker, Mary Halloran, and Greg Donaghy, *Canada's Department of External Affairs*, vol. 3, *Innovation and Adaptation, 1968-1984* (Toronto: University of Toronto Press, 2017), 429-34. See also the Yu Zhan interview on page 309.

8 The Central Intelligence Agency prepared a detailed memo on the initiative two days before Trudeau's meeting with President Reagan. It noted that Trudeau had received "a sympathetic hearing" on his mission thus far "but has won no specific commitments." It added that Trudeau "professes to be satisfied with the results." "Canada: Trudeau's Peace Initiative," in Memorandum by Office of European Analysis, Directorate of Intelligence, 14 December 1983, Central Intelligence Agency Records, CIA-RDP85T00287R000502310001-2, https://www.cia.gov/library/readingroom/docs/CIA-RDP85T00287R000502310001-2.pdf.

their countries destroyed by US and NATO nuclear weapons. Again, in the opinion of Canadian diplomats, little that was positive was accomplished.[9] The East European leaders seemed receptive to Trudeau's message, however, and when he returned to Canada, he in effect declared victory in the House of Commons on 9 February 1984. The Peace Initiative, Trudeau's last hurrah, had one final gasp when Andropov succumbed on the day of Trudeau's address in Parliament. Trudeau flew to Moscow for the funeral and had a brief meeting with Konstantin Chernenko, the new general secretary. Himself very ill, Chernenko was not one to press for détente, and Trudeau came away with nothing. Shortly after his return to Canada, he took "a walk in the snow" on 28 February and decided to step down after sixteen years as Liberal leader and prime minister.

Trudeau's Peace Initiative had been well meaning and undoubtedly sincere, but it almost certainly had little effect on the superpowers. Canada had little credit in the bank with either Washington or Moscow, and the superpowers had no intention of letting Trudeau and Ottawa meddle in their affairs. "Trudeau's impact on the [eventual] end of the Cold War was marginal," John English concluded,[10] but in Canada, much of the public had been enthusiastic, and Trudeau left office to substantial acclaim. Other assessments of the initiative, offered by diplomats and officials who had worked with the prime minister, were more sober, sometimes even damning. In this chapter, we have interviews with the senior officials who worked on the initiative or assessed its impact from Canada's posts abroad. Trudeau's own assessment may be found in the next chapter.

LOUIS DELVOIE (1939-)
INTERVIEW | LONDON, 6 OCTOBER 1987

Delvoie began his DEA service under Trudeau in Cairo and enjoyed a variety of postings, including Algiers twice, but increasingly on MBFR,

---

9   Bothwell-Granatstein interview with Henry Korn, 19 October 1987 (not published); DEA history. This was also the opinion of the Foreign and Commonwealth Office in London, where the Eastern European visits were judged as "regrettable" and "unwelcome." Paul Waldie, "Files Show What British Diplomats Really Thought of Canada in the 1980s," *Toronto Globe and Mail*, 24 August 2016, A8.
10 English, *Just Watch Me*, 601.

CSCE, and SALT. He spent 1976-78 in Brussels and was then director of DEA's Intelligence Analysis Bureau. He was the director general of the Bureau of International Security and Arms Control when Trudeau summoned him to head the task force for the Peace Initiative.

The Peace Initiative

The initiative came about at a very low point in East-West relations.[11] There had been the failure of the Gromyko-Shultz talks at the Madrid CSCE follow-on conference. There was the highly charged nature of the conference itself. There was the KAL downing. There was the total paralysis of arms control talks in Vienna and the Russian walkout. The Americans seemed to be recycling one old proposal after another. There was, too, Lord Carrington's Buchan Lecture on the dangers of "megaphone diplomacy."[12]

Trudeau called a meeting of a few ministers and senior officials on 22 or 23 September 1983. Delvoie vividly remembered Trudeau rocking back and forth in his chair, head in hands, saying that we must do something. He had in mind that ex-prime ministers such as Germany's Willy Brandt were frequently full of good international works when in retirement; why not before retirement, when they could still effect change?

Delvoie got the job of co-ordinating the task force. There was no idea where Trudeau wanted to go, just a general direction, to be consummated at a Meech Lake meeting in two weeks, about 2 or 3 October. In between, Delvoie and his colleagues from DEA, the PMO, and DND had to develop a peace plan. Achieving in two weeks what Trudeau had failed to do during the previous fifteen years seemed a bit much.

Though the enterprise seemed rather foolhardy, the task force had to come up with something, which was a blue-covered volume labelled "Proposals on East-West Relations and International Security," known informally as the

....

11 On the background and implementation of the peace mission, we are indebted to Susan Colbourn, "'Cruising toward Nuclear Danger': Canadian Anti-nuclear Activism, Pierre Trudeau's Peace Mission, and the Transatlantic Partnership," forthcoming.
12 In April 1983, the former British foreign secretary Lord Carrington delivered the Alistair Buchan Memorial Lecture in which he warned that "the dehumanization" of relations with the Soviet Union "would be the quickest road to catastrophe." R.W. Apple, "Carrington Warns on East-West Ties," *New York Times*, 24 April 1983, http://www.nytimes.com/1983/04/24/world/carrington-warns-on-east-west-ties.html.

Blue Book. It considered about twenty options and commended seven; to their surprise, Trudeau adopted them all. The date on the document was 10 October; the Meech Lake meeting was three days earlier.

What were Trudeau's motives for generating the Peace Initiative? Delvoie himself had no doubt that Trudeau was sincere. He had heard elsewhere that there was some political admixture, which was true as far as some of Trudeau's staff and ministers were concerned. But he never, ever heard it from the prime minister's lips. Quite the contrary. There were second-hand reports but nothing he had ever experienced for himself. Yes, Allan MacEachen did jokingly offer him an Order of Canada or a Senate seat if the polls went up by another five points (they had already gone up five). Why not both the order and the seat? suggested Delvoie. Sure, MacEachen replied, always provided the ratings justify it.

So the Peace Initiative was launched with the Guelph speech on 27 October. They started travelling, with the object of getting it over by 31 December. But that could not be, because of Andropov's illness; Trudeau could not be received in Moscow until the funeral. They went to fifteen capitals and met seventeen heads of government. The culmination was the New Delhi Commonwealth summit.

Delvoie did not comment about most of the heads of government. Thatcher chilled him by remarking that flowers grew in Hiroshima the year after the bomb fell. Deng Xiaoping did likewise, when he said that even if half the population of China perished, 500 million would still be left. And then there was Reagan.

Trudeau and foreign policy
Trudeau was admittedly a practitioner of "equidistance," just as the Americans suspected, and they resented it. The prime minister found Reagan's entourage appalling. He could not understand people who talked in terms of surviving a nuclear war. To the extent that he could, he resented them. He saw Reagan as "a pleasant nonentity." As a classic 1940s or 1950s small-l liberal, Trudeau found them very hard to deal with.

In fact, Delvoie saw Trudeau's own perception of power relationships as very naive. After fifteen years in office, he "didn't have that ingrained sense of how major power relations work." He believed in the power of words and ideas. At the same time, his own interest in foreign affairs was sporadic. In 1974, for example, just when Trudeau was launching his Contractual Link drive, he hadn't remembered that Denis Healey was still around the United Kingdom, still dealing with Canada, this time as chancellor of the exchequer, and would have bad memories of Canada's 1969 NATO cuts.

Not only did Trudeau think that reason should dislodge "the strenuous pursuit of national self-interest by the superpowers," he thought that dialogue in itself should produce good results. This was naive. He could not grasp why the superpowers "were unwilling to take risks for peace." His approach here was comparable to his approach to the North-South dialogue. Delvoie remembered a French diplomat asking, "How could the underdeveloped countries expect the rich ones to give up so much of their wealth to the poor ones when they could not win these prizes in war?" Yet the kind of concessions they expected were those usually extorted on the battlefield or at least under real threat.

Yet given his skepticism about Trudeau's capacity to deal with foreign affairs, he still found his peace mission not unfruitful. When told of **Gérard Pelletier**'s comment on Trudeau's knowledge of foreign policy (see page 46), prove it, Delvoie said, suggesting that Trudeau's ability could be proven by looking at the record. Nonetheless, he found the peace mission not unfruitful. Trudeau was entirely right to believe that East-West relations were in crisis and entirely right to try to start the East and West talking again. He believed, on good authority, that German chancellor Helmut Kohl was moved to take a different attitude, to further dialogue; so was Italian premier Bettino Craxi. Not that the idea was new to them, but Trudeau gave them an impetus.

On the downside was the haste and the lack of diplomatic preparations. And there was an apparent unwillingness or inability on Trudeau's part to distinguish between the societies he was dealing with. This was the American complaint of equidistance again. In approaching Reagan, Trudeau received two forms of advice. On the one hand, Delvoie urged that each power should be treated in exactly the same way and receive the same message. If this did not occur, it would get out and would discredit the initiative. But **Gotlieb** urged that if Trudeau took that tack, he'd see Reagan's eyes glaze over in five minutes flat, and the rest of the conversation would be with Secretaries George Shultz and Caspar Weinberger. Gotlieb flew down to Washington with Trudeau, who followed his advice. Delvoie had gone down the night before and lost the tactical advantage in doing so.

Another negative was the combination of public speeches and private conversations. Some leaders took badly to it.

What emerged with Trudeau in the final analysis, according to Delvoie, was a man who could give only occasional emphasis to foreign affairs. He grew to like the Commonwealth because of its informality, and he hated NATO because it was so stiff and so formal, marching to the beat of Secretary-General Joseph Luns's drum. Trudeau and Luns got to know and dislike one another in 1974 at the foreign ministers' meeting in Ottawa. There were three speakers: Trudeau, who called for détente; Luns, who gave a blood-and-guts oration that stressed the need for more weapons, NATO's weakness, Soviet strength, and so on; and James Callaghan. Luns's address seemed like an affront to Trudeau, though it may not have been. It started the two men on a downward path. They detested each other afterward. Trudeau especially hated Luns's pre-cooked communiqués.

Now, Trudeau may have misconstrued NATO. For example, he believed that the Harmel Report of 1967 called for NATO to take political initiatives, to stress its political identity. It did, but not at the expense of the military side. Delvoie himself even prepared a summary of Harmel for Trudeau but doubted that the prime minister ever read it.

Indeed, Trudeau's policies were often a contradiction in terms. Withdraw from Europe in 1969, return in 1972. People remembered, though possibly Trudeau himself did not.

Delvoie remarked on the confused nature of Canadian policy during the 1970s. We had spent several years telling Europe that we weren't interested and were cutting troops, etc., and then, a few years later, we were running after the Europeans to pledge our devotion as we sought a Contractual Link. For example, the idea of Canada asking Denis Healey for assistance with the link was ludicrous, given that he'd been so angry at our troop cuts in 1969.[13]

PETER HANCOCK (1938-)
INTERVIEW | BONN, GERMANY, 21 OCTOBER 1987

Trudeau's Peace Initiative
Referring to written sources that he had brought to the interview, Hancock stated that the key documents on the Peace Initiative were the 21 September

---

13 This paragraph is based on a conversation between Granatstein and Delvoie on 8 February 1989 in London.

1983 minutes of a meeting with the prime minister; the 22 September establishment of the Initiative Group; the 28 September covering letter on the options book generated for the Meech Lake meeting (**Louis Delvoie** to the Steering Group); and the 7 October minutes of the Meech Lake meeting.

Accounts of the initiative usually omit several important factors, Hancock said. First was that **Trudeau's** thinking on the subject began to evolve in the spring of 1982. He had been growing progressively more disillusioned with NATO and G7 meetings, and with the political level's control over the arms race, East-West relations, and the alliance. He started to come out in his May 1982 address to the Notre Dame University convocation. That speech got him into trouble. Written by Bob Fowler of the PCO after many tries by others, it raised the "equidistance" line, "which was to haunt us." But it began the process of describing superpowers as having special responsibility and asserting that arms control had to be tackled. Hancock, then in Policy Planning at DEA, had written some of Trudeau's speeches and was dragged in because Bob Fowler, the foreign policy adviser to Trudeau, never hesitated to draw on anyone who could do the job for Trudeau. Fowler and Hancock were close friends.

In addition, as the broad prime ministerial agenda unrolled after 1981, it made clear that attention had to be given to arms control and disarmament. Why? Hancock offered no real answer. He agreed that Trudeau had shown attention to the Contractual Link, to North-South, and to China in the past and didn't know why these areas hadn't been reinforced with additional efforts.

For the Williamsburg G7 summit of 1983, Hancock, **Tom Delworth**, and Sean Riley (then of SSEA MacEachen's office) prepared a declaration on peace and security, as Trudeau had asked for something more than just a talk on economics. This was a Canadian initiative, though none of the G7 liked it, the United States especially. A declaration with different text did emerge, stressing the need to press ahead on the two-track route. Everyone had learned from that, and Trudeau was not upset. But it was clear that working multilaterally was making him frustrated and was very difficult.

This was the period of the Cruise missile testing decision, stagnation in MBFR, problems in Stockholm, Reagan's harsh rhetoric, Thatcher (who later changed her tune, for which Trudeau deserves some credit), "two-track trauma," and the KAL007 shooting. All this made Trudeau wonder if the generals were out of control. It was also a period when people such as Lord Carrington (with his megaphone diplomacy comment), Robert McNamara, and George Ignatieff began crusading; they had all held senior positions.[14] In Hancock's presence, Trudeau said that "it is irresponsible for me to wait until I'm out of power to do something." He looked at McNamara, who now said he had been wrong in his earlier policies. Trudeau felt a sense of responsibility – he had to do something. But as he was Trudeau, this wasn't just a vague idea. He was the senior leader in the West, he had access to other leaders, and he was personally and intellectually endowed to intervene. Moreover, he was frustrated.

Reagan had done his part to produce this feeling. Helmut Schmidt and Trudeau had shared a sense of outrage at the ineptitude of first Jimmy Carter and then Reagan.

In July-August 1983, there was some talk of Trudeau and East-West relations. He had expressed his concerns to François Mitterrand and Thatcher.

In September 1983, Hancock left Policy Planning to become director-general for the Soviet Union and Eastern Europe. He was managing the KAL crisis when he was suddenly pushed into the Peace Initiative because of his earlier work with Trudeau. He thought that **de Montigny Marchand** put him on this job.

Planning the initiative
At the 21 September meeting, there were Trudeau, MacEachen, J.-J. Blais, **Gordon Osbaldeston, Delvoie,** Fowler, Gary Smith, Tom Axworthy, and some others. A steering committee was also set up (its members were Osbaldeston, Massé, Delvoie, Dewar, Anderson, the chief of defence staff, General Gérard Theriault, Fowler, de Montigny Marchand, and **Michael Shenstone**). The working group consisted of Delvoie, Smith, Mathewson, Hancock, and some others.[15]

Fowler was determined that this exercise wouldn't be bureaucratized by DEA, and he and Trudeau wanted ideas to come in raw form directly from individuals, rather than after being blended by the bureaucracy. It was clear to Hancock (and everyone) that he was working for Fowler, not DEA, and they dealt directly. Marchand had Trudeau's confidence, and Fowler and

---

14   Secretary of defense for Presidents Kennedy and Johnson, Robert McNamara later spoke out against his nation's misjudgments during the Vietnam War. Canadian diplomat George Ignatieff had been hawkish initially but became a disarmament advocate.
15   All these men were senior officials from DEA, DND, the PCO, and the PMO.

Marchand had confidence in Delvoie, Smith, and Hancock. These were heady days under incredible pressure – soggy pizza and warm Coke.

There were some risks in being too closely identified with Trudeau, but Hancock thought they were acceptable risks. There were also risks on the other side that Trudeau, out of frustration, might start taking positions that would put Canada at odds with NATO or cause difficulty with the United States. As bureaucrats, they had to try to prevent this.

Trudeau liked to play "Socrates of the Rideau" and took intellectual delight in asking "Why couldn't I –?" You needed good answers to deflect him.

Hancock read from the minutes of a working group meeting of Friday 23 September, convened at 10:00 a.m. During the meeting, Delvoie said that the prime minister was deeply concerned about the risks of war. The timeframe for the Peace Initiative was the next three months. There was to be consultation with the allies, dialogue with the United States, and a public dimension. Why three months? Because Trudeau didn't want the initiative to be seen as a pre-election gambit. He would allocate one hour per day to the people who were working on the initiative. (In fact, Hancock recalled, they had access to him for meetings of up to two hours.) The working group was told that the steering group would meet on 28 September and that the ideas had to be in place by then. Trudeau's first speech was to be at Guelph, and it had "to be more than just pretentious ... has to set the universe of discourse for the next five months." Fowler was concerned about options and the critical path. During the meeting, references were made to the United Nations Special Session on Disarmament and to Trudeau's 1977 strategy of suffocation.[16] This meeting produced no specific proposals.

The proposals were hammered out over the Monday and Tuesday following and probably put together around midnight on Tuesday 27 September. There was some spontaneous generation of ideas (Ken Calder in DND and Hancock had been thinking of a five-power approach to arms control for some time). Jack Toogood had been in the MBFR talks and had ideas. Delvoie was director general of the Bureau of International Security and Arms Control and had been working in Policy Planning and doing special projects for

---

16 Trudeau unveiled his "strategy of suffocation" of the arms race at the United Nations in 1977. This included a comprehensive test ban, a ban on the flight testing of new strategic missiles, a stop to the production of fissile material for nuclear weapons, and reductions in defence spending. See Geoffrey Pearson, "Trudeau and Foreign Policy," *Peace Magazine,* January-March 2001, 7.

Marchand. Moreover, Fowler and Hancock had been talking over the summer about what Trudeau could do on East-West relations. In other words, people had ideas.

The meeting produced a Blue Book that had some very brief proposals. Once agreement was reached on the items, people were detailed to draft a text that followed a specific format (background, evaluation, upside and downside, negotiability). Each proposal in the resulting tabbed Blue Book was about four of five pages long, with an introduction.

The steering committee met on 28 September to look at the Blue Book, which then went to Trudeau and the Meech Lake participants for the meeting on 7 October. The task force met on 29 September (and incorporated feedback from the 28 September meeting); it met again on 4 October.

Among the options in the Blue Book were a ban on the testing and deployment of high-altitude weapons; a five-power meeting; and tab 8, which was very controversial, on Cuban troops in Angola.[17] This didn't fly. All the other options presented in the book were thought feasible.

The Meech Lake meeting tried to decide which options were best, with Trudeau saying that he wanted further work on some proposals. Generally, Trudeau liked what he was given, liked the way it was done, and liked that he was dealing directly with a small group. He also liked the draft of the Guelph speech, which was included in the package. His contribution to the discussion, as Hancock noted while he looked through the minutes, was substantial – it consisted of asking questions and making the final "go" decision. Trudeau looked at his schedule of meetings and travel to see how the initiative fitted in. He also said that an election was likely in the spring or fall of 1984 but that the government could go another year if necessary. "We have to act as if we are eternal," Trudeau stated, "taking action now if we believe we are right."

To Hancock, Trudeau's attitude wasn't one of equidistance. He wasn't in either an anti-US or an anti-USSR mood. He was very Canadian and (like Schmidt of Germany) always aware that Canada had limited resources. But his personal standing gave us greater clout than usual. Certainly, he was aware of his standing. In fact, his European swing was put together quickly – there

....

17   Cuba intervened in decolonialized Angola in 1975 in support of leftist elements and in opposition to groups backed by the United States and South Africa. The Cuban intervention continued until 1991.

were few leaders who could get to see their opposite numbers with just a phoned request. He also had clout because he had stayed in office for such a long time.

The United States was not given a preview of the initiative. After Trudeau's Notre Dame speech of May 1982 and the Williamsburg G7 meeting of 1983, Hancock knew that the Americans wouldn't like it. However, he doubted that this had doomed it from the start. If others had seen Trudeau as a stalking horse for Washington, the initiative could have been doomed. Certainly, everyone could see the problems – Hancock, for example, worried about the leadership vacuum in the USSR – but no one who was involved in the initiative, including Trudeau, was a naive idealist.

Hancock thought the USSR might listen to Trudeau, even without US support for the initiative, just because Soviet relations with Canada regularly improved when US-Soviet relations were bad. After all, Trudeau was a NATO head of government and remained one throughout (even at Davos in January 1984, where his exchange with Raymond Barre, after Barre provoked him, caused difficulty. They had bad chemistry).[18]

After the Meech Lake meeting, there were more meetings, more cranking out of texts. The working group met solidly through the weeks of 10 and 17 October, with 17 October being the final date for the Guelph speech. That speech was given on 27 October and was preceded by guidance telegrams sent to key embassies around the world.

Going to Europe

Trudeau's consultations in Western Europe went on while Hancock worked on speech number two in Ottawa. (Hancock wrote the first three speeches and collaborated with Paul Heinbecker, who wrote much of it, on the fourth.) Trudeau was well received by Chancellor Helmut Kohl. Hancock remembered that Gary Smith and one other person went to Washington, making a special effort to deal with the Americans. They weren't well received. Lawrence Eagleburger, the under secretary of state, "of all people," spoke about Trudeau smoking pot – a little smear. Hancock did go on the Eastern European trip with Trudeau, visiting Prague, Davos, East Berlin, and Bucharest. This trip

....

18 At Davos, Trudeau asked publicly whether any US president would actually order a nuclear strike on the Soviet Union if Soviet troops moved on Western Europe. Barre, a former premier of France, reacted sharply, accusing Trudeau of weakening NATO's credibility.

had been on the original agenda as a possibility, but as the year wore on and it became clear that Andropov was not functioning, they decided to go. Trudeau liked the idea, feeling that satellites had more leeway when the Soviet leadership was weak. Over the table, East German general secretary Erich Honecker in Berlin bought the idea of the five-power meeting. Nicolae Ceaucescu, the Romanian president,[19] was launching initiatives of his own, and in Prague the Czech leadership was asserting itself under Gustav Husak. These trips were all short – a maximum of forty-eight hours in Berlin, one night in Prague, two in Bucharest.

Trudeau made sense, Hancock said. He wasn't trying for a conspiracy of middle powers in the two alliances, although there was a whiff of that. He was essentially encouraging the satellites to contribute – they were troubled by missile deployment and by the lack of movement at the CSCE (where middle powers had made some space for themselves in the past). They didn't like Reagan's rhetoric or Vice President George H.W. Bush's Vienna speech, which sounded like rollback rhetoric. And, after all, it was hard to have an East-West initiative without going to the East. If there was no one at home in the USSR, you went to the satellites. And East Germany and Czechoslovakia were sites for SS-20 deployment.

Trudeau was the first NATO head to go to East Germany. He had to mind his "p's and q's" on Berlin doctrine, but he found the East Germans very accommodating in terms of a minimum of ceremony. Communications were done directly with their ambassador in the United States, also accredited to Ottawa, by Hancock. Some arrangements were made by the Canadian ambassador to Poland, accredited to East Germany. After the East European visits, diplomats went to Brussels to brief NATO allies.

Results of the Peace Initiative

In the Peace Initiative speech in the House of Commons, Trudeau wrapped up and declared victory. But was it? According to Hancock, the initiative demonstrated the inadequacy of any foreign policy that was based on the idea of Canada as an economic animal. It also satisfied that Canadian itch to do things. And it showed that Trudeau was prepared to put his shoulder to

....

19 Nicolae Ceaucescu was general secretary of the Romanian Communist Party (1965-89) and the country's president (1967-89). In international affairs, he maintained a somewhat divergent line from that of the USSR. In 1989, his regime collapsed and he was executed by a firing squad.

the wheel, no matter how steep the hill. And, things did improve – the trend line levelled off and then rose. The formal opening at the Stockholm Conference of Foreign Ministers (a Canadian proposal) helped break the ice. Trudeau had proposed this in one speech. Stockholm got Gromyko and Shultz together, even if in acrimony. Thatcher changed her tune – in a strange way, she and Trudeau liked each other – and when she softened, Trudeau was entitled to some credit (although the Brits too were unhappy with her rhetoric). And Hancock thought that Trudeau was effective with Reagan, whose rhetoric in his second term was calmer than in his first. Trudeau had skilfully brought Reagan around to seeing that his place in history required that he deal with the USSR and arms control. He knew how to handle the president – "I know you're a peaceful man, but people don't see it like that," he said to Reagan when he saw him in Washington during the initiative. Hancock also recalled a *Toronto Star* piece of four or five years later, which noted that the initiative ideas were still current.

Hancock offered a few other points. The arms talks did reconvene – because of other reasons and Trudeau. The initiative was a good attention-getter for Canada and Trudeau. And if you're not the most reliable ally, you get a certain presence, you focus their attention. The initiative also showed Canadians that peaceniks didn't have a monopoly on peace, that their government was responsive and flexible, and could contribute to stability.

However, at the Commonwealth meetings in India, Trudeau's performance was not his best. He improvised and didn't go over. In China, **Geoffrey Pearson** preceded Trudeau's visit. He was not in the inner circle, although he had been at Meech Lake.

Assessments

Trudeau was ambivalent about DEA. The Peace Initiative was an end run around the department, one that DEA had to swallow.

Some Liberals did market the initiative for political purposes, one decision being to hold Trudeau's second speech at a November 1983 Liberal fundraiser in Montreal. But Hancock got no sense of this from Trudeau himself. And some senior Liberals were concerned about grumblings from Liberals who were unhappy with the initiative.

Hancock also alluded to individuals who had private channels to Trudeau, eminent Americans and Canadians who were scared by Reagan.

THOMAS DELWORTH (1929-2012)
INTERVIEWS | UPPSALA, SWEDEN, AND GRAINAU, GERMANY,
26 OCTOBER 1987 AND 19 FEBRUARY 1988

KAL007
At the end of his career, **Trudeau** saw the USSR not as a moral problem but as a political one. That was close to Delworth's view too. When Soviet jets shot down KAL007 on 1 September 1983, Trudeau was less concerned with the horrors of the act than with the long-term effects on East-West relations if the West reacted too stridently. That bothered SSEA MacEachen, who was more political – how would this play in Listowel, Ontario? By this time, Trudeau was a subtle player who thought in terms devoid of public applause. He was appalled by the shootdown but had to decide how far indignation and a desire to punish should be pushed. Delworth, who had the KAL007 file, had seen nothing in it to suggest that the plane was deliberately off course. His view, the Canadian view, was that it went off course in an area where US intelligence flights had gone, so the Soviets shot it down. Of course, they should have forced it down, not shot it down. On this issue, MacEachen ran the show, and the Canadian measures were the toughest of any. The shooting occurred just before the Madrid CSCE meeting of 3-4 September 1983, and MacEachen decided not to go so that he wouldn't have to hobnob with the Soviets. So Jean-Luc Pepin and Delworth went, and Pepin made a speech that forced the British, Norwegians, and Danes to toughen their own positions.

The Peace Initiative
Delworth was slightly involved in the Peace Initiative. The departmental reorganization by Marcel Massé did away with the political director post, which was his. If the old structure had been maintained, Delworth would have been involved with the initiative. Even so, the knowledge that he was going to the Stockholm conference meant that he was an adviser and that he attended meetings. He thought the initiative was viable and important. The world was nasty and bleak then, and Trudeau wasn't grandstanding. He tried to change things. If he'd succeeded, of course, he'd have been pleased to take the Nobel Peace Prize. Still, Delworth thought the DEA planners were trying to get Trudeau to do things where Canada had no clout (like the French

"force de crap"),[20] and it all ended as a busybody exercise. It was ill-conceived and it upset people, Mr. Fixit at its worst. Trudeau was right to try, but he was vain, and he overplayed the extent to which Mitterrand and others would listen. Not running it past NATO beforehand was a mistake.

Delworth said that the Stockholm arms control preparatory negotiations in November 1983 were as important as the initiative – he was the chief negotiator – as for the first time the Soviets agreed to on-site inspection on challenge. This was a Western proposal that, once accepted, would achieve more for Western security than anything Trudeau was trying to do.[21]

DE MONTIGNY MARCHAND (1936-)
INTERVIEW | GENEVA, 11 JULY 1988 AND 6 FEBRUARY 1989

The Peace Initiative
There is no arguing that **Trudeau**'s Peace Initiative was very Pearsonian. Marchand was opposed to it from the start and had said so at the first Meech Lake meeting on the subject in 1983. Trudeau "didn't like it, but he listened to me." His support for the 1981 North-South summit meeting at Cancun was also Pearsonian. Perhaps the only reconciliation of his 1968 position with his later one of 1983 was that he came to see that Canada's national interest lay in supporting high-minded international actions. There was genuine idealism here, but it was also naive and misguided as to its political repercussions on Canada. However, the fact was that the repercussions were negligible.

Marchand was one of the few of those involved from the start who expressed doubts. In his view, the political reaction in Canada would be so negative that the Peace Initiative idea would be killed abroad. He pushed hard enough on this that Trudeau finally told him to stop and to leave the political consequences to the politicians. Marchand admitted that he was wrong. He also worried that the US reaction would be very hostile if it was believed that Trudeau was trying to play intermediary. The prime minister did not understand the minutiae of arms control, but this didn't matter: the details weren't important, whereas the climate was.

....

20 A pun. The French labelled their nuclear arm the "force de frappe."
21 See Fen Osler Hampson and Michael Hart, *Multilateral Negotiations: Lessons from Arms Control, Trade, and the Environment* (Baltimore: Johns Hopkins University Press, 1999).

ALLAN GOTLIEB (1928-)
INTERVIEWS | WASHINGTON, DC, 30 JUNE 1986, 15 JANUARY 1988, AND 14 NOVEMBER 1988

INTERVIEW | 15 JANUARY 1988

The view of Trudeau in Washington
Gotlieb strongly disapproved of **Trudeau**'s Peace Initiative.[22] It wasn't even Trudeau's own idea: Jim Coutts and Tom Axworthy were responsible for it. Nor did it help that Trudeau didn't like President Reagan and held him in scorn as an actor. His flip comment to reporters at the Bonn G7 summit – "Ask Al [Haig]" – caused resentment. (One must remember that Reagan per se did not exist but was a composite of the people around him. Reagan himself may not have noticed Trudeau's slights, but the people around him did, and they were furious.)

Gotlieb got his first clue as to Washington's opinion of Trudeau during a lunch that he and his wife, Sondra, attended. At the table, Sondra was paired with Judge William Clark's wife (Clark was the second National Security Council adviser). "Your prime minister's a communist," said Mrs. Clark to Sondra. Things were so bad that nobody at the State Department had mentioned anything to Gotlieb, not even Lawrence Eagleburger, who was normally forthcoming.

Michael Deaver, White House deputy chief of staff, helped with the solution. At a party, he signalled Gotlieb over and said, "We got a problem."

"What's that?" asked Gotlieb.

"Your guy and my guy are not getting along."

"Really?"

"Your guy really upset my guy; everybody around him is upset." This occurred shortly after a June 1982 *National Review* article written by Lubor Zink had called Trudeau a Marxist, which made quite an impact.

"Well," said Gotlieb, "I'm very glad you're telling me that."

Deaver said, "We shouldn't let this go, he likes Canada, you're so important." Then he said, "My guy really likes the gestures." He suggested that

---

22 Gotlieb's views on the Peace Initiative and various events during his time as ambassador to the United States may also be followed in his *The Washington Diaries, 1981-1989* (Toronto: McClelland and Stewart, 2006).

Trudeau find a suitable occasion to drop Reagan a note. So Gotlieb relayed the recommendation, and Coutts and Trudeau were very co-operative. They wrote an appropriately friendly letter. Gotlieb said that in his opinion there was not a shred of anti-Americanism in Trudeau ...

Gotlieb on the Peace Initiative
Trudeau's Peace Initiative was "preposterous." And the idea of a five-power nuclear club was "ridiculous" and out of character for Canada to advocate. "Canadians are not a preposterous people," Gotlieb stated.

The original legitimate notion behind the initiative was to influence Reagan to change his style of discourse. When Trudeau met with him in Washington in December 1983, he handled himself outstandingly well. He realized that he was approaching from the margin and took a very soft line, starting from the premise that Reagan saw himself as a man of peace. (Gotlieb had flown down from Ottawa with Trudeau, briefing him on the way.)

The rest of the initiative was self-indulgence, high theatre. We Canadians usually act like good, modest, incremental Anglo-Saxons in our ideas. We stress professionalism and content. But on this one, for example, Thatcher and Mitterrand listened to Trudeau, but with embarrassment.

INTERVIEW | 30 JUNE 1986

The Peace Initiative in Washington
Relations between SSEA MacEachen and Secretary of State George Shultz were very warm. Then Trudeau jumped back in with the Peace Initiative and MacEachen receded. Washington hated that. It revived all the feelings of Trudeau as communist, of Canada as rogue industrial nation. The United States was in a resurgence of patriotism. The Americans did not like criticism of their foreign policies ... They rejected an apologetic foreign policy. But Trudeau came and argued for more equidistance between the superpowers in his Notre Dame University speech. Canada was good, morally equidistant, a peacemaker, whereas the others were naughty boys with nukes. "They hated that," Gotlieb recalled. At the end of the Trudeau era, the antagonism toward Trudeau was central again. Shultz and MacEachen were engaged in problem solving, as in the case of trucking – there's one off the list, what's next? But then there was this revival of antagonism toward Trudeau.

Gotlieb could not take the positive side on the initiative. It was a form of local madness to which Canadians are prone. It was not significant on a large scale. The two nuclear superpowers would not let any country get in their way, either two-bit countries like Yugoslavia or big countries like France. Trudeau claimed not to be a mediator, but he was. The five-power thing was a terrible idea. It was one of the worst ideas produced in arms control in modern times. It was just ludicrous. There was no prospect of agreement among those five, but the Peace Initiative became overly identified with that idea.

The initiative did contain one valuable notion. "I will take credit for it," Gotlieb said. Some traditionalists believed that Canada's greatest influence lay in swaying the United States. "When Trudeau came down here [to Washington], I made a tremendous effort to make him take the high road. Reagan didn't want to see him. This was a personal visit; there was no official visit in the second phase. I got him to appeal to the high ground. You are a man of peace, you are trying to get this across but it is not selling. The failure is not due to your warlike instincts. Trudeau used that line and stuck to it." It may have been helpful. Reagan significantly changed his rhetoric after that point. To some extent, it helped. But all were dead set against it and took a deep breath. The system closed to Gotlieb, he said, even the high State Department. (George Bush liked Trudeau best – he was from the old eastern establishment.) But the whole system closed to him. The visit was imposed on them. They all thought that it embarrassed the United States. Trudeau was being naughty. During the first part of his appeal to Reagan, he had to realize what was possible. His political discourse was unhelpful. The five-power idea was ludicrous, so the initiative had a bad idea as its centre. And the world tour was wrong as well – we can influence only the Americans, not the Russians, but to get declarations from the Commonwealth toward the United States was not effective. Our influence diminished but for that one appeal because of the Peace Initiative. And if you scratch hard enough, the Peace Initiative was generated not by Trudeau, but by people in his party to develop a standing in the polls, and it worked. Trudeau was sincere about it because he was a liberal moderate, but it took him a month or two to pick it up. Then when he got the bit between his teeth, he ran with it. It was always that way with him. Trudeau was not interested in the Constitution at first – he told Gotlieb that himself. The same thing was true for patriation. The only thing that interested him at first was the Bill of Rights. But he was sincere.

Trudeau's realpolitik
Trudeau had an absolute belief, like Reagan's. In the moral equivalence of the superpowers, he believed in authority and legitimacy. The USSR was a

relatively benign power. It was entitled to a sphere of influence. Trudeau was never comfortable attacking Washington on Central America or the Kremlin on Poland. He believed in vital interests and in legitimacy. He had a realpolitik view. His North-South efforts to help the starving came up later. But on basic war and peace issues, he had a realpolitik outlook. His stand on Biafra showed that he believed in the legitimacy of governments, and you don't fool around with that. He saw the USSR as a full and equal superpower entitled to *Lebensraum* and vital interests. He was uncomfortable attacking the Soviet leadership and would wiggle out of it whenever he could.

INTERVIEW | 14 NOVEMBER 1988

Gotlieb believed that Allan MacEachen had got on very well with the Americans, down to mid-1983 (see page 370).

Undercutting MacEachen

The Peace Initiative killed MacEachen's reputation. It undercut him, and "he disappeared off the screen." The whole Trudeau exercise, Gotlieb said, had an anti-American bias. The "equivalence" between the United States and the USSR maddened the Americans, who still recall it with great hostility. It was foreign to MacEachen's way of doing things. From the US perspective, it injected others into the US-USSR relationship, made it a conference matter, a frontal exercise, a matter of public diplomacy. From Trudeau's point of view, it was personal indulgence, so contrary to his cool appraisal of 1968, basing his policy on the national interest. Instead, he became "a global animateur."

GEOFFREY PEARSON (1927-2008)

INTERVIEW | OTTAWA, 30 AUGUST 1988

The Peace Initiative

Although Pearson was involved with the Peace Initiative, he was not central to it. He had returned from Moscow and was at loose ends without a job, so he was asked to help with preparations for **Trudeau**'s visits to the USSR and China. He tried to explain to Moscow and Beijing what the prime minister wanted. He saw Gromyko, for one, and told him what Trudeau wanted to raise and that he wanted to see Andropov. Gromyko was interested in

Trudeau's ideas, but he could give no assurance that Andropov would be available. Only later did we learn that Andropov was so ill he couldn't really see anyone. Even so, that Pearson saw Gromyko was a mark of the esteem in which Trudeau was held. The USSR took him seriously.

In Beijing, the PRC moved quickly. Pearson saw a political director of the Foreign Ministry (the foreign minister being out of town) and was informed that a visit could probably be arranged within three months. He told Trudeau that it was likely to be possible when he was in India, and word that it was came through there. This was exceptional speed for the Chinese.

It was a pity that Andropov was ill. That hurt the initiative. He didn't think it mattered that Washington wasn't onside before Trudeau saw the Russians. Trudeau's strategy was different.

X
The Trudeau Conversation

THIS CONVERSATION – IT WAS not an interview, Trudeau said – took place over lunch at the Ritz-Carlton Hotel in Montreal. Trudeau was accompanied by Ivan Head, who had graciously arranged the meeting, and the effect of his entrance on the other diners was palpable – every eye in the room followed him as he was escorted to our table. The discussion lasted for just under two hours.

Dressed in a suit and tie, Trudeau looked fifteen years younger than his sixty-nine years (though he had liver spots on his hands and face), and he was sharp and tough. His answers could wander, though, and he sometimes forgot questions or became confused. Head had to help him out a few times, and once he went quite astray. He was quite vain, proud of his accomplishments, and not happy about criticism.

During the interview, conducted just four years after he had left the prime ministership but referring to events as much as twenty years in the past, Trudeau's memory was generally clear. He confused Marcel Cadieux, the USSEA when he became prime minister, with Léo Cadieux, his first defence minister, and his recollection of his attitude during the Defence and Foreign Policy Reviews of his first term was somewhat imprecise. His position on Canada in NATO, for example, was surely more than nine-tenths tactical, as he put it in the conversation. But he was very clear in recounting relations with France, Paris's interference in Canada, and the rather cool French attitude to him. The French, he said bluntly, were "shit disturbers," simply ignorant about Canadian federalism and how it worked.

As for US governmental views on Quebec after the Parti Québécois victory in 1976, Trudeau said he had no reason to be confident. He knew that President Jimmy Carter's national security adviser Zbigniew Brzezinski, educated at McGill University in Montreal, believed that Quebec nationalism would triumph but thought that Carter understood the federal government's position. And the US ambassador Thomas Enders was a very able diplomat in Ottawa from 1976 to 1979; Trudeau believed that he too understood, "but you never knew with US ambassadors." The Enders interview in this volume (page 207) reveals that he understood the Quebec-Canada dynamic situation quite clearly.

Trudeau spoke of personalities abroad, notably French presidents Pompidou and Giscard, Margaret Thatcher, and Ronald Reagan, but he waxed rather more enthusiastically about Alexander Yakovlev, the USSR ambassador to Canada with whom he was friendly, and Soviet leaders Brezhnev, Kosygin, and Gorbachev. Yakovlev and Gorbachev, it was obvious, were a new breed of Soviet leaders, men who could laugh and joke while hewing to Soviet policy and changing it.

During his Peace Initiative from late 1983 into 1984, his strategy was to talk to the leaders first, then to the people. He knew that Reagan and Thatcher would not be keen, but he lined up support, and, he said, British and American rhetoric changed after his initiative.

Overall, Trudeau seemed satisfied with his policies, his impact, and his legacy. There was more than a little vanity in him and resentment still at those whom he felt had slighted him. But after some fifteen years of shaping his nation's foreign policies, he seemed pleased with his accomplishments.[1]

RT. HON. PIERRE TRUDEAU (1919-2000)

CONVERSATION | MONTREAL, 30 JUNE 1988

A lawyer, writer, and intellectual, Trudeau first won election to the House of Commons in 1965. When Lester Pearson retired in 1968, Trudeau captured the leadership at the Liberal Party's convention and began his long tenure in power. He lost the election of 1979, won the election of 1980, and after his Peace Initiative of 1983-84, he left office in 1984.

On the interplay of Quebec, Canada, and France
Asked about Quebec-France and France's improper activities, he said there was nothing secret about this. Whenever we found out that the French were doing something (such as Philippe Rossillon's efforts in Canada), Trudeau had made a public crack about it. Certainly in his view, there was little

---

1 This conversation was previously published in a somewhat extended form as J.L. Granatstein and Robert Bothwell, "Pierre Trudeau on His Foreign Policy," *International Journal* 66, 1 (Winter 2010-11): 171-81.

difference between France under Presidents de Gaulle, Pompidou, and Giscard, though it was different with Mitterrand.[2] Giscard was sympathetic to the separatists because he needed Gaullist votes. Trudeau had long talks with Giscard about this, and as far as he could tell his support was a political concession rather than a plot. The Gaullists were always plotting to get Quebec out as far as possible. Trudeau recalled a story from the time of the 1984 election, in which a very senior French minister at the UN said to **Gérard Pelletier**, "at last you may have a French Canadian as prime minister," meaning Brian Mulroney. Pelletier replied, "What about Trudeau?" The answer was that Trudeau was "an Anglo with a French name" – and this, Trudeau said, after sixteen years in power.

To Trudeau, the French were "shit disturbers," playing safe in case the separatists won their referendum so they could say they had been there to help. He didn't know how much money came from France for the Parti Québécois or whether it was government money; the RCMP couldn't find out, as they were so damned ignorant about Quebec. To him, France was always fighting for the cause of French minorities everywhere, except in France and its colonies. Moreover, the French were so ignorant about our Constitution; they didn't know of the extent of Canadian decentralization and didn't know that the Provinces controlled education, for example.

He had talked of this with Presidents Pompidou (though relations were very cool with him), Giscard, and Mitterrand. He told them that a separate Quebec would not be in France's interest, as it probably meant that English Canada, and eventually Quebec, would slide into the United States. It was not in France's interest to have one power controlling the whole continent. He also stressed his bilingualism and biculturalism efforts, which would make the French language more vigorous all across Canada. The reply from the French was not to ascribe the acts of a small group to the French government.

The 1968-69 Foreign Policy Review

Asked about the foreign policy group he had organized before he ran for the Liberal leadership, he replied that this had not started until he joined in the

---

2 De Gaulle was president from 1959 to 1969, Georges Pompidou from 1969 to 1974, Valéry Giscard d'Estaing from 1974 to 1981, and François Mitterrand from 1981 to 1995.

race; but **Ivan Head,** sitting in on our conversation, reminded him that it had existed while he was minister of justice to deal with offshore questions, constitutional questions, and federal-provincial topics. Trudeau then agreed, and there was talk about the tomato sandwiches and Cherry Blossom chocolate bars he used to serve at the lunches. Among those who participated were distinguished lawyer-scholars Jean Beetz and Gérard La Forest and Carl Goldenberg (when in town). The function of that group was to help him be a good justice minister, Trudeau said, and more enlightened on foreign policy. After he entered the race, the group changed character, and yes, he recalled **Allan Gotlieb**'s paper stressing national interests.

What had he wanted from the NATO review of 1968? He had ideas on some areas (China, recognizing the Vatican, and NATO) when he took over. Yes, he was distrusting of NATO and a bit ignorant of the arguments pro and con. He recalled the terrible speech he had ad libbed at Calgary in April 1969, on NATO. The only excuse he could offer was that he'd been skiing and that the audience wanted to hear about oil, and he didn't want to talk about oil. That speech had annoyed Head, who interjected that he'd sent a speech out to Calgary via the RCMP that didn't arrive. What Trudeau regretted was that the speech was unfair to Lester Pearson because it suggested that Canadian foreign policy had been only about NATO. Not until sometime later when he heard that Pearson was hurt did Trudeau realize that his "shallow and unfair" remarks had caused pain.

He felt then and now that Canada was just a junior partner in NATO (like everyone else except the United States). But after Calgary, he tried to play even-handed and to be a good club member.

Returning to the review of March-April 1969, Trudeau said he was probably just making a case, either because he believed in withdrawal from NATO or because he wanted to see the idea knocked down. Yes, **Paul Hellyer**'s diary did say that Trudeau was for total withdrawal,[3] but his position was nine-tenths tactical. What he really wanted was a clear examination of the facts and prejudices. Before he went into politics, his inclination was to be pro-NORAD and anti-NATO; after he got into politics, however, he began to appreciate the arguments for NATO, where we had other friends around the

---

3 Hellyer diary, 29-30 March 1969, Paul Hellyer Papers, private collection, Toronto; J.L. Granatstein and Robert Bothwell, *Pirouette: Pierre Trudeau and Canadian Foreign Policy* (Toronto: University of Toronto Press, 1990), 23.

table (though he doubted that we benefitted much from them). As it was, the United States, especially under President Reagan, wouldn't accept any views except its own.

He really didn't remember his own views in March 1969, Trudeau said, but he was clearly happy with the decision that Canada was not to be neutralist. He felt that alignment was okay. He had begun with an open mind on neutrality but accepted alignment by the end of the debate. He felt that more strongly at the NATO meeting in 1974, where he could tell the allies we had made a decision in 1969 and nothing had been heard of anti-NATO talk since, so it must have been a good decision. That helped with the allies, who saw they could trust him and perceived the wisdom of his course.

In any case, he thought that in their heart of hearts, the Europeans accepted the Canadian position in 1969. Europe was strong and very few NATO members had troops stationed outside their own borders (Head clarified that there were three – the United States, Britain, and Canada). It was an arbitrary decision to cut the NATO force in half – the point was that we were still there. And Head had taught him about the need not to be a destabilizing force – the nuclear-armed CF-104 jets.

What struck him about NATO was that so few of its members were willing to question anything. They wouldn't get rid of Joseph Luns, the long-serving secretary-general of NATO, because Washington didn't want change. There was never any real discussion at NATO summits – set speeches, a canned communiqué. At the 1974 NATO Foreign Ministers meeting that was held in the Canadian Senate, Trudeau's opening speech had made an effort to rationalize what NATO was trying to do. Kissinger had been laudatory – at last we were getting to concepts. But at a Washington NATO meeting, Trudeau remembered telling British prime minister Jim Callaghan that they should go after NATO on Mutual and Balanced Force Reductions, and their efforts at least got a decision that NATO should examine this. At the London economic summit in 1977, he had said to President Jimmy Carter that progress had been made in Washington; so now, couldn't we replace Luns? Carter was sympathetic and promised to look into it, but in the end the United States didn't want to rock the boat. He, Trudeau, had been lobbying for Peter Carrington.

Asked about **Léo Cadieux**'s threat to resign over the NATO cuts of 1969, Trudeau became confused and started talking about Marcel Cadieux, the USSEA until 1970. He and Marcel had a "terrible love-hate" relationship.

Trudeau admired his gruff style, even though Cadieux always felt superior to him. Because Cadieux was one of the first French Canadians to come to Ottawa during the war, he was always prepared to accept "shit" from him; he even accepted outright disloyalty, when he was told that Cadieux had said in Mexico that his foreign policy was terrible. He liked Cadieux; he brought a lot of French Canadians into the service. Cadieux was like **Ross Campbell** (ambassador to NATO, 1967-72), who also said disloyal things but whom Trudeau later met and liked. Independent thinkers like Cadieux and Campbell were hard to convince, but he admired them.

Trudeau then told a story about coming to Ottawa in 1949 to see about a civil service job. He was interviewed by **Mitchell Sharp,** who was then the director of the economic policy division at Trade and Commerce. A copy of George Orwell's *1984* was lying on Sharp's desk; this must be an interesting man, Trudeau thought. Ken Eaton, the taxation expert at Finance, offered him a job too. He saw Cadieux at External Affairs and hit it off badly with him – Trudeau had a long beard then, after a year of globetrotting.

Getting back to Léo Cadieux, Trudeau said he was nice but light, not an ardent Trudeau supporter. He was no astute politician, but if a lunch could save his face ... He agreed that having Cadieux leave just after Paul Hellyer, who resigned at the end of April 1969, might have looked bad. But he wouldn't change policy just to keep a minister on board.

Deterrence
Deterrence, Trudeau said, made sense in strategic terms. Intellectually, he hoped for something else, but he couldn't find any better solution to nuclear weapons. What concerned him was that Canadian policy should not destabilize things (these were Head's ideas, he added). He then mentioned Vice President George H.W. Bush telling him in SSEA Allan MacEachen's office about Reagan's Star Wars on the day that Reagan first spoke on it. Trudeau's first reaction was that Star Wars was destabilizing. It was not a good solution.

The Peace Initiative
The conversation drifted to the Peace Initiative. Trudeau had realized that he must spend time on this (he wasn't going to devote all his time to the economy once the Constitution was settled). So he got a group together, including Head, *before* the Korean Air Lines 007 shootdown, though it proceeded with

urgency after that. He wanted to lower tensions, to civilize the dialogue, to get out of the Cold War era. He himself had no idea of how to do this until the group got together.

At two preceding summits, Trudeau had expressed strong ideas on the double-track plan to limit missile deployment in Europe, stressing the need to keep disarmament moving forward. He barely recalled *Future Tasks of the Alliance,* the Harmel Report of 1967, and his heart was on the side of the peaceniks. At the 1983 Williamsburg G7 summit, Prime Minister Margaret Thatcher had accused him of giving comfort to the communists, so he knew that she and Reagan wouldn't be happy with the Peace Initiative. He had also crossed swords with Thatcher in private. Trudeau decided to talk to the leaders first and then to the people. He knew he couldn't get Washington and Westminster onside at first – get the others, then they might come aboard. On his European trip, he had not intended to visit London – Thatcher had been in Ottawa recently, and he knew she disagreed. But when he was near the end of the trip, he received an annoyed message from Thatcher, asking why he didn't plan to visit London. To Trudeau, that confirmed the rightness of his judgment. Thatcher wanted to see him because he was lining up support. That answered the critics who said it was an error to launch the initiative without US support.

When Trudeau went to Washington, he had a long talk about "the evil empire" with Vice President Bush and his officials in the White House. They were not proud of this line. Trudeau said the US and UK rhetoric changed after his visits. Bush told him that Reagan wanted peace and that what Trudeau was doing was right. For that reason, he had a lot of time for Bush.

Asked about Reagan, Trudeau was not very forthcoming. As a human being, he was okay, though no great president. Reagan had an instinctive respect for those who had won election to office. Relations between them were never nasty or discourteous. Reagan didn't contribute much to bilateral or multilateral meetings, however. At the latter, Reagan let Thatcher articulate his views.

The Soviets

Turning to the USSR, Trudeau talked of the ambassador to Canada, Alexander Yakovlev, whom he liked. In the mid-1970s, Head had told him that Yakovlev was an able guy and suggested lunching with him. Trudeau used to invite him to 24 Sussex to talk about the NATO double-track idea, human rights, and so on. Yakovlev would invite him to dinner when visitors, such as Georgy

Arbatov, head of Moscow's Institute of the USA and Canada, came through. Trudeau enjoyed caviar, he said, so he went. Yakovlev was always loyal to the party line and had good arguments, but when he didn't have to defend the system, he was open-minded. When Trudeau was in Opposition, he occasionally passed his residence, and Yakovlev would give his kids chocolate. He had only one long talk with Leonid Brezhnev during his first visit to the USSR. It was a long monologue with real sincerity on his view of the United States, not just nasty, but delivered more in sorrow than anger and in a despairing way. He met Brezhnev in Helsinki as well, went over to his seat to talk to him, and they resolved the dispute about Soviet overfishing in Canadian waters. Brezhnev picked up the phone, made a call, and it was done. Head interrupted to say that he and Viktor Sukhedrov, Brezhnev's translator and later head of the Canadian desk at the USSR Foreign Ministry, did the work on the overfishing issue, and it was the hardest time he ever had. The Russians always asked how captains at sea could possibly be controlled.

Trudeau said he had raised human rights at the Kremlin with Brezhnev and had some results, as the statistics would show. He took Brezhnev aside and said that family reunification questions had to be resolved. Brezhnev "didn't give the usual line about internal matters." He replied, "Give me the list." Trudeau felt this area was important in human and personal terms, but it shouldn't prevent talking to the USSR. The survival of mankind was worth talking about even if you disliked the Soviet attitude on human rights. Trudeau had been a little skeptical of Jimmy Carter when he made it a centrepiece of his policy, but Carter had balanced it off well, and his position helped in Latin America.

Trudeau liked Kosygin – he was Khrushchev without the rough edges, fatherly, a human being, a forerunner of Gorbachev. He was prepared to discuss things so long as USSR policy wasn't tackled head-on. He was more understanding of Canada and Trudeau personally than Brezhnev was.

Mikhail Gorbachev, he knew, was a protégé of Yuri Andropov, long-time KGB head and briefly general secretary. That was why he had lunch with him during his 1983 Canadian visit. Gorbachev was the first Soviet leader with whom one could have a to-and-fro conversation, freewheeling. Trudeau also saw him in Moscow during the summer of 1985, when he was over sightseeing with his kids. **Peter Roberts**, the Canadian ambassador to Moscow, was a friend. When Trudeau was in Yerevan, he was contacted and asked to return to Moscow for the meeting with Gorbachev. He spent a forenoon with

Yakovlev and Gorbachev, and this was very different from talking to Andropov or Konstantin Chernenko, Andropov's short-lived successor. They could laugh, joke, challenge – they knew what Trudeau had said on Poland or the KAL007 shooting. They were the equivalent of Jimmy Carter, who could take a briefing and then talk without notes. He didn't think that External Affairs had a report of this talk.

Trudeau didn't like the term "spheres of influence." There were areas of strategic importance to the superpowers. The USSR was entitled to be concerned about Poland and Afghanistan, just as the United States was entitled to be concerned about Canada and Latin America. Objectively, Canada was in the US sphere. He recalled an argument with Zbigniew Brzezinski, who had said that China, Korea, Japan, and Southeast Asia were areas of strategic importance to the United States in which Washington had the right of overview. Trudeau replied that this was too broad; the Soviets could say the same thing about China, for example. He was uncomfortable with the spheres idea – it didn't give Washington or Moscow the right in international law to intervene.

The United States and the Parti Québécois

After the Parti Québécois election win in 1976, Trudeau had no reason to be confident about the US position. No president had told him what the position was. That was why he had felt it important to speak to Congress in early 1977. By the time of the 1980 Quebec referendum, he had talked to Carter about Quebec, and he knew that Brzezinski was giving advice that nationalism would always win out. Trudeau was reasonably confident that Carter understood his own message.

Trudeau's relations with US ambassador **Thomas Enders** were fairly good, but you never knew with US ambassadors. Enders was much above the others in intellectual power and contribution to discussions. He expected Enders's judgment of Canada-Quebec would be correct. But Trudeau still felt a bit uneasy about Enders because he was a civil servant, and Trudeau was critical of American policies. Still, both Trudeau and Head agreed, Enders could deliver. He could call Kissinger ...

Conclusion

So what are we to make of Pierre Trudeau a half-century after he came to power in 1968? That he was highly intelligent, hard working, charismatic, and an untypical Canadian politician, we now take as given. At the same time, Trudeau was an adventurer in life as in politics, one who sought to change things, to look at established institutions with a fresh eye.

He became prime minister with only a global traveller's knowledge of the world, the legacy of his privileged upbringing and desire to experience different cultures. Trudeau had never studied foreign policy in a disciplined, detailed manner, though he occasionally wrote newspaper pieces or editorials on contemporary topics for his magazine *Cité libre*. After the Second World War, he had travelled widely in Europe, the Middle East, and Asia, and he had been to Moscow in 1952 and China in 1949 and 1960, when few others went there. Trudeau had studied at Harvard University during and just after the war, but he was never truly comfortable in the United States, and his knowledge of America and Americans was limited.

He had no experience or interest in the military. Trudeau had been a desultory participant in the Canadian Officers Training Corps at the Université de Montréal during the Second World War – years in which he had been cool to Canadian participation and strongly opposed to compulsory military service. In his view, the armed forces were no place for a man of intelligence.

Trudeau took office only months after France's Charles de Gaulle had roiled Canadian waters in dramatic fashion with his "Vive le Québec libre" address in Montreal. Quebec separatism and nationalism blossomed quickly, and Trudeau had withstood a barrage of bottles, fruit, and insults at the St. Jean Baptiste Day Parade only days before the 1968 election that won him a big majority. Quebec's status in Canada was the one subject on which the new prime minister held strong and well-known views. At the opening of his time in power, this was the one issue that Trudeau knew he had to address.

These experiences – or the absence of them – shaped his views on defence and foreign policy when he became prime minister in April 1968. To Trudeau, the Canadian Forces were designed more to impress Canada's allies than to frighten its enemies. And who were those enemies? He worried about violence, then epidemic in American cities, spilling over into Canada, and despite the Soviet Union's invasion of and repression in Czechoslovakia in 1968, he seemed to believe that stability in Eastern Europe was preferable to unrest. Over time, after meetings with Presidents Nixon, Ford, Carter, and Reagan, with Soviet leaders Kosygin and Brezhnev, Trudeau came to wish for "equidistance," the idea, simply put, that Canada should strive to keep as far away as possible from the ambit of both superpowers. This was difficult, given that his nation shared a continent with the United States and lay on the direct flight path from the USSR to the States. It was also virtually impossible, as Canada was in a formal alliance with Washington.

Such attitudes affected Trudeau's policies. In 1968-69, he ordered sweeping reviews of defence and foreign policy, demanding that a fresh look at the world be taken by the entrenched bureaucracies in DEA and DND. The results saw Canada cut its European military commitment to NATO by 50 percent, a move that angered allies and disheartened soldiers. Washington was not pleased: President Nixon told his newly appointed ambassador to Canada "that Prime Minister Trudeau might present special problems ... because he was at times erratic with many of the characteristics so frequently associated with intellectuals."[1] This assessment was not without merit – when a Defence White Paper of 1971 recommended that Canada's fighter-interceptors in NORAD retain their nuclear-tipped missiles, Trudeau complied despite his long-standing opposition to nuclear weapons.

If that was inconsistent (or, some might say, realistic), so too was the Trudeau government's policy regarding Europe. The Foreign Policy Review in 1970 had resulted in *Foreign Policy for Canadians,* an attractive six-pack of pamphlets that laid out the government's foreign policy vision, with a strong emphasis on trade. A few years after the NATO cutbacks, Trudeau decided that the time was right to strengthen relations with Europe. The Contractual Link with the European Community was the approach, an innovative

---

1 "Document 98: Memorandum of Conversation," 20 August 1969, in *Foreign Relations of the United States, 1969-76,* vol. 41, Office of the Historian, https://history.state.gov/historicaldocuments/frus1969-76v41/d98.

one that succeeded after enormous efforts by DEA to overcome the lingering distaste for Canada's earlier defence cuts and the absence of much interest in Europe for Canadian products other than raw materials. But the link died quickly, there being no will from Canadian business or in the Trudeau government's economic ministries, nor truly in the PMO, to make something of it. Merely securing the link, not making it work, seemed sufficient.

Oddly, *Foreign Policy for Canadians* had said almost nothing about Canadian-American relations. The United States was too omnipresent to be treated in a brief pamphlet, or so the rationale went. Thus, when the Nixon administration suddenly and without warning moved in August 1971 to deal with its balance of payments problems by hammering its trading partners with import surcharges and other measures, there was unprecedented consternation in Ottawa. The American objective was to force trading partners to adjust their exchange rates, something that Canada had already done. In effect, Canada was collateral damage, but the damage should not be exaggerated even if, at the time, Canadian ministers and officials panicked. In December 1971, SSEA Mitchell Sharp in Washington told Secretary of State William Rogers that "the President's announcement of August 15 created a shockwave in Canada ... particularly [among] the nationalists who favored reducing Canada's dependence upon the United States as soon as possible."[2] Months of acrimonious negotiations followed until, essentially, the Americans gave up. Pundits and politicians loudly proclaimed the demise of the special political-economic relationship that had been in place since 1940.[3] The Americans could no longer be relied on and, indeed, from the American point of view, neither could the Canadians. This sentiment was the genesis of the Third Option, which Sharp declared in 1972. He rejected the First Option, the idea that Canada could go it alone, and negated the Second Option, further US-Canada integration. A moderate and pragmatic course, the Third Option recognized that the policies of both the United States and Canada were rapidly changing. Unfortunately, it did not achieve much. A Contractual Link with the European Community (EC) duly appeared, and there may have

---

2 "Document 107: Memorandum of Conversation," 3 December 1971, in *Foreign Relations of the United States, 1969-76*, vol. 41, Office of the Historian, https://history.state.gov/historicaldocuments/frus1969-76v41/d107.
3 On this point, see Robert Bothwell, "Thanks for the Fish: Nixon, Kissinger, and Canada," in *Nixon in the World: American Foreign Relations, 1969-1977*, ed. Fredrik Logevall and Andrew Preston (New York: Oxford University Press, 2008), 309-27.

been better communication between Ottawa and Brussels, the EC's seat. The Third Option, in all its grandeur, was essentially dead by 1980. Trudeau recognized as much when he authorized negotiations for sectoral free trade with the United States in 1983. The Mulroney government that took power in 1984 quickly moved toward closer economic and political links with the United States.[4]

Trudeau's government was most successful in handling national unity questions. French president Charles de Gaulle blatantly interfered in Canadian domestic affairs by promoting Quebec separatism. Trudeau reacted firmly but calmly: He did not break relations with France, dismissed de Gaulle's provocations, and managed to irritate the French by extending Canada's diplomatic reach into the previously sacrosanct terrain of francophone Africa. Then he waited. De Gaulle self-destructed, and his successors had increasingly less appetite for throwing away money and prestige on a project that made no real sense, either in terms of French interests or to French voters. François Mitterrand's election as president in 1981 finished the matter, and relations with France returned to normal.

On the related question of patriating the Canadian Constitution and inserting a Charter of Rights into it, Trudeau managed a difficult situation carefully. Amending the Constitution and adding a Charter of Rights and Freedoms affected British domestic politics, for it had to pass through the British Parliament like any other piece of British legislation. The eight Provinces that opposed the Constitution, Native leaders, and miscellaneous critics from Canada fought Trudeau not in the usual diplomatic channels, but through the British political system, to the dismay of both the Canadian and British governments. In the end, Trudeau and Canada prevailed, a major achievement.

Canada's recognition of the People's Republic of China was also well managed. Trudeau ignored domestic fears that the United States would take recognition badly. As it happened, he was lucky in his timing, for very soon Richard Nixon and his adviser Henry Kissinger were hobnobbing in Beijing with the Chinese leadership. "Strictly political," Nixon said of Canadian recognition at the time; for Nixon, that was a very mild criticism – equivalent to indifference verging on admiration.[5] In fact, Canada's exchange of embassies

....

4 "Document 107: Memorandum of Conversation," 3 December 1971.
5 "Document 93: Memorandum of Conversation," 25 October 1970, in *Foreign Relations of the United States, 1969-76*, vol. 17, Office of the Historian, https://history.state.gov/historicaldocuments/frus1969-76v17/d93.

with China fitted very well into Nixon's great reversal of alliances, moving China away from the USSR and into harmony with the West. That Trudeau had gone to the USSR in May 1971, signed a Protocol on Consultations, and foolishly said in a speech that the United States was perhaps an even greater threat to Canada than the USSR, however, won him few friends in Washington. His adventurism was generally popular at home with the public, but it could have costs elsewhere.

If Trudeau had come to power with panache and the desire to change policies, he tried to leave office with similar flair in 1983-84. East-West relations were very chilly then, the superpowers planting new missiles in Europe, the Soviets shooting down a Korean Air Lines passenger jet over Siberia. With genuine sincerity, Trudeau attempted to launch a Peace Initiative, knowing that he had more clout in office, even in what he certainly suspected might be his last months in power, than he would ever have as a former prime minister. The Peace Initiative was hugely popular in Canada, the public cheering its leader to the echo, but it had little impact in Washington, Beijing, London, Paris, or Moscow, the major nuclear powers. Some smaller countries in the Commonwealth and in the Warsaw Pact satellites expressed interest when Trudeau flew in for talks, but overall the initiative had little effect. Many senior Canadian officials thought it hastily planned, badly implemented, and unrealistic. They were not wrong, though Trudeau would later justify his initiative by observing a bit wryly that there was no war and the heated rhetoric in Washington and Moscow had been toned down. Whether Trudeau accomplished even that much was impossible to determine.

Essentially, Trudeau had failed to recognize that Canada was at best a middle power, a smaller nation with little ability to alter the course of events or the policies of the superpowers. Canadians always wanted to believe that their country played a major role, and Lester Pearson's Nobel Peace Prize after the 1956 Suez Crisis had reinforced this public attitude. Certainly, Trudeau would have been pleased if his Peace Initiative had brought him similar recognition, but it was not to be. In effect, Trudeau – who had come to power scorning the Pearson government's "helpful fixer" approach – had become at best a helpful fixer to whom the nuclear powers paid little attention. The policy pirouette had been almost complete.

Still, Trudeau's foreign policy had its successes that deserve to be reiterated. Trudeau did succeed in recognizing China. That was a major achievement. His government vigorously resisted the efforts by PQ separatists to secure control over social aspects of foreign policy and to build support for international recognition of the independent Quebec they were certain was inevitable. Fighting tooth and nail, Trudeau's government won that struggle. The third major success was the patriation of the Constitution. Members of the Thatcher government were not happy with this whole process, but as Trudeau rashly stated, they simply had to hold their nose and do it. They did.

Those successes mattered, but so did Trudeau's failures. His relations with the United States had their ups and downs but can only be adjudged as unsuccessful. The Trudeau government poked the neighbouring beast with defence cuts, FIRA, the NEP, and the Peace Initiative, and the United States hit at Canada with the 1971 Nixon shokku and by freezing out Canadian diplomats in Washington. Relations with the Gerald Ford and Jimmy Carter administrations were far better than with those of Nixon and Reagan. Ford got Canada into the G7, but Trudeau talked over and sneered at Reagan in his latter summits and went nowhere.

Trudeau's summit performances also alienated Margaret Thatcher, Reagan's soulmate, and certainly she saw him as soft on the Soviet Union at a time when Moscow was pressing hard on the West. Britain mattered much less to Canada in Trudeau's time than it had done, but the Canadian leader certainly failed to build many bridges with London.

Nor did he have much success with Europe. Officials in DEA wanted to create stronger links with Western European nations and the EC, and the Third Option and the Contractual Link gave Canada just that opportunity. Trudeau deserved credit for securing the link, but he won no kudos once it was achieved by seemingly forgetting about it as his fluctuating interests shifted. Efforts to sustain the link may not have paid off, but the prime minister did not push ITC to make an effort, and ITC did not press Canadian corporations and manufacturers to turn their gaze from the south across the Atlantic. This was a lost opportunity, a failure of policy.

Nor were there any victories with NATO. By halving the Canadian troop commitment in Western Europe, Trudeau dealt a blow to his nation's standing in the European capitals. The cuts in Canadian Forces personnel as the years wore on helped not at all; nor did the mid-1970s decision to buy new German tanks help very much. To the NATO nations – and especially the United States – Trudeau's Canada was almost a freeloader.

Not that Trudeau won much regard in Moscow for his efforts. His 1971 visit produced a Protocol on Consultations that soon became a dead letter in time of crisis. There were also exchanges of academics and specialists, but nothing important resulted. Relations with the USSR could be good when

Canada-US relations were testy, but that was all. Perhaps the major achievement was that Trudeau became friendly with Alexander Yakovlev, the USSR's ambassador in Canada for ten years, and Yakovlev's experiences in Ottawa had a substantial impact on Mikhail Gorbachev and in shaping the perestroika and glasnost that helped end the Cold War.

Finally, Trudeau's Peace Initiative was a noble effort but one that achieved nothing other than to make the Canadian public feel good. Canada was not a player, and Trudeau had no magic elixir to make peace possible. He could say in later years that there had been no war and could claim that the hostile rhetoric had toned down. Perhaps he was right to take some credit for this, but when Pierre Trudeau left office at the end of June 1984, his country may have been less of a power in the world than it had been in 1968.

How could this be so? Whereas the public paid little attention to Canada's foreign policy except when Trudeau was centre stage in his crusade for peace, the chanceries of the world did. They could see that Trudeau's interest in foreign policy and defence was sporadic, his attention flowing and ebbing over his sixteen years in power. He fixated on defence for a few months, then looked away. He turned to Europe to counter the weight of the United States, then did nothing, frittering away the hard-won Contractual Link. He seemed to believe that the Soviet Union could be made civilized enough to become a better partner for Canada, but he failed to follow through, and until Gorbachev came to the fore, the USSR seemed unwilling to change course. He worried about the Americans and experimented with nationalist economic policies such as FIRA and the NEP, thus worsening Canada's situation in Washington. Even on nuclear weapons, his interest wavered, coming to full bloom only at the end of his reign. To be sure, there was plenty of idealism, there was concern for development and the Third World, and there was worry over the threat of war. But the Trudeau who had become prime minister in 1968, scorning the Pearsonian helpful fixer approach, was the same man who launched a Peace Initiative in 1983-84, an action that can only be described as helpful fixer writ large – and one effort that fixed nothing. Inconsistent is the only word to describe the foreign and defence policies of the Trudeau government.

But for Pierre Trudeau, Canada was the part of the world that mattered most. He must have known that no Canadian initiative was likely to end Great Power hostility. But he had believed that he could beat back Quebec's infatuation with nationalism and independentism, and he largely succeeded, though not permanently. On this subject and this subject alone,

Trudeau's gaze had remained constant.[6] He believed he could patriate the Constitution and give Canadians their Charter. To his credit and to Canada's great benefit, he succeeded in these aims, and they remain his legacy in a way that his foreign and defence policies do not.

As we have noted, President Richard Nixon said privately in 1969 that Pierre Trudeau "was at times erratic with many of the characteristics so frequently associated with intellectuals." Nixon may have been no one's favourite American president, but he was no fool, and he had got Trudeau exactly right.

---

6 The British high commissioner, Lord Moran, who had lunch with Trudeau during his final days in office, reported that he spoke "almost entirely about French Canada, French Canadians ... It reminded us once more what a different world even Federal French Canadians inhabit, and how they still feel themselves an embattled minority." Paul Waldie, "Files Show What British Diplomats Really Thought of Canada in the 1980s," *Toronto Globe and Mail*, 24 August 2016, A9.

Index

Able Archer. *See* NATO
Agence de coopération culturelle et technique (ACCT), 71
Aitken, Jonathan, 329
Allard, Jean-Victor, 19-20, 26, 132, 145-46, 151, 155, 164
Anderson, John F., 129, 142, 154, 161, 361; on Defence Review, 142-45
Angola, 274
anti-Americanism, 207, 370
Arctic, 56, 60, 64, 95, 105-6, 165, 274, 289, 311
Arctic Waters Pollution Prevention Act, 60
Armstrong, Elgin, 19, 135, 145, 151, 155, 163-64, 173
Armstrong, Willis (Bill), 203
Asia-Pacific Foundation, 316
Attlee, Clement, 327
Australia, 90, 97, 250, 268
Autopact, 10, 176-77, 191-93, 198-200, 202
Axworthy, Lloyd, 82
Axworthy, Tom, 99, 361, 369

Bank of Canada, 27, 31, 200, 212, 256
Barton, William, 100; on economics, 102; on Ed Ritchie, 102; on Ivan Head, 102; on Michael Pitfield, 102; on Pierre Trudeau, 101; on UN, 100-2
Basford, Ron, 327
Beesley, Alan, 60, 72, 103; on the Arctic, 105-6; on Law of the Sea, 103-7
Beetz, Jean, 93, 377
Begin, Menachem, 79, 95, 98, 121
Béliard, Jean, 21, 233, 257-58; on Allan MacEachen, 259; on Charles de Gaulle, 258; on Pierre Trudeau, 258-59

Benson, Edgar, 69, 166-67, 172, 188, 191, 196, 198, 200
Bethune, Norman, 61, 270, 308-9, 317
Biafra, 50, 57, 71-73, 372
Bissonnette, André, 54, 88-89, 150
Blakeney, Allan, 322*n*2
Bouey, Gerald, 256
Bourassa, Robert, 88, 243-44, 249, 266, 322*n*2
Brandt, Willy, 58, 356
Brezhnev Doctrine, 272, 292-93
Brezhnev, Leonid, 76, 91, 262, 270-71, 275, 283, 295, 354, 375, 381, 384
Broadbent, Ed, 330, 334, 338
Brown, Emerson, 191; on Autopact, 193; on Nixon, 192; on Nixon *shokku*, 193
Brzezinski, Zbigniew, 64, 185-86, 209, 211, 218, 225, 374, 382; on Quebec, 382
Bunche, Ralph, 100
Burns, Robert, 326-27

Cadieux, Léo, 20, 24-25, 44, 54, 65, 69, 127, 129-30, 132, 135-37, 139, 141, 143-45, 147, 150, 154, 156, 158, 161, 164, 243, 251, 300, 374, 378-79; as ambassador, 243-44; on Contractual Link, 244-45; on Defence Review, 132-33; on NATO, 137
Cadieux, Marcel, 14, 17-18, 25-26, 30, 39, 45, 47, 53, 70, 73, 89-90, 92-93, 99, 104, 113, 123-24, 144, 146, 149-51, 153, 156-57, 159, 188, 190, 196-97, 202, 233, 237-39, 277, 279, 283, 374, 378-79; character and temperament, 75-76; compared to Ed Ritchie, 67, 71; conception of foreign service, 85-87; and francophones, 92; and Jean Marchand and Gérard Pelletier, 151; and Mitchell

Sharp, 70-71, 75; on NATO, 53; and Pierre Trudeau, 18, 26, 66-67, 85-86, 279, 378-79
Callaghan, James (Jim), 61-62, 69, 77, 216, 267; and Canada, 322-25, 337, 342, 359, 378; and Pierre Trudeau, 37, 325
Cameron, David, 335
Campbell, Ross, 32, 34, 47-48, 59, 62, 65, 67, 129-30, 133, 137, 139-41, 148, 156-57, 159-60, 379; on NATO, 139-41
Canadian Forces, 15, 54-55, 127, 129, 144-46, 148, 160, 164-65, 167-68, 319, 384, 388
Carrington, Lord (Peter), 150, 325, 330, 341, 347, 352, 356, 360, 378
Carter, Jimmy, 61-62, 82, 98, 179, 185-86, 206, 209-10, 215-18, 226, 275, 378, 381, 388
Castro, Fidel, 57, 179
Charles, Prince of Wales, 331
Charter of Rights and Freedoms, 323, 328, 332-33, 339, 341, 350, 386, 390. *See also* patriating Constitution
China, 5, 9, 52, 73, 136, 176, 269, 282, 297-316, 357, 366; Cultural Revolution, 9, 61, 297-98, 307; Pierre Trudeau's visit, 308-9, 310-12, 316-17, 372-73; recognition of, 49, 60-61, 146, 289, 386-87; Russo-Chinese split, 268; two-China policy, 302, 304; and US, 305-6, 312. *See also* Taiwan
Chrétien, Jean, 65, 68, 75, 151-52, 289, 329-31, 343-45, 349-50
Clark, Clifford, 29
Clark, Ed, 97, 230-31
Clark, Joe, 13, 43, 59, 83, 230, 291
Cloutier, Sylvain, 19, 128-29, 163-64, 166-74; on Jacques Dextraze, 167; on James Richardson, 170-71; on Pierre Trudeau, 171; on procurement, 169-70; on restructuring DND, 167-68
Cohen, Mickey, 97, 230
Cold War, 5-6, 10, 18, 40-41, 76, 86, 126, 146, 176, 262, 351, 355, 379-80
Commonwealth, 10-11, 17, 50, 55, 321-22, 324, 354, 371, 387; Conferences, 34, 50-51, 321, 323, 357; and Pierre Trudeau, 23, 52, 68, 119, 123, 359, 366

Communist Party of Canada, 268
Connally, John, 177, 182, 188, 191, 193, 196-200, 202
Constitution. *See* patriating Constitution
Copithorne, Maurice, 298, 307-9; on China-Canada relations, 307-8; Trudeau's visit to China, 308-9
Cotler, Irwin, 80
Coutts, James (Jim), 63, 98, 118, 369-70
Crowe, Marshall, 42-46, 53, 58-59, 148-49, 154-57, 193, 196-97; on Donald Macdonald, 45; on Foreign Policy Review, 44; on Michael Pitfield, 43; on Nixon *shokku*, 196-97; on Pierre Trudeau, 46; on Quebec, 45
Crutchlow, Lew, 168
Cuba, 18, 56-57, 57n42, 76-77, 89, 142, 144, 223, 269, 274, 363; Trudeau's visit, 56-57
Curtis, Kenneth, 81, 215

Dare, Michael, 160, 164, 168, 172
Davis, William G. (Bill), 334, 345
de Gaulle, Charles, 39, 45, 73, 138-40, 152, 232-33, 237, 257-58, 386; visit to Canada, 20, 233-35, 237-38, 241-42, 249, 383
de Puyjalon, Henri, 144, 163
Defence Review, 52-53, 127-28, 130-34, 136-138, 142-45, 147-48, 151, 154-57, 161-65, 187
Delvoie, Louis, 355-62; on Peace Initiative, 356-57; on Pierre Trudeau, 357-59
Delworth, Thomas, 121-125, 298, 314-15, 318, 360, 367-68; on Allan Gotlieb, 124; on Allan MacEachen, 125; on Basil Robinson, 125; on DEA, 121; on Ed Ritchie, 124-25; on Gordon Osbaldeston, 124; on Marcel Cadieux, 123; on Marcel Massé, 123; on Mark MacGuigan, 124; on Michael Pitfield, 122; on NATO, 123; on the Pacific, 315-16; on Peace Initiative, 367-68; on Pierre Trudeau, 122-23; on Vietnam, 314-15
Department of External Affairs (DEA), 16-18, 21-23, 26-27, 29, 87, 99, 110-11, 127, 139, 244, 366; and patriating

Constitution, 328; reorganization, 113-16, 120; structure, 15
Department of Finance, 27, 29-30, 36, 76, 96, 99, 113, 188-89, 200, 245-46, 250
Department of Industry, Trade and Commerce (ITC), 113-15, 121-22, 200, 212, 224, 246, 250, 252, 388
Department of National Defence (DND), 19-20, 36-37, 122, 127, 139, 167-70; on procurement, 169-70; on restructuring, 167-68
Désy, Jean, 33
developing countries, 8-9, 52, 76, 83, 95-96, 99, 103-4, 250
Dextraze, Jacques, 19, 117, 128-29, 167-74; on Pierre Trudeau, 173; on Sylvain Cloutier, 172-73; on tanks, 173
Dillon, Douglas, 193
Dingell, John, 224
Dobell, Peter, 159, 164
Drury, Charles M. (Bud), 24, 54, 138, 145, 147
Duemling, Robert, 211-15; on foreign service, 213; on Kenneth Curtis, 215; on Pierre Trudeau, 215; on Quebec, 214; on Thomas Enders, 211-12
Dupuy, Michel, 160, 200, 247, 249-54; as ambassador, 253; on Contractual Link, 249-53

Eayrs, James (Jim), 140, 161
economics, 102, 115, 120-21, 176-78, 182, 187-88, 285-86
Elizabeth II, 103; and Commonwealth, 34, 322, 325-27; and Constitution, 35, 331, 344
Enders, Thomas (Tom), 71, 176, 185, 207-15, 219, 314, 374-75, 382; on Quebec, 208-11
Enlai, Zhou, 61, 298-300, 307-8, 310
European Common Market, 62, 153, 234

fisheries, 81, 195-96, 217-18, 225
Foot, Michael, 337-38
Ford, Gerald, 57n42, 61, 175, 178, 206, 226, 313, 388
Ford, John, 330-31, 342, 346, 348; on patriating Constitution, 332

Ford, Robert, 54, 65, 109, 143, 152, 154, 263-67, 294-95; on Afghanistan, 275-76; on Allan Gotlieb, 279; on Andrei Gromyko, 270; on Ed Ritchie, 279; effectiveness as ambassador, 290; on Foreign Policy Review, 273; on Ivan Head, 271-72, 279; on Mitchell Sharp, 279; Paul Martin on, 266; on Pierre Trudeau, 272-73, 277-79; on Rideau Hall conversation, 334; on Russian intellectuals, 270; on SALT, 273; on Soviet interest in Canada, 273; on STAFEUR, 271-72
foreign aid, 4, 139
Foreign Investment Review Agency (FIRA), 196, 204-5, 215, 218-19, 222-23, 229-30, 256, 260, 388-89
Foreign Policy for Canadians. See Foreign Policy Review
Foreign Policy Review, 18-19, 24, 33-34, 47, 56, 67, 89-90, 94, 107, 127-29, 146-47, 153-54, 159, 273, 376-77, 384-85; and US, 44, 129, 153, 200-1, 385
Fortier, D'Iberville, 115
France, 20, 45, 232-34; and Canadian membership in G7, 61; investment in Canada, 243. See also de Gaulle.
La Francophonie, 21, 48, 57, 71, 233-36, 239-41, 249, 259
Fraser, John, 83, 298, 304; on Taiwan, 304-7
free trade, 30, 41, 104, 200, 204, 223-24, 255-56, 386
Front de libération du Québec (FLQ), 18, 26, 70, 88-89, 98, 161, 164-65, 194, 262-63, 286

G7, 28, 97, 105, 131, 135, 178-79; representation at, 313; summits, 61-62, 79, 82, 108, 118-19, 215-16, 218-19, 378
Gabon Conference, 34, 73, 93, 239
Gagnier, Daniel, 337, 340-45; on ministerial visits, 343-45; on patriating Constitution, 340-42
Garrison Diversion, 211
Gauvin, Michel, 299, 316-17; on missing Canadians in Vietnam, 319-20; on Vietnam, 317-20

General Agreement on Tariffs and Trade (GATT), 31, 104, 191, 193-94, 197, 246, 251, 322
Gérin-Lajoie, Paul, 45
Giscard d'Estaing, Valéry, 83, 216, 233-34, 245, 247-49, 251-53, 259, 278, 313, 375-76; on Canada, 268
globalization, 8, 52
Golden, David, 155
Goldenberg, Eddie, 348-50; on patriating Constitution, 349-50
Goldschlag, Klaus, 32, 38, 65, 70, 78-80, 113, 115-16, 121-22, 245, 257, 277
Gorbachev, Mikhail, 264, 275, 277, 281, 290, 375, 381-82, 389
Gordon, Walter, 65, 67, 69, 140, 147, 151
Gorham, Richard, 299, 316; on Mitchell Sharp, 316; on Pierre Trudeau's visit to China, 316-17; on Vietnam, 316
Gorton, John, 90
Gotlieb, Allan, 33, 39, 45, 50, 51, 61, 65, 77, 119, 125, 130, 191, 216, 369; on Allan MacEachen, 220, 372; on Basil Robinson, 98; on FIRA, 223; on Foreign Policy Review, 94; on foreign service, 96-97; on free trade, 223-24; on G7, 216; on Ivan Head, 95, 99; on Jimmy Carter, 216-17, 221-22; on Marcel Cadieux, 92-93; on Michael Pitfield, 95-97, 99; on NEP, 223; on Peace Initiative, 369-72; on Pierre Trudeau, 91-92, 95, 97-98; Robert Ford on, 279
Goyer, Jean-Pierre, 159, 235
Gray, Herb, 78-79, 223, 229, 323
Great Britain. *See* Commonwealth; United Kingdom
Green, Howard, 87-88, 304
Greene, Joe, 52-53, 194
Gregg, Tom, 168
Gromyko, Andrei, 265, 291, 366, 372-73
Guang, Yao, 298, 301; on China-Canada relations, 301-4

Haggan, Reeves, 14, 73-75, 329, 334-38, 341-43, 345-46; on Ed Ritchie, 74; on Marcel Cadieux, 73-74; on Mitchell Sharp, 74-75; on patriating Constitution, 334-35, 337-38

Haig, Al, 55, 81-82, 219-20, 222, 226, 229, 369
Haldeman, H.R., 183
Halstead, John, 62, 70, 91, 107-10, 129, 152-55, 163, 245-47, 257, 277, 279-80; on Conference on Security and Cooperation in Europe, 108-9; on Contractual Link, 246-47; on Foreign Policy Review, 107, 153-54; on Michael Pitfield, 110; on NATO, 154; on Pierre Trudeau, 109, 279-80; on tanks, 108; on Third Option, 245-46
Hancock, Peter, 289-90, 359-66; and Alexander Yakovlev, 290; on Peace Initiative, 359-66; on Pierre Trudeau's visit to USSR, 289-90
Harmel, Pierre, 159
Harmel Report, 159, 293, 359, 380
Hatfield, Richard, 336
Head, Ivan, 14, 17, 22-23, 44, 46, 49-64, 69, 80, 88, 90, 93, 95-96, 99, 101-2, 105-6, 109, 117-18, 122, 127, 130-31, 133, 136-37, 144-45, 147-49, 154, 160, 162, 178, 180-90, 203, 206, 212-13, 225, 245-47, 250, 271-73, 279, 288-89, 304, 309, 312, 325, 374, 377-82; on the Arctic, 60; on China, 60-61; on Commonwealth, 50-52, 55; on Defence Review, 52-53; on European Common Market, 62; on Foreign Policy Review, 56, 127; on francophones, 57; on G7, 61-62; on Gordon Robertson, 56; on Jews, 59; on Jim Coutts, 63; on Henry Kissinger, 180-81; on Marc Lalonde, 56; on Michael Pitfield, 56; on NATO, 52-55; on Pierre Trudeau, 49; on PQ, 184-85; on Quebec, 62; on Richard Nixon, 181-83; on Thomas Enders, 185; on Vietnam, 183-84; on Zbigniew Brzezinski, 185-86
Healey, Denis, 55, 133, 141, 150, 183, 342, 358-59; as bloviator, 150n13
Heath, Edward, 322
Hébert, Jacques, 297
Hellyer, Paul, 48, 54, 65, 127, 129, 134-36, 138, 147, 377, 379; on Defence Review, 134; on NATO, 135; on Pierre Trudeau, 134

Holmes, John, 65
Hood, William (Bill), 61
Hooper, William, 264, 282-88; on communists, 286-87; on Czech invasion, 283-84; on dealing with Russians, 284-85; on intelligence, 282-83, 286, 288; on Pierre Trudeau, 285-86; on Pierre Trudeau's visit to USSR, 288
Hull, Chester, 168
Hunter, Robert, 176, 225-26, 234; on Pierre Trudeau, 226; on Quebec, 225-26

India, 104, 299, 314, 366, 373
Israel, 7, 59, 72, 79, 80, 190, 290; Canadian embassy, 98; invasion of Lebanon, 78, 102*n*12, 219; Yom Kippur War, 7, 273. *See also* Jews

Jamieson, Don, 13, 68, 88, 96, 103, 105, 109, 130, 217, 220, 279, 331; Robert Ford on, 279
Japan, 8, 33, 58, 62, 67, 83, 129, 157, 178, 181, 195*n*12, 197, 250, 271, 298, 313-15
Jews, 59, 72, 78-80, 94-95, 98, 100-1, 121, 199, 284
Johnson, Al, 168, 254
Johnson, Lyndon, 91, 267, 300
Johnstone, Bob, 114, 116, 213
Jurgensen, Jean-Daniel, 233, 236, 240, 258

Kashtan, William (Bill), 268, 293
Katz, Julius (Jules), 191, 202-4; on cancellation of Autopact, 191, 193, 199, 202
Kaunda, Kenneth, 51
Kershaw, Anthony, 342, 348
Kershaw Committee, 327, 329, 336-37
Kierans, Eric, 47, 127, 131, 133, 135, 137, 147
Killick, John, 163
Kinsman, Jeremy, 36*n*18
Kirby, Michael, 56, 334-35, 345, 349
Kirby Memorandum, 332, 335, 339
Kissinger, Henry, 7, 59, 178, 180-82, 184, 186, 196, 205, 299, 378; and Canadian membership in G7, 313; on Canadian-Soviet relations, 273; character of, 192, 273; on China, 9, 303, 304*n*8, 306, 386; détente, 10; Paris Accords, 299; and Pierre Trudeau, 180, 378; and Tom Enders as ambassador to Canada, 185, 211, 382; US and "interdependence," 8-9
Knowles, Stanley, 163
Kosygin, Alexei, 91, 275, 292; and Pierre Trudeau, 76, 262-63, 279, 381, 384; visit to Canada, 263, 265-66, 289, 294

Labour Party (UK), 337
Lacouture, Jean, 248
Lalonde, Marc, 14, 16-22, 41, 49-50, 56, 223, 227, 329; on DEA, 16-17, 68, 75; on DND, 19-20; on Foreign Policy Review, 19; on Jacques Viot, 21; on Jean Béliard, 21; on Latin America, 18; on Mitchell Sharp, 19; on NATO, 53; on Pierre-Marc Siraud, 20; on Quebec and France, 18, 20-21, 25, 45, 233
Lang, Otto, 24, 137-39; on Defence Review, 137-38
Latin America, 7, 18, 65, 78, 146-47, 186, 215, 382; and Foreign Policy Review, 129, 200
Laubman, Don, 134
Law of the Sea (LOS), 103-7, 115
Leduc, François, 235, 237-38
Lee, Kuan-Yew, 51
Léger, Jean-Marc, 241
Léger, Jules, 47, 65, 73, 94, 234-35, 243
LePan, Douglas, 93
Lévesque, René, 68, 214, 228, 258, 323, 326, 347; speech at Economic Club of New York, 209-10
Levy, David, 277
Liberal Party, 6-7, 16, 272, 326, 354, 375
Linder, Harold, 188
Loiselle, Gilles, 118, 326-27, 336, 342
Lumley, Ed, 79, 114, 124, 224, 229-30
Luns, Joseph, 55, 123, 150, 160, 359, 378
Lynch, Charles, 46, 59
Lyon, Peyton, 76, 104, 108, 162

Macdonald, Donald S., 19, 30, 35, 39, 44-45, 47, 52, 54, 60, 64, 69, 96, 106, 117, 133, 135-37, 156, 163-66, 170, 173-74, 179, 215-16; on the Arctic, 64; on Defence Review, 128, 136-37, 161-65; on Elgin Armstrong, 164; on G7, 215-16; and Pierre Trudeau, 297, 300

MacDonald, Flora, 78
MacEachen, Allan, 13, 59, 63, 65, 68, 72, 83-84, 117, 125, 196, 213, 218, 220-22, 227, 229, 258-59, 277, 285, 288, 329, 332, 357, 367, 370, 372, 379
MacGuigan, Mark, 13, 75-84, 97, 114, 118, 124, 222, 226-27, 276, 328-32, 341; on Allan Gotlieb, 78; on Cuba, 77; on dealing with Great Britain, 328-31; and developing countries, 76; on fisheries, 81; on G7, 82-83; on Ivan Head, 80; on Jews and Middle East, 78-80; on Michael Pitfield, 79; and Moscow Olympics, 76; on NEP, 226-27; on patriating Constitution, 328-29, 345; on Pierre Trudeau, 77; on the press, 83
Manthorpe, Jonathan, 345-46
Massé, Marcel, 15, 79, 115-16, 120-21, 123, 238n6
Marchand, de Montigny, 114-21, 254-57, 330, 361-63, 368; on DEA, 120; on FIRA, 256-57; on France, 257; on G7, 118-19; on Ivan Head, 118; on Jewish lobbying, 121; on Peace Initiative, 368; on Pierre Trudeau, 121; on tanks, 117; on Third Option, 254-56
Marchand, Jean, 13, 45n28, 65, 71, 89, 131, 134, 151, 239
Marshall, Chuck, 143
Martin, Paul, 36, 39, 47-48, 54, 60-61, 63-70, 76, 87, 92-94, 100, 105, 137, 147, 156, 159, 162, 191, 239, 265-67, 285, 299-301, 304, 315, 323-27; on Alexei Kosygin's visit, 265-66; on Allan Gotlieb, 65-66; on Allan MacEachen, 68; on the Arctic, 60, 64; on Basil Robinson, 66-67; on China, 299-300; on Commonwealth, 323-27; on DEA, 65; on Don Jamieson, 68; on Donald Macdonald, 69; on Foreign Policy Review, 67; on Ivan Head, 63-64; on Jean Chrétien, 68; on Léo Cadieux, 69; on Michael Pitfield, 65; on Mitchell Sharp, 63, 68; on monarchy, 326; on NATO, 64-65; on Pierre Trudeau, 67-68; on Robert Ford, 266-67; on Ross Campbell, 67
McIlraith, George, 48, 48n34

McKinney, Russell, 201-6; on FIRA, 204-5; on Marcel Cadieux, 202-3; on NEP, 204-5; on Nixon *shokku*, 202; on Taiwan, 206
Meagher, Margaret, 5, 306
Meekison, Peter, 338; on patriating Constitution, 338-40
Megarry, Roy, 336, 336n13, 344
Meir, Golda, 59
Menzies, Arthur, 65, 300
Mitterrand, François, 83, 119, 253, 257, 259, 361, 368, 370, 376, 386
Mondale, Walter, 186, 206, 218
Morin, Claude, 21, 27-28, 210, 238n6, 238-40, 340
Mowat, Farley, and USSR, 274
Mozambique, 274
Murdoch, Robert, 129, 151, 157-58, 160; on Defence Review, 157; on Léo Cadieux, 158; on NATO, 158; on Ross Campbell, 157
Murray, Geoffrey, 44, 56, 67, 94, 130, 146
Muskoxen, as factor in Canadian-Soviet relations, 274

Nara, Yasuhiko, 298, 312; on Pierre Trudeau, 312-14
Nasser, Gamal Abdel, 100, 274
National Energy Programme (NEP), 41-42, 53, 97, 109, 204-5, 218-19, 223, 226-27, 229-31
Nef, Edward, 224-25; on fisheries, 225; on oil, 224
Nixon, Buzz, 43, 142
Nixon, Richard, 7, 273, 302; and Canada, 189, 192, 200, 384; and Pierre Trudeau, 181-84, 187-90, 193, 201, 390; on recognition of China, 9, 302, 304, 306, 386-87
Nixon *shokku*, 8, 177-78, 188, 191, 193-94, 196-99, 200, 202, 245, 250, 385, 388
Non-Group. *See* Privy Council Office
North American Air Defence Command (NORAD), 126, 128, 145, 158, 161-62, 187, 377-78, 384
North Atlantic Treaty Organization (NATO), 16, 31, 36, 46, 52-55, 82, 91-92, 107, 129-33, 136-38, 146-48, 152-53,

157-58, 164, 187, 232, 262, 283-84, 286, 293, 296, 321, 362, 365, 374, 377-78, 388; Able Archer, 353; attitudes towards, 10, 14, 47, 97-98, 112, 126, 139, 144, 190, 359-60; commitments, 15-16; cuts, 15, 64-65, 67, 127-28, 133-36, 140-41, 154-55, 158, 160, 174, 183, 190, 259, 271, 358, 378, 384; meetings, 40, 109, 123, 135, 139-40, 149-51, 159, 219, 346, 360
nuclear weapons, 126, 128, 161-62, 184, 247, 269, 275, 312, 353-55, 357, 370, 379, 384, 387, 389; and China, 354; cruise missile testing, 82, 223, 362n16; and NATO, 53; and USSR, 142, 354-55, 364n18; warheads in Canada, 6, 53, 55, 161-62, 384
Nutt, Jim, 144, 154, 157
Nyerere, Julius, 51

oil, 7-10, 42, 179, 186, 195, 199, 204-5, 208, 219, 377; crisis, 224; prices, 9, 207, 223, 230
Olympics (1976), 57n42
Osbaldeston, Gordon, 30, 41, 79, 113-16, 120-1, 124, 361; on DEA, 113-16; on Marcel Massé, 116; on Michael Pitfield, 114
Owen, David, 61, 68

Parti Québécois (PQ), 25-26, 28, 62-63, 184, 208-11, 243, 323, 328, 374, 376, 387-88; and United States, 382
patriating Constitution, 328-29, 332, 334-35, 337-42, 345-50, 350
Peace Initiative, 40-1, 112, 155, 218, 221, 312, 351-57, 359-366, 367-73, 375, 379-80, 379-80, 387-89
peacekeeping, 128, 139, 155, 183-84; in Egypt, 100
Pearson, Geoffrey, 38, 89, 97, 109, 124, 264-65, 276-77, 279, 294-96, 366, 372-73; as ambassador, 295-96; on Peace Initiative, 372-73; on Robert Ford, 294-95
Pearson, Lester B., 6, 17-18, 22, 32, 35, 58, 74, 85-86, 93-94, 101, 127, 142, 146-48, 164, 239, 265, 306, 326, 387; and China, 299-300, 302, 304; on Foreign Policy Review, 67, 89; and Paul Martin, 39, 74, 77, 147, 159; and Pierre Trudeau, 16-17, 22, 31, 34, 57, 94, 122-23, 297, 377; and Temple University speech, 150
Pearsonianism, 93, 115, 118-19, 286, 368, 389
Pelletier, Gérard, 13, 45-48, 71, 89, 131, 134, 147, 152, 234-37, 239, 241, 358, 376; on Foreign Policy Review, 47; on La Francophonie, 234-35; on Pierre Trudeau, 46-48
Pennefather, John, 163, 165-66
People's Republic of China. *See* China
Pepin, Jean-Luc, 138, 138n9, 156, 188, 196, 289, 300, 313, 367
Peres, Shimon, 59
petroleum. *See* oil
Pipes, Richard, 276
Pitfield, Michael, 11, 14, 27-43, 79, 90, 95-97, 99, 102, 110-11, 114-16, 122-23, 148, 210, 227; on Allan Gotlieb, 33, 39; on bilingualism, 33; on DEA, 29, 32-33, 37-39; on DND, 36-37; on Foreign Policy Review, 33-34; on free trade, 41; on Lester Pearson, 35-36; on Marcel Cadieux, 39; on NATO, 40; on NEP, 41-42; and Pierre Trudeau, 122; on Pierre Trudeau, 31, 34-35; on PMO and PCO, 35; on Quebec, 34
Pompidou, Georges, 45, 233, 242, 244; and Pierre Trudeau, 375-76
Porter, William, 196, 207
Post, Richard, 206, 212; on anti-Americanism, 207
Prime Minister's Office (PMO), 14, 16, 18-19, 32, 80, 122, 133, 152, 162, 212, 246, 279; and Ivan Head, 63, 80, 95-96, 117-18, 136, 144; and PCO, 22, 35
Privy Council Office (PCO), 14, 23, 27, 36-37, 50, 96, 110-11, 117-18, 127, 146, 148-49, 152, 156; and Marshall Crowe, 42-44, 155, 193; and Non-Group, 44-45, 53-54, 90, 127, 133, 144, 149, 154; and PMO, 22, 35
Progressive Conservative Party (PC), 13, 83; and UK Conservatives, 348
Pym, Lord, 333, 341, 345-47, 349; on patriating Constitution, 347-48

Quebec, 6, 20-21, 27-28, 45, 61-62, 71, 79, 91-93, 185-86, 208-11, 233, 239-44, 251, 253, 257-58, 326, 336, 375-76; comparisons with Bangladesh, 57-58; in DEA, 17; intelligence about, 25-26; nationalism, 18, 31, 235, 383; and Pierre Trudeau's legacy, 386-89; and provinces, 340, 342, 347; referendum (1980), 323, 328; separatism, 57, 85, 248, 323; and US and separatism, 208-9, 213-14, 217, 221, 225-26, 374-75, 382; and USSR and separatism, 268

Rabinovitch, Robert, 97
Ramphal, Sonny, 325
Reagan, Ronald, 10, 80, 119, 179-80, 218-20, 228-29, 275-76, 361, 375, 388; and Pierre Trudeau, 76, 82, 112, 354, 357-58, 366, 369-71, 380; on Star Wars, 221-22, 351, 379
Reid, Escott, 299
Reisman, Simon, 43-44, 90, 181, 188, 191-93, 195-200, 250, 254; and John Connally, 188, 197, 200, 202
Rhodesia, 51, 55, 321, 325
Richard, François, 117, 122
Richardson, Jim, 19, 47, 117, 136, 170-72, 174
Ridley, Nicholas, 341, 346, 349
Ritchie, A. Edgar (Ed), 67-68, 70, 74, 87-91, 101-2, 124, 184, 188-191, 194, 199, 203, 245, 279-80, 288; on Autopact, 191; on FLQ crisis, 88-89; on Foreign Policy Review, 89-90; on Ivan Head, 190; on Michael Pitfield, 90; on Mitchell Sharp, 88; on Nixon *shokku*, 191; on Pierre Trudeau, 87, 189-90
Ritchie, Charles, 54, 139, 197
Roberts, John, 35, 82, 144, 328, 331, 341, 343
Roberts, Peter, 264-65, 276, 280-1, 381; as ambassador, 281; on Pierre Trudeau, 280; on USSR, 281
Robertson, Norman, 23-24, 23n6, 29, 31, 34, 37, 67, 89, 94, 120; and Marcel Cadieux, 85
Robertson, R. Gordon, 21-28, 42, 44, 50, 56, 91, 93, 99, 106, 110-11, 148, 166, 335;
on communism, 26; on DEA, 21-23, 26-27; on DND, 21-22; on Foreign Policy Review, 24; on Léo Cadieux, 24-25; on Mitchell Sharp, 24-25; on Norman Robertson, 23-24; on PCO and PMO, 22; on Pierre Trudeau, 23-24; on Quebec, 25, 28
Robinson, H. Basil, 32-33, 53-54, 66-67, 74, 92, 94, 98-99, 111, 125, 141, 145-53, 156, 213, 300; on Defence Review, 147-48, 151; on Foreign Policy Review, 146-47; on Mitchell Sharp, 151; on NATO, 53, 149-50
Robinson, Paul H., Jr., 179, 227-30; on FIRA, 229-30; on NEP, 229-30
Rogers, William, 177, 183-84, 191, 193, 201, 203, 385
Ronning, Chester, 57, 300
Roquet, Christian, 88-89
Roy, Jacques, 122
Royal Canadian Mounted Police (RCMP), 25-26, 212, 237, 276; and Pierre Trudeau, 164
Rusk, Dean, 66, 265, 267, 300

Schmidt, Adolph, 182, 189, 196
Schmidt, Helmut, 40, 62, 82, 164, 178-79, 216; and Pierre Trudeau, 108, 119, 217, 226, 234, 260, 361
Schneppen, Heinz, 259-261; on FIRA, 260; on Third Option, 259; on Pierre Trudeau, 260-61
Scowcroft, Brent, 61, 185, 190, 206
Seaborn, Blair, 70, 294
Sears, Robin, 338
Sharp, Daisy, 151
Sharp, Fred, 143, 151, 163-64, 167, 172
Sharp, Mitchell, 6, 13, 19, 56, 65, 68-75, 88-89, 101-2, 129-132, 140-41, 144-47, 156-57, 200-1, 285-86, 319, 385; on Biafra, 71-72; on Defence Review, 130-32; on FLQ, 70; on Foreign Policy Review, 129; on Geoffrey Murray, 130; on Jews, 72; as minister, 274-75, 279; on monarchy, 326; and Pierre Trudeau, 24; on Pierre Trudeau, 6; on Third Option, 200-1
Shenstone, Michael, 144, 154-57, 162, 361; on Defence Review, 154-57

shokku. *See* Nixon *shokku*
Shortliffe, Glen, 114
Shultz, George, 203, 220-21, 358, 370; on NEP, 223, 226
Siraud, Pierre-Marc, 20, 241-43
Smith, Arnold, 57-58, 236, 324
Smith, Gary, 361-62, 364
Smith, Gordon, 110-13, 128-29, 159-65; on DEA, 110; on Defence Review, 127, 161-63; on Foreign Policy Review, 159; on Michael Pitfield, 110-11; on NATO, 160; on Pierre Trudeau, 112-13
Smith, Richard, 230-31; on NEP, 230-31
Smith, Rufus, 186-89, 192-94, 203, 213; on Defence Review, 187; on Nixon *shokku*, 188
Soviet Union. *See* Union of Soviet Socialist Republics (USSR)
special relationship, 189, 198, 200, 219, 250
STAFEUR, 129, 140, 143, 146, 152-54, 155-56, 157, 245, 271-72
Stanley, Tim, 160
Starnes, John, 65, 89
Stevens, Geoffrey, 105
Stoner, Gerry, 42-43, 148
Strategic Arms Limitation Talks/Treaty (SALT), 273
Strong, Maurice, 96
Sutherland, Robert, 143, 151

Taiwan, 269, 297-99, 301-3, 305-6; exclusion from Montreal Olympics, 57*n*42, 206
tanks, 10, 108, 117, 160, 165, 170, 173-74, 388
Tassé, Roger, 335
Taylor, James (Si), 38, 78, 115, 244, 291-294; invasion of Czechoslovakia, 292-93; service in Moscow, 292
Taylor, Kenneth (Ken), 206
Thatcher, Margaret, 16, 95, 130, 328, 347*n*17, 348*n*18; disapproval of Trudeau, 388; at G7, 388; meets Pierre Trudeau (1980), 323; and Pierre Trudeau, 83, 118-19, 348, 380
Third Option, 10, 33, 130, 189, 195, 200-1, 207, 234, 244-46, 250, 254-56, 259-60, 273, 278-79, 385-86, 388; and Contractual Link, 62, 62*n*55, 109, 117, 152, 155, 160, 200, 234, 244-47, 249-53, 259, 357-60, 384-85, 388-89

Third World. *See* developing countries
Thorson, Donald, 327
Towe, Peter, 61, 96, 197-99, 202, 218, 222; on Nixon *shokku*, 197-99
Treasury Board, 53, 74, 165-8, 170, 173, 212
Tremblay, Paul, 88, 94, 152, 271
Trezise, Philip, 191, 198
Trudeau, Justin, 3
Trudeau, Margaret, 312-13, 315
Trudeau, Pierre, 374-82; A. Edgar Ritchie on Trudeau, 87, 189-90; and Alexander Yakovlev, 290, 380-2, 389; and Alexei Kosygin, 76, 262-63, 279, 381, 384; Allan Gotlieb on Trudeau, 91-92, 95, 97-98; on China, 9; and Commonwealth, 23, 52, 68, 119, 123, 359, 366; de Montigny Marchand on Trudeau, 121; on deterrence, 379; on divided countries, 58; and Donald Macdonald, 297, 300; early life, 85; on Foreign Policy Review, 376-77, 384-85; and Georges Pompidou, 375-76; Gérard Pelletier on Trudeau, 46-48; Gordon Robertson on Trudeau, 23-24; Gordon Smith on Trudeau, 112-13; Heinz Schneppen on Trudeau, 260-61; and Helmut Schmidt, 108, 119, 217, 226, 234, 260, 361; and Henry Kissinger, 180, 378; Ivan Head on Trudeau, 49; Jacques Dextraze on Trudeau, 173; Jacques Viot on Trudeau, 248; and James Callaghan, 325; Jean Béliard on Trudeau, 258-59; John Halstead on Trudeau, 109, 279-80; legacy, 382-90; on Léo Cadieux, 378-79; and Lester Pearson, 16-17, 22, 31, 34, 57, 94, 122-23, 297, 377; Louis Delvoie on Trudeau, 357-59; and Marcel Cadieux, 18, 85-86, 378-79; and Margaret Thatcher, 83, 118-19, 323, 348, 380; Mark MacGuigan on Trudeau, 77; Marshall Crowe on Trudeau, 46; Michael Pitfield on Trudeau, 31, 34-35, 122; Mitchell Sharp on Trudeau, 6, 24; Nara Yasuhiko on Trudeau, 312-14; on NATO, 10, 377-78; Paul Hellyer on Trudeau, 134; Paul

Martin on Trudeau, 67-68; on Peace Initiative, 379-80; on PQ, 382; Peter Roberts on Trudeau, 280; and Quebec and France, 375-76, 386-89; and RCMP, 164; and Richard Nixon, 181-84, 187-90, 193, 201, 390; Robert Duemling on Trudeau, 215; Robert Ford on Trudeau, 272-73; 277-79; Robert Hunter on Trudeau, 226; and Ronald Reagan, 76, 82, 112, 354, 357-58, 366, 369-71, 380; Rüdiger von Lukowitz on Trudeau, 260-61; on Soviets, 380-2; Sylvain Cloutier on Trudeau, 171; Thomas Delworth on Trudeau, 122-23; and US, 95, 112, 181, 210, 248, 263, 314, 370, 382-83; and UN, 11, 67-68, 101; visit to China, 308-9, 310-12, 316-17, 372-73; visit to Cuba, 56-57; visit to USSR; 58, 91, 262, 288-91; William Barton on Trudeau, 101; William Hooper on Trudeau, 285-86

Turner, John, 65, 138, 187; and George Shultz, 203

Turner, Vernon, 225, 276, 290-91, 318; on Russia desk at DEA, 290-91

Union of Soviet Socialist Republics (USSR), 9-10, 126, 176, 217, 262-65, 351, 388-89; academic exchanges with, 274; and the Arctic, 60; attitudes towards, 59; economy, 9-10, 276, 293; invasion of Afghanistan, 296; invasion of Czechoslovakia, 71, 140, 271, 283-84, 292-93, 384; Moscow Olympics, 75-76; poverty, 274; Trudeau's visit, 58, 91, 262, 291; and US, 273, 351, 372

United Kingdom, character of British, 335. *See also* Commonwealth

United Nations, 46-47, 100, 232, 300, 362; and China, 9, 297, 300; and Pierre Trudeau, 11, 67-68, 101; Security Council, 102

United States, 7-9; and Canada, 41, 52, 77, 148, 175-80, 206-7, 213, 221-22, 388; and China, 302-4, 312; and Foreign Policy Review, 44, 129, 153, 200-1, 385; investment (*see* FIRA); and Peace Initiative, 370-1; and Pierre Trudeau, 95, 112, 181, 210, 248, 263, 314, 382-83; and Quebec, 208-9, 213-14, 217, 221, 225-26, 374-75, 382; and USSR, 273, 351, 372

Vance, Cyrus, 80-81, 101, 183, 186, 206
Vanier, Georges, 33, 35
Vietnam, 7, 58, 66, 188, 204, 269, 285, 298-300, 319-20; International Commission for Control and Supervision, 183-84, 201, 299, 314-15, 317-19; and UN, 101
Viot, Jacques, 21, 247-49; on Pierre Trudeau, 248; on Quebec, 248-49
von Lukowitz, Rüdiger, 259-61; on FIRA, 260; on Pierre Trudeau, 260-61; on Third Option, 259

Wadds, Jean, 5, 331, 335-36, 340-41, 346; as high commissioner, 331*n*11, 336, 344; and Margaret Thatcher, 331*n*11
Wade, William, 336
Warren, Jake, 99, 191-92, 196, 254, 257
Watt, Ron, 335
Wells, Thomas (Tom), 345-47; on patriating Constitution, 345-47
Whelan, Eugene, 264, 323-24
Wilson, Harold, 51, 267, 322, 349
Withers, Ramsey, 19-20, 169
World Court, 60
Worthington, Peter, 277
Wright, Hume, 44, 90, 155

Yakovlev, Alexander, 76, 263-64, 280-81, 284, 287, 375, 380-81; and Pierre Trudeau, 290, 389
Yalden, Max, 17-18, 93, 238-41; on La Francophonie, 239-41; on Marcel Cadieux, 239
Yandell Elliott, William, 180
Young, Andrew (Andy), 101, 103

Zedong, Mao, 9, 298, 307
Zhan, Yu, 298, 309-12; on China-Canada relations, 309; on Pierre Trudeau's visit to China, 310-12